Sha Tau Kok

ver

ng

Plover Cove

Tolo Channel

Long Harbour

Tolo Harbour

Tide Cove

Chek Keng

'Croucher's
Beach'

Tin

Sai Kung

High
Island

Kau Sai

Port Shelter

Lung
Shun
W a n
Hoi

Silverstrand Bay

LOON

Kai Tak Aerodrome
Victoria Harbour

Ngam
Tau
Sha

Junk Bay

erry

North Point

al

Happy Valley

toria Peak

Shaukiwan

HONG KONG

Deep Water
Bay

se Bay

Tai
Tam
Bay

Shek O

Cape D'Aguilar

Stanley

WAGLAN ISLAND

PO TOI ISLAND

Chandler's
Ford

EASTLEIGH

ENGLAND

SOUTHAMPTON

New
Forest

Fareham

THE SOLENT

Gosport

Lymington

Cowes

Portsmouth

Ryde

Yarmouth

Carisbrooke
Castle

Newport

Sandown

ISLE OF WIGHT

Shanklin

Ventnor

Whitwell

The Quest of
Noel Croucher
Hong Kong's Quiet Philanthropist

In his long life Chater had two 'students' —
Sir Robert Ho Tung in the nineteenth century,
Noel Croucher in the twentieth.
Both became millionaires...

— *Austin Coates*

The Quest of
Noel Croucher

Hong Kong's Quiet Philanthropist

Vaudine England

Foreword by Dr Elizabeth Sinn

香港大學出版社

HONG KONG UNIVERSITY PRESS

Hong Kong University Press
14/F Hing Wai Centre
7 Tin Wan Praya Road
Aberdeen, Hong Kong

© Makale Limited 1998

ISBN 962 209 473 2

Printed in Hong Kong by United League Graphic & Printing Co. Ltd.

CONTENTS

ention the name Noel Croucher in Hong Kong today, and chances are you will draw a total blank. More likely than not, the person you address will repeat the name, followed by a big innocent question mark — 'Noel Croucher?'

Among students and academics, in particular those in the fields of science and medicine, the chances of finding some familiarity with the name are slightly better, but only just. Usually the mention of Croucher's name would induce the same predictable admission of ignorance, but when I add, 'You know, Noel Croucher of The Croucher Foundation,' instantly, my addressee's face would light up. Relieved, the person would exclaim, 'Oh, *that* Noel Croucher!' But knowledge of the man seldom goes beyond that, either.

How interesting to note that it is mainly through The Croucher Foundation that Croucher the man is remembered in Hong Kong at all! For someone who lived for so long in Hong Kong, played such an active role in the business world and contributed so much to its charities — indeed, who was reputedly at one point the richest white man east of Suez — why has he not become a household name, like Y.K. Pao, Li Ka-shing, Lord Kadoorie or Robert Ho Tung?

If Croucher had had a street and park named after him — like Paul Chater, his mentor in the rough and tough world of stockbroking, or E.R. Belilios, for whom a school was named — would he have had a better chance of imposing himself on the collective memory of contemporary Hong Kong?

Who *was* Noel Croucher?

Born in Eastleigh, a small railway town near Southampton, in 1891, he came to Hong Kong in the mid-1900s and started his slow but sometimes spectacular climb up in the world. This biography reveals him struggling from modest beginnings and ending up not only as the Chairman of the Hong Kong Stock Exchange but the Commodore of the socially prestigious Royal Hong Kong Yacht Club. And, in due course, he became one of Hong Kong's biggest philanthropists.

Croucher's story is, in many ways, a typical rags-to-riches story, but it is also more than just that.

The search for Noel Croucher takes us to unfamiliar territory on many levels and we are reminded of how little, in fact, we know about Hong Kong's history. The relatively few histories of the region concentrate on the leading companies which helped to lay Hong Kong's foundations — companies like Jardine Matheson & Co., the Hong Kong & Shanghai Bank and Swire's — and this is perfectly understandable. What the quest for Croucher does, on the other hand, is to help uncover the activities of second- and third-line firms in Hong Kong, companies such as Benjamin & Potts, China Provident Loan and Mortgage Co., and Croucher & Co. which, in one way or another, also played a part in building up Hong Kong's financial and economic infrastructure. In the process, we gain a more detailed picture of Hong Kong's business world.

In particular, we witness the development of Hong Kong's stock market from an ad hoc gathering of brokers wheeling and dealing in the streets, observing only those rules they set up for themselves, to one of the world's largest and most sophisticated financial arenas.

It is a compelling story, packed with action, as we watch Croucher negotiate his way in the market over the years, first as a trainee stockbroker trying to make the big time, and as a small shareholder challenging the privileges and wisdom of company directors, and finally as chairman of the Hong Kong Stock Exchange itself. More than just a ripping yarn, this is a chronicle that serious scholars of Hong Kong's business history should take note of.

In addition, the Croucher story reveals a social world that has been overly simplified and stereotyped. The humble circumstances of the young family, headed by his stepfather, living in very modest Morrison Hill Gap, force us to re-examine the life of the British lower classes in Hong Kong. We are often led to think that in the colonial days, the British not only governed the place and dominated the social hierarchy, but that they all lived easy, balmy lives. Too often, we read only about the life of the taipans and their senior staff, governors and their entourage; we imagine only the merriment and luxury, and to some degree, the mindlessness, of life on the Peak.

Croucher's story, however, points out that there were *the other* British groups, poor whites, who, lacking the social ties through school, family and club, had to fend for themselves, relying on hard work, cunning or chance, to survive at the other end of the social scale. In the frontier atmosphere of early twentieth century Hong Kong, even poor Chinese could, to a large extent, rely on various social networks to alleviate the migrants' disorientation and hardship in a strange place.

The situation of many poor whites, by contrast, was frequently marked by emotional isolation and social helplessness; on top of that, they were subject to the resentment of other whites for 'letting the side down in front of the natives'. The Croucher story provides information and food for thought for social scientists to proceed deeper in the analysis of class relations within the European community in early Hong Kong.

It also prompts us to re-examine race-class relations between Chinese and non-Chinese.

Significantly, this book opens with Croucher visiting Deanna Lee, the daughter of his good friend Dick Lee, one of Hong Kong's leading Chinese businessmen. Croucher's lasting friendship with the Lee family, beginning with Dick's father, Lee Hysan, underlines the contradictions of the Hong Kong experience. As a colony and capitalist economy, Hong Kong was widely presumed to be full of fierce economic exploitation, unrelenting racial tensions and brutal social discrimination. Yet, Hong Kong had other faces too. This story allows us to see that Hong Kong was also a place where lasting and caring friendships that crossed the boundaries of race and culture occurred.

Moreover, Croucher's own charitable works — and, indeed the charitable works of many other non-Chinese philanthropists — effectively illustrate intercommunal caring in Hong Kong society. By actively supporting the Royal Society of St. George, he aided his own British people. But more importantly, by endowing The Croucher Foundation with the bulk of his estate, a foundation organized specifically to support Hong Kong students and academics in their scientific and medical pursuits, he made an important statement about his commitment to Hong Kong and its people — they were *his* home and *his* people, too.

This book may be seen as an attempt to reinstate Noel Croucher in history, to rescue him from oblivion. Of course, for the moment at least, he is not completely forgotten. His family and many of his friends remember him. The fact that much of this book is based on their memories testifies to this. But most of the time, the knowledge of each individual is patchy and fragmentary. Even those who remember some aspects of his life, some episodes, in great and vivid detail are completely unaware of other aspects. No one has the whole story.

In the course of time, myths have grown up around Croucher and taken root. The most circulated stories include the one about his coming to Hong Kong as part of a circus and the one about him dying of a cold because he was too parsimonious to take a taxi. To many, it is irrelevant if these 'facts' are accurate or not. It is enough that they are spicy and colourful and fit the tellers' preconceived image of the man. No one has the whole story, but for most people, the myths suffice.

Taking up the many loose threads of people's memories, the author weaves them into a large tapestry. The gaps are filled by research at archives and libraries, through private holdings of letters and photographs, and by cross-checking the interview accounts. Not only do we now have a more complete picture of Croucher's life, but as its more obscure aspects emerge, it seems that we also find a more fascinating man than perhaps the mythologizers would have us believe. We find a man with a lifelong passion for poetry and genuine thirst for knowledge. We find the labour recruiter in the First World War, and more importantly, we find early signs of his humanity in his interaction with the Chinese 'coolies' who were his wards.

Above all, the book reveals the philanthropist, who not only gave his money to worthy causes, but also his time and affection to his beneficiaries. To him, they were not just so many pairs of hands reaching out for dole, but real people, and he cared for them as real people.

This book will not replace myths about Croucher. Histories that pay careful attention to factual accuracy do not replace myths. For those who care about 'what really happened in the past', however, this book is important for setting the record straight. But, it is more than this. Croucher's extraordinary life is a prism that reveals, in all their myriad colours, the many faces of Hong Kong's past — forgotten, obscured, undiscovered faces. For those who feel that history should be constantly re-explored and re-interpreted, the Croucher story, in providing new information and new perspectives, can be both a challenge and a boon.

Elizabeth Sinn
July 1998

AUTHOR'S NOTE

ust three brown envelopes provided the basis for research into Noel Croucher's life and times. They contained papers from the Royal Hong Kong Yacht Club, a collection of unnamed and undated photographs, and a miscellany of pictures and papers collected from Noel's office when he died. Then Florence Lo, Croucher's former office assistant, found the Index Book — Noel's contacts list from 1977. And luckily, journalist Kevin Sinclair had written a double spread for the *South China Morning Post* on Noel Croucher's death in 1980. So we could begin.

First thanks must go to Anthony Tsui, director of The Croucher Foundation, for being the most civilised 'boss' this writer ever had, and for asking Dr Elizabeth Sinn to find a biographer. First thanks also, to the Revd Carl T. Smith, a dear family friend, adviser and mentor throughout this project — and for introducing me to Dr Sinn a dozen years ago. Thanks, of course, to Dr Sinn, for all her advice.

The trustees of The Croucher Foundation, especially Lord Butterfield, insisted from the start on the integrity of our research for which, indeed, deep thanks. They were brave enough to let me reach my own conclusions, and have not censored a sentence of the result. Their support over two years is truly appreciated.

Many exciting discoveries were made with the help of Florence Lo. As the late Lord Todd said, 'she knows her onions alright!' Extra thanks also to all Noel Croucher's staff, past and present.

To Joan Scrivener, my thanks know no bounds. She freely shared twenty-four years' worth of private letters, pictures and personal details, adding unprecedented depth and understanding to our knowledge of our subject. She was and remains a true friend to Noel Croucher.

Special mention goes to Richard Croucher, Noel's son, who

generously shared letters and long dinners, answering questions few people would care to answer about their lives. He has supported this research throughout.

Hundreds of people responded to requests for information and interviews, most of them mentioned in the text. To all of them we are greatly indebted. Of special help were members of the family to which Noel belonged — Betsy Treadgold in Devon, Doris Webb and her daughter Pauline Lacey in Southampton, Doris Croucher and her daughter Jennifer Kang on the Isle of Wight. Penny Croucher of London also squeezed in the time to talk, for which many thanks.

For sheer delight under the guise of interviews, my thanks go to Lady May Ride in Bournemouth, Dr Edith Waldmann of Lyme Regis, Anne Sorby in Kent, Jack Potts in Hampshire and to Pat Loseby. Cynthia and Brian Johnson, Alan Adgey-Edgar, George Stewart, Elizabeth and Allen Mills, Gerald Carey, Marjorie Bray, Bill and Andrin Blauuw, Jack Hobbs — our list could go on and on. Some names will not be found in the text, such as Professor Jim Cummins of London, David Li Kwok-po of the Bank of East Asia and Betty Wei Peh-t'i. I am very grateful to members of the Lee Hysan family — Dr Deanna Lee Rudgard and Ansie Lee Sperry especially. Anne and John Marden deserve special thanks, as does a particular lady of Hong Kong who chooses to remain nameless. My greatest regret was missing a chance to talk with Austin Coates. He died five days before we could meet again. For his life's work and writings, and his friendship with Noel, our thanks.

Among various willing research assistants, Angela Trevor, the Family Historian in Hampshire, deserves top billing. She tirelessly pursued every lead imaginable on a most elusive subject. Gordon Cox, found through the very helpful women of the Eastleigh Museum, is another enthusiast, and the best guide to old Eastleigh. Tim Hughes, a researcher at the Public Records Office at Kew, and Donna Lawrence at the Maritime Archive in Newfoundland perused endless lists and documents. Jason Wordie, Hong Kong's unique resource on colonial and military history, has helped out at every stage.

For timely assistance, my thanks to photographer Hubert Van Es, to editor Paul Bayfield, to Lucy Gamage at the *South China Morning Post* library, to Gillian Chambers, Philip Bowring, David Baird and Frank Bren, and to John McGlynn, of Lontar publishing foundation in Indonesia. To Iris Hay Edie Knapp in Jamaica, many thanks for the delightful film rolls from 1930s Hong Kong. To Kees Metselaar, and to my parents, very special thank yous.

Many institutions gave assistance to this project, and lest we forget, the world's postal services deserve a serious vote of thanks. Not one of 391 identical letters sent around the world to names from an out-of-date address book went astray. Rare and valuable documents or pictures, sent unregistered from far-flung places, all made it intact to base. Email helped too, but the thrill of a battered envelope from an unknown place is hard to beat.

To the Public Records Office system in England, my thanks not only for the information, but for its ready, democratic accessibility. In particular, the Isle of Wight Records Office did valuable work under straitened circumstances. Thanks also to the offices at Winchester, Southampton and Kew. The Family History Centre of London, Guildhall Library of the City of London, Greenwich Maritime Museum and the Imperial War Museum are excellent resources. To the nameless bookseller who directed me to the Charing Cross public library on the performing arts, my thanks. It was a special joy to sit in the old domed Reading Room of the British Library at the British Museum. Thanks also to the P & O Steam Navigation Company Archives, the Cable & Wireless Company Archives, The Rothschild Archive, Jardine Matheson & Company, the Woking Homes, the Nuffield Foundation, the School of Oriental and African Studies in London, to Edwin Green at the Hong Kong Bank archives in London, to Cambridge University Library, Rhodes House at Oxford and Hazlitt's Hotel in Soho.

In Hong Kong, thanks are due to the Hong Kong University Library — especially the Hong Kong Collection and Rare Books Room — and to the librarians at The Helena May. Thanks also to the History Department at the University of Hong Kong, the Public Records Office, Hong Kong Museum of Art, to Charlotte Havilland at the Swire Group Archives, Mrs Welland at the China Coast Community, to the Royal Hong Kong Yacht Club, St. John's Cathedral, the Hong Kong Jockey Club, the Royal Society of Saint George, the Hong Kong Club, and last but not least, the Foreign Correspondents' Club of Hong Kong.

Vaudine England
August 1998

The Croucher Family Tree

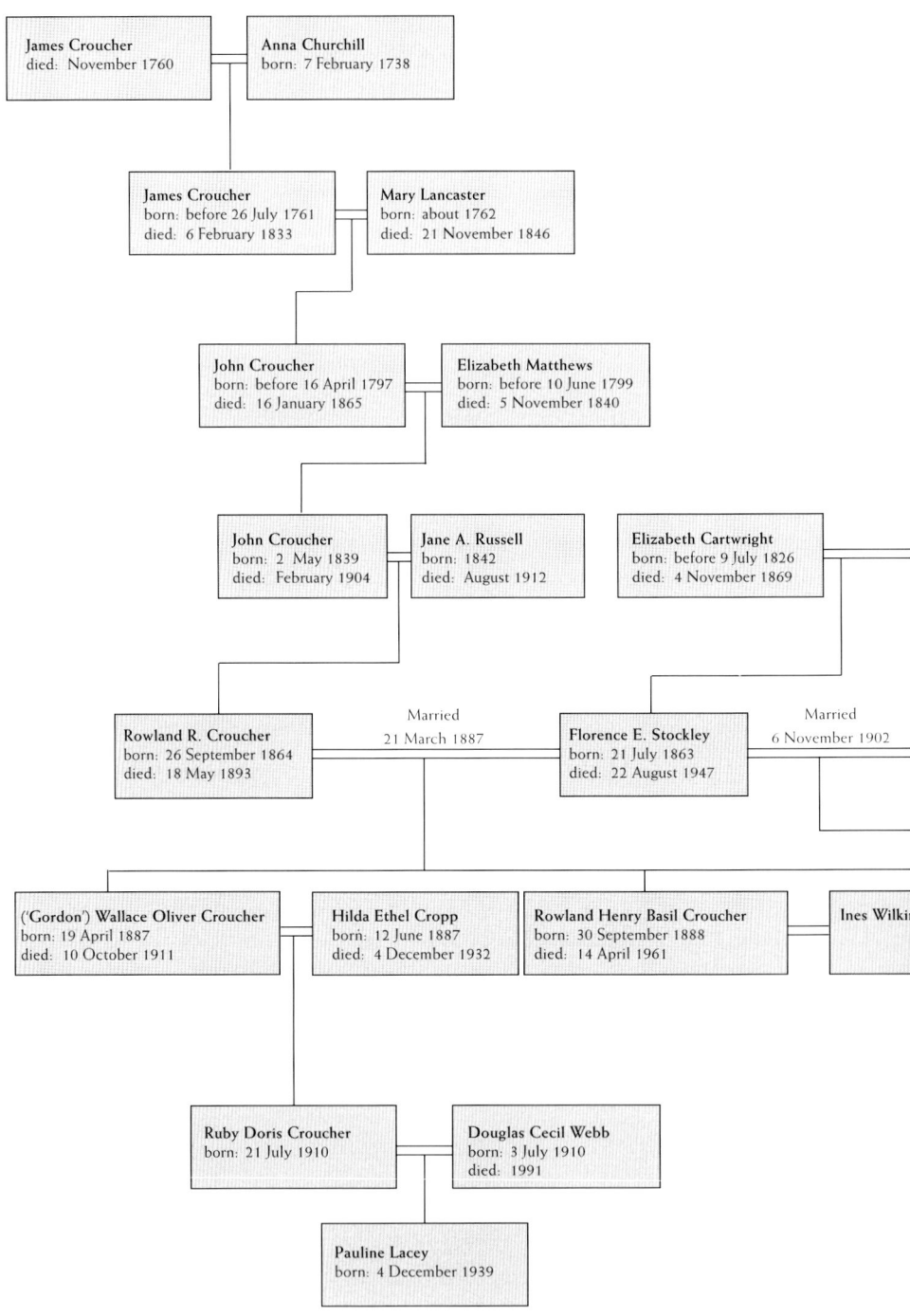

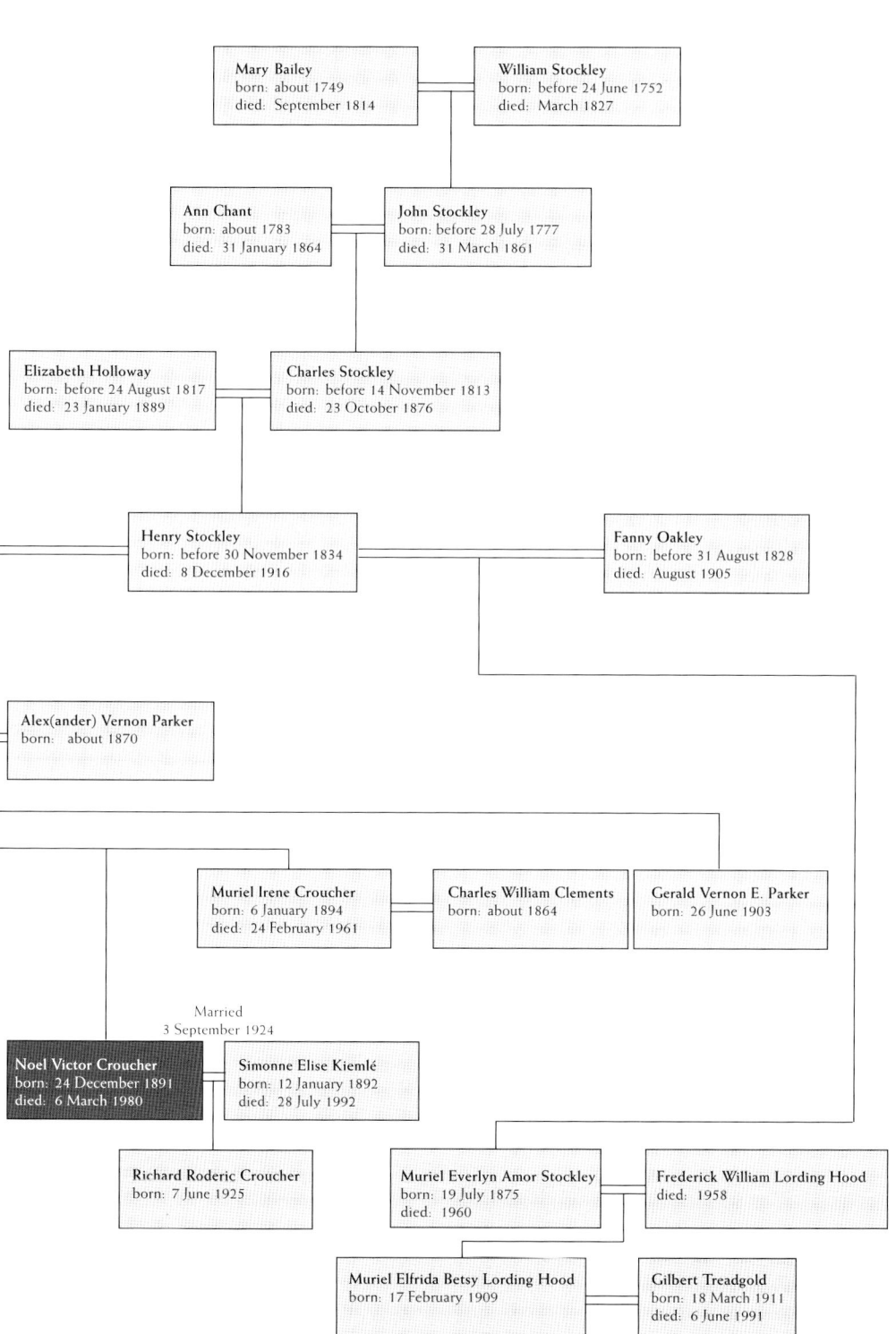

CHAPTER ONE

ISLAND ORIGINS

Some people are curious to know something about their ancestors, without any idea of being snobbish. — Noel Croucher[1]

n the early 1950s, a dashing Englishman in his sixties hired a smart sports car to motor down the coast of the Isle of Wight through the quiet towns of Shanklin and Ventnor. He was Noel Croucher, successful businessman and philanthropist from Hong Kong, taking time for a sentimental journey back to the villages of his father's family. Few people realised he even had a family. But as Noel ambled over the steep hills and gullies he knew, as usual, exactly what he was doing.

His smart car brought him to the island village of Shanklin. Here he paused, collected his bearings and drove to the exclusive girls' boarding school nearby. He was to pick up the daughter of one of his closest business friends from Hong Kong, the legendary Richard or Dick Lee. Noel Croucher was here to show young Deanna Lee the sights in style.

At this stage in his life, Noel Croucher was rich and well-known, entrusted by tycoons with their daughters. The young student he visited that day, now Dr Lee Rudgard, remembers her girlfriends envied her the flashy car and escort:

> During those years [1952–57], in the summer, 'Uncle' Noel would visit to take me out to lunch or afternoon tea. He had an Aston Martin. We'd have a nice lunch and he impressed all the girls with the car. I know my father got on very well with Noel, because only very good friends were introduced to me at school.[2]

There was another reason why Noel would visit this area. He wanted to make a connection between his fascinating life in Hong Kong, the city where he rose from poverty to the Peak, and the homely groups of cottages back in England where he knew his roots lay. In passing through Ventnor in his sports car, he was discovering his ancestors.

Noel Croucher was established in the colony of Hong Kong as a rich mixture of old China hand, ancient mariner and Scrooge. No one knew where he came from, but many were the long evenings at the Bowling Alley Bar of the Hong Kong Club when rumour swirled about the true story of Noel Croucher. Some said he was an orphan, a Jew or an officer's son. Others insist he first got to Hong Kong in a travelling circus. Those who know of the namesake of Chater Road, Sir Paul Catchick Chater, recount the story of how young Noel impressed Sir Paul over a shares purchase and so won a place under the great man's wing.

Noel could have been or done all of these things, but in fact, he did perhaps one.

He was indeed an old-timer on the China Coast, arriving from England near the turn of the century and living to a ripe old age on the Peak. But much of him was a mystery. When he died in 1980, he was regarded with fascinated awe and occasional distaste. Alongside his undoubted business acumen, Noel's character had quirks which defied expectations.[3] Worth a fortune by anyone's standards, he lived alone, frugally, and rarely bought a round of drinks. Known widely as tight-fisted, he frequently, and in secret, gave immense amounts of money and time to his chosen causes. Though a charmer, well-groomed and debonair, he could not find a woman with whom to share his life. Money mattered more than mere class in a colony, yet Noel was looked at askance.

In his public life, he hobnobbed with taipans, the self-styled merchant aristocracy of the China trade. He talked with Governors, knew Chinese warlords and was a firm fan of Joan Fontaine. When Noel was not sailing in the harbours of Hong Kong, his strong personality led the market in the Hong Kong Stock Exchange.

But little was left to show from this life — a miscellany of loose papers, letters and pictures to fill just three brown envelopes, an old contacts book, and the casual hyperbole of hearsay recounted by those who knew him. Which of the many legends was true? What, apart from the money, did it all add up to?

Walk along St. Catherine's Street in Ventnor today and a more different world to Hong Kong can scarcely be imagined. Here on the southeast cliffs of the Isle of Wight fresh winds bluster the walker, the sun shines on clumps of trees, waves are crashing below. A car can hardly squeeze along the street and it's so quiet the local radio from the back of a house a block away can be heard distinctly. Narrow little houses stand side by side, with names like Sea Breeze or Providence Cottage. It's a five-minute walk to the centre of town, where a couple of streets offer a rare books shop, a tourist office, novelty stores and tea rooms.

Few people are about nowadays, although the young woman stacking deck chairs on the beach is hoping for a summer onslaught. Back when Noel Croucher's father was growing up there in the mid-1800s, Ventnor was just becoming known as a fresh, healthy resort. There were beneficial sea breezes on the Esplanade, and curtained changing pavilions on the sand for respite between morning and afternoon teas. Many came to Ventnor as consumptive convalescents, to stay at the pioneering Royal National Hospital on the cliffs. As the *Ward Guide Book* to the Isle of 1906 declaimed, 'Ventnor, like the familiar garden flower, turns always to the sun.' Made alluring by the title, 'The English Madeira', Ventnor was snug, secluded, even stylish.[4]

Karl Marx retired to Ventnor under treatment for headaches and bronchial trouble. Swinburne, Keats and W.S. Gilbert lived here, as did Dickens who, appropriately, started writing *Great Expectations* here. The Isle of Wight gained new allure when Alfred Tennyson made his home here. Then Victoria came.

Queen Victoria, Prince Albert and five children found the pomp of Windsor an impediment to domestic bliss, notes Lytton Strachey's astringent biography of the Queen. So they removed themselves to the estate of Osborne on the Isle of Wight, where family cares and delights could be indulged to the full. 'The middle classes, in particular, were pleased. They liked a love-match; they liked ... the regularity, the plain tuckers, the round games, the roast beef and Yorkshire pudding of Osborne ... duty, industry, morality and domesticity triumphed... The Victorian Age was in full swing.'[5]

Noel Croucher wondered if his family was part of the Huguenot diaspora — many Crouchers of Hampshire and the Isle of Wight did arrive in that way.[6] His fascination with family history is shown in the letters Noel wrote to people such as the vicar at Yarmouth in 1969. He explained that his papers had been lost during World War II, 'and I don't think I shall be able to get a record back to 1440 when John Croucher was Dean of Winchester Cathedral'.[7]

Noel was onto his trail, albeit without all the clues or tools to hand. Importantly, to Noel and to our story, his roots were deep in English soil. Not all of the Isle's many emigrants ever managed to return. But Noel Croucher loved to revisit the Isle of Wight. He told friends how he came from near Carisbrooke Castle, where King Charles I tried in vain to escape from a meeting with Cromwell's axe in London. The castle stands, in glorious countryside, and Crouchers live in its lee.[8] Noel Croucher, the millionaire yachtsman of Hong Kong, also kept photos in his office of friends on their yachts at Cowes. He enjoyed the aristocratic yachting crowd there, knowing his humble start just round the coast at Ventnor.

Here then, lived Noel's forebears. His father, Rowland Russell Croucher, came from a strong line of seafarers, on an island with a rich history in shipping, smuggling and piracy.[9] Rowland was son of John Croucher, mariner, ship's captain and hotel-keeper, also of Ventnor, whom we can trace all the way back at least to James Croucher (circa 1760–1833) and his wife Mary Lancaster. Indeed, most Crouchers on the Isle go back to James, mariner of Yarmouth. He was a respectable man, being churchwarden in 1795–96. Half a dozen different Croucher families live on the Isle today and there are recollections of Croucher's Post Office.[10]

Rowland's mother was Jane Ann Russell, daughter of Jacob Russell of Whitwell, three miles (five kilometres) inland from Ventnor. Trade directories for 1857 through to 1891 list Jacob Russell as shopkeeper, grocer and baker, Maurice Russell as dairyman and James Russell as grocer. Modern-day Whitwell has but one shop left. Residents recall the milk delivery from Russell's farm, in milk pails hung from a yoke, and the cheese made at Russell's dairy, known locally as 'rock' due to its hardness. The Russells also walked into Ventnor with baskets of eggs.[11] Few strangers passed through the village in those days, 'one of the quietest, drowsiest, prettiest spots on the Isle'.[12]

On Christmas Day, 1860, John Croucher married Jane Russell in the Anglican parish church of Whitwell. They lived for at least a decade on St. Catherine's Street, Ventnor. After the ninth child, they moved house almost yearly, in and around Ventnor. John branched out from his family's main work on the sea, so his son, Rowland, learned the craft of baker and confectioner. He was probably the lad who delivered bread to the hospital on the hill — where he was soon to be dazzled by a redhead.

Beyond the steep and narrow roads of the town are Ventnor's Botanical Gardens, basking in the sun. Here, before its demolition in 1964, stood the Royal National Hospital. Opened almost a century earlier by Arthur Hill Hassall it was built on the then novel concept of having separate rooms for tuberculosis sufferers. Even the kitchens were underground so that patients would breathe fresh air.

Here, in 1881, worked a sharp, determined young woman christened Florence Emma Stockley, known to her friends as Floss. She was born at 4 Cavendish Grove, just off Wandsworth Road, South Lambeth, London, on 21 July 1863, back when her father was an engine driver at the nearby railway works. She became housemaid at the hospital at the age of seventeen and her boss was Dr Sinclair Coghill who had worked for several years at the Shanghai General Hospital.[13] Perhaps his stories of the East were the first inkling that Noel's mother had of life outside England. The hospital was also host to performing troupes and travelling players — an apparently friendly community of staff and patients, a village on its own.

Vivacious Floss soon met sensible Rowland. Indeed she was pregnant when they married on 21 March 1887, at his family's little house on the cliffs of Ventnor. Their first child, Wallace Oliver, arrived on 19 April, thereafter to be known as Gordon,[14] then Rowland Henry Basil (known as Basil) arrived on 30 September 1888.

It was time for the young family to move, so off they went to the mainland where new opportunities for work were beckoning. The railways had just come to Eastleigh, a country area north of Southampton and, conveniently, it was Eastleigh where Floss' family was based. Here, on Christmas Eve, 1891, Noel Victor Croucher was born.

Eastleigh Railway Station, signs of progress all around, still relies on the original metal poles of 1841 to hold up the platform shelter.[15] Along the main Leigh Road, skirting the park with a bandstand in the middle, is a statue of a railway man, the roots of the town's early prosperity. The old Salvation Army Hall is now the museum, which traces the rapid growth of Eastleigh from a manor farm into the bustling town of today. The key fact about Eastleigh soon becomes clear — it is relatively new, less than two hundred years old, with few feudal dynasties or traditions. By the time of Noel's birth, Eastleigh had only just graduated to a town of six thousand people. Reports of the bustling community insist: 'Victorian values shone through everything'.[16]

With the opening of the London-Southampton line in 1840, Eastleigh became an important railway junction. But the move of the London and South Western Railway's Carriage and Wagon Works to the town in 1891 made it a magnet to new labour and young families. Rowland Croucher got a job as a Permanent Way Inspector, checking land where new tracks would be laid. His father-in-law, Henry Stockley, had driven trains to the same station.

Housing was in short supply, 'and controversy centred on the deplorable state of the unmade streets and lack of street lighting, and the lack of adequate drainage and sewage in the town'.[17] But the young family managed to find a home in the terraced houses of the time, at 6 Wykeham Villas, on High Street.

Anecdotes suggest Noel Croucher well remembered his maternal grandfather Henry Stockley, whose white beard in later years gave him an imposing air of distinction. Born in the village of Mottisfont, near Winchester, in 1834, Henry descended from a long line of Stockleys who, at various stages, appeared quite well-off, with land-holdings to pass on for generations.[18] One William Stockley, who died in 1744 in Kings Somborne, Hampshire, had a freehold estate, including meadows, a malt-house, orchards and estates.

Five generations later, Henry Stockley's first marriage was to the well-educated plumber's daughter Elizabeth Cartwright. It produced, among others, one Florence Emma Stockley, known to us already as Floss. Elizabeth died when Floss, her daughter, was only six years old. Within a year Henry married again.[19]

Noel wrote in 1971: 'When my mother [Floss] died [in 1947] she gave my brother Basil a family Bible which he gave to me. It is a large one and was presented to Elizabeth Cartwright ... in 1856. I think she was a Sunday School teacher and was born in 1826. It is rather dilapidated, but the names of her children and when they were born are entered there. I believe she was a cultured lady and played the piano very well — how she got married to Henry Stockley, Lord knows, he must have had a way with him...'[20]

Floss' family, led by the redoubtable Henry Stockley, had moved down to Eastleigh in the early 1860s, presumably for the railways.[21] When Noel was born on the High Street in 1891, his maternal grandparents, the Stockleys, lived on Market Street just around the corner. Judging by where marriages and births took place, both sides of Noel's family, the Crouchers and the Stockleys, appeared to be Bible Christians, a society which later formed part of the United Methodists.

Noel first learned about upward mobility from old Grandpa Stockley. Henry's father, Charles Stockley, was a publican and gamekeeper, and for some reason Henry grew up with his maternal grandparents, Joseph and Frances Holloway of Mottisfont. At the risk of getting ahead of the story, Henry, like Noel, was working by the age of about sixteen. Henry appeared in the records as an engine man and commercial traveller, but within a decade was recognised as a 'Gentleman'. Huntin' and shootin', visiting the racetrack and sporting clubs of Chandlers Ford, Henry Stockley became a big man in Eastleigh. He liked to walk down the middle of the road.

'Oh golly he thought he was the earth,' remembers his granddaughter, Betsy Treadgold, chatting decades later in her sun room at home in Devon. 'He was like Floss you know — terrible! When I knew him he was a bookmaker and he used to go hunting and he used to go fishing and he used to go to all the race meetings, and that's why he moved from Southampton to Eastleigh because Eastleigh was a big junction, and you could get to Salisbury Races, get to Dene, he had shoots in Dene, he had shoots in Bishopstoke.

'Always, if he wasn't at a race meeting he was at a shooting. He had his own shoots, he and a few friends, and he had a keeper and a keeper's cottage. I used to go there when I was a child. He used to rear pheasants and have a shoot after. My grandfather, he belonged to several hunts. And we had all these jolly stuffed animals all round the place, a stag, a hare, a fox, he had a case of 'em, a hall full of 'em, pheasants, partridge... My mother got fed up with it.'[22]

By the end of the nineteenth century Henry had built three houses in a row, numbers 65, 67 and 69 Leigh Road, one of which is the Labour Party office of Eastleigh today. One of Henry's brothers, Peter, was head gamekeeper to the Marquis of Bath residing at Longleat House. The other, Joseph or Josiah, was gamekeeper to the Duke of Somerset's riding estate at Stover.

Henry achieved a state in which he no longer needed to work. His recreational pursuits were engrossing, perhaps aided by the 'pass' available to former workers on the railways. But Henry was a strict and cantankerous father. He horsewhipped his sons and locked up his daughters, and when his wife Frances was poorly in 1905, he insisted the band playing in the park be kept silent until she recovered. The newspaper notice of 21 July 1905 reads: 'Mr Henry Stockley begs to apologise to the inhabitants of Eastleigh for being the cause of the Band not playing in the Recreation ground on Wednesday due to serious illness in his house.' Notwithstanding these efforts, Frances died the next month.

'I thought Grandpa was Master of the Hursley Hunt, or maybe the whipper-in,' wrote Noel Croucher decades later. 'I remember all the hounds in front of the house and I was only about six at the time and wore a red pinafore. Aunt Flo Wilkins [half-sister to Floss] and her husband would come for a visit and your mother [Muriel Everlyn Amor Stockley] of course was there — she had lovely fair hair and a good figure...'[23]

A certain imperiousness marks Noel's memories of Grandpa Henry, and he was an autocratic landlord. 'Our villa was the third one up,' said Mrs Treadgold. 'We had quite a decent garden [on Leigh Road]. But my grandfather also had to have a stable. So instead of the poor people next door having a decent garden, half of their garden was where Grandpa built his stable. They had only half a garden. So we had a stable, and horses. I know Mother used to say the horses used to come up on Easter and have a hot cross bun at the back door and that sort of nonsense. We only left the villas, sold them, in 1958 or '60, and they're still there.'[24]

Betsy adds Grandpa Henry was a regular at the Conservative Club just down a lane from their house on Leigh Road. 'My grandfather and me, aged four or five, and two retriever dogs, used to go there every morning for him to have a "two of Scotch" while I played ball there with the dogs. I have been told some members objected and Grandpa threatened to buy the place and turn them out! The "Con Club" as it was known is still the same ... the large building at the end used to be a Wesleyan Chapel, but was bought by the Eastleigh Masons and became the Masonic Hall. They used to hold meetings in the Council Chamber and my grandfather was a member, also my father and my husband.'

Floss, Noel's mother, was one of the few who dared to stand up to her father Henry Stockley. She was the wild, rebellious one. She answered back, she fought back, and it seems she eventually fled, displaying a determination and a dramatic streak which were to stand her in good stead in the years that followed. 'The only thing I remember about Floss,' says Betsy Treadgold, 'is my mother saying, oh Floss is terrible, she wants to rule everybody. And then Floss disappeared from view.'

Mrs Treadgold also recalls a story told to her by Floss about the latter's alleged attendance at a reception given to mark Princess (now Queen) Elizabeth's wedding. It cannot, unfortunately, be true as the wedding took place after Floss' death. But for the insight it gives into how Floss was regarded by her relations — as they clearly believed the story easily — here it is:

> I tell you what SHE says she did, and I quite believe her ... the Princess
> was wed, and spent her honeymoon at Mountbatten's place in Romsey,

six miles from Southampton. Floss was going to the wedding. They had a church service, and the Queen spent her honeymoon at Romsey Abbey, and had a reception, all with tickets. So Floss said she was going! We didn't take much notice. Anyway she turned up and 'Oooh, it was marvellous,' she said. I said, 'You can't get in, how could you get in?' She said, 'Of course I got in!' She always dressed in black satin, all in satin, and one of these hats with a feather you know, and she had a walking stick, and she turned herself up and if somebody said something to her she said, 'Out of my way man!' and man got out of way for Floss! My mother said, 'That's Floss all over.' She was a big woman, tall.[25]

Rowland Croucher, the young baker Floss married on the Isle of Wight, unfortunately barely makes it into this story. Two years after young Noel was born, he died of jaundice.

Here began a difficult time for young Floss — she was three months pregnant with her fourth child, a daughter named Muriel Irene. Irene's birth is a rare clue to Floss' whereabouts following her widowhood. The address from which she registered Irene's birth, on 6 January 1894, was 105 Pyle Street, Newport, Isle of Wight. Why she went there is a mystery.[26] Irene was brought up by relatives on the Isle and certainly Noel, her brother, knew little of her.

Noel's early childhood in a new, growing town, with a grandfather of personality and an elusive mother, was profoundly disrupted by the death of his father.

Vague family memories suggest that mother Floss, at least, was living in Southampton rather than Eastleigh by the turn of the century. Or perhaps the newly widowed Floss, with three or four young children to bring up, stayed at her father's house on Leigh Road, Eastleigh, leaving new daughter Irene behind on the Isle. Or perhaps she kept all her children on the Isle of Wight. What school records survive, reveal no sign of Noel Croucher and his siblings either in Hampshire or on the Isle of Wight. At some point, however, Floss ran away to the music halls and theatres of Southampton, and one reason was probably the stern character of her father, Henry Stockley.

'Oh my mother had a frightful time,' said Mrs Treadgold of Muriel Stockley, Floss' half-sister. 'She was brought up so strict. Grandpa was terrible. I think that's probably why the girls left, you see. I think they probably fled the so-called nest, because their father was so strict. They went off the rails.'[27]

Of course that's not quite how the Eastleigh newspaper saw it in the obituary published on Henry Stockley's death in 1916:

> Death has removed another of Eastleigh's oldest residents, Mr Henry Stockley, who passed away on Friday last at the ripe old age of 82. He was well known and greatly respected. For many years he has resided at 'Moreton', Leigh Road. Up till a few years ago, he was a keen sportsman with his gun and a follower of the Hursley Hounds for many years. Familiarly known as Harry, he had a wide circle of friends while he was also a Freemason...[28]

Noel's formative years were thus spent under the influence of two strong personalities — his mother's and his grandfather's. Whether he grew up more in Henry's household, or with his mother, his childhood memories were focused on the Solent, stretching north to Eastleigh and south to the Isle of Wight. These are the areas he chose to visit, decades later, as a successful man of Hong Kong.

A key point of his upbringing was its instability — the early loss of his father, the apparent moves from place to place, and the lack of educational opportunities. Certainly Noel learned his 'three Rs' somewhere, how to go to church regularly and to dress smartly at all times. According to existing records, he was not placed in an orphanage or home or workhouse — at least his family background was solid enough to save him from that.[29] But whatever caused his mother's rupture with her father's household, it seems likely Noel's schooling, and sense of security, would have suffered.[30]

Anecdotes later recounted by Noel Croucher suggest he did spend some early years back on the Isle of Wight — one meeting he had there stayed in his mind throughout his life. This was the encounter he told special friends about, his meeting with an old woman on the beach of Ventnor. He was a lad of about six years old (circa 1897), playing on his own in the sand. It was a blustery, lonely sort of day. The woman had a dog at her heels and her short, stocky form was swathed in vast cloaks of black. The mysterious woman chatted with the young boy, probably about the dog or the weather, then moved on. Later, Noel was told he'd been talking with Queen Victoria.[31]

A chat on the windy beach one morning was not all that Noel absorbed from Queen Victoria's reign. He grew up with notions of

Victorian propriety mixed with a heavy dose of survival instinct. He became what his own family felt to be a Victorian patriarch — God-fearing, intimidating, forever impossible to please.

How deeply such attitudes had sunk into his make-up can be seen in the gift he gave to his son, Richard, in the 1930s, when Richard was about to be sent off to school. It was the book called *John Halifax, Gentleman* by Mrs Craik,[32] a bestseller in the mid-1800s. It is an epic based on the fine upstanding character of John Halifax who overcomes all manner of disadvantages through sheer, dogged hard work, and triumphs by becoming a rich and respected patriarch in a manor house, forever admired for his moral uprightness and business acumen.

Moral tone and keen determination are key themes. At one point pondering how to get through a dense yew hedge which is fifteen feet high and fifteen feet wide, John Halifax, our hero, 'smiled — there was no "giving up" in that smile of his. "I'll tell you what I'd do — I'd begin and break it, twig by twig, till I forced my way through, and got out safe at the other side." '[33] Chapter One opens with pithy, preaching dialogue: 'Sir, I want work; may I earn a penny?' asks the impoverished but very proper John Halifax. 'Lad, shall I give thee the groat now?' the man of affairs replies. 'Not till I've earned it, sir,' says John.

John Halifax is the archetypal self-made man, constantly striving to improve himself and his station. The book applauds the egalitarianism that allowed a poor boy to get ahead. It also upholds the 'old-fashioned' notion of nobility wherein a gentleman not only had money and power but also a deep sense of responsibility to the community, a commitment to 'his people'. In Robert Denniston's introduction to Mrs Craik's book, he notes, 'so far from being a forerunner of the Classless Society he is rather a messenger of hope to those who try to raise themselves from the station to which they were born.'

The book is steeped in the characteristic paradox of Victoria's reign. It extols honesty and hard work, for capitalist gain, defending a cruel hoarder of flour during a famine, for example, in the name of private property. It also shows our hero, John, risking the lives of his own children in order to aid an ailing servant child in his home. The message made its mark on Noel Croucher. In the fly leaf of the book, specially for his son, Noel Croucher had written: 'Good Better Best, Never Let Me Rest, Till my Good is Better, And my Better Best'.[34]

John Halifax got ahead only partly through his own probity and perseverance — it also mattered that originally, his family was respectable. Noel Croucher was keen to discover his family history, corresponding with many over the years on the subject, yet he had no time for snobbery. Certainly, in the large figure of Henry Stockley, and the Crouchers of the Isle of Wight, he had little to be ashamed of.

Another key to John Halifax's success was education. His ability to teach himself to read and write was the secret to his rise in stature and wealth throughout his life. The idea was that men could better themselves. 'Self-help, self-reliance, entrepreneurship, individual charity (rather than a state dole), law and order, family discipline and a stricter sexual morality were the principles that enabled the Victorians to make hitherto undreamed of progress...'[35] As the nineteenth century progressed, men believed in tradition, in 'Merrie England' and in *noblesse oblige*, at the same time as they found ways to harness science, technology and labour for a better future. The England Noel was born into was riding high on the glories of empire and ambition.

However cheerful Noel's early years might have been, life changed dramatically, when Floss took another bold step. On 6 November 1902, she married again. This time she had found a man called Alex Vernon Parker, listed as an actor on the marriage certificate. They were both in Southampton, but what they lived off is anyone's guess. How did she meet this man? And where did he come from? Mr Parker is the most mysterious of all. He appears, plays a brief but crucial role, and he disappears. It is to him that we owe Noel Croucher's arrival in Hong Kong, but in ways Alex Parker could hardly have imagined.

As for Floss, she had done it again — she was pregnant when she married Alex Parker. Betsy Treadgold says: 'I remember Mother saying, oh, Parker wasn't anything, just an out-of-work actor. Why Floss ever married him...! She was very very close, Floss, frightfully autocratic. Oh dear. I had an idea what she was like!'

Parker does not seem to have been such a good actor as his new wife. Able to put on airs and graces, she could perform on life's stage with no tremor of fear. She would not be down and out, she could talk her way out of anything bad and sweep her way into anything good. She knew the impact of appearance, of a straight back and a bold mien. Noel got his unconventional start in Hong Kong from his stepfather, but he learned style and quickness of eye from his mother.

The family legend is that Alex Parker joined the army as an officer and was posted to Hong Kong with his family. Alas, the lists of officers (army and navy) held by the Public Records Office at Kew feature no A.V. Parker. What happened first was the arrival of Gerald Vernon Ephraim Parker, a half-brother to Noel. He was born to Floss and Alex Parker on 26 June 1903 in Southampton.[36] He was the only relative, apart from Noel's wife, whom Noel was to list in his will.

The Croucher-Parkers were still in England in late 1904, according to a press cutting kept by Mrs Treadgold in Devon. This reports her mother's wedding in Eastleigh in August 1904. Among a list of Stockleys and other guests were Mr and Mrs A.V. Parker, attributed with giving a silver teapot to the married couple.[37] One more clue to the family's whereabouts comes from a letter Noel Croucher wrote in which he recalled seeing Betsy Treadgold's grandmother, that is Henry Stockley's second wife Frances, lying in state after her death in August 1905.[38] She died and was buried in Eastleigh, so Noel at least believed he was still in the Southampton neighbourhood in late 1905.

According to surviving family members, Alex Parker did enlist, but in the ranks, and was indeed sent out to Hong Kong. One version has it that he might have found Flossie a bit too hot to handle (or had it just slipped his mind in the rush?) as he did not leave her any address where she could find him in the East. Some women would have taken the hint, but not Florence Emma Croucher-Parker. The story goes that she 'upped and offed and followed him!'[39]

However it happened, a carefully posed photograph has survived which tells an almost convincing story. It shows a well-dressed Floss with Alex Parker and the various children, appearing to be settled for life in Southampton. The direct eyes of young Noel show little inkling of the dramatic changes in store.

CHAPTER TWO

POOR EUROPEANS IN THE COLONY

All Hong Kong is built on the sea-face; the rest is fog.[1]

Above all, steer your way carefully through the destroying fog of Hongkong snobbery.[2]

uch though we would love to describe Noel as a keen-eyed lad, leaning over the rail of a ship as it steamed into Hong Kong harbour and imagining his glorious future as a multimillionaire on the Peak, an exhaustive search of shipping lists has produced no evidence of just when and how Noel Croucher first saw his future home. Had he sailed out in style, he would have been easily traced. But Floss and her children, though intrepid, were certainly not travelling first-class.[3] What is clear, however, is that Noel's stepfather was in Hong Kong by 1905, and Noel himself by 1907 if not before, both dates being much earlier than the alleged arrival in 1910 which has made it into legend.

The image we have of the early British colonials is that they were a high-stepping lot. They sailed first-class, stayed at the Hong Kong Hotel, or up at the hotels on the Peak. Newly arrived single men — fresh from public school or the City — would be met by a company contact or someone who knew their fathers, and taken straight to the Hong Kong Club. Here they would meet anyone they needed to know, find a place to stay, and have a ready-made society to walk into. Scores of servants, subservient natives, lavish ease of living — all this could be taken for granted. So long as the young man did not offend, and could hold his own at the club bars or on the cricket pitch, then his future fortune was assured.

The most important fact of all about Noel Croucher is that this is *not* how he started out in Hong Kong. On the contrary, Noel did not or could not join the Hong Kong Club until he was thirty-seven years old, almost a quarter of a century after he arrived in the colony.[4] He was not prominent enough to get his own pew at St. John's Cathedral before the seat-naming ritual was discontinued in 1929. He did not live on the Peak until twenty years after his arrival in Hong Kong and then only briefly. He did not secure his settled home there on Mount Cameron Road until well after World War II. He certainly had not been to public school back home, and no personal connection or introduction was awaiting him in Hong Kong. Nor was there any ready-made society for this odd young family to fit into when they arrived. There is no record of their arrival, and no record of where they first stayed — it was no doubt a small boarding house, perhaps in Kowloon or on the outskirts of the respectable parts of central Hong Kong.

By August 1907, however, the Croucher-Parker family lived at 12 Morrison Hill Gap, Hong Kong.[5] The area was named after the first Protestant missionary to China, Robert Morrison. Coincidentally, Ethel Morrison, the well-known brothel Madam, lived at 33 Morrison Hill Road, and a sketch of her home shows a simple terraced house with balconies.[6] Another resident was Mr Van Eps, the undertaker. In the 1890s this area, on the boundaries between Wanchai and Happy Valley, was home to wharfs, godowns and coffin repositories. New houses were built around 1903, by a group of related Chinese families, probably terraced. On Morrison Hill itself were six homes for Jardine's staff, and the land further along at East Point was owned by Jardine's.

In between the godowns and the mansions was the swamp of Happy Valley, drained to form a semi-industrial area of lumber yards, steam laundries and warehouses, and the racecourse. Noel's early home was near what was then the foreshore, close to the Royal Hong Kong Yacht Club where Noel was to spend so much of his adult life. Several Portuguese and English families lived where Morrison Hill Road connected with Wanchai Road.

This was not a salubrious neighbourhood.[7] Although trams had made their debut in 1904, trundling from nearby Causeway Bay to West Point, it was on the outer edges of respectability. Noel's family was in that half-invisible subclass of poorer whites, barely recognised by their richer compatriots or by the Chinese. Expatriate communities on the China Coast were confined and self-absorbed, often paralysed by the need to maintain the white man's decorum and prestige in the East. To ignore the poor whites around them seemed a deliberate policy of the colonial leadership, in the name of imperial prestige. 'A working class European was excluded from both polite European and Chinese society; he was forced to live in his own constricted social world, a type of marginal man.'[8]

Unlike their Chinese counterparts in Hong Kong, poor whites had no family or community in which to survive and find strength. They were rejected by their own, that is by other whites, for 'letting the side down in front of the natives'. Indeed, a rich white man in turn-of-the-century Hong Kong could be seen chatting to a rich Chinese, before he would be seen talking to a poor compatriot.[9] Discussing the class of European workers then residing in Hong Kong, W.K. Chan notes, 'their numerical insignificance apart, their economic inferiority and low status excluded them from the European merchant class, while their racial and cultural characteristics made it difficult for them to be assimilated into the Chinese working class.'[10] As for interrace relations, 'it is important to remember that, from earliest days, Chinese were, if anything, more socially aloof from foreigners than vice versa...'[11]

Quite why Hong Kong society should have been so hierarchical is a subject of academic debate. Perhaps for the 12,000 Westerners in a city of 500,000 Chinese, rituals of social class and a fetish about status were statements of Englishness.[12] Whatever the theory, the reality of class division within the expatriate society had a large impact on Noel Croucher, affecting his personal and business dealings throughout his life.

At the top end of colonial society were the senior civil servants and proprietors of the old hongs or trading houses. Such people stayed for several decades in Hong Kong, but still saw England as home and aimed to retire there. In Hong Kong's subtropical suburbia, a newcomer found acceptance and professional advancement if he had the right background, that measured by Debrett's peerage and the annals of public schools. The only difference in Hong Kong was that without such a headstart, success, though still very hard to achieve, was not impossible. Longevity on the China Coast gave a person a certain kudos, but without good class origins and wealth, such longevity would only make the person a character, not a respected leader of society.

In the top merchant class, by contrast, was the seeming permanence of the old firms, the old names, '...the Wodehouses, the Bell-Irvings, the

Keswicks, the Hancocks, the Pearces, the Lammerts, the Dennys, and many more — father and son, uncle and nephew, spanning long unbroken stretches of the colony's life. Indeed, whereas in the case of the Chinese population it is the rapid increase in numbers that catches the eye, with the Europeans it is the limitation of numbers and, within that select circle, the constant repetition of old names.'[13]

Of these top merchants, some were not even English — wealth was (and is) accorded great respect in Hong Kong, and could mitigate many sins. When Thomas Ash Lane, a Scots mariner, and storekeeper Ninian Crawford first set up as ship chandlers — Lane, Crawford and Co. — they were despised as mere plebeians in trade. But once their descendants made a fortune, social acceptance was achieved. Sir Paul Chater was a leader of society due to his wealth, vision and mercantile power, even though he was an Armenian from Calcutta.

The merchants were the aristocracy of the China Coast. 'As far as they were concerned, although Hong Kong was nominally founded by Captain Elliott, it was founded *for* them.'[14]

Military officers could join the good clubs and go to the Governors' balls. But the mass of middle- or lower-ranking soldiers formed a community of their own, mostly in Kowloon. Being an army wife could be a position of solid, if not stolid, respectability. But it was not as lucrative or stylish as that of the Europeans on Hong Kong-side. As for the missionaries, they were in a curious grey zone in class terms. Individuals were admired for their scholarship, daring explorations of the interior, perhaps even for their faith. But they were difficult people to know. Their priorities were so tiresome — no fun, few parties, certainly no money.

Professionals forming our next layer of white society were lawyers and doctors, followed by engineers, ship captains, highly skilled works managers, and the journalists of Hong Kong's free-wheeling publishing industry. Such men could rise from works foreman to manager or member of the board through merit and knowledge, thanks to the prospects for upward mobility afforded by a colony. There were also settled communities of Parsees and other South Asians. A larger influx, of Portuguese from Macao, was led by such names as d'Almada e Castro, Braga, Noronha, Soares and Barretto. 'The Portuguese element, it may here be noted, forms no inconsiderable portion of the better class of residents settled in Hong Kong.'[15]

For the dregs of Hong Kong society, one went to the streets west of Central to the area bounded by Hollywood Road, Wyndham Street, Graham Street and Wellington Street. On Lyndhurst Terrace, European prostitutes lived and died. The lowest white men went further west, to gin shops, opium or gambling dens. 'Beachcombers' drifted from port to port across the Pacific into the East, taking life's chances and usually losing the bet. They were 'mostly merchant seamen of various nationalities who had either jumped ship or missed the sailing of their vessel because of drunkenness. They were ... creatures of the night, emerging at dusk to solicit alms from sympathetic noctambules. During the day they lay low because if observed by a European policeman they were usually arrested and charged with vagrancy.'[16] Hong Kong was an excellent place in which to avoid a shady past, 'a place where money and bluff and a measure of chicanery helped to compensate for deficiencies in birth or education.'[17]

Hovering between the skilled workers and the destitute, was a narrow band of unskilled, little-educated, but just-respectable people. These Europeans were neither mission nor military, neither tutored nor aristocratic. Here we find the white policemen,[18] the working sailors, the overseers of local labour, and the clerks. Here, if female, were the milliners, the governesses and the nannies. Here too would be Alex Parker, his wife Floss, with sons Gordon, Basil and Noel Croucher, perhaps daughter Irene, and baby Gerald Parker.

While a small crowd of prominent Europeans lived in the same neighbourhood, went to the same church, shopped in the same few shops and recycled the same gossip, young Noel Croucher lived on the outskirts of town and was regarded by the toffs as white trash. And here stepfather Alex Parker played his typical role in history — propelling those around him to great heights through his failure. Much as his acting career appeared to have gone nowhere fast, so too did his military, if it ever occurred. Given his marriage to Noel's mother in Southampton in November 1902, the birth of son Gerald there in June 1903, his apparent attendance at a wedding in Eastleigh in August 1904, and the time it would have taken for a passage to Hong Kong on a troop ship, he could have barely lasted with the army more than a few months, if he enlisted at all.[19]

In April 1905, Alex Parker was appointed to the civil service in Hong Kong, as one of several second-grade overseers in the Public Works Department. This was the lowest position a white man could have. By 1 August 1905, he was confirmed as a second-class overseer in the department.[20] Lethbridge quotes an overseer saying in 1902 that 'any

European here — it doesn't matter who he is or where he is picked up — can be put on a job and is termed an Overseer'.[21]

Public Works was a very busy department. The early 1900s showed a high death rate from plague, severe damage was regularly caused by typhoons, particularly in 1900 and 1906, and flash-floods and strong winds brought down many of the poorly constructed buildings in the Chinese quarter of the city. Shipping and small sampans, on which whole families lived, suffered huge losses. Following reports on sanitation by Osbert Chadwick (1882) and Professor W.J. Simpson (1903), the Public Works Department was surveying and hopefully clearing the slums of Hong Kong to allow for the building of sewers and proper homes.[22]

Noel Croucher's stepfather probably supervised Chinese workmen. It is unlikely he would have been tied to a desk — that was for more senior clerical staff. His role, though humble, was based on that grand imperial assumption that having a white man shout orders in an incomprehensible language will steel the resolve of the labourers to perform.

From the family's address and Parker's occupation, it is clear that young Noel grew up in lower-class limbo. 'The higher orders of government officials and the executive personnel of the big business houses had homes built for them on the midriff, bosom, shoulders and head of the Peak, leaving all that was sordidly commercial or commercially sordid in the unmentionable nether regions below.'[23]

Noel Croucher started in these 'nether regions below' and he never forgot it. Churches and the Mission to Seamen, and groups such as the Hong Kong Ladies' Benevolent Society, were rare beacons of charity to the down-and-out European, even if a cup of tea and a moral lecture were less fun than a night flat out in an opium den. Noel was later to add to their work, partly through the Royal Society of Saint George. He knew of the invidious position endured by poor whites in the colonies and was to become known to friends as a man who would help others to get home, on the quiet, with dignity intact. He seemed to harbour special concern for those Westerners who had somehow fallen from grace.[24] Such compassion had no doubt been nurtured early on.

The visual impact of Hong Kong on a virgin eye has prompted some to compare the sweep of peak and harbour to Genoa or to Gibraltar 'but far, far, finer'.[25] Others say the layout is best understood by comparing

Hong Kong to the Isle of Wight, and Kowloon to Portsmouth and the Portsdown Hills. Perhaps this helped Noel feel at home.[26]

Little else would have been familiar. Back home, Noel's place was clear — he was a younger son of a fascinating mother who, recently remarried, chose to follow adventure rather than the rules. Noel's maternal grandfather had progressed to 'Gentleman', a basis Noel's mother Floss could have built on had she married well. Instead, she took the high-risk route to a new life. Perhaps she was looking for Alex Parker, or perhaps Hong Kong had an allure of its own.

At this naval and commercial terminus of the Suez Canal, moored to England by its electric cable, steep streets of steps were arched over by trees, creating tropical colonnades. Turn-of-the-century Hong Kong was in the throes of recovery and change. The British government had chosen 1891 (incidentally, the year of Noel's birth) to celebrate Hong Kong's 'Jubilee' to mark fifty years of existence.[27] Perhaps the overambition of that choice — the Treaty of Nanking was not signed until 1842 after all — accounts for the ups and downs that followed. Along with the typhoons and outbreaks of plague, activism for local reforms had begun. These led to the appointment of Mr (later Sir) Catchick Paul Chater along with the Jardine's representative J.J. Bell-Irving as the first unofficial members of the Executive Council. Away from the mainstream, and largely unknown to the non-Chinese community in Hong Kong, republican revolution was fomenting (under Dr Sun Yat-sen) and was to succeed in 1911.

In the last years of the last century, Hong Kong had grown apace. The granite praya, the busy wharves, smart office buildings and a new statue of Queen Victoria were complemented by the opening in 1898 of the Hong Kong Club, or 'New Club'[28] — a stately building opposite the future Court House. Resident members were admitted by ballot and required to pay an entrance fee of $30 and a monthly subscription of $4.[29] The highest villages of the Peak and Magazine Gap now boasted two hotels and an excellent road, according to the *Chronicle and Directory* of 1897,[30] while the city of Victoria comprised a four-mile stretch of closely built houses, rising in tiers up the hillside from the sea. Kowloon was gradually being developed. The New Territories were only just becoming more than a wild hinterland, the ninety-nine-year lease granted by China to Britain dating only from 9 June 1898. Docks and warehouses were host to a harbour full of shipping.

By 1902, work had begun on a network of reservoirs. In 1903, a path-breaking public health ordinance was passed, and building began on a new Post Office, Supreme Court and Government Offices. The first reclamations in Victoria, along the waterfront of central Hong Kong, were underway. So too was the argument over having military lands and a planned naval dock, right in the prime area between the central business district and its eastern hinterland, effectively blocking any natural mercantile expansion. The merchants lost to the military. Eighty years later, Noel's papers still included a clipping about the military lands dispute. Alongside the bonded warehouses, Hong Kong was building its first industries: a cotton mill, a flour mill (its creator, A.H. Rennie, drowned himself in 1906), a tannery, two sugar refineries and, further afield in Macao, a cement works.

Perhaps Alex Parker found the work not to his liking. Perhaps, as with so many others, he drank too much. 'Less than half of the European subordinate staff who came to Hong Kong survived to earn their pensions; the rest died, were dismissed, or were invalided out of the service, and most of these casualties were caused by excessive drinking.'[31] Maybe he succumbed to local delights in the brothels of Western. Or perhaps he was part of the scams all around him — public health laws were widely disliked, corruption was rife and by 1906, scandal had engulfed the department. In 1907, a Commission of Enquiry found 'much irregularity', with inspectors colluding with building contractors. 'The powers intended for use in public health were made the subject of private gain.'[32]

Whatever the cause, Alex Parker got the sack early in 1908. The best possible view we can put on this is that, under a contract, his time was up. Alternatively, he may have misbehaved. The records do not tell us.[33] When Alex Parker lost his job, the precarious position of his young family can readily be imagined. The family faced desperate times.

Who could Alex Parker or Floss turn to for help? Unsubstantiated rumours about Noel's mother cover boarding houses, dance troupes and travelling players. As for Alex Parker, his patchy career supervising Chinese work gangs out in the open air is the last sighting of the man. Once he was dismissed from the Public Works Department in 1908, no record in Hong Kong or England makes any reference to our Alex Vernon Parker, dead or alive.[34]

As for Floss, now laden with young children and perhaps debt, her outlook was grim.[35] So too was Noel's. Without an immense determination on his part, there would not now be a story to tell. At this point in his life, Noel had few natural advantages and key among those few was simply the fact that he was in Hong Kong. He had an unstable family background, a lack of positive role models, at least on the father's side, and he may well have developed an early sense of exclusion, of not belonging, of being not quite up to scratch. Most significantly, Noel was forced into poverty and hard work by the age of fifteen.

It is not even clear if Noel had much education. Several old friends believe Noel went to school in Hong Kong, others say he never made it at all. Noel's son, Richard, believes his father had been to a school in East Dene, Hampshire, 'with patches on his pants'.[36] When Eugene Yourieff arrived in Hong Kong from Tsingtao in 1938, he carried a letter of introduction from his sister's mother-in-law, Mrs Catherine Wheen, to Mr N.V.A. Croucher, then Commodore of the Royal Hong Kong Yacht Club. Mrs Wheen, born Lee-Jones, was the daughter of a magistrate in Hong Kong, and had grown up partly at the flat her father's job gave them at the Central Police Station. Mrs Wheen told the young Eugene that she had gone to school in Hong Kong with Noel, and it was thought to be Central British School. 'They were good friends,' said Mr Yourieff of Mrs Wheen and Noel Croucher.[37] The impression Mrs Wheen and others had of Noel was that he was an orphan.

One is reminded of the story of *John Halifax, Gentleman*. In that stirring tale, the hero goes without food and warm clothes, so that he might teach himself to read and write by candlelight on dark, cold nights, after he has spent the day collecting skins for a tanner's yard. His reading included *Pilgrim's Progress, Robinson Crusoe, Arabian Nights*, and the Bible. Pride of place went to Shakespeare — an interest Noel Croucher was to share, and to institutionalise through the Royal Society of St. George.[38]

Noel had no easy education dropped into his lap. Whatever he learned, he managed despite his family and despite his circumstances. And, as with John Halifax, he 'possessed to the full that "business" faculty, so frequently despised, but which, out of very ordinary material, often makes a clever man; and without which the cleverest man alive can never be altogether a great man.' Indeed, 'few as were his years, he had learnt much in them. He was at heart a man, ready and able to design and carry out a man's work in the world.'[39]

We must deduce that Noel went to school at some point because he certainly knew his figures and had no trouble multiplying fractions — his future success in accruing wealth bears ample testimony to that. But he was never happy with his writing ability, and he developed a reputation for brusqueness on occasion which his closer friends saw as an attempt to hide the weakness. 'I'm a very poor letter writer,' wrote Noel to a friend once. 'But I evidently size up matters pretty well — while many good correspondents would and do make a hash of things.'[40]

In the 1950s and 1960s, whenever Noel was outraged by some iniquity, he liked to vent his anger in the letters columns of local newspapers. Each time, he took his draft letter to a friend for improvement. 'He was very lacking in confidence regarding his ability to put things in writing. So his letters to the editor went through me or Peter Griffiths [late senior partner of Wilkinson & Grist solicitors] for polish.'[41] Frederic A. Silva, a broker working two doors down from Noel's office in Holland House, was another friend who helped 'dress up his anonymous vituperative letters to the Editor'.[42]

These men saw the passion Noel had about education. Noel was vividly aware that he had missed out in this area, and he strove to overcome the handicap. No doubt this early disadvantage, caused by the poverty of his family, was what decades later led to his use of his wealth to provide others with the opportunities he had missed. His later philanthropies seem linked directly to his own experience.

'He worked his way into the closed European society, above and beyond the Chinese. He came from the lowest level and people don't acknowledge their poor beginnings. He wasn't anything.'[43] That Noel Croucher became something is due to his hard start in the colony. He was a self-made man.

CHAPTER THREE

FROM MACAO
TO MYSTERY

Gem of the orient earth and open sea

Macao! that in thy lap and on thy breast

Hast gathered beauties all the loveliest

Which the sun smiles in his majesty![1]

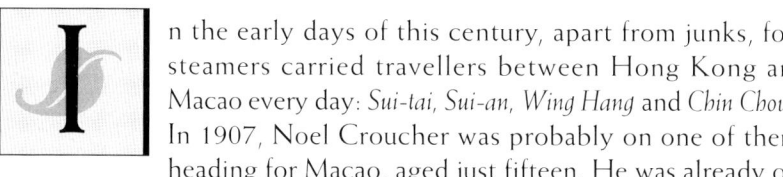

n the early days of this century, apart from junks, four steamers carried travellers between Hong Kong and Macao every day: *Sui-tai, Sui-an, Wing Hang* and *Chin Chow*.[2] In 1907, Noel Croucher was probably on one of them, heading for Macao, aged just fifteen. He was already out to make a living to support his hard-pressed mother and his siblings, apparently the only one to do so.

Few writers have pretended the journey to Macao was a scenic joy, although a guide book in 1893 describes the river steamers of the Hong Kong, Canton and Macao Steamboat Company Limited as 'magnificent' and the route 'extremely interesting and pleasant'.[3] Travellers gazed at the nondescript, apparently empty islands dotted across the murky swell, hoping the pirates or typhoons left them to an uneventful trip of about four hours, depending on the tide.

The city Noel arrived in was a slumbering relic of the China Coast trade, the loser in competition with its rival Hong Kong. It was exotic — peopled by Chinese, Portuguese, Indians, Persians, Armenians, Dutch, Africans, mixtures of them all, and more. It was also home to the hybrid Macanese, product of unions between Chinese and Portuguese, whose families had long acted as facilitators of coastal commerce, be it in tea, silk, ceramics or opium.[4] Macao consists of a tip of the Chinese mainland

and a few small islands including Taipa and Coloane. At the turn of the century, the Praya Grande — that sweep of bay and promenade now destroyed by reclamations — was the first sight to the visitor.

Whereas Hong Kong was the new town with a mere half-century of building behind it, Macao was the grand old dame of the China Coast, with rotting Portuguese mansions, imposing forts, the Cathedral and four parish churches, an impressive temple to the sea goddess Tin Hau and a Catholic seminary. Here the painter George Chinnery chronicled the homes and faces of the Europeans and their ships, the labour of old Chinese amahs, the dignity of coolies, the money-changers in back alleys, the swaying form of old robes or rickshaws. It was once dubbed the 'Holy City'. European visitors would hardly have thought of gambling which was then largely a Chinese preserve. Then and now Macao is a haven for all manner of neighbours seeking respite from political or financial restraint. Perched between empires of East and West, it holds a special place in the annals of the China trade.

As Hong Kong grew, albeit slowly, into a key harbour, Macao's role as a refuge persisted. Besides, Hong Kong was rather dull — suffused with the bureaucracy of a self-regarding British empire, constrained by notions of proper behaviour irksome to free spirits.[5] Macao exists in counterpoise to all empires around it — long a haven for remnants of the Portuguese empire from East Timor to the Caribbean, and for exiles of China, Russia and North Korea. From earliest times, missionaries, too, found inspiration in the separateness of Macao.

The enclave of Macao also gave respite to residents of the treaty ports up the coast of China. For them, it offered rest and a change of air. Naturally, they needed hotels, preferably managed by men who knew what comforts Westerners wanted. 'There are two good hotels at Macao, the Boa Vista erected on a hill near the southern extremity of the city, and Hing Kee's hotel on the Praya Grande surrounded by trees and facing South East', reported *The Hong Kong Guide* of 1893.[6] By 1907, one of three such hotels was the Macao Hotel, formerly Hing Kee's, 65 Praia Grande, owned and managed by William Farmer.[7]

Hing Kee Hotel was regarded as one of the oldest in Macao, owned by Pedro Leong Hing Kee, 'a chubby and cheerful Chinaman'.[8] In the 1880s, it 'was the inevitable meeting place for the Portuguese civil servants who had been sent out from the metropolis, the English from Hong Kong, who came to spend the weekend in Macao, and the occasional western traveller in search of the exotic'.[9] It was not at first a luxury hotel, but specialised in wholesome comfort and cleanliness. The covered balcony was home to soft chairs and rattan sofas, the food was good, there was an old harpsichord for dances and several baby tigers, pets of the owner. In 1894, the poet Camilo Pessanha stayed at Hing Kee's because it was cheaper than the Boa Vista, at just forty patacas a month for full board and laundry, excluding wine.

Mr Hing Kee must have tired of the hotel trade, as he relinquished his landmark in 1903 to Mr Farmer. A veteran of the hotel business, Farmer had worked in Australia before arriving in Hong Kong in 1890 to work at the Victoria Hotel, then the New Victoria Hotel, where he became proprietor by 1898. Four years later, he built on his partnership with one Mr Madar to join with the prominent Parsee Dhunjeebhoy Dorabjee to manage the smart King Edward Hotel, centrally located at 3 Des Voeux Road, Hong Kong.

Less than a couple of years later, William Farmer had taken one of those steamers to Macao, which then boasted a population of about seventy-five thousand.[10] He took over Hing Kee's, well placed at the heart of the waterfront, renaming it the Macao Hotel. Mr Farmer knew his market well, and had an able Armenian manager, Earl Granville Jordan. He usually had at least one other foreigner on staff with him. In 1906 there was a Mr J. Manders humbly designated Runner.

In 1907 he employed Noel Croucher, Clerk.[11]

Exactly what Croucher's job would have entailed is unclear. The Macao Hotel was the busiest in town at the time, routinely hosting more guests than its competitors. Noel may have been tucked away in a back office, keeping the books in order, but it is likely he at least exchanged small talk with some of the guests passing through from Canton or Hong Kong.

Given the divisions of language and culture between local and Western communities, the business of supplies to the hotel and employment of local staff would more naturally have fallen to the Macanese or Chinese staff of the hotel. Perhaps Noel spoke some Cantonese at that time enabling him to be of some use in such matters, but if so, he lost the ability later in life. His salary is likely to have been very low, his living conditions simple. He probably ran errands for the Western guests, for a tip or a pat on the head.

Perhaps it was here that Noel Croucher first saw or spoke to Robert Shewan, George Potts, or the other men who held the keys to his future. It is tempting to think that when the famous Armenian of Hong Kong, Sir Paul Chater, passed by the hotel he would have talked with his compatriot, the hotel manager E.G. Jordan, and learned of the existence of a promising young English boy newly arrived.[12] The sight of Noel at work in the hotel would have been an unusual one, and a few questions as to why and how he was there are only to be expected.

Life was full of surprises on the Macao waterfront, and no doubt Noel kept his eyes wide open and watchful. Fresh air was of critical importance, as seen in this complaint lodged by Noel's boss, William Farmer, to the civil administration:

> May I be permitted to address you about a delicate matter in the hope that you will have this complaint sent to the proper quarters and the nuisance rectified.
>
> Several ladies complained of the coolies and others committing nuisance in front of the Macao Post Office on the stone pier that leads on to the water. It is very embarrassing and obnoxious to ladies who come here to spend a few days holiday and are offended by such sights from daylight to dark, the coolies and others having no decency at all, and do not mind if ladies and children are near.
>
> Then when the breeze blows from the south (the very breeze which people come to Macao to enjoy) the air is laden with the disgusting smell from the stone wall which is the receptacle for numbers of coolies and others daily. The sun having poured on that part all day would dry any germs and cause them to circulate through the air and be not only a disgraceful nuisance but also a grave danger to public health.
>
> Apologising for troubling you with this unsavoury subject and begging that you will do your best to lodge this complaint where it will receive due attention... (Signed: William Farmer)[13]

An advertisement in the *Daily Press* extolled the amenities of Noel Croucher's first known place of employ:

> MACAO HOTEL (late Hing Kee's):
>
> This favourite and long-established Hotel is situated on the sea-front, commanding a magnificent view of the harbour and adjacent islands, and is open to the cool southerly breezes in summer.
>
> The Bedrooms are large, cool, airy, well ventilated and handsomely furnished. The Cuisine is excellent and is under direct European supervision.
>
> Picnic, Boating or Shooting Parties specially catered for. A commodious and comfortable stern-wheel Houseboat, with sleeping accommodation for six passengers and every convenience, is provided for the use of visitors, at reasonable rates.

A Military Band plays in the Gardens, close to the Hotel, three times a week. Sea Bathing. Steamers to and from Macao every morning and afternoon.

W.M. FARMER, Proprietor. E.G. JORDAN, Manager.[14]

The Military Bands were indeed a draw. Two-hour concerts included waltzes and polkas, along with operas and the occasional marches. Noel would have heard popular Western classics of the time, played either by the Garrison of Macao Band or the Orchestra of the Police Corps of Macao. On 22 March 1907, for example, the opera was *Gioconda* by Ponchielli. On 4 April 1907, the programme ran from a 'Pot-pourri', a waltz and a mazurka, to Bach's bolero, 'Reve de Juanite'. Each performance ended solemnly with the Hymno Nacional.[15]

Such delicate entertainment was no doubt seen as an improvement on the hotel site's original role as a billiard parlour under the aegis of the enterprising Pedro Leong Hing Kee. He was to branch out after selling the hotel, into auctioneering and an ice depot. His business as valuer and commission agent was carried on after his death in 1911 by his son who later secured agencies for China Mutual Insurance Company Limited, Canton Navigation Co. Ltd., Hong Kong Ice Co. Ltd., and Dairy Farm Company. Peter Hing Kee established the first garage for cars in Macao in 1916, with American cars for sale.[16]

It is not inconceivable that Noel Croucher learned some of his first lessons in trade and financial services through his early exposure to connections such as these. Interestingly, the companies which Noel first chose to patronise as a stockbroker include Green Island Cement Company and Hong Kong Canton & Macao Steam Boat Company. The latter he had already used as a passenger. The former he would have heard of and perhaps visited, as the island referred to was not the Hong Kong knoll of that name, but Ilha Verde in Macao.[17]

How deep an impact Macao made on Noel Croucher can be seen in one of the few pieces of paper which he kept for himself and which survived his death. This is a report titled 'A Little about George Chinnery and the Fearons', typed probably by Noel on his old manual machine. Three pages are held together by a rusting pin, and they are the blue, small-sized sheets of paper which Noel used for private notes throughout his life. He had corrected his own grammar in the typescript with a dark pen and the spacing between words is erratic:

Chinnery arrived in Macao in 1828[18] after a decline in his fortunes in India. He had become the great friend of Christopher Fearon, an English merchant in Macao, and accompanied him to China. At Macao, he lived for several years with Christopher and his wife, Elizabeth (née Noad, of Bath, Somerset). The Fearons built him a studio in their garden, and his first pictures were painted here. The first of these was the lovely portrait of Elizabeth (now in the possession of her great-grandson, in Maidenhead). This picture has never left the family, but two other pictures (as far as is known) were done of Elizabeth, and were probably sold in New York in 1898, when Elizabeth's son, Robert Fearon died. The portrait, now in Hong Kong, is almost certainly one of these....

Elizabeth Fearon was one of the first three women who went to visit their menfolk working in Canton, when it was forbidden for Western women to set foot there, a point Noel made in his notes.[19] It's clear Noel was attracted by the boldness and bravery of this unusual woman.

The family portrait of her in Maidenhead shows her as a highly-spirited beauty, and is one of Chinnery's loveliest pictures. Chinnery became the godfather of Elizabeth's son, Robert, and both her sons (Charles, the elder, and Robert) were taught drawing by ~~Chinnery~~ him [sic] in the garden studio. Incidentally, this studio is often referred to as 'a wayside temple' in picture catalogues! ...

Noel's notes go on to discuss the provenance of several Chinnery drawings, ending with:

ELIZABETH FEARON, born 22/10/1794. Married 14/5/1818. Died 31/3/1838. Buried in Macao.

Elizabeth Fearon was buried in the Protestant Cemetery in Macao, a famous resting place which fascinated Noel.[20] Here the graves of people such as Chinnery, Swedish trader Anders Ljungstedt and the missionary Robert Morrison can be found, beside the delightful Camoes Gardens. Not only did he make notes about people buried there, but Noel was good friends with Sir Lindsay and Lady May Ride, who dedicated years of research to the lives of those in the early foreign trading community, named on the gravestones in Macao.[21] Noel's friendship with the Rides was to bear remarkable fruit, in the genesis of The Croucher Foundation — but that is getting ahead of the story.

Inscriptions at this most historically interesting cemetery in the East testify to the often tragically brief but God-fearing lives of the staff of the East India Company and, later, of Protestants of all nations and professions. A chapel adjoins the entrance, bordered by flower gardens and graced by the shade of banyan trees. At the Camoes Gardens, pathways lead up to a grotto made from huge boulders in which stands a bust of the poet Camoes. It is a place which retains a rare charm. Across the path, old men of the neighbourhood gather to this day for a talk or a smoke, near the wall on which are engraved poems and inscriptions in Chinese, Portuguese and English — including Bowring's *Sonnet to Macao*.

So evocative was this spot in Macao that Noel remembered and returned to it, again and again, throughout his life. Here was a man moved by the romance of a sheltered haven of beauty, peace and poetry. Perhaps here he nourished his strong Christian faith, perhaps here a homesick Noel found space when daily life as a hotel clerk left him desperate or unhappy. He was so enchanted by the grotto and its poetry that he brought special friends to this spot half a century later.

One such friend is Joan Scrivener, a sparkling woman who knew Noel's family back in Hampshire and so had a letter of introduction to him when she came to Hong Kong for a friend's wedding in 1956. Noel provided benign escort to the young Joan as she enjoyed her first-ever trip to the East, and her visit to Macao over the New Year of 1957 holds a firm place in her memories. In the letters which Noel wrote to Joan after this trip, it's clear that Noel still held that emotional connection with the Macao cemetery, the grotto and the poetry.

Noel fluently described various spots in Macao including the facade of St. Paul's for Joan's benefit as she was labelling her holiday snaps back in England. Then he waxed lyrical about his favoured place in Macao: 'the bust in the Grotto shown in your picture is of the Portuguese poet [Luis] Camoes who was exiled from Portugal about 1600 [actually 1556] to Macao. He wrote the epic poem "Lusiad" [Os Lusiadas] the most famous in Portuguese literature. There's a poem on the pedestal by a former Governor of Hong Kong — "Ode to Macao".

'I read it first many years ago, before you were born [thus before the 1920s], and the lines impressed me [so] much that I never forgot them. If you remember I repeated them to you before we came to the Grotto:

> Gem of the orient [earth] and open sea,
> Macao! that in thy lap and on thy breast
> Hast gathered beauties all the loveliest.'[22]

This gives a fascinating hint of a young Noel first reading this poem in Macao during his earliest sojourn there in 1907. His quotation in the letter omitted the word 'earth', implying he was indeed relying on memory and not a book. His friendship with Joan was cemented by this shared rediscovery of a special spot from his youth. More, Noel revealed himself here as a sensitive man, one drawn by beauty and culture.[23]

An interest in such history, and in the personalities preceding him on the China Coast, recurred throughout Noel's life. Teresa Price of Lammert Brothers Auctioneers believes she has a couple of Chinnery sketches from the auction of Noel's house seventy-seven years later.[24] Noel the yachtsman sailed many times to Macao and his yacht *La Cigale* won many races there.

One wonders if Noel ever told his friends, decades later, about his first period in Macao, but it seems unlikely as no one has any recollection of it.[25] One friend, for example, was the late F.J. Gellion, an engineer who became head of Macao Electric Company before World War II. Gellion's house, 'Sky Line', still stands today and is an impressive, starkly white Bauhaus mansion on the hill above Bela Vista Hotel. Gellion lived for about thirty years in Macao and so he must have been able to share much old local lore with Noel Croucher.

He was a generous host in later years, opening his large house to visitors from Hong Kong, including Noel.[26] 'Gellion had a fine house on top of the hill in Macao. The usual drill was, we took a boat about teatime from Hong Kong on a Saturday afternoon. We dined at his house, and then he often went to bed. The rest of us did what we felt like, we went out and had fun,' recalls G.O.W. Stewart, formerly of the Hong Kong and Shanghai Bank. 'Very often, we'd find Chinese doctors at Gellion's breakfast table. They were doing voluntary work and Gellion was so kind-hearted it was no trouble for him to provide hospitality.'[27]

When Joan Scrivener and Noel went to Macao, they stayed at the Boa Vista but only because Gellion was out of town, as Noel's correspondence shows: 'By the way, my friend who lives in that wonderful House in Macao — where we called and I signed my name in his book on New Year's Day — returned from England and Lisbon yesterday and said as I knew he would — why didn't you stay in my House and keep the servants on their toes — I wish we had.'[28]

But Noel would not have been able to make a sentimental journey back to his first workplace, even had he wanted to. Seven years after he worked at the Macao Hotel, it became the New Macao Hotel, and by 1928 it had become the Hotel Riviera. After 1966, the site became home to the PRC Bank which was once again rebuilt in the mid-1990s. Following the latest waves of reclamations in Macao, Noel Croucher's once-scenic waterfront hotel would be several blocks inland, and anyone seeking the fresh southerly breezes of summer would be better advised to find a site less subject to traffic jams.

_♫ ♫ ♫_

Perhaps young Noel felt the hotel business was not for him, or perhaps a guest one day prompted him to think again about prospects in Hong Kong. It is worth reporting that Lady May Ride recalls Noel telling her that he met Sir Paul Chater when he was sixteen years old.[29] Whatever the reason, Noel did not last long as a hotel clerk. On 7 August 1907, he joined the colonial government of Hong Kong, once again as a clerk, but now at the Post Office.

Noel joined the government as a very junior one of many clerks described as 'Fifth Grade'. Noel was hired on the same day as and worked alongside one Ed. Laurence Stainfield, aged seventeen, about whom more is known than about Noel at this stage. Ed. was a grandson of George Stainfield, a hotel-keeper in Hong Kong and an undertaker, among other things. His wife ran a boarding house for a while. They were obvious members of that little-known class of the respectable poor in white Hong Kong, giving another clue to Noel's status.[30] Noel's only relative in government, stepfather Parker, was but a lowly overseer in public works, hardly likely to offer Noel much chance of advancement.

The business of the mail between outposts of empire in the early years of the century would have given Noel a hands-on introduction to the details of trade, geography and global shipping. The Trans-Siberian Railway was completed in 1903 and by 1912 it was carrying all overland post, and the Kowloon-Canton Railway opened in 1911. Prior to these advances, all post went by ship.

Yet it was not as simple as it sounds. The Post Office had stumbled into being in the first years of the colony: 'Pre-payment of postage was not mandatory and it was often left up to the addressee to pay for the delivery. Nor were there regular mail carrying steamships in operation. Mail was usually loaded on to a passing clipper or steamer. On occasions even warships were pressed into service as mail carriers. This system did not lend itself to reliability or regularity.' Letters were lost, or stuck to each other by their sealing wax, and the first London-appointed Postmaster General was dismissed for the 'general want of confidence' in him. He died four days later.[31]

By the 1860s, a letter took three months to reach home from Hong

Kong. It went by steamer to Singapore, Ceylon and Aden, then overland to Suez and from Alexandria to Southampton via Marseilles. If put on a train in Marseilles, it would arrive in London five days faster. The Suez Canal opened in 1869, to be used on a regular basis by 1874, speeding post further. Getting from Britain to Hong Kong was only part of the journey — post delivery to the treaty ports was left in the hands of the British consuls, and many merchants were used to making their own arrangements. Packet agents then came into being with the Post Office's blessing, a system which continued until 1922 when all postal agencies in the treaty ports were closed.[32]

The Post Office building in which Noel worked was opened on New Year's Day back in 1846. It was a grand building near Pedder's Wharf, on the corner of Queen's Road and Pedder Street. Built in classical style with columns, it was designated a branch of the General Post Office in London (until 1859 when the Hong Kong Government claimed control). But by the 1890s, the place was described in Dickensian terms: 'The Assistant Postmaster General has to be content with a high stool and a desk in a recess which overlooks a stand frequented by cacophonous chair bearers'.[33] Worse, the old post office was no longer on the waterfront due to successive reclamations. This mattered, as launches, then as now, took the post direct from the post office to ships, and later, planes.

Although mooted early in the century, the 'new' Post Office was not completed until 1911, well after Noel's time as a clerk. That new building, demolished only in 1979 for the construction of the underground Mass Transit Railway, was a distinctive granite and Amoy brick pile which the established broker Noel Croucher was to use years later for business telegrams and letters to his wife.

Noel's clerical duties were focused on the post between Hong Kong and home. The Peninsula and Oriental Steamship Company ran a government-subsidised post service, a monopoly later broken by the French Messageries Maritimes Line. For them as for all shipping, piracy and the weather were constant hazards. The arrival of a mail ship was of such importance as to warrant announcements in the daily newspapers, days in advance. This gave people time to write letters ready to be taken home. Noel's tasks probably included the meeting of these ships, giving him an early introduction to the bustle of Hong Kong harbour.

The mail was a focus of colonial life, more so before Hong Kong could provide what the Europeans felt were vital to life in the East. Ladies seeking new fashions to be presented at a Governor's ball had to wait for the mail to arrive, as did business tycoons seeking new finance or instructions from partners at home. Here the fifteen-year-old Noel would have come to know the names of, or perhaps delivered packets to, the elite of Hong Kong. If at a desk or long wooden counter in the post office building, he could well have been using an abacus for his sums, as these wood and bead frames were not superseded until the 1940s.[34]

But he did not last long in the job. Perhaps the salary of $480 — significantly designated in local currency and not in pounds sterling — was just not enough. Perhaps the business of sorting others' letters was too humdrum. The Civil List of 1907 states Noel Croucher was 'Discharged' from the Post Office on 6 November 1907.[35]

And this is the last we see of Noel Croucher for three long years, until the records reveal his arrival in 1911, in more senses than one, as an assistant in one of the biggest firms in Hong Kong — Shewan, Tomes & Co.

Where did Noel go in these years? He turned sixteen in December 1907, and from then until he was nineteen years old, there is no record of his whereabouts. We know his stepfather was sacked in 1908, perhaps throwing the family, already on shaky ground, into desperate straits. Perhaps Noel went back to school, or worked for a concern which felt no need to be in the Directory. His former boss, William Farmer, now ran a hotel on Shameen Island (the international settlement in Canton). But there is no record of Noel's name there or anywhere.

One can only imagine what Noel's intrepid mother, Floss, was doing to hold it all together. One surviving family member recalls hearing that 'Floss shipped her blackwood furniture to Canada'. Perhaps the whole family moved to Canada, which might explain why Noel's half-brother Gerald Parker later married and had three daughters there.[36] If so, Noel had enough gumption to bring himself back to Hong Kong by 1911 if not before.

Noel's son, Richard, believes his father was gun-running for warlords across the border in China, but the time and place are not quite right. There were traders in Hong Kong and Macao willing to sell arms to whichever side could pay, and perhaps Noel Croucher's first deals were of such ilk. He used to tell a story of how he rescued a warlord of Canton from a hotel fire in Hong Kong, so presumably he was acquainted with some of them. He is also said to have known T.V. Soong — the financier-brother to the three famous Soong Sisters who between them married Chiang Kai-shek, Sun Yat-sen and wealthy H.H. Kung.[37]

Someone Noel counted as a close friend in later years was William Henry Donald (1875–1946), an Australian journalist and rare teetotaller. 'Don' worked on the *China Mail* in Hong Kong at the turn of the century, before becoming involved in Mainland politics, and was 'a curious combination of rebel and diplomat, of sage and jester.'[38] He was laughed at for being so interested in China, but went on to become an adviser to Viceroy Chang Chen-chun in Canton (circa 1903), then to the republican leader Sun Yat-sen, to Marshal Chang Tso-lin and his son the Young Marshal Chang Hsueh-liang, and finally to General Chiang Kai-shek. Don was a special friend to Madame Chiang, whom he had known from her childhood through her father Charlie Soong, a supporter of revolution in China. But there is no firm evidence to link Noel with China's civil war.

The years 1908 to 1911 must remain a mystery — one of those mysteries which Noel Croucher may never have wanted us to dispel.

HEADS I WIN, TAILS YOU LOSE

O ne possible answer to the mystery comes in an anecdote which Noel Croucher told friends over the years. It refers to his meeting with the most important man in his life, the grand old man of Hong Kong, Sir Paul Chater. Sir Paul was one of the founders of today's Hong Kong — its cosmopolitan port, bustling community, churches and racetracks, primary trades and industries. Sir Paul made Hong Kong — literally — for he pioneered the reclamations of Central and the development of Kowloon peninsula, putting up his own money whenever government proved shy.

Austin Coates, the late and brilliant chronicler of life on the Coast, had this to say on the subject of Noel Croucher and Sir Paul Chater:

> In his long life Chater had two 'students', in the Chinese meaning of that word: Sir Robert Ho Tung in the nineteenth century, Noel Croucher in the twentieth. Both became millionaires, and both acknowledged the debt they owed to Chater as their real mentor in the world of finance.

Sir Robert Ho Tung was the leading non-European of Hong Kong and founded a dynasty which remains prominent, wealthy and influential to this day. He was the first Eurasian to be allowed to live on the Peak, and from a beginning as compradore to the 'noble house' of Jardine Matheson & Company, Sir Robert built an empire. Noel Croucher, by contrast, is now little known.

Without doubt, Chater was a name to conjure with. And Noel Croucher did just that. The story about the meeting — before, during or after the year 1910 — has no doubt evolved over the years. It goes something like this:

On a quiet day in Central, Hong Kong's business district, the great

Sir Paul entered the brokerage where Noel was working and demanded that a certain block of shares be bought for him. The upstart Noel thought he knew better than Sir Paul however, and told him so, saying, 'I wouldn't buy those shares if I were you, sir!' Such impertinence could scarcely be tolerated, but the big man chose to listen.

As it turned out, young Noel was right. So Sir Paul soon made his way back to that junior clerk and gave him more of the much-sought-after Chater business. Chater saw that by following Noel Croucher's suggestions, he would make a lot more money. There began a relationship through which Noel was to attain prominence and acclaim as a financier, even social acceptability.

Neither man knew it, but the chance Noel hoped for had arrived. Chater might well have seen a shadow of his younger self. Noel understood the market, and knew what he was talking about — though how he managed it and where on earth he had sprung from were anyone's guess. Chater was already a major philanthropist, adviser to the Governor, patron of horse-racing, art, religion and the temples of Mammon. It was easy to pick up a bright lad, to use him and train him and for him to get ahead.

From this encounter, everything else followed, according to Noel's account. Chater left more of his investments in the young man's hands, used him as runner or messenger, and gave him the protection of his name about town. From this came the right contacts and an education for life. Noel needed little else. From then on, he had to do only what he did best — collect information, build and maintain an enviable knowledge of people and events throughout the East, and keep his eyes always open for a good trade.

So who was Paul Chater? Seekers of any biography or study of the man will be disappointed — mere sections about him appear in the general works on the period. This is even more surprising when eulogies of his day are found — they assumed that 'the future historian of Hong Kong will find his task as regards the past sixty years a sinecure, for the record of Hong Kong will be a replica of the career of Sir Paul Chater'.[1]

Catchick Paul Chater, born in 1846 in Calcutta to a prominent family of Armenian merchants, arrived in Hong Kong in April 1864. He was the youngest of thirteen children. 'The history of the Chater family, on his mother's side, goes far back into that of the opening up of India to British commerce.' But his parents died when he was just nine years old. He became a scholarship boy at a school in Calcutta, where he also learned cricket, making him, 'by dint of perseverance and merit of an exceptionally high order, the architect of his own fortune, having practically risen from the lowest rung of the ladder to the very highest in the commercial world of Hong Kong.' Chater also set an example by his 'princely donations to temples of learning and places of divine worship'.[2] It will be no surprise that in Chater's life story is yet another reminder of Noel Croucher's fictional mentor, John Halifax.

Aged eighteen, the future Sir Paul was an assistant in the Bank of Hindustan, China and Japan. He stayed with the family of his sister, who was mother of a Dr Jordan, but when they left Hong Kong he went to stay at a cheap boarding house on Wyndham Street. In two years he was in business on his own, trading bullion and exchange, investing all the while in land. A lifelong partner in business and philanthropy was Sir Hormusjee Mody. Chater was also close to the prominent opium-trading family, the Sassoons. Within ten years he was seriously rich. 'C.P. Chater was himself without any substantial means, and his rise in the commercial world of Hong Kong was nothing short of brilliant.'[3]

A look back on his achievements shows above all his great prescience — or was it opportunism? The *China Mail*[4] reported that Chater used to spend evening after evening in a sampan in the shadows around the Kowloon shore, as if he was fishing. In fact he was taking soundings in a search for water deep enough to cope with ocean-going steamers. He found what he was looking for and hence the Hong Kong and Kowloon Wharf and Godown Company came into being.

Though he took enormous risks, each step in hindsight seems part of a clear-sighted vision of what Hong Kong would need next. 'He is at the head of everything there; no enterprise gets on without asking his assistance. Shipping, banking, international companies with their heads in London or in Paris — he is in them all... He is the father of everything in Hong Kong...'[5] On Chater's death, the Governor, Sir Cecil Clementi KCMG, recalled that when he first set foot on Hong Kong soil, he stepped on land created by Chater's reclamations. Chater proposed the creation of new land in 1887, later travelling to England to secure approval. 'The work was concluded in 1905, and the result has been an addition to the Colony of considerable foreshore upon which have been erected some of the finest hongs in the East.'[6] Chater's contribution hinged on his idea that marine lot-holders would themselves fund the works while the land remained ultimately under government control. This cut through swathes of delay and red tape at last. He also initiated the Wanchai reclamations.

In 1886, Sir Paul took a seat on the Legislative Council vacated by

F.D. Sassoon, a seat he held until commitments to higher office intervened. He was already a Justice of the Peace. Now he became one of the first two unofficials appointed to the Governor's inner cabinet, the Executive Council, where he served from 1896 until his death in 1926. The other unofficial was the head of Jardine Matheson & Company. High office of a different order saw Chater installed as the District Grand Master of the Hong Kong and South China English Constitution of the Freemasons, in 1881.

It was Sir Paul who first suggested to the government that new lands should be acquired beyond Kowloon, namely the New Territories. He built St. Andrew's Church in Kowloon, chaired the Queen's Jubilee and Diamond Jubilee committees, and was knighted in 1902. He was a steward of the Jockey Club for over a quarter of a century. At his home, Marble Hall in Mid-levels, he accumulated a collection of art, lithographs, maps and curios regarded as pre-eminent in the Far East.[7]

Catchick Street in Kennedy Town is another reminder of Chater — he reclaimed twenty-six acres there. He was the driving force behind iron mining in the New Territories, coal mining in Tongkin (in French Indo-China, thus earning the Legion d'Honneur from a grateful France) and a cotton spinning factory, in addition to his founding roles in the wharf company and Hongkong Land Investment & Agency Ltd.

Chater worked with Jardine's through the wharf company, and was personal friend to William Keswick and John Bell-Irving (another unofficial on the Executive Council). With Bell-Irving and Bendysche Layton, a partner in Gibb, Livingston and Company, Chater set up the Hong Kong Electric Company. Recipients of his philanthropy included the University of Hong Kong (along with Mody), St. John's Cathedral, St. Andrew's, and Kowloon Union Church. Sir Paul also built a lavish bungalow in Kowloon, where he entertained anyone from kings to clerks.

There was simply no better man in Hong Kong for the young Noel to meet. Had Noel Croucher been able to pluck a perfect patron out of the air, he could not have done better than to find Sir Paul Chater.

Noel picked up some lessons in style (first learned at his mother's knee) at Sir Paul's dinner table. A memorable description of dinner at Marble Hall is provided by Commander C.H. Drage: 'With H.E. to lunch with Sir Paul Chater, a coloured magnate and the multi-millionaire of Hong Kong. He has a lovely house full of wonderful china, and gave us an excellent meal with superlative wine... His collection of china is well-known and, though much of it is said to be faked, the pieces are really beautiful, but the furnishing of the rest of the house is in atrocious taste.'[8]

Years later, Croucher told friends he stayed at Marble Hall with Sir Paul's blessing when Sir and Lady Chater were away on trips. He would have enjoyed the view from the terrace, five hundred feet above sea level, the cards, dining and billiard rooms, spacious verandahs, two acres of garden, wine closets and sweeping stairways. Marble Hall was built near the end of the nineteenth century out of stuccoed brickwork, with the main staircase executed in polished Italian marble. The interiors were finished in mahogany and teak.[9]

When the indispensable author Austin Coates wanted to explain some Chater stories to a fellow historian, he said, 'My principal source is the late Noel Croucher, who died here a few years ago, a multi-millionaire.'[10]

In that letter he wrote: 'To give an idea of how close Croucher was to Sir Paul and Christine Chater, in his very first year here they asked him to take over Marble Hall, their palatial residence on Conduit Road — it was about the same size as Government House — while they were away on their annual summer visit to Europe; and he did this for several years thereafter. There was little about the Chaters which Croucher did not know; he was "family"... I should explain that when Noel Croucher and I were together we talked nineteen to the dozen on everything you can think of about Hong Kong's past, hardly pausing for breath.'

When Chater died, on 26 May 1926, Noel Croucher was among the prominent names of the colony who gave a wreath.[11] He claimed the big old desk in his office had been Sir Paul's own desk. Noel's interests in later years were focused on companies in which Chater played major roles — the docks, utilities, property.

Noel did not have a proper education, his family was broken, he was a long way from home, and his prospects were poor. His contemporaries in business were all middle-class and aspiring, he was son of a railwayman and stepson of an unemployed actor. Yet he became Commodore of the Royal Hong Kong Yacht Club, owner of half a dozen horses, the most important individual client of the Hong Kong Bank, and to this day, one of Hong Kong's most lavish philanthropists. Not bad for the lad who, like Oliver Twist asking for more, presumed to talk back to Sir Paul.

The story told by Noel takes us only so far, however. If he was already a broker when he met Sir Paul, then how did Noel get started in business? More, if he and Sir Paul met over a shares purchase, it might place the story in about 1915, when Noel was formally working in a brokerage.

But Noel himself told special friends that he met Sir Paul when he was sixteen years old, thus in Macao, in 1907.

If indeed the two men met in 1907, then it was most likely over the counter at the Macao Hotel — this is feasible, and a story backed by hearsay. A meeting at the Hong Kong Post Office feels less likely as Sir Paul would hardly do his own post. Perhaps a meeting led to Noel serving as a runner for Chater at the stock exchange or a general messenger around town, in the years 1908 to 1910, before being recommended by Chater for his first 'proper job' in 1911. That would account for the mystery years, as such a position with Chater would not be in formal records.

Or perhaps the two men met in 1910, as Austin Coates believed. If so, we can only imagine what Noel was up to before then — perhaps he was hanging around the stock brokers' gutter of Ice House Street,[12] learning the business from the street up, and Chater saw him there.

A favourite story for many old-timers is that Noel arrived in Hong Kong with a travelling circus. The late Eric Cumine said so: 'There was always an anecdote but Noel would neither deny nor confirm it. Maybe he couldn't remember anyway! He had a long innings through almost half of HK's history... Our informant ... says he came to HK with a travelling circus at the age of sixteen [thus, 1907] and was messenger for Sir Paul Chater from whom he soon learnt where was what and the cut and thrust of the rialto which gave him the know-how to gather his millions... He is now one of the greatest benefactors to this city. The Croucher Foundation is worth about a billion HK dollars...'[13]

In support of the story about Chater wanting some shares, is the recollection of Noel's lawyer at the time of his death, Ian MacCallum: 'He told me that Paul Chater came by to buy some shares. Chater was very impressed by Croucher's advice. So Croucher set up on his own, with Chater as his major client.'[14]

Suffice to say, Noel Croucher knew Sir Paul, and from 1911 onwards, Noel had a career to be proud of. He joined first the premier trading firm, Shewan, Tomes & Company, founded by another exceptional self-made man, Robert Shewan. In those early days of Hong Kong business, firms grew up around key personalities, and dabbled in all aspects of money-making, from import and export to manufacturing to shipping to agency work. Strengthening the argument that Chater helped Noel get this job is the fact that Chater was a good friend and business partner to Shewan. Austin Coates pointed out the interests they shared — key among them the concentration of docks and development on Kowloon which was then barely known to the people across the water in Victoria.[15]

Noel learned about business and responsibilities from Sir Paul. He learned brinkmanship from Robert Shewan — about how far one could go, what could be done without censure. By 1911, the name Noel Croucher appeared among the forty-three staff members listed for Shewan, Tomes & Co. To progress from hotel boy in Macao to assistant at the top trading company in Hong Kong was the first vital leap in Noel's career. Without this introduction to the colony's business life, it is unlikely he could have gone on to join the prestigious Benjamin & Potts brokerage four years later. Be it by scheme or happy chance, Noel was on his way. He had found a channel in which his talents could come to the fore.

'He was very tight when he was young, he saved every bit of money,' recalls his office assistant Florence Lo. 'He used to tell me how he had not much money in the beginning. He had enough for food for one week — but for bread and water only. After a week of that, he had made enough to buy one share in Hong Kong Bank for himself. There were not many companies to invest in at first either...'[16]

The significance of his new job at Shewan, Tomes & Co. cannot be underestimated — it was here that Noel served as apprentice to the China trade. Shewan, Tomes & Co. was the direct heir to the venerable Russell & Company, the oldest and one of the biggest American firms on the China Coast. Robert Shewan had started out as a clerk for Russell & Co.[17]

As with the aristocracy of the day, Russell & Co. had a prestigious name but was losing money. In the glorious prose of Walter Feldwick:

> For long it was among the more important of the pioneers of foreign trade with the Empire, but though highly successful for a number of years, it ultimately fell on evil days. It was on its ashes that the firm of Shewan & Co arose, retaining many of the interests of the defunct firm and launching out from time to time in various directions with marked success. It [Shewan, Tomes & Co.] occupies a prominent position in general commercial and financial circles, and owns ... enterprises which have brought much profit to the shareholders and fame to the promoters and managers. The firm has branches and agencies throughout the Far East — from Tientsin in the north to Manila and the Straits Settlements in the south...[18]

Robert Shewan and his twin brother, William, were born in London on 13 November 1859. Of Scots stock, Robert arrived in Hong Kong on 14 February 1881. Within a decade of joining Russell & Co. he had taken it over.

In 1892, the same year as Russell & Co. was declared bankrupt, Shewan & Company started business at 37 Wyndham Street. In 1895, Charles Alexander Tomes joined the firm, and it became Shewan, Tomes & Co. Interestingly, 1895 is also the year which Austin Coates described as 'a year of commercial disaster and despair'. While Britain was at its zenith, Hong Kong seemed to be digging its own grave: 'There had been wild speculation in such things as Australian gold where there was none, Malayan gold where there was none either, Borneo plantations where there was no plantation work force, and so on.'[19] And in 1894–95 the Sino-Japanese War was underway.

In Shewan's memoirs of his half-century in Hong Kong,[20] he recalled four brokers sharing a room during this bad patch and others turning up uninvited at meals. In passing, he noted that two old firms had not survived the crash — Adamson Bell & Co. and Russell & Co. Though his room-mates were falling by the wayside, Shewan hung on and turned the experience to good account.

Robert Shewan was not the type to give up. At this point, his firm was 'an extremely active — even aggressive — enterprise'.[21] He had a finger in every pie, dealing in raw silk and piece goods, tea, matting, firecrackers, rattan and more. Then he branched into imported cottons, woollens, hardware, glassware, flour, hemp, raw sugar, wine and spirits. Soon he began acquiring agencies which made the firm a lynchpin in shipping, insurance, manufacturing — all vital if Hong Kong was to grow out of the slump. Shewan himself had meanwhile become Consul for Chile no doubt as an aid to trade which might have been more difficult for a Briton. On 10 June 1908, the offices formerly occupied by Shewan, Tomes & Co. on the first and second floors of 14 Des Voeux Road were offered for let. The advertisement in the *Daily Press* told those interested to 'Apply to the compradore of E.D. Sassoon & Co, Queen's Rd Central'.

This is a useful indicator of the series of interlocking relationships within the small business community of Hong Kong. A mere handful of names recurs — on each other's boards — performing different functions for each other, all working within a small physical radius. The clubs, the Freemasons, the Church and a range of sporting events all bound these men into a tightly-delineated merchant class, and their interests as merchants overrode boundaries of race.

Shewan, Tomes & Co. had four directors: Robert Shewan, C.A. Tomes, A. Babington and H.R.B. Hancock. Among the names are those of families which recur throughout the Hong Kong establishment for years. Of the partners, only Mr Tomes sinks without trace.[22] Mr Babington left his name on a Hong Kong pathway, suggesting either he lived there or was responsible for development in the area. As for H.R.B. Hancock, his father, Alfred, was a bill and bullion broker in Hong Kong. Alfred and his brother Sydney were partners of the firm, A. and S. Hancock, of Queen's Road, Hong Kong which was still active in 1940. By 1906, Alfred Hancock had clocked up more than fifty years in Amoy and Hong Kong.[23] One of his sisters, Edith, married the Colonial Secretary, James Stewart Lockhart, in 1889, the man first in charge of the New Territories and later Commissioner in Weihaiwei.[24] The Lockharts' hospitality at their Peak mansion, Ardsheal, was well-known for its openness — Chinese guests were welcome, so were intellectuals and China watchers, government officials and compradores.[25]

However Noel Croucher joined Shewan, Tomes & Co., here he had the opportunity to start making the contacts necessary for business in Hong Kong.

On Shewan's death in Hong Kong on 14 February 1934 at the age of seventy-five, an article described Shewan as one of the most prominent men in the colony. The piece described him: 'To those who knew him in the nineties of the last century, there was no more outstanding figure and more loving personality in the Colony than the deceased gentleman. Outstanding in his ability, lovable in his modesty, the late Mr Shewan was one of the finest of characters.'[26]

Unlike others around at this time, Shewan was keen on building the colony. To him, and to the more illustrious Sir Paul Chater, credit must go for backing the major advances of the time — reclamation, electrification, industrialisation. Both men served on the Legislative Council and on many company boards. In one of many examples, Shewan was at the 1896 Annual General Meeting of Sir Paul Chater's pioneering Hongkong Land Company, building the central business district on new land.[27]

Shewan, one-time director and chairman of the Hong Kong and Shanghai Banking Corporation[28] and active in many of the sporting clubs in the colony, interested himself in a key group of companies: Green Island Cement Company, Hong Kong Rope Manufacturing Company, China Light and Power Company, China Provident Loan and Mortgage Company (formed 'with the object of financing men of small means to build and own their own homes'),[29] Sandakan Light and Power Company, and China Underwriters Limited. Shewan, Tomes & Co. managed the most important early industries of Hong Kong.

Young Noel was a ready learner — an almost identical list could be made of his future interests. Noel retained a close involvement with China Provident throughout his life and was a member of its board for many years. It appears to have been his first and longest-running directorship.

Noel's first-ever attendance at a company meeting was at the dramatic Green Island Cement Company meeting in Hong Kong in 1911.[30] He was aged just nineteen. This company's history is another example of Shewan and Chater's association. The company was Macao's first excursion into heavy industry when established in 1889, with headquarters in Hong Kong. Limestone from quarries in south China and clays recovered from the harbour were used to make cement. For about fifty years, the plant supplied cement to Macao, Hong Kong and various parts of East Asia including Japan. The company manager's imposing mansion was a centre of Macao's social life at the turn of the century.

Green Island Cement Company had its ups and downs and in 1895, Shewan & Co. (predecessor to Shewan, Tomes & Company Limited) was appointed General Manager. The former managers advised Shewan, 'there was nothing in the company: they were sick of it', but he was not daunted. In 1896, Mr (later Sir) Paul Chater became a director and in 1897 the board decided to open a new works in Hong Kong, acquiring a large and valuable site at Kowloon. It has remained the only cement manufacturer in Hong Kong ever since.[31]

Shewan, Tomes & Co. also managed the Philippines Steam Shipping Company, the Canton Land Co. Ltd., Wei San Knitting Co. Ltd. and the Equitable Life Assurance Society of the United States. It was agent to four shipping companies, eleven insurance firms, and several pioneering industrial concerns (covering mining machinery, cable manufacture, concrete reinforcement, British Westinghouse Electric & Manufacturing Company, and the Hong Kong Electric Tramway Co. Ltd.). It is hard to imagine a better training ground for a bright young lad, a quick learner and one ambitious for advancement. He was lucky to be in an office responsible for a very broad range of activities, thus gaining wide exposure to the ways of Hong Kong's industry and trade.

Noel's work would probably have begun down on the docks. Junior staff were usually deputised to meet ships arriving in Hong Kong harbour, to deliver messages and perhaps arrange transport for anyone important on board. At the age of twenty, this was likely to be good fun, especially for someone with the seas of the Isle of Wight in the background for contrast.

If ledgers had to be filled back at the office, then Noel would have been in the original St. George's Building, somewhat different to its modern counterpart. Then, four high floors boasted verandahs along two sides above a pavement colonnade. Rattan blinds or canvas awnings were drawn over the shuttered windows on bright days. Inside, a waist-high iron railing divided separate departments in the otherwise open-plan office. Long-corded lamps suspended from a white moulded ceiling. Fans, if one was lucky enough to have one, were of the desktop metal variety. A stone-floored machinery department contrasted with Mr Shewan's personal office — here were sofa, armchairs, access to a private verandah, a fancy clock and barometer, several paintings and one telephone.

By the time Noel joined this office, Shewan was not only a leading businessman but a maverick, someone prepared to buck authority while making a fortune. In 1901, for example, Shewan had founded China Light & Power Company by purchasing a failing power station in Canton while retaining its agency for electricity. Power supplies commenced to Kowloon in 1903. Shewan was the company's first chairman and remained so for over thirty years. But the utility struggled at first. At one stage, Shewan fought off demands for its liquidation by claiming a contract had been won to supply the newly completed Kowloon-Canton Railway — a characteristic overstatement on Shewan's part, alas.

By 1932 the principal shareholders, members of the Kadoorie family, who retain control to this day, decided they wanted to run it themselves. Shewan was asked to leave, so he demanded a parting gift of $1 million. China Light balked at this seemingly excessive amount and took the claim to court. More fool they. Shewan's sums were more accurate but still too conservative, the court decided, ordering that Shewan be paid $2 million instead!

This then was the man for whom Noel Croucher began working in 1911 — brash in business and dashing enough to get away with it. But what sort of business world was young Noel Croucher entering?

Unremitting growth in Hong Kong was but a distant dream one hundred years ago. In the 1890s, Austin Coates reported that Hong Kong was in its lowest and longest slump from 1889 to 1896: 'Many Europeans gave the place up for lost and left; others slipped away before landing in the debtors' court. Business was in total stagnation; capital dried up; stock market losses were horrendous, frequently total; apparently stable companies collapsed by the week. On top of it all, in 1894 there was an epidemic of bubonic plague...'[32]

Shewan survived such vicissitudes, perhaps partly because he trod a fine line through the shoals of business ethics. He helped set the tone in the world young Noel had joined, a tone best sensed in the famous trial of 1889, Potts versus Rustomjee — the 'Corner in Ropes' affair. This scandal occurred near the end of the life of Russell & Co. when young Shewan worked there. It exposed how businessmen operated in Hong Kong, implying that even if not illegal, it was scurrilous and bordering on the immoral. The case was about the existence of a 'corner' in the market for shares of the Hong Kong Rope Manufacturing Company. In modern parlance, it was a successful case of insider trading, through which Shewan and friends accumulated all the company's shares so as to manipulate prices and the market.

A memorable account[33] shows, among other things, that the ways of business were helpfully vague for Shewan: 'I have no record to show any transactions; I do all my business with orders on the compradore and square up at any time. I may owe him a few dollars now. I have no cheque book...' In Shewan's memoirs,[34] however, he describes the 'very pleasant help' afforded by the Compradore system: 'No visits to one's "uncle"; all you had to do was to tell your creditors to take it to the Compradore who never said a word till China New Year came round. Then, when he handed you a long account of receipts and payments it invariably ended with the words, "balance forward no got". As it was certainly "no got", we could only leave him to carry it forward.'

Shewan saw the whole Corner affair as very successful, even though it led to court action. 'I fell ill and had to go to Japan and smile now when I look back and see my evidence being taken while I lay on my back on the floor of the Court and Wotton, our solicitor, administering sips of champagne from time to time.

'When the case came on in Court, all Hong Kong was there and no work was done that day in mercantile offices. It was decided that in what I had done I had only protected the Rope Coy's [sic] interests against the "Bears". However, as there were only 3,000 shares in the Company and we held contracts for 3,500 we were not worrying!'[35]

Mr J.J. Francis, QC, appeared for the defendant, S. Rustomjee, in an action brought by George Potts, then an employee of Russell & Co. Potts was suing (for $5,600) because he had ordered shares in Hong Kong Rope Manufacturing Company from Rustomjee which Rustomjee had been unable to deliver. In the meantime, the value of the shares had increased, and Potts wanted the profits he saw as rightly his. The nub of the case was that when Potts had ordered the shares, he knew that their value would go up because, as it happens, the Rope company was managed by Russell & Co. Potts was accused of having inside knowledge of a likely high dividend on Rope company shares. The argument went further, to assert that Potts' order for the shares was part of a conspiracy led by Shewan, for the purpose of creating a 'Corner in Ropes'.

This case lays out most debates of relevance in the shares business, particularly that thorny issue of knowing at what stage acting on personal judgement is no longer a case of good business sense, but a disreputable dose of 'insider trading' instead. Potts' defence relied partly on assertions that he made his own judgement on the value of the shares, thereby concluding on his own that they were likely to increase in value. Where is the line between a good broker and a sneak?

Francis, addressing the jury made up 'of mercantile men', had no hesitation in calling the broking business a game and a gamble. 'They all understood', the *Hong Kong Telegraph* reported him as saying, 'that the greater portion of the share traffic was done for the sake of doing business, and that many of the transactions would not hold good in a court of law, but were conducted on the principle of honour.' That in itself was acceptable, he allowed, as in a 'game of poker, in which all sorts of bluff and pretence were fair... But every poker player or share speculator would draw the line at swindling and cheating. Every man was at liberty, as far as his own actions went, to manipulate or try to deceive his opponent, but no man, or set of men, must "pack the cards" ... no one would hesitate for a moment to draw the line at going outside the rules of the game...'

Although this case took place just before Noel Croucher was born, it provides a special insight into the business morality of the day, as well as the operation of the share market in Hong Kong. (It also shows how there is nothing new under the sun.) The case involved a rack of names comprising the broking elite, from whom Noel was to inherit skills, style and values. What we know of his upbringing shows he had a grounding in solid propriety and God-fearing respectability — at least until his mysterious stepfather brought the family out to Hong Kong. Then Noel entered this world of men who made fun of the court, sipping champagne while reputations were vilified.

In defence of Potts, Mr Pollock (instructed by the solicitors Wotton & Deacon) summed up that the attempted shares deal 'might not be a very moral transaction; but they had to draw the line between what the law allowed and recognised and what it did not...' Of course Potts and Shewan had inside knowledge of the Rope company, 'and there was really nothing in law to prevent their utilising that knowledge'. This was not good enough for the *Hong Kong Telegraph*, which commented, 'neither are we acquainted with any such prohibitory enactment, outside the unwritten but universally recognised laws of honour and common honesty.'

The paper decried the 'unblushing effrontery unparalleled in the history of local share gambling, [which] was avowed with the greatest coolness imaginable... It would seem that certain brokers in the colony frequently figure as principals in transactions where they also act as brokers, and they consider this perfectly legitimate ... the witnesses pretended to regard it as a mere matter of course.'

Haranguing the 'moral pestilence' of these 'daring speculators', the *Telegraph* editorialised further, stressing that Shewan and Potts were by no means on their own in their behaviour: 'There is scarcely a public company or merchant's office in the Colony where general share speculating is not rampant, to the neglect of legitimate business.' More, the paper went on to recall that in the course of the trial, a list of 'good names' was referred to which Potts and Shewan had used in attempts to get a bank loan. 'Who were "the good names" offered as additional security to the Manager of the Chartered Bank when these two salaried clerks [i.e. Shewan and Potts] tried to negotiate a loan of something like a quarter of a million of dollars? Why were these "good names" not forthcoming?'

Why indeed? The implication was that exposure of such 'good names' would have damaged the public's view of the colony's elite, who apparently were involved in or sympathetic to the dubious activities of the brokers. The added implication is that if one has a 'good name', one can get away with all sorts of financial shenanigans and not suffer exposure.

The 'heads I win, tails you lose' philosophy displayed in the trial had hardly been banished from broking more than a century later, but such newspaper prose is alas a thing of the past. Defining the 'corner' for its readers, the *Telegraph* wrote: 'In plain English it is a combination, by persons who doubtless consider themselves models of honour and probity, to obtain money under false pretences... The very men who have been liberally paid to advance and protect the rights of the shareholders have made a common practice of ignoring everything but their own personal interests, and have unscrupulously enriched themselves at the public expense.'

This stern judgement did not appear to damage Robert Shewan or his companies in any way. On the contrary, the case demonstrated the incestuous nature of daily trading in the colony, and showed a crowd of daredevil men prepared to cock a snook at stuffy moralisers, all in the name of the game. This was a small clique, with Shewan prominent, and it was this clique to which Noel Croucher gained entry. Not surprisingly, 'the rise of Shewan, Tomes & Co was spectacular as by the early twentieth century, it became one of the major firms in the Far East.'[36]

It may seem paradoxical, yet apt, that Shewan inspired young Noel in another way too: 'In private life it was said that he [Shewan] was of a very unassuming character. It is literally true; his private benevolence knew no bounds. Many are those who retain grateful remembrance of benevolence received from the kind hands of the late Mr Shewan. Widowed mothers, orphan children, will bend their knees in prayer to the memory of one who dispensed his benevolence with one hand unknown to the other.'[37]

Though Shewan, Tomes & Co. records did not survive, it was a corporate force in Hong Kong for most of Noel's life. Severely damaged during the Japanese occupation (1941–45), the firm was acquired in 1951 by Wheelock Marden & Company chaired by George Marden. He is another important man in Croucher's life, of whom more later. By 1967, it was reported that 'the pattern of progressive, up-to-date business method started so long ago by Samuel Russell has continued through to the present and Shewan Tomes is still one of the most forward-looking companies in the Colony.'[38]

Shewan, Tomes & Co. served the purpose for Noel Croucher. During these years, he took major strides not only in his business life, but in his personal life too.

Florence 'Floss' Croucher, Noel Croucher's mother, in Ventnor, 1933.

The Croucher-Parker family, Southampton, circa 1903. From left: Noel's stepfather, Alex Vernon Parker; Basil; mother Floss; Wallace Oliver; and Irene. Sitting in front is Noel Croucher.

Hong Kong Panorama, 1890. (Courtesy of the Government of the Hong Kong Special Administrative Regio...

Post Office and Macao Hotel on Praya Grande. Macao.

The Macao Hotel and Praya Grande. (Courtesy of Arthur Hacker/Stockhouse.)

Elizabeth Cartwright Born July 6th 1826
at 10 Minutes before 8 in the morning
and Named at St Lawrence Church
in the City of Norwich

Henry Stockley Born the 25th October 1834
at half past 4 in the Afternoon

Henry Stockley Born the 25th october 1834
at half past 4 in the afternoon

Henry Stockley departed this life December 8th 1916
and was buried in Eastleigh Cemetery December 12[t] 1916

Harry Charles Stockley died on Thursday March 22[n] 1917
and was buried in Southampton Cemetery March 27[t] 1917

Frontispiece to the Stockley Family Bible, where births, deaths and marriages were recorded,
starting with Elizabeth Cartwright's marriage to Henry Stockley and including the birth of Floss.

Noel Croucher, Hong Kong, 1915.

Hunting in the New Territories.

Party time at Marble Hall, Sir Paul Chater's residence. Noel Croucher is standing, second to the left. (Courtesy of the Government of the Hong Kong SAR.)

Sir Paul Catchick Chater. (Courtesy of the Government of the Hong Kong SAR.)

Noel Croucher (left) and Walter H. Adgey-Edgar, aboard S.S. Ionian,
on the way to war with the Chinese Labour Corps. The cargo of 'coolies' is seen at left.

Noel Croucher in officer's uniform for World War I, 'after being in the East so long and getting a lot of England knocked out of me. The girls said I was different to the homeside Englishman, and I suppose I was.'

Chinese labourers loading munitions under supervision, World War I.
(Courtesy of the Imperial War Museum, London.)

Labourers taking a break with a Chinese newspaper.
(Courtesy of the Imperial War Museum, London.)

*Noel's neighbourhood, Hong Kong in the 1930s. On the left is Union Building
(now Swire House), in the middle is Gloucester Hotel and on the right
is the old Post Office (now Worldwide House).
(Courtesy of the Government of the Hong Kong SAR.)*

The young family: Noel, Richard and Simonne Croucher at home, 1925.

Opening of the new Stock Exchange Building, 1934, at 10 Ice House Street.
Exchange chairman, George Potts, has the pipe. Noel Croucher is on his right.

Noel Croucher, Hong Kong, 1925.

Noel Croucher, sailing, 1925.

Simonne Elise Croucher, née Kiemlé,
Hong Kong, 1936.

*Simonne Croucher, at the penthouse, with the Hong Kong
& Shanghai Bank at back left, Hong Kong, 1938.*

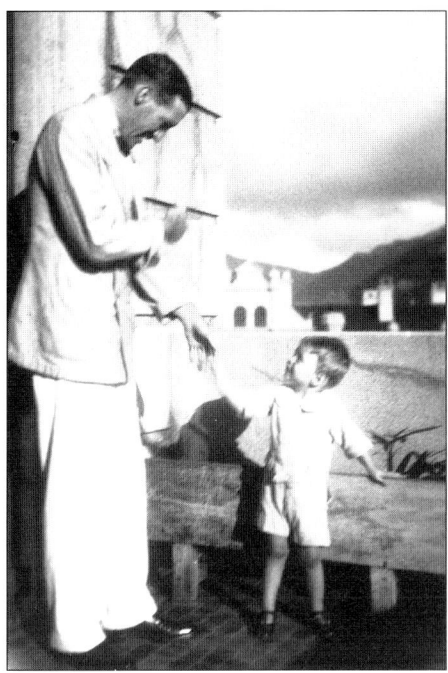

Father and son, at the
P & O Building penthouse, 1927.

Simonne and Noel Croucher, Hong Kong, 1938.

Simonne Croucher with Iris Hay Edie Knapp, Gloucester Hotel, 1930s Hong Kong.

CHAPTER FIVE

FUN AND GAMES

he year 1911 was an eventful one for the China Coast and for Noel Croucher — socially and professionally. The Kowloon-Canton Railway was completed and coronation celebrations were held. The political and trade environment in the Pearl Delta was perhaps never more unstable than after the 1911 revolution.[1] The next year, when Noel could have had little idea of its future significance to him, the University of Hong Kong was opened (on 11 March 1912).

The year 1912 holds interest in the Croucher chronicle for another reason. It is the year in which he later told some friends and colleagues that he was a shipping clerk for Butterfield & Swire.[2] Unfortunately, a picture of the staff of Swire, taken in 1912 and neatly labelled, shows the chief shipping clerk to be J.W. Crouch — not Noel Croucher.[3] This is one of those very feasible legends created by or about Croucher, which turns out to be untrue.

As in so many legends, there is a weak link to truth which may have inspired the tale, or at least helped muddy the waters later on. Perhaps Noel saw the picture or heard of the name so similar to his own and found a way to use it, to bolster his non-existent curriculum vitae. Or perhaps the story was just confused by chroniclers decades later. As to why he repeated the story, anyone knowing the stature of the Chief Shipping Clerk for Swire in 1912 need not ask. It was indeed an unlikely role for a mere stripling of twenty-one years old who certainly had not been to the right school.

Graduating from the Shewan school of commerce in 1915, Noel joined that small crew of financiers grouped under the partnership of Benjamin & Potts. Here he was to catch the eye of George Hutton Potts, the man we already met in the Ropes affair.

But before then, and at the early age of twenty-two, Noel Croucher came of age in several ways. In 1913, he made his first appearance on the jury lists of the colony, registered as living at 3 Calder Path, between Macdonnell and Kennedy roads. At this address was Tower House owned by Mrs Ada Charlotte Sachse, a Scotswoman wed to a German who worked for Arnhold, Karberg and Company. She ran several respectable boarding houses, including the Craigebourne Boarding House on the Peak and the Kingsclerc Hotel on Kennedy Road. Noel moved from Tower House after a year, however. In 1914, his address was 9 Garden Road, known either as Harperville or Harper's Villa, owned by Li Tsze-chiu and managed by J.H. Seth. This too appears to have been a boarding house or bachelor's mess, handy for young men making their way in the city.[4] From 1916, Noel's address was the Hong Kong Hotel.

He also joined two institutions — the Hong Kong Volunteer Defence Corps[5] and the Royal Hong Kong Yacht Club.[6] The regiment then was as much a social club as it was an outlet for militaristic tendencies. Here young men without other ways to get ahead could meet and mingle with officers, and with the middle and upper classes of expatriate society. As a gunner, Noel was at the lowest rank, in the cheapest social club in town. There were regimental parades and drill nights, but there were also balls and access to recreational facilities. Noel stayed with the Volunteers until World War I, but played no part in it thereafter. By the time the next war took place, he was too old for active service.[7]

A mere snippet from Noel's military career, on a piece of paper he kept all his life, reveals that he was the subject of a Field-General's Court Martial in 1914, but no records exist to tell us more. Considering Noel was made an officer three years later, his 'crime' was too minor to get in the way — perhaps a Negligent Discharge (firing one's gun wrongly or too soon), or failing to turn up for a parade or drill night.

Of far greater significance was Croucher's membership of the Royal Hong Kong Yacht Club. In no other activity, bar moneymaking, did Noel invest so much of himself. Sailing was his primary form of recreation, and the yacht club the site of his greatest enjoyment and challenge. It is also where his philanthropic urges found early expression in his virtually single-handed post-war rescue of the club. Did Noel love sailing because it was in his blood from his ancestor mariners on the Isle of Wight? He could not afford his own yacht at this stage, but he could crew on others' yachts, spending his weekends on the water, exploring the bays, coves and islands that made Hong Kong such a beautiful place in those days.

It seems fitting that Noel pursued a sport which, though often requiring teamwork, was not necessarily a team sport. He had not been at school long enough, let alone at the right schools, to learn or to love games such as cricket or rugger. Sailing is a sport for individualists and for people prepared to dare the elements and their own skills in competition of yacht against yacht, helmsman against helmsman. No wonder it suited Noel Croucher.

Another clue to why Noel may have turned his eyes to the yacht club was the active participation in its activities by his bosses. A.L. Shields, who was to succeed Robert Shewan as a partner in Shewan, Tomes & Co., was a keen sailor who later became Commodore of the club in the years 1927–28 and 1932–36. Another company man, C.A. Tomes, was sailing by the turn of the century. In 1904, the Governor's Cup was won by *Haidee*, owned by George Potts.[8]

In those days, the Royal Hong Kong Yacht Club had premises at North Point (in a building now used as a government supplies depot). But a threat to the club's dominance existed in the form of the Corinthian Yacht Club, home of smaller, cheaper yachts from 1904. As a result, the 'elite' joined the Royal Hong Kong Yacht Club, while those with perhaps a more untrammelled sense of fun joined the Corinthian. By 1920, the rift between the two clubs was solved through amicable merger, but it is interesting to see which way Noel's aspirations inclined, back in 1913.

Sailing had been underway on the China Coast well before the settlement of Hong Kong. The Canton Regatta Club (later renamed the Canton Rowing Club) was formed in 1837, while rowing and sailing were also enjoyed at Macao. The first official regatta in Hong Kong was organised by the Royal Navy in February 1845. By 1864, the colony's keen yachtsmen instituted the first race outside the limits of Victoria Harbour, sailing right around the island. By the end of 1869, the Hong Kong Yacht Club formally came into being as an entity distinct from the Victoria Regatta Club. (The latter had begun life as purely a rowing club. It became the Victoria Recreation Club, which exists to this day in Deep Water Bay.)

Not surprisingly, sailing was pursued by the same names involved in setting up the colony: Jardine, Dent, Keswick, Linstead, McMurdo, Lammert, Hazeland, Sassoon, Lapraik, among others. Francis H. May (later to be Governor of Hong Kong) was Commodore of the Hong Kong Yacht Club from 1896 to 1907 and wrote a book titled *Yachting in Hong Kong, 1849–1904*. In 1894, the club received Queen Victoria's permission to fly the Blue Ensign and to use the title 'Royal'.

Meanwhile, the acquisition of the New Territories in 1898 opened up a vast hinterland of beautiful bays and beaches where cruising could take place (as opposed to racing). In later years, Noel wrote about his intense enjoyment of such excursions, and remembered some of the best trips in his letters:

> I went out sailing ... and when I was a long way out the wireless weather report said the Black Ball had been hoisted meaning a strong wind was expected. I had to pick up anchor and go to a more sheltered spot. It certainly blew and I had to get back home on Sunday night, whatever the weather. *La Cigale* went like a bomb, but going round the back of the island the strong gusts from the hill sides blew one of my sails out. It didn't matter as it is as well to know the halyards wanted renewing. I had a swim in the evening and another in the morning and it was cold.[9]

> ...the weather was uncertain owing to a prevailing typhoon in the offing, but the weekend bid fair to be nice, without a cloud in the sky and the azure blue of the hills after the heavy rains, and the clear jade green water at the solitary sandy beach — with sand as fine as pepper and as white as ... [illegible] — it's out of another world.[10]

Anyone else sailing in the pre-war days knew that Noel Croucher had found his own favourite places around Hong Kong. One of them became known as Croucher's Beach, or sometimes, La Cigale Bay. It was at the top of Rocky Harbour (Lung Shun Wan Hoi), between Ki Yan Siak and Sai Wan Tsui:[11]

> It was a lovely weekend I spent in my own particular Bay. The evenings are long and it's dark about 8.30 — by that time I've had a snack and am lying in the cockpit which is boarded over with mattresses, looking right up to the starry heavens. Perfectly silent, with just a light sarong on and nothing else ... one can lie and contemplate the infinite. In the morning, a swim. At seven, breakfast, reading, another swim, then upsail to another place and a pleasant sail home in the evening.[12]

As in the examples of poetry Noel kept to remember these early pleasures, his enjoyment of sailing gave him a special insight into the joys of nature and of the rare opportunities on offer in early Hong Kong. He took a sensual delight in the exertion and in the relaxation, savouring these good times for years to come.

Noel had also begun to explore the hinterland and had some idea of the Middle Kingdom, because, sadly without elaboration, he wrote to a friend in 1976,[13] that he had visited China: 'China had her wall in 2000 BC if I remember correctly. I went there in 1913 and to the Ming Tombs.' His old friend Arnold Graham also believed that Noel had visited Miyajima in Japan at this time.[14]

It was probably in these years that Noel Croucher got to know Sydney Chynchen, agent for North China Insurance Co. Ltd., in Alexandra Buildings from 1908 on. The Revd John Chynchen recalls a cocktail party held by Lord and Lady Kadoorie, when Noel became excited on hearing John's family name. Noel immediately buttonholed John to say, 'My best friend was Chynchen at Union Insurance, from 1911 to '35. We did a lot together.' John Chynchen's grandfather, born in 1848, was Samuel Chinchen [sic], a colourful character who had two legitimate sons among others. He then married the cook and had four more children, the youngest of whom was John's father. 'It was one of Samuel's two sons who Noel knew — my half-great uncle,' he says.[15]

One of the daily complexities of life for Noel was the chaos of currencies in which business was done. 'In Hong Kong itself, when I took my letters to the post and gave a dollar to the clerk to pay for stamps, I had to wait while he bit it, tried with an acid, weighed it, and gave me change, not as though my dollar were a dollar, but according to its weight, which was 96/100ths of what it should have been. This was no exceptional case, but was the practice gone through in every instance.'[16] Commerce required the 'chop' of the issuer as a guarantee of the silver's fineness. All calculations had to be made on the spot. 'With the various provincial currencies behaving, in the days of the warlord type of local governors, rather like the seed that fell upon stony ground, springing up overnight and withering away again in the noonday sun, no man of substance would hold his money reserves in anything but solid silver...'[17]

Up and down the China Coast, expatriates lived with the possibilities of sudden alarms requiring flight from local political upsets. In Hong Kong the sense of threat may not have been so violent, but a ghetto mentality was common. Life was luxurious and exotic. It was also nasty, brutish and often short.

Part of the traders' moral insouciance (if we may call it that) might be excused by the feeling that life was indeed precarious. The value systems of the surrounding alien culture (that is, of the Chinese) were so different or so incomprehensible, and the possibilities so huge, it was little wonder that one's own values might alter over time. Little wonder too that what might appear to be self-evident rules of conduct back home became laughable or impracticable abroad. Once a foreigner starts broadening the mind enough to take in the new environment, some effort is required not to lose all one's moorings at once.

It is this which often gives expatriates, wherever they are, a sense of freedom (on a good day) or a confused sense of loss (on a bad one) — comprising the dangerous appeal of living in foreign parts. As Gompertz puts it: 'Although there was plenty of gaiety, there was often a feverish phreneticism about it. We were so often on the brink of something — we knew not what.'[18]

Noel Croucher was on the brink of a lifetime of moneymaking in Hong Kong. It will be seen that, compared to some of his role models, he lost less of his probity than might be expected. He did become a 'permanent expatriate' of course — indeed, having started abroad so young he had little choice in the matter. He had gained acceptance in the world he found through the good offices of Chater and Shewan, and was now ready to move further into the belly of the beast of finance.

CHAPTER SIX

JOBS FOR THE BOYS

oel Croucher joined the stockbroking firm of Benjamin & Potts in 1915 and worked at this premier establishment until 1932. Within two years of leaving Benjamin & Potts, he set up Croucher & Company, the vehicle through which he traded in the world's companies and currencies until his death in 1980. Whereas he gained his grounding in trade — shipping, construction, industry, mining and raw materials — at Shewan, Tomes & Co., Noel Croucher learned more precisely about stocks, shares, currency and deal-making at Benjamin & Potts. He had secured the necessary introductions in his early twenties. Now he could build on these beginnings, nurture his own network of clients and become 'one of the boys' in business.

There is a school of thought which holds that Noel Croucher actually made his money in Shanghai, appearing in Hong Kong as an already rich man. The wild and sophisticated image of Shanghai then, Paris of the East, contributes to this myth, as anyone who knew Noel Croucher in only his last few decades saw in him a throwback to a more stylish and eccentric time. Some perhaps saw the more fluid morality of Shanghai, especially in financial matters, as more appropriate to their notion of Noel than staid Hong Kong. Yet another school of thought holds that Noel Croucher was a Jew, and the usual stereotypes about moneymaking no doubt played a part in this legend.

But the starting point of these assumptions is inaccurate. He might well have spent time in Shanghai (and the friend, Arnold Graham, who might have told us more about it, sadly passed away in 1996). But Noel's one proven link to Shanghai was through Benjamin & Potts, and that indirectly. He was not Jewish at all as far as family history goes — but the scene he joined with Benjamin & Potts was a largely Jewish one, albeit with strong Anglophile tendencies.

In Shanghai, several families were accruing wealth in cosmopolitan style. There were the Kadoories, the Sassoons, the Potts, the Hayims, among others. These families formed one of several networks in business on the China Coast which produced, among other things, the broking firm of Benjamin & Potts. Many records and attic treasures were lost in Hong Kong and Shanghai during wars and revolutions, but thanks to an unforgettably titled autobiography and the records of Carl T. Smith, the genesis of this firm can be traced.

To start with a personal view of one side of this famous broking partnership, we can turn to George Hayim's autobiography — *Thou Shalt Not Uncover Thy Mother's Nakedness*. George Hayim recounts how his grandmother had left Baghdad 'for Bombay, where her brother, a friendly, rich, round man, called Benjamin Sassoon, had an import-export business with Shanghai, where he also had an office... Uncle Benjamin also had a stockbroking business in Shanghai, called Benjamin & Potts, Potts being a distinguished Christian and an old Harrovian. This was to alter our destiny: I was named George after him; my father [Ellis Hayim] became an Anglophile and joined the firm in Shanghai.

'Father had drive and ambition. The stock exchange was small and when six or seven Baghdadians yelled out in Arabic and no one else understood, they made a killing. Within a few years of his marriage, Father had become a millionaire.'[1]

Ellis Hayim was a key part of the Shanghai crowd. He was born in Baghdad in 1893, was a partner of Benjamin & Potts, and chairman of the Shanghai Stock Exchange at one time. The family moved to Hong Kong in the 1950s. His wife, young George's mother, Flora Kate (Mimi) Elias, died ten years earlier than her husband, in Rome in 1967. She features in the book *China Races* by Austin Coates,[2] as a pioneer in the female ownership of racing horses, although her son's autobiography suggests this was merely one of many talents.[3]

George Hayim's 'Uncle Benjamin', from whom the brokerage was to take its name, was in fact Solomon Sassoon Benjamin. He was born in 1862, and arrived in Shanghai in the late 1870s in the employ of David Sassoon & Co. He later joined the Hong Kong Stock Exchange, returning to Shanghai in 1900. He had married the only daughter of Mrs Abraham Van Nierop of Bayswater, London, in August 1891. The next year, domestic tragedy struck twice. First his wife, Fanny, aged twenty-four, died giving premature birth to a son, and by November, the son died after a life of just four months and three days. Within a few years, Benjamin married again, and his wife Dolly went on to provide him with a daughter and two sons, all the while making a fortune in Shanghai. He outlived Dolly too, in elegant retirement at Villa Edgerton, Roque-brune Cap Martin, until he died aged seventy-two on 14 March 1934, after a life rich in financial daring and vision.

In this era of trade, the importance of personal ties was overwhelming. A further look at the Benjamins shows how: Maurice Benjamin, son of Benjamin David Benjamin, was the director of the Shanghai Land Investment Company in the mid-1920s and was once a member of the Municipal Council (1920–21). Early family members include: A.E. Benjamin, formerly representative of Judah & Co. in Macao and an assistant at D. Sassoon Sons & Co. in Hong Kong (1850–60s); Jacob Benjamin, assistant in the firm of Ezra and Judah Co. in Canton (1854); Ezekiel Sassoon Benjamin, a merchant at 3 Pottinger Street (1860s); Joseph Benjamin, assistant at E.D. Sassoon & Company (1899–1912); another David Benjamin, assistant at Taikoo Sugar and at E.D. Sassoon & Company (1889–91); and David Hai Benjamin, an estate agent in Shanghai who killed himself in 1935.[4]

In this fascinating mosaic of companies and blood brothers, the Hayims and Sassoons were good friends, as were the Sassoons and the Benjamins. D. Sassoon Sons & Co. was one of the first Jewish firms in Hong Kong, founded by David Sassoon and expanding from Canton to Hong Kong in the 1850s.[5] Born in Baghdad in 1792, David Sassoon moved to Bombay in 1832 and embarked on the China trade with a fleet of opium clippers, branching into banking and property. Around 1860, his son Albert took over, achieving great wealth and a knighthood.

Another son, Elias David Sassoon, set up E.D. Sassoon & Company in 1867. He too dealt in opium, from a well-guarded warehouse on Pedder's Hill alongside Wyndham Street. He traded in yarns and moved into banking, all the while tapping the pool of young men of fellow Jewish families such as the Benjamins.

Of course, the Sassoons were good friends with the Kadoories, another legendary family on the Coast. Divisions sometimes arose — perhaps over observance of the Sabbath or the conduct of a deal — but these leading figures of finance were interrelated and, in Shanghai at least, lived near each other. The tangled web embraced not only Jews, but Sir Paul Chater, a Christian. Chater's own start in business was backed by the Sassoons, his seat on the Legislative Council had been Frederick Sassoon's and he willed effects and responsibilities to Sir Victor Sassoon.[6] Meanwhile, the brothers Ellis and Elly Kadoorie were first employed by the Sassoons. Longevity in business required people one could trust.

It is worth noting that when Noel entered business, he did not join any johnny-come-lately outfits — he joined this financial aristocracy of interlocking ties, the leaders of which were begetting dynasties which would last throughout all manner of upheavals over the decades. This circle of contacts was a survival technique — little wonder that Noel wanted to join it.

As for the Potts, the other half of the Benjamin & Potts brokerage, here Noel Croucher formed another vital connection. The Potts family hailed from Firby Hall, Bedale, Yorkshire — the home of Lipton Hutton Potts. He was Master of the Hunt but found time to have twelve children, including sons William Hutton, Ronald Maitland, Peter, George Frederick, Alex Cumings, and Patrick Cumings.[7]

William H. Potts, the elder brother, was born in Sunderland in 1846 and lived for seventy-two years.[8] He came to Hong Kong in the 1880s and became a partner in Linstead & Davis (the precursor to Peat Marwick, the accountants). It was primarily a property agency which also dabbled in other business interests.[9] He began his career as company secretary to Selamar Tin Mining Company Limited, in Hong Kong in 1889 — at least he was in tin, and not ropes that year. After a spell at New Balmoral Gold Mining Company, he joined Dairy Farm Company in 1898–99. Not until 1900 did he choose to return to the broking business, by which time his younger brother George had already made his mark.

George Frederick Hutton Potts was born eighteen years after brother William, in 1864, and died on 4 January 1937. During that lifetime, George Potts pursued business and family interests in lavish style. He managed to straddle various different worlds — from the colourful crowd of Shanghai traders, to the bureaucrats of Hong Kong, to the smart vacationers on the English coast. This George was educated at Harrow, worked in an insurance firm in the city, and arrived in the East at the age of twenty-one. For five years he worked for Russell & Co. — the firm where Robert Shewan had worked, and where they both became involved in the 'Corner in Ropes'. 'A Harrovian was trained to make a buck,' said his late son, Jack Potts, speaking of students at Harrow public school in England.[10]

George Potts became share and general broker on his own account on 16 April 1890.[11] He took as partner one C.S. Barff, and his firm briefly became Potts & Barff, at 7 Praya Central, Hong Kong. By 1892, George Potts had joined forces with a Mr Danby while Mr Barff had disappeared, making the firm Potts & Danby.

Solomon Isaac Danby had also featured in the 'Corner in Ropes' affair.

As with the Benjamins, Danby had started in business as an assistant in E.D. Sassoon & Company (in 1886). He was also part of the Jewish broking crowd: Solomon Sassoon Benjamin, S.I. Danby and E.S. Kelly were trading under the name of Benjamin & Danby. Ellis Kadoorie had chosen to obscure his Jewish roots by calling himself Kelly in business, but resumed his Hebrew name in 1901.[12] In 1890, that partnership had been dissolved:

> Partnership of S.S. Benjamin, S.I. Danby and E.S. Kelly under style Benjamin & Danby, Dissolved, March 31. Hong Kong business will be continued by S.S. Benjamin and E.S. Kelly, as Benjamin & Kelly.[13]

By then joining up with George Potts after that, Danby, in effect, brought two networks together, linking George Potts to the Shanghai brokers in a partnership of great promise. But, unlike these colleagues, Danby's fortunes wavered. He almost sank without trace: by 1895, his lawyer had to publish a debtor's petition in which it was explained that Danby had narrowly averted bankruptcy — but only through the help of his friends.

Those friends were as tight-knit as ever. In 1896, George Potts joined the firm, now named Benjamin, Kelly & Potts. Not the eldest of the Potts, yet George was the dominant Potts about town. He did not forget his brothers — in 1900–01, William worked at Benjamin, Kelly & Potts at Queen's Road Central, before joining Linstead & Davis. Meanwhile, George's youngest brother, Ronald, was employed from 1897 to 1901 with Benjamin, Kelly & Potts, following a stint in the South African constabulary. In 1902, he worked for W.H. Potts & Co., before his premature death clouded by suggestions that he was drunk at the time.[14]

The work was varied. 'Benjamin and Potts played a somewhat similar role to a merchant bank as an underwriter, for it helped establish China Light and Power Company Limited in 1901.'[15] When the new daily newspaper, *South China Morning Post*, was in financial difficulties a month after it made its appearance on 6 November 1903, it turned to Kadoorie of Benjamin & Potts, requesting a guarantee of an overdraft against the unissued shares in the company.

George Potts settled into the broking business, having apparently found the kind of people with whom he could work. The *Daily Press* picked up the plot in 1906:

NOTICE

The partnership of BENJAMIN, KELLY & POTTS has this day expired by effluxion of time, and Messrs S.S. BENJAMIN and G.H. POTTS have been appointed Liquidators in Shanghai and Mr E.S. Kadoorie as Liquidator in Hongkong, and they are respectively empowered to receive all monies due to and to pay all monies owing by the late firm of BENJAMIN, KELLY & POTTS. The successors of the Firm are Messrs S.S. BENJAMIN and G.H. POTTS, in Shanghai, and Messrs E.S. KADOORIE & CO in Hongkong, who are prepared to carry on BROKERAGE Business as heretofore.

Hongkong, 31st March, 1906

NOTICE

I, the Undersigned (formerly Partner in the Firm of BENJAMIN, KELLY & POTTS now dissolved) have this day established myself as SHARE AND GENERAL BROKER in Hongkong and will carry on the business under the style of E.S. KADOORIE & CO.

E.S. KADOORIE

Hongkong, 1st April, 1906

NOTICE

We, the Undersigned (formerly Partners in the Firm of BENJAMIN, KELLY & POTTS now dissolved) have this day established ourselves as SHARE AND GENERAL BROKERS in Shanghai, and will carry on the business under the style of BENJAMIN & POTTS.

S.S. BENJAMIN
G.H. POTTS

Shanghai, 1st April, 1906[16]

Business developed so well that there was found to be room in Hong Kong for both firms, and Benjamin & Potts opened its own Hong Kong office. It was this which Noel Croucher joined. Described as share and general brokers, the office in the smart new Prince's Building[17] was headed by S.S. Benjamin who nonetheless remained based in Shanghai, and George Hutton Potts now often in Hong Kong. George's brother P.C. Potts was next on the staff list, followed by H.R.B. Hancock, R. Pestonjee, N. Croucher and J. Mackenzie.

How did Noel come to the attention of George Potts? It was a small community. Potts might have come to know Noel through Robert Shewan, Potts' colleague years ago at Russell & Co. Or perhaps the overlap in the person of H.R.B. Hancock can account for it — he too was at both Shewan, Tomes & Co. and Benjamin & Potts. As for Rustom Pestonjee, he had started as a clerk in the Sanitary Department in 1898, to become one of the colony's leading stockbrokers. Himself a Parsee, he married a well-born Filipina, Carmen Sanchez, in 1912.[18]

George Potts became a leading figure in the colony. 'Sir Paul Chater used to come and stay with us in England,' recalled George's son Jack. Jack Potts remembered the detached two-storey mansion in spacious grounds which was home in Shanghai, the family holidays in Weihaiwei and Tientsin, his mother's pioneering ownership of the latest car models in Shanghai, and phalanxes of servants lined up across the lawn, weeding. George Potts could not stay in England if he wanted to avoid paying tax, so was reputed to hold the record for the number of times he had crossed the Atlantic. He had travelled in every Cunard ship, and the Potts family albums include many menus, captain's table seating arrangements and other mementoes of this civilised way to travel. The family home in England was at Frinton-on-Sea and, leaping ahead of the story here, 'I think Noel would see us during school days, when we were living at Frinton,' said Jack Potts. 'Dad [George] had the personality, but Noel was very smart'.[19]

George Potts married 'Dolly' Esme Stuart Wallace on 11 April 1906. Her father was Captain F.H. Wallace of the China Merchants steamer *Haw-an*. Their first son, George Ronald Hutton Potts, was born in Shanghai on 14 February 1907. Next was Reginald Hutton Potts (3 February 1910), and the third was Jack Yuan Hutton Potts, born in Shanghai on 6 August 1913.[20]

As for another of Jack's uncles, Patrick Cumings Potts, he was a clerk in his brother's firm in 1902, and on his death in February 1941 left his estate to his brother's youngest son, Jack. Jack recalls how 'P.C.' had a delightful bungalow at Fanling, in the then rural New Territories of Hong Kong, and mostly lived out there in the countryside, hosting great golf and hunting parties on the weekends.

Finally, one brother of George Potts had a lasting impact on Hong Kong although he never went there, namely Alec Cumings Potts, for he was the father of Alec Hutton Potts, who carried on stockbroking in Hong Kong well after World War II. Noel Croucher worked closely with Alec Potts in later years, and thus encountered another neatly intertwined group of Jewish families in Hong Kong — the Weills and the Odells and their famous houses in Pokfulam. Alec Potts married Susannah Weill in December 1928, and she was the daughter of Mr and Mrs Albert Weill. Albert Weill was manager of Sennet Freres and Company, jewellers in Hong Kong (formerly Levy Hermnos & Co.).[21]

Meanwhile, Susannah's sister, Sophie, married Harry Odell in January 1921 at Hong Kong's Ohel Leah Synagogue.[22] The reception was held at the bride's mother's residence, 'Alberose', at Pokfulam. This is one of the houses referred to by chroniclers of Hong Kong during World War II: 'They had a sumptious [sic] home, with furnishings in exquisite taste, their servants had remained with them throughout,' wrote Ellen Field. 'Grandmother Weill, elegant and gracious, always made me think of a "grande dame" — a French countess still ruling in her chateau despite the invaders. When we went we were always invited to spend the whole weekend with them. We found it heavenly...'[23]

'Susie [Susannah Potts] came of an international family,' wrote Emily Hahn, recalling those who kindly gave her and her new baby a home. 'Her mother, Mrs Weill, was born in Stamboul. I don't quite know how that works out with the fact that she met the French Mr Weill in Shanghai or Harbin or Hong Kong, but it does, and they married and had four children and settled down in Hong Kong with a jewelry [sic] shop, after wandering about the Far East long enough for Mother Weill to have learned to speak Japanese, Cantonese, and goodness knows what else... Mamma still ran the lot of them. She owned a plot of ground out near the Queen Mary [Hospital], in the lovely countryside, and on this ground she built two large houses, one just above the other on a steep slope.

'Susie, the baby, married Alec Potts, a Yorkshireman. Susie and Alec were old friends of mine from those long-ago days when I followed the horses. Alec was very horsy and had been a "starter" for the races for as long as I could remember...'[24]

The Potts family recur throughout our narrative. Well into the 1960s, they were still worthy of newspaper attention. For example, Peter Potts, the son of Alec and Susie Potts, revisited Hong Kong in August 1964.[25] Then aged thirty-three, Peter had been at school in Shanghai when the Japanese war started. 'He somehow managed to get to his parents who were interned in Stanley Camp which I think was quite an achievement and equal to J.G. Ballard's achievement [as recounted in the book and film *Empire of the Sun*],' recalled his cousin Jack.[26]

Noel Croucher not only entered an atmosphere of high finance when he joined Benjamin & Potts in 1915 — he was also entering a new social scene. George Potts clearly had 'class' and a great deal of style. His impressive bearing, his patently British mode of respectability, his public school background — all this was vastly attractive to his various partners in business who, in the more uptight mores of that day, might have felt the need to 'improve' on their roots. George had started a horse-racing stable in Hong Kong on the side, and Austin Coates lists his name alongside those of Ellis Kadoorie and Hormusjee Mody as a leading horse owner of Shanghai by 1908.[27] The Potts home in Hong Kong (circa 1917) was 'Clovelly' on May Road.

The entry of Noel Croucher into this elite — led by a large personality, handling the monies of the establishment — was an early recognition of his talents. Noel could not have got this job if he had not already displayed native cunning, financial astuteness and at least minimum acceptability among the money men.

One way Noel achieved this is found in newspaper reports of the annual general meetings of prominent companies. Noel first went to a company meeting, as far as we know, at the age of nineteen, in 1911. It was an epochal meeting for Green Island Cement Company, featuring heated argument and controversy. Noel was listed as 'N.V. Croucher' among those present, implying he was already a shareholder.[28] This was early in his career at Shewan, Tomes & Co., and might have been an office duty or a sign of extracurricular enthusiasm. He was at meetings of the Green Island Cement Company in 1913 and 1915. By the latter, he had become N.V.A. Croucher.[29] The name Amor was from his mother's stepfamily, perhaps to give him gravitas in the grown-up world of finance. His frequent attendance at such meetings helped build relationships which would last for years to come.

At these meetings, Noel Croucher was in the company of Sir Paul Chater, naturally, Robert Shewan, A.L. Shields, H.R.B. Hancock, David Landale of Jardine's and many more. Dr Joseph W. Noble was usually present — he had accumulated holdings and directorships across the economy of Hong Kong, effectively rescuing at least two firms, namely Dairy Farm, Ice and Cold Storage Company, and the South China Morning Post. Noel was also seated near Ho Fook and Lo Shiu, the former being a younger brother and the latter a brother-in-law of Sir Robert Ho Tung. Many of these names recur throughout Noel's life. Some were to become good friends.

The Ho family, the Li family (soon to co-found the Bank of East Asia with the Kan family) and, a few years later, the Lee Hysan family gave Noel a premier introduction to the Chinese elite too. These links also show the degree of continuity in Hong Kong. Patriarchs of these major merchant families were making their way at this time, accruing wealth and establishing dynasties which remain powerful to this day. Noel Croucher knew these men when they were starting out. Now, almost a century later, it is a descendant of Lee Hysan, Lee Hon-chiu, who chairs the Hong Kong Stock Exchange. The late Ho Shai Lai remembers it was Noel who helped him sort out his Jockey Club membership after a long absence from Hong Kong:

'Although he had always been a close business friend of my father, the late Sir Robert Ho Tung — after all, Mr Croucher was a very successful trader on the stock exchange and his name often came up during dinners with my father — my career took me away from Hong Kong... He was invited to dine at my home on the Peak one evening, [and] he urged me to own a race horse... He took it upon himself to reactivate my membership and succeeded in two days... He was a close associate of my father for many years. They had worked closely together.'[30] Noel was to acquire the position of trusted uncle to some of these people, accepted by the families' second and third generations because he had known their fathers.

As an indication of how such things were measured, the accountant and founder of Lowe Bingham & Mathews, Arthur Lowe, had achieved 'Man of Means' status by 1912. 'He enjoyed a position of some standing in Hong Kong business and social circles. He was a member of the Hong Kong Club, the Peak Club, the Jockey Club (where he raced a couple of ponies), the Golf Club, the Football Club, the Yacht Club, the Freemasons, and so on. He had an attractive house and garden on the Peak...'[31] He had been a Justice of the Peace since 1906, so was able to stand for the JP's seat on the Legislative Council in 1920.

When Noel Croucher joined Benjamin & Potts, he was not yet a member of the Hong Kong Club or the Jockey Club, so he was not mingling with the inner sanctum yet. But he was sailing and those he had not met either at sea or in the boardrooms he could meet at the dinner table of Sir Paul and Lady Chater at Marble Hall. He was a lot closer to success than might have been expected of the former post office clerk and hotel boy.

The most significant aspect of his time at Benjamin & Potts was probably the introduction it afforded to the stock exchange — an institution Noel was to dominate for decades, as chairman and broker extraordinaire.

We have already seen the state the exchange was in, in 1889, through the scandal in court about business methods and morality caused by the 'Corner in Ropes'. See how durable the key personalities were — George Potts was now a widely known and well-liked man on the Coast, more than twenty years after his youthful appearance in court. In such a small society, the dominance of one or two such men can be easily imagined. No wonder the world of business seemed a closed shop to anyone outside it, an interlocking maze of relationships, with unusual and complex notions of debit and credit.

So how had the trading in stocks and shares evolved since its dirty laundry was exposed in 1889? It had begun back in 1866, a year after the first Companies Ordinance was passed.[32] By 1874, about thirty brokers were listed, five of them claiming to deal specifically in stock and shares: Joseph Theophilus Chater (brother to Sir Paul), G.A. Kneebone, Hormusjee N. Mody, John Robinson, and Sharp & Co. Trading took place either at the Hong Kong Club or in the gutter: 'the Stock Exchange of Hong Kong is the gutter ... extending from the Club for about a hundred yards down Queen's Road ... filled with Britishers, Germans, Anglo-Indians, Chinese from Canton, Armenians from Calcutta, Parsees from Bombay, and Jews from Baghdad...'[33]

An eyewitness account of Hong Kong's market at this time comes from Walter Young — a man newly embarked on a career in the East, having warmed a seat in a bank in the city before getting his first posting to the Philippine Islands. His sojourn in Manila and Ilo Ilo was delightful and he was most distressed to be sent up to Hong Kong. It was 'a fall greater than that of Lucifer'. Recording his first impressions, he mentions the 'brokers of the produce and exchange variety, and whom we bank men naturally look down upon...' Years later, after suffering various crises in his career, Young confesses, 'I longed to get back to the more reputable life of a bank man compared to that of a kerbstone broker.'[34]

His bitter thoughts about kerbstone broking were formed in Hong Kong. He describes the 'heads I win, tails you lose' system as something he first encountered in the East, referring to the 'others [who] chucked their decent jobs and started as brokers, for the only capital required in this business is a penny washing-book and a pencil, and sometimes with this modest equipment, an elastic conscience and plenty of cheek, fortunes are made.' Young's descriptions conjure up another world. Dashing from an unfortunate meeting with an unreliable client, 'I jammed on my sun helmet, jumped into the first rickshaw and shouted to the coolie... I felt so bad ... that on my way back to the bank I stopped at the Club to get a refresher and buck myself up for the next interview with the boss. There I found the early-drinking birds all alive and cheery...'[35]

But the scandal of 1889 was to have far-reaching implications. In 1890, a bill was laid before the Legislative Council, entitled 'An Ordinance to Amend the Law in respect of the Sale of Shares in Companies Registered under the Companies Ordinances 1865 to 1886 and in other Joint Stock Companies'. The declared point of the bill was to 'prevent the sale of shares of which the vendor is not in possession at the time he enters into a contract or which he has not under his control ... by compelling the vendor to list on any contract of sale the actual numbers or other identifying marks of the shares.'[36] If this was not done, the contract would become null and void.

The First Reading of the Bill was on 21 July 1890, when the acting attorney-general referred to the need to stop 'the great gambling in shares which took place last year ... which led to great abuses and evils and to the ruin of many... Two or three large operators and moneyed men having sold largely for delivery at future dates can no doubt in Hong Kong rule the market, and by continuing to sell they lower considerably the price of the stock they are dealing in...'[37]

The Stockbrokers' Association came into being on 3 February 1891, initiated by Sir Paul Chater with a total of twenty-one members, all of them European. Not until 1914 was its name changed to the Hong Kong Stock Exchange. This fraternity was very much against the bill, and J.J. Francis QC was employed to argue on their behalf — the same man who had appeared for Rustomjee against George Potts in the 'Corner in Ropes' affair. Francis said the bill would impede trade and infringe on freedom to trade, noting that laws in England similar to those proposed for Hong Kong had long been repealed because they did not tackle the real problem. Referring to his clients he said, 'They admit that very great evils do exist in this colony and that those evils arise out of transactions in shares and stocks, and, to put it plainly, out of excessive speculation and gambling in shares and stocks...'

'The evil it is desired to stop,' said Francis, 'is what is commonly known as selling short, that is, a man going into the market and selling shares he has not in his possession and has not under his control at the moment, and which when the time comes he must go into the market and buy...'[38] The link to the Ropes scandal was obvious. One result was that the Government passed the Companies (Sale of Shares) Ordinance (Number 5) to stop gambling in shares.

Just how Hong Kong's share market was perceived to operate comes up in Walter Young's discourse on the theme of a particularly raunchy night out on the town: 'The Chino-Portuguese den was situated at the far end of Queen's Road, in a neighbourhood swarming with Chinese and mongrel Macacos [sic], a turbid and flat-faced blend of Confucius and Vasco da Gama. The smell of this quarter was genuine old Oriental; by *instink* [sic] we knew we were inhaling Kipling's best East-of-Suez brand — the real Rudyard. This part of the town was very different to the Rue de Joie — or Gage Street — where the imported expensive American princesses held their nightly drawing rooms and murdered the Queen's English.

'These fascinating "horizontals" made handsome incomes, except during the periodical financial crises in the Colony brought about by the expert manipulations of the share market by two local Eastern foreign potentates. These philanthropists every few months made a raid on all the young men's savings and built hospitals and universities with the money — thereby they acquired merit, great titles and exceeding fame in the land...'[39]

His travails and excesses as a young banker in the colony, tracing a cheque forger through the sin holes of Tai Ping Shan and Macao and observing startling ladies of the night and the lounge lizards of the Hong Kong Club, all make a ripping yarn today. Young Walter was swept along in the giddiness of the broking world in 1890s Hong Kong. He tells how it changed his life, mostly for the worse.

In 1915, Noel worked in a stock market which had only recently recovered from the trauma of legislation. Since new rules on the trade of shares had come into force, 'not even chicken food could be picked up there in the broking,' reported Mr Young.[40] Despite earlier disdain for brokers he had been so attracted by potential profits from the share market that he had quit his proper job to become a share pusher. Referring to the late 1880s he wrote, 'there was great activity in the share market, and brokers were making ten times as much as a bank accountant. Things went pretty well with me for a couple of years until the Honourable Soapy Jim, a gentleman with exquisite manners, and a member of the Legislative Council, introduced and carried a local Act which made time bargains illegal. Although this modern Lord Chesterfield gambled freely in opium, he had religious objections to speculation in shares for future delivery.

'This beastly Act of his ruined all the broker-wallahs, because share business on a strictly cash basis did not produce enough to pay laundry bills. Some men were lucky to get back to their old jobs, others kept the wolf from the door by petty clerking, while many nearly starved. One kept himself alive by playing the piano behind a screen in a maison de joie.'[41]

By 1914, the body now named the Hong Kong Stock Exchange had about fifty-five companies listed. Many of these survive in some form today — Canton Insurance Office Ltd. (absorbed by Lombard which was itself absorbed by Jardine's), Hong Kong Rope Manufacturing Co., Hong Kong and Kowloon Wharf and Godown Company, Hong Kong Electric, Hong Kong Land Investment and Agency Co., and Union Insurance Society of Canton Limited. Noel was to play a large role in the future of Union Insurance. He got to know these companies well, and to become deeply involved with several of them.

The exchange moved from Alexandra Buildings to 10a Ice House Street in 1914, the street around which Noel Croucher's business life revolved for the rest of his life.[42] Trading at this time was a cosy and leisurely affair: 'the promoters of a new company or of an existing firm seeking limited liability would let it be known among their friends or associates that a new company was about to be formed and that they were prepared to accept applications for shares.'[43]

Members met twice a day, at 10 a.m. and 2.30 p.m., for a call-over of share prices, in between visiting their clients. The mode of transport was rickshaw (jinriksha), with the number of runners used to push and pull giving some indication of the broker's sense of his status. It was a small crowd of men who all knew each other, and business was personal, a matter to be discussed over a drink or two, or in daily chats at each other's offices. 'In a typical day, a broker might after the first call over pay a visit to a particular client, leaving the topic of share trading until after a general discussion of social or political affairs. And there would certainly be no desperate rush to execute the client's order. A suitable deal might not, on occasions, be struck until a few days later, when, typically, the broker would take his rickshaw back round to the client to advise him personally of the terms.'[44]

Business conducted at such a gentlemanly pace was regarded then as now, as at least respectable, but perhaps not much more than that. Are we to see these early brokers and the web they wove in the financial life of Hong Kong, as merely a bunch of clever cohorts in shady wheeling-dealing? Not at all — aside from the popular argument that anyone making a lot of money must be crooked.

Naturally Hong Kong did attract adventurers, buccaneers, swindlers and crooks, rendering definition more difficult. Following extensive study of such matters, Henry Lethbridge concluded that 'those who aspire to great wealth must exempt themselves from the commonplace morality of the herd though that does not mean they need be criminal... It is extremely difficult to draw fine distinctions between such social types as the adventurer on the one hand and the businessman, the speculator, the shady financier, and the crook, on the other.'[45]

We need only know that high finance was in the hands of a small cabal, and Noel Croucher had entered the cabal.

CHAPTER SEVEN

WITH THE 'COOLIES'

THE HAPPY LABOURER

In the Middle Kingdom he was born,
Frail life, left alone, forlorn;
Among the millet, rape and rice
He seemed unworthy at half price;
Uglier than the dust he seemed:
Love was not his, dead or dreamed.

Among a million little lights
He flickered, hardly shone, at night,
And his lean body manlier grew
All unaware, pale blue to blue,
And blue to grey, boyhood to man,
A godless uneventful span.

Until one day the Great White came
And gave his pattern mind an aim;
And sent him packing overseas
With a hundred thousand more Chinese;
And landed him in warring France
To do his bit and take his chance.

With pick and shovel, pole and spade
The Happy Labourer, born not made
Bears his burden and does his bit —
With nimble limb and nimble wit,
Side by side with Tommy he toils
All unaware for immortal spoils.[1]

oel Croucher joined Benjamin & Potts brokerage one year into World War I, keen only to build a portfolio of clients and shares.[2] At first, business seemed little affected by war. But then, companies defined as German, such as the trading and shipping firm Jebsen & Company, had to be liquidated by government-appointed British firms. The patriarch, Jacob Jebsen, was interned, his property confiscated and his ships which had not reached neutral ports captured and sunk.[3] The war hurt friendships too — suddenly old (German) friends must be ignored if one was to support the (British) war effort.[4]

Trade was difficult under the new conditions. Business aside however, the war gave Noel a new, exotic opportunity for upward mobility. For his military assignment, beginning in 1917, was to recruit Chinese 'coolies' and escort them to the Western Front. (The contracts signed by Chinese labourers specifically used the word 'coolie', even though many of those recruited were not from the labouring class at all, being school teachers, soldiers, bakers, cabin-boys, farmers, laundrymen and more.)[5] Once there, Noel was to supervise the labour of these hard-working men, so as to help free up British fighting men for the serious work of war. His was a supportive role, rather than combative.

In addition, his friendship with a French family, begun as a result of his wartime presence in France, was to change the course of his life.

As the endearingly paternalistic Daryl Klein would have it, the business of sending Chinese labourers to the Western Front was a new and exciting aspect of the vast imperial mission of Britain to civilise the world, in the nicest possible way. For Noel Croucher, it was time to use what small advantage he had gained from his life in the East. Through the Chinese Labour Corps, he bypassed the training and background usually needed in order to become an officer. Noel did not speak much Chinese, but that was not the point. Anyone with experience in 'handling natives' was able to leap-frog into a commission, get transport to the Front, and, who knows, maybe help fight the war.

What was afoot was the recruitment and transfer of 100,000 men from a neutral nation, China, to the allied effort in France. Once there, the Chinese could free up British men for the trenches just when a shortage of manpower was becoming crucial to the Allies. Britain's organised labour was not going to let foreign labour into the country, but France had no such qualms. The Chinese Labour Corps was officially formed on 21 February 1917.

David Stephen Robertson, British military attache in Beijing, designed the system to import Chinese labour.[6] The existence of a British-leased territory near Beijing, Weihaiwei, provided a useful starting point. Sir James Haldane Stewart Lockhart, Commissioner of Weihaiwei, helped implement the scheme. The War Office also sent out their own representative, Thomas Johnstone Bourne. A latent motive of the scheme was to spread British influence within China. It followed others already in place to import labour from within Britain's sphere — from Egypt, India, Malta, the West Indies, Mauritius, the Seychelles, Fiji and South Africa. Chinese workers were regarded as more sturdy and tough than others, more willing and available, and less expensive.

The idea of exporting Chinese labour was hardly new — a vast trade already took place through Macao, Hong Kong and other ports. This organised export of Mainland emigrants to mines, railways and commercial centres of the West had been underway for decades. The extreme hardship and risk of travel was outweighed by the prospect of the earnings, some of which would filter back to the impoverished Chinese provinces.

The fact that China was neutral in the war to begin with, prompted the creation of a system whereby Britain offered contracts to individual volunteers in Shantung province — rather than negotiated a formal treaty between states. China could have interfered with this new export of men had it wished, but did not. 'At first the local authorities objected to the recruitment plan, and arrested two Englishmen found looking for recruits outside the leased territory, but the Chinese Foreign Ministry requested them not to interfere.'[7] Technically, China avoided violating the conventions of neutrality. Then it also declared war on the central European powers on 14 August 1917. (Weihaiwei remained a British possession for thirty-two years, until 1 October 1930.)

Weihaiwei lacked a pier, railway and roads, but it had the barracks built (and never used) by the Witwatersrand Native Labour Association of Johannesburg for the shipment of men to the mines of South Africa.[8] Advertisements were posted in tea houses and the like, and recruits for war work poured in. Some of the men's wives were even more delighted — one commented that the British government was wonderful, firstly for taking her husband away, and secondly, for paying her for the pleasure![9]

The theory was that labourers would work as civilians, well out of range of enemy action. In fact, though not subject to all the rigours of military life, the 'coolies' were 'placed' under military law on arrival in France. This was one of several ways in which the apparently benign arrangement was modified unilaterally, after the 'coolie' signed a contract. The contract required the 'coolie' to profess he was a 'willing labourer', and many new rules and definitions were created by the British administrators so as to protect the scheme from criticism.[10] Critiques there were of course — the contract was ambivalent, unclear, too easily adapted by administrators for their own ends. Some argued the contract used by France for its labourers offered more civil rights than did the British.[11]

More recent commentary on the fate of Chinese 'coolies' has compared British complaints about human rights abuses in China to the British treatment of the Chinese eighty years ago. 'The conditions of their indenture to the British Army were as shameful as slavery, but this was regarded by the government as different. This was war, old chap,' wrote Danny Buckland in *The Independent*.[12] For an account of contrasting tone, one can turn to 'The Story of the Chinese Labor Corps — A Highly Efficient British Organisation to Protect the Personal and Financial Interests of the Chinese Coolies Laboring Behind the Lines in France'.[13] Here, photographs of happy smiling Chinese men show their apparent delight in the entire process, and the author goes so far as to describe the 'coolie' barracks at Weihaiwei as 'the gateway to an Eldorado'.

Throughout the history of the Chinese Labour Corps, the single most important factor governing the flow of 'coolies' to the front was the availability of shipping. Fears of attacks on shipping routes had to be allayed. More significant was the competition for ship space between the Allies, and between the need for men, food and matériel. Recruitment of Chinese stopped early in 1918, at least partly because America had joined the war and needed ships to cross the Atlantic too.

Fifty-seven years after Noel first saw service in World War I, he wrote down his recollections of the experience for the book by Michael Summerskill called *China on the Western Front*. While the Chinese 'coolies' were not used directly as cannon fodder, it was the graves of Chinese still existing in France which set Mr Summerskill off on his investigations. His pioneering zeal in researching this little known subject must be applauded, not least because he stimulated Noel Croucher into writing his own recollections of the experience.

The covering letter Noel sent to Mr Summerskill was dated 3 December 1974: 'I enclose what little I remember of my time with the C.L.C. [Chinese Labour Corps], it does not add much, if anything to what you already know. Please excuse the typing but I am short of staff just now.' The story is best told in his own words, so we quote it in full:[14]

When the War started, the Hong Kong volunteers were put on a war footing and a few left for Home to join up. This depleted the garrison and permission had to be obtained to leave, otherwise replacements had to be brought from England. I obtained permission and Sir Claude Severn, the Colonial Secretary, suggested that I went to Weihaiwei with others and take charge of Chinese Labourers recruited from the mainland, for service in France. There were only three of us: Charles Gordon Mackie of Mackinnon Mackenz [sic], and Hanry Dennys [sic], a solicitor. We were given a commission of 2nd Lieut. We thought that after arriving at Noyelles, the receiving depot, we could return to England and join the Army and have 4 months training. We left early 1917.

We arrived at Weihaiwei in a Coastal ship and put up at the Kings Hotel managed by a Mr Clarke, who had a brother in the Shanghai Stock Exchange.

A Camp had already been prepared to receive the labourers. As you probably know, there was at one time a Weihaiwei regiment with British Officers and N.C.O.s [non-commissioned officers] — quite a number of Chinese who had served were enlisted. R.F. Johnson [sic] who later became tutor to the young Emperor was the British Administrator at the time.[15] It was interesting to see these sturdy sons of the soil. Most of them had not seen a 'fan kwai lo' [foreign devil, i.e. Westerner] before. When coming into camp they were poorly dressed & wore a queue. Several long huts had been specially prepared. The men disrobed before entering and had their queue cut and took a hot shower and then they gathered a blue uniform and a cap and shoes and left at the exit where several looking glasses had been placed. They would not believe their eyes nor their friends' at their appearance. They were then formed into platoons and drilled for hours and hours. After a few weeks the C.P.R.[16] *Empress of Asia* called at Weihaiwei and 3,000 men embarked below deck. There was no trouble at all during the trip to Vancouver where a special train was waiting to take us to Montreal or Nova Scotia, where we boarded the Aberdeen S.S. *Ionian*.

After two days out the Captain told us he had instructions to be at a certain position at a certain time, 4 p.m., where he would be met by two Destroyers. By then we were entering the dangerous zone and joining a convoy. A sharp look out was kept for submarines, and ship lights were out at night. We were making for Iceland and saw the Northern Lights. Sometime later it was reported a 'U' Boat was in the vicinity. It was only too true — a torpedo was seen coming towards us. Fortunately it missed us, but it struck the Union Castle liner *Armadale Castle* which sank. Nothing was mentioned in the Press about the sinking until three months later. We expected one of the other ships in the convoy would stop and rescue any survivors, but if they had, they might also be torpedoed.

In due course we arrived in Liverpool. The officers had a few days' leave and later reported at Noyelles. When I reported to the Captain of the Company I was assigned to, he was in his tent fiddling about with his revolver. I saluted and presented myself. I evidently took him by surprise — a shot was accidentally fired which went through my hat. I was not a bit perturbed, but my Captain was speechless for a while. When he did recover the first words were 'For God's sake, say nothing about this' and I didn't until he passed away.

I was appointed to No. 53 Company C.L.C. which consisted of 376 'coolies' plus British N.C.O.s. We were sent to Vendroux, a place between Calais and Guines, where there was a very big dump alongside a canal. Barges would come up from Calais and Bologne to be unloaded and reloaded onto trains. Sometimes we would go to Les Attaques where Gas Cylinders were handled. On one occasion a number of 'coolies' went down the hold and when the time came to go back to camp several were missing. They were in the hold gassed, but they recovered.

After a time, the 'coolies' selected their gangers and everybody worked as hard as they could for about 10 hours a day, with a minute or two off occasionally to drink a cup of tea. Some 'coolies' were bigger and stronger than others, but every one did their very best. I well remember a barge loaded with flour from Canada — each bag weighed 90 or 100 lbs. I had seen 4 bags being carried on the shoulders of men from the barge to a railway truck 20 feet away, but usually 2 or 3 bags were carried. After a while it was decided that to encourage them, an extra load was given and when done they could go home, which usually meant an hour earlier. After a while it was decided that if a certain job took 9–10 hours going all out, an extra quantity would be thrown in and they could go back when their work for the day was finished.

I remember when the big push was on, March 21st 1918. After finishing we were called out again to empty some barges. Two hundred yards away there was a British Labour Corps composed of London Dockers doing identical work unloading flour. We had been going hard at it since early morning and the gang was promised that when they had done so much more they could go back to camp.

The British Sergeant had them ready to go off when a Blue Tabbed Major Blair-Taylor came up to me and said 'What do you mean sending these men home don't you know there's a war on, tell them to go on working'. I declined to do so and said an Englishman's word was respected by the Chinese and I couldn't go back on it. We had emptied two identical barges full of cargo, while the Barge further up, worked by the London Dockers, was only half done. I told him I did not come 10,000 miles to be ordered to break my word. Nevertheless he ordered Sergeant Gallaghar to get the 'coolies' back to work but they refused and appealed to Daran [me] which as you probably know is Mandarin for Senior Official.

At last they were ready to march back to camp. Major Blair-Taylor said he would report me. He was on his horse and as he rode away somebody threw a brick which hit him in the back. This held up things but eventually we got back to camp. No one would say who threw it. The London Dockers were still at it 4 hours later, most of them carrying one bag.[17]

Some time before this the Germans had bombed Vlamertinge and Poperinge. The Chinese were working behind the lines and I heard 123 were killed. This was reported to the Chinese Embassy in London and afterwards the Chinese were not allowed to work so close to the front. We were also bombed, losing about 20. They were buried in bits and pieces in a common grave. I recall inspecting the huts one raining afternoon with my interpreter when I saw a 'coolie' with a bamboo pole and a piece of rope in his hand slowly walking around as if looking for something. I asked what he was doing out in the rain and he told the interpreter that many of his friends had been killed by the bombs and buried altogether in one pit and in bits and pieces and he was going to hang himself and be sure of joining his ancestors in one piece. The poor chap was slightly deranged and I spoke to him about how foolish it was to hang himself when it was raining — why not wait until it was a sunny day and then hang himself to join his ancestors in one piece. He thought a little and said to the interpreter, 'Daran is right. I will wait until it is fine.' He was sent to a mental hospital shortly afterwards.

On another occasion some medical supplies etc. had to be unloaded and transferred. They were found to include certain brandy and whiskey and some of the cases were damaged and the contents consumed by the 'coolies'. Later on, the effects caused a lot of trouble. The military were to be called in and the trouble makers were sent back to their huts. I asked permission to go along with the interpreter. The majority in the hut had come over from Weihaiwei with me and on several occasions I used to tell them stories[18] through the interpreter, which amused them. When I entered the hut they shouted 'Daran Daran' and became happy to see me. After a while, talking and smiling, I got the interpreter to stand on a box and told him to ask if they remembered Weihaiwei and coming across the Ocean, and they became attentive. I reminded them of their villages and their parents and how unhappy they would be if they did not receive the monthly allowance because they were drinking. This had a marked effect. Many of them had gone to sleep from over indulgence, but the others quietened down and it was not necessary to bring in the military.

Before parading for work they would have their early morning meal and then march to their job, but on one occasion they refused to eat or work. Meals were served to groups of 12; food — rice etc. being brought from the kitchen. I was asked to find out what the reason was for not eating their food. I guessed somebody was doing a bit of squeeze and suggested this and had the quantity of food served out checked. It was found to be underweight — the cooks were selling part of the ration to some French peasants. The cooks were sent away to another camp for such offences. I can't remember what the 'coolies' were paid, but 20 silver dollars a month was paid to their dependents and it meant a lot to them.

I was always complaining about the cooking and I was made Mess President. Among the German prisoners of war was a chef who had been in a leading London Hotel and I took him on in place of our Chinese cook. Well, what Fritz did with our rations plus a few extras was out of this world. This was the first meal after I was made Mess President, but alas Fritz did not stay with us long. I found Col. Grant Peterkin had snaffled him but I found another substitute from the P.O.W.s. On another occasion, when there was the usual sick parade of the P.O.W.s, one man was examined and the doctor could not find anything wrong. But the chap insisted, in German, and was told by the M.O. to report to the orderly room where he was found to be an Englishman who spoke German like a German, and had been used by British underground or intelligence. This was the first opportunity he had [to say so], being among those who had been taken prisoner and serving with them.

The M.O. orderly room was about a mile away. On another occasion I was on my way down the long road when I saw a dozen German P.O.W.s approaching who had been sent down there in charge of our N.C.O. who happened to be very small and had joined the Bantam Brigade if you remember. Well, he was carrying his rifle when he left in charge of the P.O.W.s but evidently the long walk there and half the way back was too much for him. Now one of the Germans was carrying his rifle, and a big 6 1/2' German was carrying the Bantam on his back. It was usual when a group of German prisoners were passing an officer for the one in charge to order a 'eyes right' and a salute, but to save embarrassment the German N.C.O. gave the order 'eyes left' so I would not notice our N.C.O. being carried.

Not far away from us, an American group of 27th Company Engineers pitched their tents. They had picked up a piano somewhere and when I passed, somebody would be playing in the officers' mess. So I suggested we bring the Piano down to our mess and have a sing song — but this couldn't be done as the player was only a private. We had a man who could play, so the piano was brought down — but our man had no music and couldn't play without it. Fortunately the American then brought another officer with him and, after chow supplemented with a special kind of whiskey, we had a good sing song and the pianist played all the popular songs. I told my American friend he was lucky to have another pianist who was not a private. He said 'Oh no we haven't, I lent him my uniform. We are not so stuffy as you limies and in civil life I'd be working under him'.

You would not, I am afraid, find very much of interest in what I have written but I must thank you for giving me the opportunity of looking back on those far off days and recalling events.

The records section of the Ministry of Defence in Britain confirms the bare details of Noel Croucher's account. He was appointed to a Temporary Commission as 2nd Lieutenant on the General List for employment with the Chinese Labour Corps, on 14 May 1917. He embarked in China per S.S. *Empress of Russia* on the same day, and disembarked on 2 July 1917 — the files do not say where. Noel was posted to the 53rd Company Chinese Labour Corps on 23 July 1917, was promoted to Lieutenant at some unknown date, and was released on 2 February 1919. He returned to Hong Kong soon after, travelling on the S.S. *Baltic* on 10 March 1919.[19] His address on discharge was recorded as 118 Divehaine Road [illegible], Wimbledon, Surrey.

But there is more to the story. Some say Noel was disappointed at the task he was given during World War I.[20] Contemporaries such as George Marden were daredevil men in their flying machines for the embryonic Royal Air Force. As he notes in his account of events, Noel had hoped merely to deliver the 'coolies' to their destination, before joining the Army and being trained for 'real' war work. The use of white men to oversee the Chinese mirrored what Noel's stepfather had done in the Public Works Department in Hong Kong a decade earlier — hardly a cheering reminder for a man just beginning to make his own, more successful, way in Hong Kong.

It all seems rather odd. Noel spoke little Chinese, relying throughout on an unnamed interpreter. The system was fixed, all he had to do was keep an eye on things. Presumably the British feared Chinese loyalty could not be assured. The episode drips with imperialism. Noel was a junior clerk in a brokerage firm, with no meaningful experience of managing staff. He had simply been on the China Coast for a while, which may, or may not, have developed sensitivity in him towards things Chinese. His account of the loading and unloading work says 'we' worked all day, but Noel had time to think of the food and music.

Noel had a sense of responsibility to 'his' people — his pride in their greater strength and efficiency over the London dockers is appealing. It foreshadows an idea he was reputed to have put forward many years later, at least in the Hong Kong Club, when Nelson's Column in London's Trafalgar Square needed renovation. He suggested that Chinese should be used for the job — they could erect their bamboo scaffolding and clean up the column much faster and cheaper than any other group, Noel believed.[21] And indeed, the Chinese on the Western Front were highly regarded by anyone who had dealings with them. They did not only carry heavy loads — they were mechanics, cooks, vegetable gardeners, bootmakers and tailors. They test-drove tanks, repaired roads and built aerodromes.

As for the Chinese workers' heroism, reports abound of when Germans appeared to overrun a camp only to face Chinese fighting them with picks and shovels. 'When the violence of war came near, the Chinese do not seem to have faltered. During one battle, a British officer commanding a group of Chinese labourers was gassed and could not move. Though surrounded by German soldiers, the Chinese stood round him and fought the Germans.'[22] Some groups of 'coolies' mutinied, others protested for better conditions. Some preferred to implement their own punishments on their fellows, others had no chance and were left puzzled by the alien systems of the West. As a result of various disturbances by the end of 1917, an analysis of the 'coolies' discontent listed twenty causes, eight of which referred to the quality of men in charge, or rather the lack of men who could move easily among the Chinese and who could garner their respect.[23]

Though Noel was young and relatively inexperienced, he did understand motivation: that men work faster if they can rest earlier. And he knew how to quell disturbances in a Chinese population — threaten their families. However 'coolies' were paid and looked after, that grip over their families at home was a vice from which they could not extract themselves. Having once volunteered, they laboured in a war which had little to do with them, and had less physical and judicial protection than white fellow-workers. A mutiny in Boulogne by the Chinese resulted in twenty-seven unarmed strikers being shot dead on the spot — had they been white, they would at least have had the 'luxury' of a court martial.[24]

When Noel quietened the drunken 'coolies', it is notable they still responded to any concern about their families amid the bombs and madness of war. More, it shows Noel himself had strong notions about family responsibilities. He was a patriarch by instinct, yet without a family to call his own.

Patronising pride in the 'coolies' reappeared decades later when Noel was outraged at the incursions of trade unionism into business:

> I wish the Dockers could be shut out and all ships on their way to London be diverted elsewhere, and those laid up must wait until the Dockers see sense. It's a pity we couldn't send 100,000 Chinese Dockers over — they would do twice the work in half the time. During the 1st World War, China sent 100,000 over to France to work. On one occasion, some barges had to be emptied... The same conditions in every respect were given to the men from London Docks (all in Khaki). They took nearly twice as long, none carrying more than one bag, and just sauntering across to put one bag into the train. This is true in every detail... Of course one couldn't bring Chinese labourers to England but if we only could, what an example.
>
> Love, N.[25]

Noel appears to have made the best of his posting, remembering the moments of humour, and revealing his streak of the rebel within. He had no trouble talking back to authority in the form of Major Blair-Taylor, and was eager to defend the underdog. One wonders just who threw the mysterious brick at the back of the departing major. His account of the American pianist's new clothes seems admiring — it makes the point that military rank was not sacred, and that the skills and standing of men in civilian life were just as, if not more, important.

Noel was an overseer, not an overlord, he took orders from English officers. He defended 'his' Chinese, after all he was there because of the Chinese men's qualities, not so much his own. In later years, the story of Weihaiwei and the 'coolies' became part of Noel's repertoire as a raconteur. (His account shows he was a storyteller to the 'coolies' too.) At the time, the episode perhaps showed Noel how non-normal he was, in his hybrid, hard-won state in the tropics.

More light is shed on the labourers' story by the period piece written by Daryl Klein. We must recall that Klein's constant references to the childlike nature of the Chinese men, who seemed to be ever smiling dumbly, was actually meant as a *defence* of the Chinese. He dispelled most cliches about 'China-men' in the course of his narrative, pointing out that Chinese do *not* all look alike, and lamenting that he and his colleagues were at fault for not knowing the language. He admired what he called the 'coolies' philosophical-ness, at the same time as admitting one could not know their real feelings without knowing the language. Obvious though such views are, Klein was radical to express them in 1933.

Yet, Klein's and no doubt Noel Croucher's views on 'coolie' labour were formed underneath an all-embracing, unchallenged umbrella of empire. 'He [the Chinese 'coolie'] seldom gives way to an expression of surprise, but, like a child, he is taking it in all the time, he is changing under the influence of a new vision, and there is not a coolie in France today who, when the war is over, will not go back to his country a better man for his exploits abroad, a progressive spirit, and the possessor of clean habits. That is not to say that he left China a barbarian ... today we have outgrown this puerility, but still retain a deep distrust of the coolie and his ways. Nothing could be more unfair. The coolie whom we trained and brought to France is a simple, jolly fellow. He is content with the very simplicities of life; he steals, but not overmuch; he is to be trusted. He is extraordinarily happy; he grins and grins; he is good to his fellow creature....'[26]

Noel Croucher did not write much about the time before embarkation. But Klein, at the same rank as Noel, went into detail. The men were not armed and had their own 'mess' to rest in far away from the 'coolies' crowded barracks. Klein was not at Weihaiwei, but at the second depot set up for recruiting and transporting the 'coolies', at Tsingtao. The white men in charge at Klein's depot ranged from a displaced Russian officer, joined up for the passage back to Europe, to a misplaced missionary from Japan, to a merchant from Manila.

Klein ebulliently tackled the status question head-on when a colleague described with disdain their 'mess of lance-corporals'. Klein argued that herein lay its charm. 'We are from all parts of the Far East and of all classes. We grade from a pinkish weak-jawed voluble Irishman who chatters about *gurgling* his throat after shiftin' round with them dirty coolies, to Captain Linen himself, who parades in spurs, smokes Egyptian fags, speaks nothing but persuasive Mandarin to the natives and nothing but King's English in the mess.'[27] Klein's concern that officers in the Labour Corps were of lesser import than officers in the regular army was probably valid, concluded Summerskill.[28]

But there were other ways of seeing the difference between officers at the Front and officers in the Labour Corps: 'The fierce joy of encountering the enemy face to face, and driving him visibly to demoralisation and defeat, is denied the Labour Officer; not for him the exultant agony of the advance under the barrage of the guns, the wild thrill of battle, the glory and stimulus of victory.'[29]

Klein and his colleagues were told not to put too military a construction on their duties, partly so the Chinese would not fear going near the trenches. 'And do not think of yourself as a C.C. [Company Commander], but as a supervisor of labour, a ganger par excellence, a glorified stevedore.'[30] There were fears too, that officers working on the labour battalions would not know how to behave once in the presence of 'real' officers: 'I hear that C.L.C. officers, owing to their lack of training, are apt to flatter the ranks on occasion and offend the powers that be. So that we may not be classed with stinking fish, the Assistant-Adjutant of camp — a man who knows, having become an officer at home in the normal way, escaping the incubator process associated with the C.L.C. — has drawn up for us a list of Do-Nots, which list we zealously peruse nightly before retirement.'[31]

The Reverend in Klein's mess wondered out loud one night about why young men were working with the 'coolies' instead of joining full combat regiments at home. Others thought life in a C.L.C. regiment was akin to ostracism, socially, forever more. But a returned officer put them straight: ' "We're treated as any other wee officers of the army and we work just as hard as most... Our job," he went on, "is a special job. None but a mon [sic] who has lived out East could do it. All his civilian life out East is a training. Remember that." It was something worth remembering, to be sure, and none spoke for a little while.'[32]

Klein further exposes the complexities and humour of racial and class confusion in a cameo about 'Joe' the ship's English carpenter: 'They [the Chinese] cannot place him. He is too shabby and workaday-looking to be a company commander; too skilful with his saw (as they soon see) to be a foreigner. So they ingeniously conclude he is a Chinaman in disguise. The fact that his lingo does not seem to be immediately intelligible ... confirms them in this opinion.'[33]

As for the white man's work, it was a matter of organising hundreds of men 'in the raw' who were to be 'hammered and coaxed and cursed into a disciplined body of men.' Competition raged between officers as to how many canes they broke on backs, legs, shins, even the heads of those who misbehaved. Sentries in and around the camp were to prevent the escape of the homesick, lovelorn or otherwise fed-up, as the men were subjected to the Sausage Machine — 'a process which turns an ordinary uninviting workaday "coolie" into a clean, well-clothed and smartly active human being. An astonishing process which is doing a great good for a corner of China.'[34] In return, the 'coolies' earned separation money, known as allotments, given to their families in China,[35] plus free passage, food, clothes, and the prospect of earning one franc a day once in France.

The Sausage Machine involved medical examination, haircut (loss of queue), hot bath (a great vat, into which several plunged at once), new clothes, vaccination, the welding of a brass bracelet with a number on the wrist, and the start of decent food and military drills. Then the men were packed shoulder to shoulder in triple-deck bunks which outsiders might think insanitary: 'For Europeans it would be; for Chinese it is passably snug — and snugness is all that is looked to.' Stowing 'coolies' on board a ship was referred to as packing: 'The coolies ... are so much cargo, live stock, which has to be packed away, so many head in a hold...' With the aid of Malacca canes and gloved hands, Klein's company created a record, 'stowing away no less than 1,700 coolies in an hour and thirty-five minutes.'[36] In an interesting aside, he noted that the crew of the ship was Cantonese (from southern China), and these men were at loggerheads with the northerners, for what he saw as racial rather than political reasons.

A phrase book written by a British major for those in charge of the Chinese labourers in this martial enterprise offered its students phrases such as 'Less talk and more work', 'The inside of this tent is not very clean', 'You are very undisciplined, and if you are not more careful I will be compelled to punish you', 'This latrine is reserved for Europeans and is not available for Chinese'.[37]

Ruminates the romantic Klein: 'They are a race of Peter Pans, never having grown up. Nightly I thank God they are not going to be soldiers. Never a man would reach the trenches alive. I see their fate at the hands of a colonel ignorant of their psychology. They would be shot at dawn by battalions. Yet, if Wells is right in saying that laughter will end this war, the C.L.C. *may* do it.'[38] At the same time, Klein feels sorry for the men as they were brutally given internal and external medical checks — 'all to ascertain if he has a sound enough body to work in the fields and by the canals of France. As if he hadn't garnered the harvests of twenty years in China!'[39]

The admiration Klein expressed for the Chinese labourers in their novel working environment was mirrored by Lloyd George. He wrote in his memoirs of how brave the Chinese were under fire compared to other auxiliaries. The problem was that the death of a Chinese seriously disrupted the work at hand as 'they would all break off work to attend the funeral, and neither threats nor cajolery had the least effect on them, nor would bombing or shelling by the enemy scatter their cortege, until the obsequies had been duly completed.'[40]

Noel's memories of these events were of great help to his friends and help reveal him to us. A sporadic correspondence which Noel kept up with W.H. Adgey-Edgar was rooted in their shared experience of the labour battalion. W.H. Adgey-Edgar was born in Newchwang, north China, of missionary stock and was a 2nd Lieutenant in the Royal Inniskillin Fusiliers before joining the Chinese Labour Corps. 'He and my father remained close friends, however they met, until the death of my father,' notes his son, Alan Adgey-Edgar.[41] A letter by Noel to 'My Dear Edgar' on 19 November 1976 reads as if he was helping Adgey-Edgar to remember the crazy times. Picking up the story when their ship was crossing the Atlantic, Noel wrote:

> When we got in the danger zone we would be sitting in the saloon and I noticed that Mackie used to get rather fat and put a tube in his mouth. He had an inflatable shirt which he blew up as, if we were torpedoed, it would keep him afloat. You remember we went very far north and saw the Aurora Borealis...

On the subject of the time when he and his men were bombed, Noel was more eloquent to his old friend than he had been to Summerskill:

We suffered severe bombing one night and 23 were killed out of 160, and some places like Poperinge and Audricque got it worse. I was next to a German Prisoner of War Camp and one night we were bombed and I fell into a ditch just in time and the bomb dropped into the Prisoner of War Camp killing many. After the bombers had gone I got up from the ditch and walked into the camp where the dead and wounded were sprawled about. I took the cigarette I was smoking and put it between the lips of a chap who just barely touched it with his hand. When it became light enough we went to see what the damage was and I saw this young German soldier with my cigarette in his mouth, dead.[42]

A tantalising last sentence is attached to this letter: 'Do you remember,' wrote Noel to Adgey-Edgar, 'R.F. Johnstone [sic]? I think he was Colonial Secretary in the Hong Kong Govt. and then became Commissioner at Weihaiwei...' He had mentioned Johnston in his account for Summerskill and the repetition here does at least raise the possibility that Noel Croucher met or knew one of the most fascinating characters ever to be associated with Weihaiwei. A Scots-born son of a lawyer, Johnston was a brilliant Oxford graduate who came to Hong Kong as a civil service Cadet in 1898. He was Assistant Colonial Secretary, 1900–04, and for some time private secretary to Governor Blake. Made Commissioner's assistant in Weihaiwei, he arrived in May 1904. Later he got a better offer: Johnston, a renowned Chinese scholar, was tutor to the last emperor.[43]

In a lengthy letter to W.H. Adgey-Edgar,[44] Noel had a suggestion to make which unfortunately he ran out of time to implement:

Wouldn't it be a swell idea if I came home and advertised in *The London Times* inviting all those who served in the Chinese Labour Corps to have a Chinese Dinner in a Chinese restaurant — with the usual round of Yum Sings (drinks with bottoms up) — ...Did you ever meet a David Lancaster who was in the C.L.C. He has written a small book on Chinese stamps... Do you ever [hear] anything of those who went home or who joined the Labour Corps? There was a chap named McGuire who used to train horses in Shanghai and Peanut Way from Tientsin — Harker-Tayler from Mukden — Jowett — Boyd...

A favourite memento of the war, kept by Noel Croucher all his life, was a copy of the famous 'Special Order of the Day', issued by the

Commander-in-Chief of the British Forces, Sir Douglas Haig, on 11 April 1918. Germany had swept the Bolsheviks out of the war and secured the Eastern Front, and were now turning their might onto the Western Front in March 1918. It was a defining moment:

SPECIAL ORDER OF THE DAY:
To All Ranks of the British Army in France and Flanders.

Three weeks ago to-day the enemy began his terrific attacks against us on a fifty-mile front. His objects are to separate us from the French, to take the Channel Ports and destroy the British Army.

In spite of throwing already 106 Divisions into the battle and enduring the most reckless sacrifice of human life, he has as yet made little progress towards his goals.

We owe this to the determined fighting and self-sacrifice of our troops. Words fail me to express the admiration which I feel for the splendid resistance offered by all ranks of our Army under the most trying circumstances.

Many amongst us now are tired. To those I would say that Victory will belong to the side which holds out the longest. The French Army is moving rapidly and in great force to our support.

There is no other course open to us but to fight it out. Every position must be held to the last man: there must be no retirement. With our backs to the wall and believing in the justice of our cause each one of us must fight on to the end. The safety of our homes and the Freedom of mankind alike depend upon the conduct of each one of us at this critical moment.

General Headquarters, Thursday, April 11th, 1918.

The scale of the German attack coupled with the numerical weakness of British and French forces made it a very close-run thing. There were many heroic stories — despite the immense German force, British troops resisted with style, singing hymns, blowing trumpets, even as tens of thousands were taken prisoner.

'On the Western Front, the situation was worsening for the Allied forces. On April 10 the British were driven from Messines, which had been gained at such cost nine months earlier... For six days the Allies struggled to defend successive lines behind the river Lys. On April 11, Haig issued a famous Special Order of the Day.... Commented Vera Brittain, whose hospital wards, crowded with badly wounded men, were now much nearer the front, "there was a braver spirit in the hospital that afternoon, and though we only referred briefly and brusquely to Haig's message, each one of us had made up her mind that, though enemy airmen blew up our huts and the Germans advanced upon us from Abbeville, so long as wounded men remained in Étaples, there would be no 'retirement' ". [45] It was this moment Noel chose to preserve.

Another item he kept was a poem, and by now we should not be surprised. Noel loved the language, the ideas, the emotions of poetry. As with the poem he remembered from Camoes Grotto, his copy of this poem featured minor slip-ups in typing. In Macao, Noel appreciated beauty and peace. Now, with the strain and devastation of his first war behind him, his response to the heartache, loss and death-defying courage he had shared and seen was *Flanders Fields*:

> In Flanders Fields the Poppies blow
> Between the crosses row on row
> That mark the place.
> And in the sky the larks still bravely singing fly
> Scarce heard among the guns below.
> We are the dead. Short days ago we lived
> Felt [sic] down, saw sunsets glow
> Loved and were loved and now we lie in Flanders Fields.
> Take up our quarrel with the foe
> To him with failing hands we throw the torch
> Be yours to hold it high.
> If ye break faith with us who die
> We shall not sleep though poppies grow in Flanders Fields.
>
> By John Macrae (1872–1918)

CHAPTER EIGHT

THE TWENTIES —
TO THE PEAK

 n France, Noel Croucher got to know the family of a lacemaker of Lyons called Kiemlé. He recounted in a letter to a friend written half a century later that he was lucky to meet an English-educated Frenchman, near to where he was stationed in the war. Noel, newly elevated to officer class, no doubt welcomed the chance to share a drink and a chat with someone different.

Soon this man took Noel home to meet his family. As told in Noel's blunt prose, this family was later to become intimately connected to his own:

> My wife is French. Her family had a Chateau some distance from Guines which is about 7 miles from Calais. She went to Battle Abbey School & her 2 brothers to Kings School Canterbury. They were in the French Army & one happened to be a Liaison Officer who I became friendly with. On an off day he took me to visit his parents & there I met his young sister Simonne who had returned home owing to the War.
>
> When I had a chance I would visit her home — but never went out alone with her. The French as you know were either very strict where their daughters were concerned or the other way. If we went out we had a chaperone. Well when the war was over I came back to Hongkong and continued to keep in touch as I did and still do with many old friends. So when I returned to England in 1924 on leave I let Simonne know as I was going over to France to visit the old places, the cemeteries...[1]

Between 1919, when Noel was repatriated to Hong Kong, and 1924, when he made a return visit to the Kiemlés, this bright young man pursued his career at Benjamin & Potts with vigour.

In July 1919, he might have watched the fireworks sizzling over Victoria Harbour to celebrate the end of war. If he did, the glitz did not deflect him from a greater purpose: that of securing a terrific bargain at a sale of German custodian property. This was the beautiful and already record-breaking yacht, *La Cigale*. The fourteen-ton cutter was built in 1897 by Hong Kong and Whampoa Dock Company for Captain Carey and W.H. Wickham at a cost of $2,000. It was forty-six feet long, thirty-four feet on the waterline, and carried 1,800 square feet of sail. *La Cigale* changed hands several times but just before the war was owned by a German who had set the Round the Island record in her in 1913. Noel Croucher got the yacht for $1,000.[2] He was to race, party and create legends on board for decades to come.

'He so relished telling us how, on his puny salary, when he was young, he could, on a weekend, sail his boat from Causeway Bay to Deep Water Bay, play a round of golf and waiting for him was his mafoo[3] with his horse to ride back to Happy Valley. He really delighted in those carefree days.'[4]

Post-war euphoria was setting in. The Bank of East Asia opened its doors in 1919, with a group of bright young Chinese in charge — the scions of the Li, Kan and Fung families. They were to become good contacts and friends to Noel. It was a fiction that all wealth and power was in the hands of the British. The percentage of Chinese and Eurasian holdings in premier companies was growing, and the battering of British interests during the war had left the field more open.

Noel was part of most blue-chip activity in the Hong Kong market. Just before the war, he had attended his first Hong Kong Bank meeting (in February 1917), and so began a key, lifelong relationship.[5] Noel was never a director of the bank but was reputed at one time to have been able to buy it. Now interested in the shipbuilding firm Hong Kong and Whampoa Dock Company, he learned enough to make a real contribution to a chronicling of Hong Kong's past. In the company history *Whampoa, Ships on the Shore*, Austin Coates had this to say:

> I would like in particular to thank Mr Noel Croucher, whose formidably accurate memories of Hong Kong go back to the day of his first arrival here in the year 1910 [sic]. I am grateful to him not only for valuable information provided, but also for the propulsion given to me by his consistent interest in this history.[6]

Meanwhile, the Hong Kong Stock Exchange (known formally as such from 1914) still had no Chinese members. Such a situation hardly accorded with the growing prominence of Chinese wealth and power. So an alternative, the Hong Kong Share Brokers' Association, was formed on 1 October 1921.

After the war, Noel continued to diversify his portfolio,[7] and at first the mood was positive. The Hong Kong Hotels meeting in 1921 heard of the growing popularity of Repulse Bay and thus the opening up of the south side of the Island. Negotiations began for the purchase of a 'particularly fine site at Kowloon' for the future Peninsula Hotel.[8] In 1924, Noel became a shareholder of Hongkong Land Investment and Agency Company Limited — the brainchild of Sir Paul Chater and vehicle for his visionary reclamation ambitions.[9] Formed on 2 March 1889, the company linked Sir Paul with the taipan of Jardine Matheson and Company, James Johnstone Keswick. It was, and remains, one of Hong Kong's leading landowners, at least in the central district of Hong Kong.

Business was easier once the cable from London to Singapore was installed (in 1922), which reduced the time it took for a telegram to get from Hong Kong to London to a mere nine hours. Yet, the first signs of unrest occurred among 'Native Labour', in what was to become the Seamen's Strike. In 1923, at the Hong Kong Canton and Macao Steamboat Company meeting, Noel heard of the notorious piracy attack against a company steamer, *Sui An*, on 19 November 1922.[10]

At the beginning of June 1923, a sad event brought the colonial elite together — the funeral of 'one of its best-known and best-liked business men', the Hon. Mr Arthur Lowe, of Lowe Bingham Chartered Accountants. Noel had backed Lowe a few times in company business. Lowe had been Commodore of the Royal Hong Kong Yacht Club, a director of the Hong Kong Hotels Company, and president of the Lawn Bowls Association of Hong Kong. The attendance list for his funeral, headed by Governor Sir Edward Stubbs, Colonial Secretary Sir Claud Severn and Chief Justice Mr H.H.J. Gompertz, is a road-map to status in the colony. Members of the Potts family were there, and the companies Noel worked for and invested in were well represented. Noel Croucher, however, did not feature as an individual — not yet.[11]

Noel was just starting out in business. Judging by his letters, he was also starting to get around town in this pre-marital phase. The naivete or nerves betrayed in later accounts of his engagement suggest he lacked experience with women. Yet he had joined the Hong Kong Volunteer Regiment back in 1913 and would not have been the first to have done so for social reasons. His letters also mention 'my old girlfriend, Rheta Hazeland'. She was the eldest daughter of Ernest Manning Hazeland of Hong Kong, himself the seventh son of a police magistrate.[12] Her father was a civil engineer and architect, born in 1870 and educated at Diocesan Boys' School, Hong Kong. He was also a keen sailor who Noel probably knew through the yacht club.

Noel Croucher often dropped the line that 'his old girlfriend' married a submarine captain in Hong Kong who retired as a Chief Admiral and became Lord Ashbourne. Years later, Noel expressed his increasing loneliness as his contemporaries were dying off around him: 'My very very old friend Mr Hazeland — whose daughter married Gibbs, a Naval Lieutenant in 1924 — would have been 107 on February 21... Mr Hazeland was born here...'[13]

Western women in the colony were in the delightful position of being vastly outnumbered by the men. They could pick and choose between officers, wealthy merchants, rising civil servants and more. Some came to Hong Kong in the 'fishing fleet', seeking husbands among the eligible bachelors of empire who, though happily consorting with non-European women, could not contemplate marrying an 'oriental'. Mixed marriages were greeted with shock if not outrage by both Chinese and English communities, and terminated a young man's climb up the social hierarchy. No doubt Noel too was prone to 'Yellow Fever'.[14]

Prostitution thrived in the colony, ranging from 'high class honey' managed by Ethel Morrison, who had lived near to Noel's first home at Morrison Hill, to all manner of dens further west. Where Lyndhurst Terrace meets Hollywood Road was 'The Line'. Brothels offered white women from America, Russia, England and Australia. Ethel was Russian, blonde and buxom and 'no history of a Hongkong company between the wars would be complete without her'.[15] When the trade was criminalised in 1932, many moved their business to Happy Valley, near the racetrack. Ethel passed hers on to one of her American 'girls' (Rosa Lewis) who ran it until the 1940s.

Instead of courting the right girls in Hong Kong Noel, the loner, took the Trans-Siberian Railway back to Europe. In 1923–24, this involved sailing to Shanghai, there changing ship to reach Vladivostok, where the train began. (Passenger planes did not reach Hong Kong until the late 1930s.) On this trip, Noel explored Moscow and once again, his memories show his appreciation for music and art:

> I first heard the Grand Magnificat in Moscow about 1923 in the famous Cathedral of St Basils. Although the Foreign Press were full

of stories about how the Communists were pulling down the Churches and there were pictures in the London Press, This Cathedral was packed and I had to stand at the back.

The acoustics were perfect and the Metropolitan Bishop or whatever he is called, walked up the aisle in rich robes with acolytes holding them and with candles burning. Then a far off choir was heard & later another from it seemed further still, until 7 choirs joined in unison — all from different parts of the Church. When I got back to England I stayed at a lovely guest house near Hadley Wood... [Signed] Plac d'Croix.[16]

The Russians made a deep positive impression, as Noel described in a separate letter of 1962, almost forty years after the trip: 'Next time go to Moscow,' he advises his friend Joan Scrivener who had just returned from a holiday in Gibraltar. 'You will enjoy it I'm sure. I was there a few years after the revolution — 1924 — and again some years later, & intend going again. Enormous changes have taken place & whatever Kruschev & other leaders say & do, the Russian people I find very charming — they want to live in peace like the rest of us...'[17]

One wonders if the timing of Noel's trip to Europe was connected to the British Empire Exhibition, to be held at Wembley Park from April to October 1924, under the patronage of HRH the Prince of Wales. 'Father,' recalled Sir Robert Ho Tung's daughter Jean Gittins, 'was very pre-occupied with the Exhibition at Wembley and we were soon taken in and shown around. There was a section specially for Hong Kong to display its then small array of industrial products...'[18] Or perhaps Noel's trip had something to do with a serious back injury. In his old age, the back injury was to cause severe pain, prompting a letter to a friend in which he writes, 'It was an old trouble I had in 1924 when I fractured my back. I was in hospital for 3 months in plaster...'[19] In another letter he comments that 'the well-known Sir Robt Jones gave me the "all clear" in 1924'.[20]

When Noel arrived in London in 1924, he was thirty-two years old, had survived a war, bought a yacht and established himself in Hong Kong business. And yet, 'Noel was strange because he was one of those people who almost accepted the inevitable in a strange way. You expect him to be a real mover and shaker but actually there were some aspects of his life that he never really got a grip on at all. His personal life was the main one,' recalls a friend of Noel Croucher from the last years of his life, Elizabeth Mills.[21]

Remembering the letter Noel wrote to a friend about how he first met Simonne, it is time now to pick up the story, in his own words, about what happened on that trip to France and England. He had told Simonne and her family he planned to drop by and revisit the cemeteries. But, according to the way Noel tells it, he got rather more than he bargained for:

> Well I made a date and when I got there I found a group of people congratulating me (mostly in French) on my engagement to lovely Simonne. You can imagine the situation I was in. Not a word had been mentioned about marriage, or written — & there was I, an Englishman confronted to deny all this, which I could not do — so after a while some members of the family came over to England & we were married in a Registry Office. (She was a Catholic.) Mind you she was a lovely girl — strictly brought up, but I was married against my will, although I was very fond of her.[22]

Written in the 1970s, this letter goes on to betray Noel's bitterness about this area of his life. But at the time, in the heat of war, the friendship of the Kiemlé family must have been a source of comfort and enjoyment for Noel. He stayed in touch with the Kiemlé son, Marcel, and admitted his affection for the woman who was to become his wife. Perhaps his explanations to a male friend are disingenuous — it is easy to fudge or distort weak moments in one's youth. We can never know Simonne's side of the story and, as in any relationship, there was no doubt fault and misunderstanding on both sides.

Enough has been written about the effects of war, especially of World War I, on an entire generation of men and women. The solace of an attractive Frenchwoman and her family was a boon for the young Noel Croucher, himself plunged into alien territory and duties. Another attraction must have been that Simonne was 'musical'. She played the piano and passed on the gift to her son Richard. And Noel loved music and the arts from an early age.

Remembering Noel's lack of education, one wonders how he communicated with the Kiemlés. But given the schooling in England of the Kiemlé offspring, the language used was probably English. It would not be surprising if a language gap had contributed to what he later said was a monumental misunderstanding. Perhaps too, he knew little of the rules governing respectable behaviour with women and had unwittingly crossed an invisible line.

In letters from the last years of Noel's life, he again refers to the marriage: 'My wife was a very nice girl but I had never thought of getting married to her and when I did she had to come to England and we were married in a Registry Office. All marriages are happy to begin with — and mine was, but there was the feeling that it had been arranged. Well, c'est la vie.'[23] He was fond of quoting a line he had heard somewhere — that the state of marriage is akin to that of a besieged citadel: everyone outside wants to get in, and everyone inside wants to get out.

'So they got married. And they were given by the bride's father a case of Napoleon Brandy ... a dozen large bottles of pre-first world war Napoleon brandy, which clearly he treasured. That's a very spectacular and delightful present.'[24]

Noel's wife, Simonne Elise Kiemlé, was described as twenty-six years old on the marriage certificate, but in fact she was just eighteen days younger than her husband, aged thirty-two. Her father, Auguste, was described as a lace manufacturer. Noel and Simonne were married on 3 September 1924, at the registrar's office in St. Marylebone, London. 'And then he took his bride and he took his brandy and he got on a ship and headed back to the Far East... They went back and set up house together.'[25]

Indeed they did, but one wonders how keen Noel was on the idea of marriage anyway, as he left it until his early thirties and then might have avoided it if he could. Nor should it be forgotten that his own broken home had hardly given him a positive role model of happy marriage or true love. Part of the problem was Simonne's unclear health trouble which Noel, in his laconic way, 'got used to'. In the words of a letter he wrote on the subject:

> She returned to France every year & was home when the last War started & I was interned here for 4 years. During that time I did not receive a single letter[26] — though my Mother wrote very often through the Red Cross like the others... Well Simonne came out after the War for a short while & returned to England where she has been ever since. The last time I was home was in 1965 & I stayed at the Carlton Club & saw her once.[27]

Mr and Mrs Croucher settled into Hong Kong and at last they reached the Peak.[28] One year later, on 7 June 1925, Noel's only child, Richard Roderic Croucher, was born in Hong Kong. He was christened at St. John's Cathedral, and the address on the birth certificate was simply 55

The Peak. This was Des Voeux Villas on Mount Kellett, Royal Building Lot Nos. 50–6, owned by the astounding E.R. Belilios who, among many other things, commuted by camel and funded causes such as female education.

The Peak, twelve thousand feet above sea level, was the pinnacle of social achievement, and to some it still is. Then, it was an elite reservation for foreigners. With its inaccessibility, fresh air and racial exclusiveness, the appeal was obvious — to white people.[29] Before the Peak Tram opened in 1888 getting home involved the sweated labour of two or three Chinese runners, carrying one's sedan chair up incredibly steep and narrow pathways. Temperatures were markedly cooler, making it a perfect spot for that favourite aspect of empire — the hill station. The Governor moved up to Mountain Lodge in each year's murky, torpid season, mirroring the Viceroy's retreat to Simla in the fierce Indian summer.

As transportation improved and more wives dared to stay in Hong Kong the year round, the Peak became the place for settled and genteel residence. Homes were built in gracious style with verandahs, lounges, English gardens, boxes in which to drop calling cards, and music rooms. There was the Anglican church, the Peak Hotel, a hospital and sanatorium, recreational facilities — plus dances and dalliance at the Peak Club, opened in 1902. Some wives whiled away their days in interminable bridge tournaments, others with croquet, tennis or tea. For the ideal picture of childhood on the Peak, the memoir by Phoebe Whitworth must be consulted.[30] She was one of the daughters of a future Governor of Hong Kong, Henry May, and his wife Helena, who founded the Helena May Women's Institute in 1916. Other childhoods were more traumatic with memories of snakes in the grass, and of the fog for months on end.

Such dubious delights had never been Noel's, of course, but now he could pay for such things for his son. Although this sojourn on the Peak was not permanent, Noel was, for a while, one of those taipans in the making who, as he stepped off the Peak Tram at Victoria Gap station after a day at the office, 'was in Surbiton or Wimbledon, in an atmosphere as truly British as roast beef or muffins...'[31] So began what Richard Croucher now recalls as an idyllic childhood. He had his own nurse who was sent back to England only when Richard was big enough to go to school in Hong Kong: 'When you were old enough Sikim your nurse went back to England & the Amah took you to the Army School...'[32]

Perhaps the move to the Peak had been premature — after all, the twenties were years of economic losses for many — for the young family soon moved downhill again, to take up residence in the penthouse of the P & O (Peninsula & Oriental) Building in Central. Jury lists show that this was Noel's registered address from 1926 to the War, apart from one year of absence in 1931 and one year at the Hong Kong Club in 1932. This stunning apartment had a balcony running around four sides where the young (and, one fears, precocious) Richard could ride his bicycle at will. Noel Croucher had not far to walk to the stock exchange on Ice House Street.

These were busy years for Noel. On Boxing Day 1924, he had made news in his yacht, *La Cigale*, winning his favourite Macao race, which at last had been revived. Local reports noted that 'the "joss" experienced differed very much with each boat, but everyone had a great sail and an enjoyable experience.'[33] The seventy-one-mile course from Murray Pier to Macao began at 7 a.m. There were six yachts competing: *Azuma* owned by S. Berg, *Coquette* owned by F. Oliver, *Feather* owned by A. Ritchie, *Irene* owned by Captain Arthur, *U and I* owned by H.S. Rouse, and *La Cigale* owned by N.V.A. Croucher. *U and I* and *La Cigale* were the favourites, with *U and I* initially in the lead.

'When an hour away from Macao, we saw the high peak of *La Cigale*. She was bearing back for the north of Lantao and had evidently not long rounded the mark. Through the glasses, we saw *U and I* round and *Azuma* was ahead of us by nearly half an hour... *La Cigale* finished at 1 a.m. on Saturday, *U and I* at 3.30 a.m. Thus Mr Rouse's boat just failed to beat the crack boat and Mr Croucher's *La Cigale* becomes the first holder of the Potts trophy.'[34]

Noel was sailing in triumph with two stockbroking colleagues — P.C. Potts and F. Lenfestey. According to Potts, their win was a sign 'that the Lord looks after his own'.[35] High times indeed — newly married, soon to be a father, and winning races in his yacht — Noel's cup was getting full.

It was at this time, too, that Noel and Simonne Croucher were regarded as one of the best-looking couples in town. They partied, she danced, he sailed and made money, and little Richard was sent to Garrison School just near the Peak Tram terminus. We know too little about Simonne, but must note in passing the transition she had made, from her provincial French home to the high life of Hong Kong between the wars. Sadly, she never enjoyed sailing, thus excluding herself from her husband's primary obsession apart from making money.

Simonne, by all accounts, was attractive, vivacious, even dashing. But some recollections of her do feature the ultimate English insult: 'She was loud, she was common.' The point is not whether she *was* 'common' or not, but that she was perceived by some sections of society as such.[36] Some people now admit the English colonials were narrow-minded enough to be snobs about the French.

'Simonne was dark, tall, very talkative, nervous, very hospitable. She liked a good time, and had very pretty clothes. [But] I don't think she fitted at all. He of course fitted with big business,' recalls Diane de Precourt, whose late husband, Claude, was with the then Bank of Indo-China (now Banque Indosuez), in the Far East. Claude and Noel sailed together and discussed world affairs. 'I think there was a kind of affection [between Simonne and Noel]. No doubt she irritated him, and so he did her probably, because he was always so calm and smiling and good-tempered and perhaps that made her impatient.'[37]

From Noel's letters and the stories he told close friends, it seems Simonne may also have been ill. How far we can trust these stories is unclear. Some record Simonne as epileptic, but her son Richard insists she was in fine health, merely persecuted on occasion by her husband. Such subjects are not for us to judge. Meanwhile, Richard was sent to school in Tsingtao, with its good year-round climate. Most expatriate children were sent away to school, separating parents from their children often for years at a time. Parents feared (with due cause) the health threats posed by the colony — cholera, dysentery, smallpox, leprosy and typhoid, all fatal then.[38] Simonne managed an annual trip back home to France.

One story holds that Simonne ran a popular boutique at Repulse Bay Hotel, selling ladies' 'notions', accessories and lingerie.[39] The shop was said to be well known, as Noel was well known. But, expected to make her own way with the snobs of white Hong Kong, Simonne was ill-suited to shine. Being a trophy wife was no fun, as many wives in expatriate Hong Kong would concur today. She stayed in Hong Kong only until it was time for young Richard to go to school in England. The next war broke out while she was visiting her family in France, so she moved to England and spent the World War II period in a house in Guildford, near London.[40] Apart from a brief, unhappy visit to Hong Kong after the war, she lived in a house for which Noel paid, at 33 Eaton Square, London, until she died.

Simonne cropped up later in Noel's life and letters as a source of irritation and occasional concern. He was annoyed by what he saw as constant requests for money, then bothered when she had not written for a year and he heard from someone else that she had suffered a bad fall months before. Naturally, others will tell you she was kept on far too tight a budget by her strict and grumpy husband, and it was little wonder he had no woman to live with for the rest of his life. There are recollections of the stupendous rows between Noel and Simonne in the first year after World War II, echoing along the corridors of the Repulse Bay Hotel.

Simonne was not without the instinct to fight back: in a letter Noel wrote to his son in 1974, he records receiving a letter from Simonne in which she tells a sad vignette of Croucher married life. On being introduced to someone, Simonne was asked if she was married to 'that awful man in Hong Kong'. She lost no time in passing the comment directly on to the 'awful man', her husband Noel. And he lost no time in spreading the bile onward towards his son.[41]

In Noel's will, Simonne got a small amount to live on, which lawyers later negotiated to increase to pay for an urgent eye operation. She died in London on 28 July 1992. Her death certificate gives her date of birth as 12 January 1892, so she had lived to the ripe age of one hundred — longevity was reputed to run in her family.

Noel was not the only man in the East to be without his wife — far from it. Geography solved many a major marital incompatibility and let the men play while the wives brought up the children. Always the excuses of bad climate and alien ways could be used to explain away many a marriage breakdown. But few men reached the top of Hong Kong without the 'right' wife, and only Sir Paul Chater got away with living with a woman who only later became his wife.

To speculate, just for a moment: if Noel had found a wife from a good Hong Kong family, someone at ease on the China Coast, there seems no doubt that Noel might have managed to build one of those great dynasties of the East. He nurtured strong patriarchal instincts, as we shall see, but he lacked the venue in which to express them. He was ambitious and would have loved to found a dynasty. In later years he signed some letters 'Tai Pan', but in fact could not lay claim to it without a large firm or family behind him.

❧ ❧ ❧

Far from inspiring either sentiment or passion, his marital episode demonstrates the extent to which Noel Croucher was instinctively a loner. He did not even join the Freemasons. Most leaders of business and society were adherents of Freemasonry, starting with Sir Paul Chater and including most male members of the establishment. It was and is an important form of social cement on the China Coast.[42] But Noel Croucher never joined the Freemasons — even though his maternal grandfather Henry Stockley had been a leading Mason, and some of Noel's Chinese contacts, such as Lee Hysan's son, R.C. Lee, were Masons.[43]

Noel preferred to go his own way, and soon became known as an eligible partner or guest, good to have at a party. Some friends' recollections are of a 'bit of a lad' who 'cut a dash' with the ladies, squiring many a beauty around town and making assignations in quiet bays on his yacht. Others see him as a lonely, alone sort of man. Indeed the two views are not incompatible. Most women thought him dashing, suave and well-behaved. In the words of a woman who met him in the fifties, Noel Croucher was 'Fascinating!'

According to Noel, she was not alone in this view. 'I too could write a book,' he ruminated in a letter, 'or could give a wealth of experiences to a ghost writer and it would be very readable — When I was young I met many well known personages, not only met them but went around with them believe it or not. You won't remember Elinor Glynn and the great Anne Pavlova, & Pearl White & I had a letter from Joan Fontaine only yesterday hoping I had not forgotten her.'[44]

The death of the Duke of Windsor in 1972 prompted Noel Croucher to reminisce on his meeting the then Prince of Wales who was briefly to be King Edward VIII in 1936 before the abdication following his marriage to Wallis Simpson. Noel recalled: 'I remember his visit to H.K. on his way to Japan, 1921–22. All the young girls I had booked to dance with at the Ball were pinched by Mountbatten, his ADC, and I was left without a dance. I knew Mrs Simpson, née Warfield.'[45]

The visit of Edward lasted two days in April 1922. The Prince covered a lot of ground with dinner at Government House and a Community Ball on Friday 7 April.[46] It must have been at the Community Ball where Noel was thwarted on the dance floor. As for dinner, Noel had kept the seating plan for it and noted in a letter to a friend that 'when the Queen visited us in May [1975] with Philip, Government wanted to know who was with the Prince of Wales when he came here in 1922. They had a photograph and did not know who the others were in the group except the Governor, so I had to give them the names.'[47]

There is no sign of Noel in the seating plan, but Noel knew Captain, later Major-General, Sir Robert Neville, Aide de Camp to Governor Stubbs in the years 1922–25 and later a Governor to the Bahamas. Two letters survive in which Sir Robert thanked Noel for sending copies of a

Progress Hong Kong pamphlet: 'In case you would like it I enclose the names of the people in the Prince of Wales group in Hong Kong 52 years ago. Again I do hope that you will let us know when you are in this country — should love to see you again and get you to come down here for lunch...'[48]

Wallis Simpson was in Hong Kong at this time too, arriving on 8 September 1924. She was there as part of American intelligence courier work, in which navy wives were used to carry messages to American forces in China. Her trip was described as 'one of the great experiences of her life',[49] but we fear this had more to do with the political and sexual turmoil she allegedly got involved in on the Mainland than with any chance meeting which may or may not have occurred between her and Noel Croucher. She stayed briefly at the Repulse Bay Hotel, visited Shanghai and Peking, and met Sir Victor Sassoon.[50] Her journeying provided such intense gossip and speculation — about her 'intelligence' work and alleged visits to exotic Hong Kong brothels — that anyone in the area must have felt they had known her.[51]

As the 1920s marched on, and members of high society frivolled away the days and nights, Hong Kong grappled with political and financial upheaval. The number of brokers continued to grow. By June 1924 a third exchange opened — the Share and Real Estate Brokers Society of Hong Kong. Shares were being bought and sold three months ahead, a practice which caused severe liquidity problems when the General Strike of 1925 hit Hong Kong.

The mechanics' strike action in 1920,[52] followed by the Seamen's Strike of 1922, helped radicalise the relationship between the very poorly-paid labourers and the aloof European employees.[53] Then on 30 May 1925, British-led police in Shanghai shot and killed several workers and the anti-foreign 'May 30th Movement' was born. Resentment against foreign intervention in China engulfed Canton too, when Anglo-French troops on the island of Shameen shot at Whampoa cadets, leaving fifty-two Chinese dead, on 23 June. The strike had just begun, on 19 June, and the Shameen Incident, as it came to be known, intensified the turmoil which was to last for the next sixteen months.

The Nationalist-led government of Canton could not control much beyond its southern provincial borders, as self-seeking military leaders looted the Chinese countryside. Communist influence was rising, especially after the arrival of more than a hundred Russian agents led by Michael Borodin. The luxury and privilege of the Foreign Concessions became easy targets. Sun Yat-sen's death in March 1925 ignited a bitter power struggle in Canton, and neighbouring Hong Kong could not escape the consequences. Poverty and violence ruled the majority — the country ached like a mouthful of bad teeth.

Seamen were again in the forefront of agitation, but this time virtually every occupation was affected. Pressure was brought to bear on Hong Kong's Chinese workers so that even house servants on the Peak left their posts, thus bringing the message literally into the breakfast rooms of the colony. And the message, precisely? Along with better pay and conditions, the strikers demanded equality of treatment for Chinese and non-Chinese in Hong Kong and the freedoms of residence, speech and association for Chinese. Other demands included an end to child labour; abolition of the deportation law; an end to maltreatment and torture; rent reductions; the right of Chinese to live on the Peak; and more.

Transport seized up, cargoes were left on the docks, night-soil collection came to a smelly halt. Schools closed early that year and by 19 June, staff had walked out of the Peak Hotel. Violent intimidation was used by Canton strike leaders to get Hong Kong's population on their side. Hong Kong workers were also inspired by patriotism, their own bad pay and conditions, and a sense of solidarity with their compatriots across the border. Anti-foreignism was not a Mainland monopoly.

Some colonialists needed only such chaos to shine. European managers wore shorts to save laundry, and one eminent doctor carved the joints at the Hong Kong Hotel. The Royal Navy ran Star Ferry under armed guard. Accountants drove trams, lawyers carried ice, stockbrokers and bankers became couriers. We hope Noel savoured the chance to return to his early career as a post office clerk, dropping cables and messages around town.[54] Elegant white wives eschewed finery for aprons, waiting on table at Cafe Wiseman.[55] Peak ladies shared the unaccustomed task of babysitting. The Hong Kong Volunteers were called out and neighbourhood teams formed to keep basic services running.[56] Governor Stubbs declared a state of emergency, empowering police to search for and destroy subversive materials and to censor the post.

Interestingly, there were no defections of Chinese from the Hong Kong Police. Shouson Chow and Robert Kotewall, both unofficial members of the Legislative Council, helped produce anti-strike propaganda, thus placing loyalty to Hong Kong above loyalty to their compatriots in China. Many Chinese braved terror by serving in the St. John's Ambulance Brigade or similar services. Yet others returned to their families in Canton — by mid-July 1925 more than 80,000 had done so. The strike evolved into a boycott (announced on 6 July 1925) which brought Hong Kong's economy to the brink of collapse. It meant Hong Kong's lifeblood, its entrepôt trade, virtually dried up overnight. Food prices rose, land values collapsed and banks became vulnerable again.

How could such a state of affairs be allowed to continue? The European powers including Britain all recognised the government in Peking and communicated diplomatically with it. But Peking had no sway over Canton, where government seemed either unable or unwilling to suppress the boycott pickets. 'Until Canton once more secures control within her own borders Hong Kong is bound to experience greatly restricted business activity.'[57]

Most companies Noel was involved with suffered severe losses. Dividends dwindled to nought. But Noel himself came more to the fore. At a 1925 meeting of the Hong Kong, Canton and Macao Steamboat Company, he made his debut as a speechifier, seconding the speech of the chairman, the Hon. Mr Percy Holyoak. Here we find an early exposition of Noel's business philosophy, which we might call the Croucher Caution. Praising the company's past sense in creating reserves, allowing the balance sheet to display continuing health, he said:

> You always have to prepare in the good times for the times that are bad because the bad times always do come — they follow rapidly after the good times.[58]

The bad times continued. By October of 1925, the stock market had suffered an overall depreciation of forty percent in the value of stocks and shares traded, and the bankruptcy court was handling twenty cases a day.[59] On New Year's Day, 1926, a devastating fire took hold of the Hong Kong Hotel, perhaps the occasion when Noel helped save 'a Canton warlord' from a desperate fire in a hotel in the 1920s.[60] Caused by fused wires in the lift shaft, it took two days to be quelled. Furniture and fittings were strewn along Pedder Street and Des Voeux Road — but afternoon tea was still served and Bessie's Bar offered drinks as usual.[61]

'Respectable' Chinese tried to mediate in the strike and boycott, through the Chinese Chamber of Commerce. Others organised scab labour on behalf of the government, unwilling to see their progress, albeit under colonialism, whittled away by chaos. The appointment in 1925 of Chinese-speaking Sir Cecil Clementi as Governor helped too — he set about establishing communication with the authorities in Canton. Following the coup there on 20 March 1926, through which General Chiang Kai-shek gained ascendancy in Mainland politics, a negotiated end was possible. The Strike Committee and Strikers' Delegates Congress, meeting in Canton, decided it was all over, on 10 October 1926.[62]

This trauma was when Hong Kong came of age. Key segments of the Chinese community had decided that despite obvious flaws, the way in which Hong Kong was ruled was more amenable to their interests than the radicalism over the border. 'It was not a case of either sincerely admiring and uncritically accepting a foreign regime or not, but rather one of weighing the advantages that accrued from living in Hong Kong as against China or some other country... A [colonial] government which made no appeal to democratic ideals, that accepted a wide gap between rich and poor, did not seriously affront prominent Chinese, so long as they as a group did not become less rich.'[63]

The gradual decline of European dominance of Hong Kong can be traced from this pivotal moment. Chinese participation in every avenue of Hong Kong life was now an established fact, and a new generation of Hong Kong Chinese was growing, influenced by the ideals from the Mainland yet determined to assert themselves in their home of Hong Kong. Newly united in adversity, European and Chinese elements in what had been a scrappy, transient sort of place, were beginning to coalesce into a more integrated and sustainable community. Thus, starker delineation of classes in society — of employed and employing, of rich and poor, and the rise of a Chinese middle class — helped blur other lines of schism such as race. For better or worse, Hong Kong began to nurture its own identity.

Noel and Simonne became parents one week before the strike began, so Richard's first years of life were marked by danger on the streets, limited home help and, in the next few years, the discomfort of water-rationing and drought. Everyone was affected by the unrest. For months the broking community was scrambling to liquidate its settlements in some way. Only cash business was transacted and the fervour in the futures market was dulled for a considerable period. When forward business resumed, it was at a reduced volume, finally coming to a stop in 1933 when twenty-four-hour settlement became the rule.[64]

Noel Croucher had already made himself heard at company meetings, routinely seconding proposals or moving the adoption of a report. But in the late 1920s he embarked upon what was to become a characteristic habit — that of asking sticky questions. Naturally this had its uses, but

Noel managed to put people's backs up, too. His instinct was to back the small shareholders, the underdogs, against the entrenched establishment, as well as simply to protect his own investments.

In May 1926, he was on his feet at the Hong Kong Hotels Company meeting, asking that reconsideration be given to the question of an interim dividend. He was wonderfully polite, acknowledging the 'heavy handicaps under which the company has laboured', yet hoping the corner had been turned. 'I should like to ask therefore if the chairman could give us his idea of present possibilities, provided that he is causing the Board no embarrassment by doing so.'[65]

Noel Croucher came into his own at the meeting for Green Island Cement Co. Ltd., on 30 March 1927: 'The closing down of the Deep Water Bay works was advocated by Mr N.V.A. Croucher when he put a series of questions regarding the conduct of the Company's affairs...', began the newspaper report.[66] Indeed, Noel's questions were pithy. He had clearly done his research. He asked for exact costings of various works, criticising the profits as too small, and expressing 'the share holders' view' that the Deep Water Bay works be given up. He had greatly detailed information — the length of delays in construction, the wastes of time and money down to precise figures — and wanted to know why new jobs were created in hard times which were not found necessary in good. Amusingly, the man forced to answer Noel was none but his former boss, Robert Shewan.

Sad news was to follow: the death of the man who Noel Croucher credited with setting him on his path in Hong Kong. Sir Paul Chater died on 27 May 1926. Columns of newsprint went on with lists of those who gave wreaths, long tributes and outpourings of adulation for the man who, more than any other, had laid the foundations of Hong Kong.[67] Sir Paul left instructions that he be buried within twelve hours of his death, and his timing was such that the stock exchange was opened that day only to be closed again straight away. Arrangements were hasty, and a funeral held that same evening. It was as if the man who had created and moved markets in life was determined to do the same in his death.

Noel Croucher paid tribute to Chater's importance to him throughout his life. Whatever the facts of their first meetings were, Noel saw in Chater the man who had picked him up from the metaphorical gutter and guided his early steps towards fortune and civic commitment. His loss was no doubt a deep one.

Could the concern thus induced be the reason why Noel failed to win the next Macao race? In 1925, *U and I* was the winner, but this lapse was more than made up for by a brilliant performance the next year. In 1926, *La Cigale* won the Macao race emphatically, by setting a new record of twelve hours, twenty-three minutes and sixteen seconds. This took eight minutes off the record set by *Naiad*, forty-nine years previously.[68] At the yacht club, Noel gained access to good company from around the region — the first Interport was held in that year. Sailors and rowers of Canton, Manila and Hong Kong competed on a glorious afternoon with Governor Sir William and Lady Peel presiding. The season, November to April, was opened and closed with regattas usually attended by the Governor and his lady.

The next year saw Noel take a significant step — he became a company director for the first time. It was China Provident Loan & Mortgage Company Limited, a firm he was to stay in close touch with for decades to come (not least because it too practised cautious Reserves policy).[69] Noel attended meetings of the Hongkong Land Investment & Agency Company (which had just bought Prince's Building for $3 million), and the Hong Kong & Shanghai Banking Corporation. Also in 1927, he bought a chunk of land in Kowloon for $1,760,000.[70]

For what appears to be the first time, Noel was present at the Union Insurance Society of Canton meeting on 25 May 1928. His relationship with this company was to cause drama after the next war, with Noel carving out a leading role for himself in the company's fortunes. At the fourth yearly meeting of the Hong Kong Tug and Lighter Company in 1928, it was Robert Shewan's turn again to suffer Noel's caustic tongue. Shewan admitted the company ran at a loss but, in a delicious circular argument, said there need only be greater demand for its services for the position to improve. This was not good enough for Mr Croucher, who did not mince his words: 'It seems that our Company is run solely for the benefit of our Directors and General Managers...'[71] Noel saw the company had borrowed in order to pay the directors' fees, and was not pleased. 'I feel that only when our Company is on a better footing that the Directors should draw their fees again.'

Not surprisingly, the directors felt differently. But one year later, at a meeting he did not attend, the same company succumbed to voluntary liquidation, perhaps vindicating Noel's concern.

Before the dramatic twenties could close for Noel, he was to play a part in a sadly sensational event — the death of leading patriarch and businessman, Mr Lee Hysan. How Noel came to be involved tells us much of his activities and connections beyond the small circle of English life in the colony.

Lee Hysan had been involved in the opium monopoly for Macao through his Yue Seng Company, and was busy dealing with would-be competitors in the still-lucrative and legal trade. As part of the process, he made an appointment for tiffin at the Yue Kee Chinese Club, on a lane near no. 196 Wellington Street in central Hong Kong. It so happens that Noel was in the habit of also taking tiffin at the Yue Kee Chinese Club. It is not certain that he was there that day specifically to meet Mr Lee. But his routine of being there was known among leading Chinese, implying a strong relationship between Noel Croucher and the Chinese tycoons of the day. (No wonder he had such detailed and reliable information about the inner workings of trade and the companies in which he invested.)

The club's locale was interesting: 'Kau Yu Fong Lane was formerly a somewhat notorious street, being the rendezvous of undesirable characters, especially members of alleged secret societies. This was the case some years ago but since more business premises have been opened in the immediate neighbourhood the street has become a mere quiet backwater, little frequented.'[72]

Before Lee Hysan could get settled for a cup of tea he was shot dead at point-blank range. 'The assembly of well-known Chinese businessmen who take tiffin in the Club were not molested. But before they or the servants could do anything, the murderer had got outside. Then he dropped his revolver at the top of the steps and vanished. ...Mr Lee had hinted lightly in the course of conversation that danger lurked in the air and his friends had persistently warned him not to visit the club — on account of its dark approaches...'[73]

Lee Hysan's daughter, Ansie Lee Sperry, says it was Noel who telephoned the police. 'From what I gathered from Noel's description of the day that Father was murdered — Noel had gone to the Yue Kee Chinese Club ... to have tiffin which he apparently did often. Father also went there regularly and surely it must have been at this club that Father and Noel had many business discussions and became friends. If I remember correctly, Noel telephoned the police after they learned that someone was seriously hurt by gunfire. What a terrible shock to find out it was his friend, Lee Hysan.'[74]

The murderer was never found, and it was assumed that Lee Hysan's drug world connections were responsible. One news report made a tantalising reference: 'It has been ascertained that the last place visited by Mr Lee Hysan before going to Wellington Street was a share broker's offices in Ice House Street.'[75] Perhaps Noel was not at the club at all but was the last person to speak to Lee Hysan?

The sudden death plunged the Lee family into financial difficulties, which Noel Croucher played a sympathetic role in helping to sort out. Family members recall Noel seemed to know exactly what Lee Hysan owed. 'I was astonished when he told me the exact sum Father had borrowed from the Hong Kong & Shanghai Bank.'[76] Lee Hysan had bought Jardine Hill with its no. 1 and no. 2 houses for the taipans, heralding the family's dominant role in real estate ever since. The Queen's College-educated patriarch bought the land behind East Point which became the famous Lee Gardens, home to Lee Theatre and now a shopping hub.

Noel's friendship with this leading Chinese family, as with several other families, led to his role as a trusted friend and adviser to the next generation. Lee Hysan's son Richard C. Lee (Dick Lee) was to turn to Noel in those first difficult days after his father's death and, decades later, he was to ask Noel to visit his daughter Deanna Lee at her boarding school on the Isle of Wight. And in the decades to come, a strong business relationship developed, notably through their joint presence on the board of the Hong Kong & China Gas Company.[77] Another son, J.S. Lee, recalls, 'Noel always spoke of my father in the good old days.' 'Lee Hysan? Noel knew him, knew the family. He knew how they got their money and he knew their background,' says a former broker, F.A. Silva.[78]

🕊 🕊 🕊

As significant as anything else in this decade was Noel's achievement of membership in the Hong Kong Club. This he managed by 1928,[79] and the contrast between tiffin at the Yue Kee Chinese Club and tea at the Hong Kong Club no doubt amused him. The latter is the oldest club in Hong Kong, formed in 1844 at what used to be the site of King's Theatre, Queen's Road Central.[80] It took its present site on Jackson Road, facing Statue Square, in 1897. Referring to this structure, architect-chronicler Eric Cumine noted its 'out-of-date elegance even when it was new! It was designed in a kind of Renaissance style during a period when its charms had faded and Britain had taken to a Gothic revival.'[81]

Noel Croucher's favourite spot in later years was the Bowling Alley Bar. The spacious verandah, where men could lounge at will and watch the harbour from a shaded vantage point, was also a special place. The club became Japanese naval headquarters during World War II, at which point most of its records were allegedly lost. The club has long been the home and symbol of Hong Kong's colonial elite — which may help explain why so few records were discoverable in the days of imperial decline in the 1980s and 1990s.

The club's membership was specifically defined according to race and sex, as well as status. Chinese could not join the club until after the war, by which time many had found more amenable havens of prestige. It was also long famous for banning the presence of women although it does now admit 'Lady Subscribers'. In the era we are talking about, the word 'women' was wrong, of course, as one was either a lady, or not, as Noel's former boss, Robert Shewan, argued so eloquently in the 1890s: 'The committee ought to ask themselves — how are you going to discriminate as to who are the ladies? Is the answering of that delicate question to be left to the head-boy or the steward? ...Are we going to have the gilded youth of this colony bringing ladies of the ballet in here to supper after the play?...'[82]

The Hong Kong Club was not just the social centre of expatriate Hong Kong, but its nerve centre. Membership included top taipans and officials of the day, and was easily withheld from anyone thought undesirable. The endless gossip and scandal generated in its bars and lounges played a more important role in regulating 'gentlemen's' behaviour than any statute in a law book. Narrow worlds defined narrow rules and the pressure of conformism was great — transgressions resulted in social death, which, considering the links between business, political and social power, could have a direct impact on one's ability to get a loan. 'It was a deliberately created gentlemen's club, members being artificially created gentlemen.'[83]

The paucity of records makes it impossible to reveal who might have sponsored Noel Croucher for membership of the club back in 1928.[84] Perhaps his contacts in business and at board meetings had opened the way, or a friend at the yacht club, or a connection from his days as a British officer. Perhaps, it was simply that he had become a director of a company one year earlier. The club boasted accommodation, bars, restaurants, billiard tables, electricity, and a library, not to mention the scores of servants. By the time Noel died, he was an icon, famous for his tricks or cheats at Liar's Dice, and was regarded as a venerable eccentric.

As the 1920s drew to a close, Noel could look back on his most successful decade so far. Now a husband and father, company director and club member, he had reason to feel he was riding high. This decade also showed the makings of his fortune to come. To all those who wonder how Noel Croucher got rich, the old-fashioned values of thrift, alongside scrupulous research and analysis, were key. Being assertive, questioning and sometimes rebellious also had something to do with it — here was a man prepared to challenge the status quo.

Noel had learned early on about the need to put something aside for a rainy day. He knew profits must be earned, losses minimised, and debt avoided wherever possible. These were precisely the priorities overtly espoused by the board of the China Provident Loan and Mortgage Company, of which he was a member. And there is very little difference between such values in the corporate world and the lessons life had taught him when he had been down and out.

Those lessons made him more earthy, practical and direct than his colleagues — much to their chagrin. Getting rich was not a game to Noel Croucher, nor was corporate life a privilege which this man would take for granted. He expected to have to earn his advancement. Noel Croucher was not swayed by the mere mystique of money. He worked at it.

CHAPTER NINE

THE THIRTIES —
CHINA COAST FINANCIER

he biggest thing on Noel Croucher's mind as the 1930s began was no doubt the collapse of the New York stock market in October 1929. Whatever his personal exposure had been to that market, few investors would have been in any doubt about how far-reaching the Crash of '29 was to be. Worldwide depression set in, and eventually reached Hong Kong. By the end of the decade, war was on almost every horizon — in Europe, in China, in the Pacific, and in Hong Kong too. Yet it was in this decade that Noel Croucher took the final leaps necessary to ensure his position in the top financial circles of the East: he established his own company, was made a Justice of the Peace, became Commodore of the Royal Hong Kong Yacht Club, helped open the new Stock Exchange Building, and established a reputation for fearless insight into business affairs.

He also had a good time. Anyone still living who recalls those halcyon days before the war sees them through the glow of moonlight on champagne. Never were parties so spectacular, dresses more gorgeous, the drinks more powerful nor the gossip more salacious. Noel and his wife Simonne were still a couple at this stage and 'dashed good looking' by public repute. They lived in the centre of town, at the P & O Building penthouse, and Noel's office was not far away, in the Standard Chartered Bank Building.[1]

The hub of the city of Victoria's social life was the Hong Kong Hotel which, in addition to being listed as Noel's formal address on the jury lists from 1920 to 1925, was home to the famous bar known as Gripps.[2] For balls, tea or dinner dances, Gripps was the favourite, along with the Rose Room and Roof Garden of the Peninsula and the Repulse Bay Hotel ballroom. If Noel was already a member of the Royal Society of Saint George, he would have been at the annual St. George's Ball in 1930 where revellers heard stirring speeches: 'The society of St George exists for the purpose of strengthening the sentiment of English nationality... St George is representative of individual effort... I venture to suggest that St George did not sit on a committee and vote for somebody else to slay dragons.' Beefeaters, military bands, English town crests and flags were all gathered around a huge emblem of Saint George as reference was made to Wordsworth and Shakespeare on the theme of 'This blessed plot this earth, this realm, this England.'[3]

Hong Kong remained a destination for a flow of film stars, and royalty still made its way to Hong Kong. Naturally, Noel Croucher made sure he was there. 'I danced with Princess Marina when she visited Hong Kong some years ago,' Noel wrote to a friend. 'I knew Prince George the husband very well. He was in the Navy in 1932 (I think it was). My wife — who is French & quite in demand in those far off days as she was very vivacious — well, he would often ring up and come along. I did not know that Princess Marina had a slight limp due to Polio when young but one doesn't notice it. Prince George was very gay & quite a handful, did all kinds of pranks, like any other young chap.'[4] Here Noel is referring to the son of King George V who was made Duke of Kent in 1934 and was killed while on active service in the Royal Navy in 1942. Princess Marina of Greece and Denmark was married to him in 1934, after this remembered visit of Prince George, and lived until 1968.[5]

In 1932, the spectacular double wedding, which bound together the Kan, Li and Fung families of the Bank of East Asia, took place at St. John's Cathedral. Ivy Kan and Doris Li married the twin sons of Fung Ping-shan, but it seems this was one big event which Noel missed.[6]

In that year, however, Noel almost disappeared forever in the South China seas. It was the time of the Macao race again, but this year there was almost no wind and a tide which was far too strong for safety. 'Grave fears were entertained at one time this morning for the safety of the crews of two of the yachts so long overdue in the annual race to Macao and back. The whereabouts of 12 of the 14 competing yachts was known, but *La Cigale*, with N.V.A. Croucher aboard and *Azuma*, with Mr E.B. Lambert in charge and Mr C.J. Cooke also aboard, were unaccounted for and distress signals had been observed by the occupants of another yacht early yesterday morning.'[7] Planes from the aircraft carrier, HMS *Hermes*, were sent out to search for the missing yachts.

Just before the newspapers went to press, news was received to calm all fears: 'Mr Croucher stated that he and his crew aboard *La Cigale* found themselves off Tai O in dead weather this morning and decided to abandon the attempt to finish. *La Cigale* has therefore been left temporarily at Tai O, the crew having landed and taken a ferry to Hong Kong. *Azuma* finished the race. Mr Lambert landed on the shore opposite Capsuimun this morning and came in by bus. Mr C.J. Cooke remained on board and brought in *Azuma* at 12.27 p.m.'[8] Unlike most of the other yachts, Noel Croucher was purist enough in those days to have no engine or auxiliary power sources on board. If it was not possible to sail, and one had to get back to the office, then a local ferry was the only option.

Aside from racing yachts, Noel was getting to know the horse-racing crowd.[9] Indeed, almost all his important contacts were part of the racing scene at Happy Valley. Sir Paul Chater went to his first race meeting in 1865 and ran his own stable along with Sir Hormusjee Mody, winning every race of any importance. He was a steward of the club for nearly fifty years. If the relationship with Chater was as strong as Croucher would have us believe, it might have been the grand old man himself who put young Noel up for membership.

A day at the races was a great opportunity for people to mix — all classes, races and competitors in varied fields went to the races. Undated and unlabelled photographs show Noel Croucher at the races, on friendly terms with prominent punters, such as Dr Honourable Sir Sik-nin Chau CBE JP, the leading ear, nose and throat specialist. His son, Kai-bong Chau, confirms that Noel Croucher was a firm family friend in those early days. 'I remember Uncle Croucher vaguely from my childhood,' he says, referring to the years just before World War II. 'He was very debonair, very well-dressed, a family friend. I remember Auntie too — she was a French woman, with very big eyes, very tall and dark, oh, very French! He was a fond uncle to me, a perfect gentleman.'

Kai-bong Chau recalls that Noel 'liked to make the ladies laugh', and often took Kai-bong's mother and her friends out for tea at Gloucester Hotel for ice-cream, scones and club sandwiches. Perhaps this was after the war, but whenever it was, the teas were delicious and the tai-tais always amused. 'I was the youngest son, the cakes were wonderful! And he called me Junior,' Mr Chau recalls.[10]

It may have been friends such as these who encouraged Noel to join the Jockey Club, or maybe it was Noel's stock exchange colleague, George Potts, a keen sportsman in Shanghai, Macao and Hong Kong: in February 1931, George went to see the Governor of Macao, and secured a racing concession for what became the Macao Jockey Club.[11]

Horses could never compete in Noel's mind with the joys of sailing, however, and he might have joined the Jockey Club — as many did and do — as a statement of social arrival rather than for love of horses or gambling. Innate conservatism shows through in any account of Noel Croucher and the turf. He did not really like to gamble at all, risking only small sums as play bets, because it was the thing to do. He was never reported to be at the racetrack for the dawn training sessions loved by his mentor Sir Paul and any other keen horse-owner. And he always warned his staff not to waste money on gambling.

Clearly demonstrating which love came first in his life, he named almost all his horses after sailing terms: *Mainsail, Bowsprit, Full Sail, Hurricane, Windward* and *Topsail*. One horse was named *Sandy Bay*, but the reason for that must wait.[12] For the moment we need only say that he knew those people at the top of the Jockey Club between the wars, and the Jockey Club was one of the most powerful institutions in Hong Kong.

In these years, the sporting men of the colony formed another brethren which met on the weekends in the far-flung New Territories, under the auspices of the Fanling Hunt. Started by Dr Pierce Grove and a sharebroker in 1924,[13] and later dominated by Hunt-master Alec Hutton Potts, this gathering featured the chaps and their friends in plus-fours enjoying that very English pastime of riding after the hounds, following their exertions with vast picnics or dinners and perhaps a dance or two. None of the photographs, kept in leather-bound volumes still held by Alec Potts' widow Rosie, show Noel.[14] According to Rosie Potts,[15] her husband occasionally rode Noel's horses at the Jockey Club, suggesting that even if Noel did ride occasionally, he was not so enamoured of the experience to let it take over his weekends as well. Besides, he had a beautiful yacht to sail.

Outside observers of Hong Kong at this time saw it as a brittle, boring and superficial sort of place. Social circles were small, and conventions writ large. Compared to Shanghai, Hong Kong was still not up to much as a city. The late Lord Lawrence Kadoorie described Hong Kong as 'a sleepy little place. Before the war I remember one night in Hong Kong standing on the deck of one of the President boats going to Shanghai and there was an American near me. Eleven o'clock, everything in Hong Kong closed down. And he looked at the lights and he said, "the best illuminated cemetery in the world"! That was a sort of feeling that you had.'[16]

Another sort of feeling was that Noel Croucher, despite everything, was still not quite up to scratch in some circles. Anecdotes recall how members of the Butterfield & Swire or Jardine fraternities saw Noel as being 'from the other side of the table'. While people like the Potts, for example, were creating a social success of everything they did, Noel was making money or messing about in boats. Many of his friends had assumed he was Jewish — Noel's attitude was described by some as 'a Jewish attitude'. Perhaps what they meant was that Noel, who lacked the security of a true home, seemed more determined than others. Many Jews, as others, were highly successful in Hong Kong, then as now, showing that regardless of social attitudes, one could still get ahead. Noel knew many successful people and was rapidly joining their ranks.

Yet, Hong Kong society remained segregated and riven by convention. There were the government circles, the top taipans' crowd, the education and missionary people, the armed forces, and many other cliques. 'Before the war I suspect there was more of a social caste system among the Europeans. I would have thought that between the wars Noel was still probably a bit of an outsider. Probably after the second war it wasn't nearly so bad. By that time he was so well-established financially anyhow that presumably, you know in Hong Kong, so long as you're rich enough, you've made it regardless of your background. But not between the wars.'[17]

A select crowd took stratification a few steps further — out to Shek O, the fishing village on the southeast tip of Hong Kong Island. Even today, membership of Shek O Golf and Country Club is rigorously exclusive. Then, people such as shipping taipan Haakon J. Wallem and his son Nordahl built sprawling homes with tennis courts, sweeping lawns and swimming pools. Their names feature in Noel Croucher's address book with the home phone number for their house at no. 1 Shek O. The parties were tremendous affairs — as the scars of the champagne corks on the ceiling of the Wallem home attest — where casual still meant jacket and tie, and the women were fashionably languid.[18] At the yacht club, while class distinctions were not wholly lost, they were at least drowned from time to time on the ocean wave and at the bar.

As for any inkling of the momentous events due to change all their lives — Hong Kong's gadabouts were a blank. Part of the fun of the parties must have stemmed from the liberal attitudes of Hong Kong's barmen. Today's 'optics' which measure out alcoholic doses from the bottle did not exist then. Instead, the bar boy would hand over the whole bottle to the customer who then poured his own. Gimlets were the Hong Kong drink — gin with bottled lime squash and ice. And there was Black Velvet, that heady mixture of Guinness and champagne. People met at each other's homes, but more often at their clubs, at Gripps, at Jimmy's Kitchen, or on launches (junks) hired for the day.

Behind the parties and lavish teas, the storm clouds of the 1930s were gathering. In business, the outlook was grim and even Noel went through a difficult patch in this decade. The global depression was exacerbated by Britain's departure from the gold standard and a consequent fall in sterling at the decade's start. The anti-Japanese trade boycott by China increased traders' woes. Trade contracted; tariffs, embargoes, quotas and exchange restrictions multiplied. And a cable between Hong Kong and Europe cost $3 per word.

In this murky atmosphere, Noel worked, most likely on foot or by rickshaw: 'Bullion and exchange brokers in Ice House Street dashed between banks in company rickshaws with highly polished brasswork trim and low seats designed for getting speedily in and out. Francis Zimmern recalls that in 1941 the Hong Kong Stock Exchange had only six telephones for sixty brokers, a fact which made rickshaws essential.'[19] Alec Potts owned a beautiful weather-proof rickshaw. 'Every morning, before the exchange opened, he would go round town in it, block by block, taking orders, rather like a milkman. That was the start of business for the day,' recalls Peter Vine.[20]

Noel was still on staff at Benjamin & Potts but seems to have built an enviable list of contacts, including unparalleled sources of information. He was diligent in his attendance at company meetings, giving us clear indications of his growing contacts with the business elite, both British and Chinese.[21] On 1 April 1931, he was confirmed as a director of China Provident Loan & Mortgage Company, at which he heard that the company's affairs were at last turning the corner, thanks to the pursuit of prudence and liquidation of loans.[22]

The style of moneymaking was very different in those days. Daily business was in the hands of each company's compradore — the Chinese manager whose unique position, akin to that of a middleman, relied on his ability to understand and communicate to foreigners the intricacies of the China Coast trade. They employed a large number of staff of their own, often dominated by members of their own families, and usually rose to positions of great wealth and influence. The Ho Tungs, just one example, were compradores to the Hong Kong & Shanghai Banking Corporation, where ledgers were made with a Chinese brush instead of pen and ink, and the abacus used instead of a calculator.

Alongside his regular attendance at the meetings of Green Island Cement Company, Hongkong Land, Hong Kong Tramways, and Hong Kong & Shanghai Hotels in 1932, we can see proof of Noel's shareholdings in the Bank of East Asia from this year, too.[23] The recent death of Mr

Fung Ping-shan, a founder-director of the bank, was noted with sadness. Noel was one of the earlier non-Chinese investors in this bank. He was friends with the patriarchs as well as the junior generation of the top families involved.

His old bugbear about directors' fees[24] emerged again, however, at the meeting of the Douglas Steamship Company Limited, and his experiences with this company appear to show how, following a strict telling-off by Noel Croucher, the company at last managed to improve its management and, ultimately, its balance sheet. 'Mr Chairman,' he rose to say, 'I notice in the account that you have allocated a sum of $30,000 to leave pay and pension reserve. A like amount was transferred last year, which I consider out of all proportion to the Company's profit... No-one would object to generosity during a boom, but I think in times like the present, strictest economy should be practised... No dividend has been paid to shareholders for eight years and the steamers appear to have been run solely for the benefit of the managers, staff and compradore...'[25] He had no fear of consequences here — once again he was on his feet to defend the shareholders.

He noted too that the steamers stood in the books at twice their market value when in fact they were all over thirty years old and needed to be replaced. When the chairman, A.H. White, tried to explain that such matters were being examined, Noel replied, 'Yes, I understand that, but we cannot go on doing this Mr Chairman. Our entire capital is only six lakhs, and we are spending it all on the officers and crews. All leave etc., should be suspended straight away. I don't think the floating staff have borne the sacrifices the shareholders have during this period of depression. I trust that something drastic will be done Mr Chairman.'[26] All Mr White could do after this was to say 'Yes'. Once again Noel had spotted extravagances and was blunt enough to demand changes.

By the next year, the company's position had improved and Mr Croucher was moved to pay a tribute to the efforts of the special consulting committee. But, he could not help adding, 'Although the past year reflects in some degree the economies which have been made in the running of our fleet, I trust our general managers will not be relaxing their efforts in this direction.'[27] In 1934, he went so far as to congratulate the management 'on the handsome profit obtained in spite of dull trade, keen competition and general unrest. We have to go a long way back to find such gratifying results... I fully endorse the conservative policy of the Board in deferring payment of a dividend, and also in writing down the value of the fleet to a figure more in keeping with their market value.'[28]

By now, Noel had reached a position of influence in the company, and the results proved his sense of economy to be worthwhile. Sure enough, by 1935, a dividend was declared for the first time in more than a decade. In Mr Croucher's seconding speech, he revealed he had personally inspected one of the company's new ships, *Haitan*, an acquisition he praised highly, and congratulations were shared all round.[29] Douglas Steamship was victim to the generally poor trading conditions, and too-prevalent smuggling contributed to a loss in 1937, but Noel could not resist the homily: 'It is fortunate that our consulting committee and general managers made provision in the past which has enabled them to meet these abnormal conditions.'[30] In the years to come, Noel kept harping on, and praising, the 'prudent' policy to consolidate reserves — not surprising, since it was his own policy from the start. China Provident Loan & Mortgage Company was another rare company which could report substantial increases in profits.[31]

During the early years of this decade, Noel started relationships in business which were going to be significant to him for years to come. Along with his first appearances at the Bank of East Asia meetings, for example, there was his first appearance as a shareholder of Dairy Farm, Ice and Cold Storage Company Limited, where one of his colleagues was Mr B.W. Bradbury — the future butcher at Stanley Internment Camp and founder of the Bradbury Trust which supports elderly people of Hong Kong, among other things. Noel was subsequently to play a key role in the take-over of Dairy Farm by Hongkong Land.[32]

In 1934, the new Stock Exchange Building was opened,[33] and at last, Noel Croucher was to take his own seat in it. He formed his own company — Croucher and Company — through which he traded for the rest of his life. Pre-war company registration records are all lost, and the directories for 1932 and 1933 appear to have mislaid Mr Croucher. But on his reappearance in 1934, the directory had this to list:

> CROUCHER & CO., Stock, Share & General Brokers,
> (Member, Hong Kong Stock Exchange) — National
> City Bank Building; Teleph. 20211; Cable Ad:
> Crostock; Codes: Broomhall, Bentley, A.B.C. 6th etc.
> > N.V.A. Croucher, principal
> > C.C. Blake, signs per pro.
> > H.Y. Yuen, interpreter
> > Wong Ah Kow, book-keeper
> > Mrs Lai, stenographer[34]

Establishing his own company was probably a long-standing ambition. Noel was not the sort to be taking orders from others, or to be bogged down in bureaucracy. He had flair and individuality, and was probably stubborn and arrogant enough to give it a try. But it is worth wondering if he also knew somehow that he had to go his own way. After all, sixteen years at Benjamin & Potts still had not made him a partner, or even someone trusted to 'sign per pro'.[35]

'I always thought he had learned his market sense at Benjamin & Potts, that was the real street work, going round on behalf of B & P, he was doing it on a commission. No, he wasn't made a partner. Well, they took him on as a runner, and so it would be a long time before they would accept him, knowing how things were, what attitudes were in those days,' comments Guy Sayer, formerly of Hong Kong & Shanghai Bank.[36]

We can assume a certain drive on Noel's part because these were bad times in which to start a new business. The rise in the value of silver, emanating from the United States' policy of buying up silver with a view to raising its price, caused China to de-link its currency from silver, forcing Hong Kong to follow suit. By March 1935, the Hong Kong dollar rate was unprecedentedly high: HK\$8/£1.[37] In November 1935, China moved to a managed currency, causing a big disparity between the value of Hong Kong's and China's currencies. Hong Kong's currency was encouraged to depreciate to HK\$16/£1. The subsequent budget chaos was tackled by a levy on civil service salaries and new taxes on drinks, tobacco, petrol, and higher estate duty.

'All I know is that Noel had some very hard times in his early days and he was so short of money, he used to live on his boat which was moored at the Royal Hong Kong Yacht Club in Wanchai until he was able to live on land again. We all found that quite "shocking" as the waters in that causeway were nothing short of putrid on a hot day at low tide,' says Norma Rasmussen.[38] Another source is Robert Minnitt: 'I remember there was a time when Noel was a bit poor in actual fact, living very quietly. There was a time when it wasn't all that easy. Then things improved. Well, Hong Kong as you know is the sort of place where you can be rich one day and poor the next!'[39]

Perhaps in the financial turmoil, there was new opportunity for Noel. After all, flux in the currency markets and financial policies of the USA, Britain, Hong Kong and China created fresh room for manoeuvre for the canny speculator. Noel might not have fancied a punt on the horses, but he was so steeped in the markets that moving his currencies around would have been an occupation of calculated risk.

Through the company meetings too, he got a view of the dramatic events in the region — a connection which kept Noel more informed than many in Hong Kong. At a Hotels Company meeting he heard about how the Sino-Japanese War in and around Shanghai was damaging its properties there, especially the Astor House Hotel. Noel's investment interests were focused on utilities, on infrastructural companies, and on basic services such as transportation — and through such a breadth of interests he could expect rich returns.

Noel's boldness was justified by 1937, when trade began to recover. And though the outbreak of war between Japan and China was generally deplored, honest entrepreneurs had to admit it was good for business. 'Much trade was diverted through Hong Kong from Shanghai, refugees began to flood into the colony, and their expenditure swelled the government's receipts from indirect taxation and caused a new boom in land sales. Expenditure also rose, both on new public works and on civil defence against a possible Japanese attack.'[40] In these pre-war years, Noel must also have gone to the Philippines where he invested in shares. He later recalled what a modern city Manila was before the war.

As if Noel did not have enough on his plate, in 1935, he was made an unofficial Justice of the Peace. This involved several responsibilities at the same time as it gave the office-bearer that cachet of absolute respectability. Noel could not have acquired the honour without the recommendation and backing of senior members of the community — influence from the right quarters would have been crucial. 'The general requirements for the appointment of a Justice of the Peace are that a person should be of integrity and has the capability and willingness to serve the community. The primary duty of Justices of the Peace is to visit prisons, hospitals and other social institutions to ensure that the rights of inmates are safeguarded.'[41]

As Hong Kong developed, so too did the duties of Justices of the Peace — now, JPs visit new housing estates, neighbourhood police units, street markets and squatter areas. They raise the profiles of government campaigns, such as 'Keep Hong Kong Clean', and check that dangerous slopes and street lighting are fixed. They acquired responsibility, too, for checking on the special conditions under which people are detained by the Independent Commission Against Corruption.

Back in the 1930s, as now, a key task for JPs was to visit prisons to check on the welfare of those incarcerated. Visiting a prison was hardly a pleasant experience. A rare account from the inside comes from a man already expelled for his anti-imperialist writings in Burma, who was forced to spend a night in Hong Kong:

We were herded into a police station which was about as comfortable as a pigsty, and quite unceremoniously slammed in the clink. ...

As we peered round inside, a sixteen watt bulb illuminated six prisoners sleeping on the floor in the fifteen-square-metre cell. When we were told to enter, they all woke up with a start and looked up at us, revealing heads swollen with dropsy. With the two of us, there was scarcely enough space for everyone to sit down. In one corner stood a tin night-soil bucket. A large section of the floor around it was soaking wet, obviously with urine that had spilled from the bucket. There were also a couple of banana-shaped turds lying there conspicuously in the middle of the floor. The room stunk... Our detention house in Burma was a lot better than this place in Hong Kong...[42]

There was more to being a JP than the duties, however. In a discussion of the relationship between civil servants and rich traders, James Pope-Hennessy, grandson of a Hong Kong Governor, mentioned Governor Bonham's creation of 'fifteen Justices of the Peace to be his special advisers, thus creating, in succession to the merchant princes of former days, an untitled commercial aristocracy. This was all very well for the fifteen Justices and their families, but it aroused keen resentment amongst the many other wealthy merchants who were not chosen and it laid a solid foundation for that form of social snobbery which, theoretically based on freedom of access to a Governor, has ever been a hallmark of small British colonial communities...'[43] A look at the list of unofficial JPs in 1941 does, indeed, bear this out — it is a who's who of the business community at the time: Ho Tung, Kadoorie, Compton, Arculli, Dodwell, Dowbiggin, Hancock, Kotewall, Pearce, Newbigging, Pollock, Potts, Ross, Ruttonjee, Sorby, Shields, Li, Lo, and Tse.[44]

Noel took his JP duties seriously, referring to them in letters throughout his life. He learned of subjects such as drug addiction and disadvantaged citizens which were to become increasingly important to him in his future activities as a philanthropist. He had just become fully established as an independent businessman, was of rising prominence at the yacht club, settled in to the Hong Kong Club, and circulating well in business circles. This is the first sign of his truly civic instincts, and it appears as soon as can be expected in a man who had to make his own way from scratch.

In the years that followed, Noel pursued investments in the group of blue-chip companies which constituted the basis of Hong Kong's economy: the Hong Kong and Kowloon Wharf and Godown Company, the Tramways, Hongkong Land, China Provident, the Bank, Green Island Cement, and more. Of course, these were only some of his Hong Kong investments — tracking what he invested in around the world is far more difficult.

Noel's Index Book included names of broking firms across Canada, Australia, Europe, the Bahamas and Bermuda, even New Zealand, suggesting his financial horizons were by no means restricted to Hong Kong or the East. He was believed to have been, at one time, the largest individual shareholder in the Canadian Pacific Railway Company — that massive company which had straddled the North American continent by rail and owned a fleet of popular liners which brought many people to Hong Kong and home again. (The ships also transported Chinese coolies to France in World War I, one of them, *Empress of Russia*, carrying Noel Croucher, too.)

'Croucher once told me that the two most successful investments he ever made in his life were, one, in the Canadian Pacific Railway and two, in Rothmans Australia, which he bought at an absolutely ridiculously low price and it multiplied about 25 times. He had a very large stake in that.'[45]

At the Annual General Meeting of the Hong Kong Telephone Company, Noel heard of the new technology allowing communication with various cities in China by radio-telephone for the first time.[46] The Hong Kong Realty & Trust Company revealed plans for the Lido at Repulse Bay — a fifty-metre swimming pool, open-air dance floor, terraces, lawns and restaurants.[47] Back in town, the popular and newly renovated Cafe Wiseman was due to reopen within a year, 'the location and name being synonymous some twenty years ago'.[48] This was made possible by the vacation of Lane Crawford's basement and ground floor by its previous tenant, the Hong Kong Stock Exchange.

The exotic-sounding Sandakan Light & Power Company also attracted Noel's interest. He heard its chairman A.L. Shields (a name we know from the offices of Shewan, Tomes & Co.) say: 'It is difficult to make any forecast about the future but I believe there is a more optimistic feeling in British North Borneo than there has been for the last few years.'[49] Noel's involvement in this company may have stemmed from the fact that China Provident held an investment in it; it also had historical links to Russell & Co.[50] In another link, Guy Sayer believes that returning members of the Chinese Labour Corps, in which his father was involved, were given land in British North Borneo after World War I.[51]

By 1937, Hong Kong & Whampoa Dock Company announced its first dividend in twelve years, while the Sandakan firm, which had not achieved a return for its investors for fifteen years, finally managed one in 1938.

Throughout Noel's career at company meetings over these years, what comes across is his diligent, persistent research. This man wanted to know all about whatever was going on. It can be seen how he put some people's backs up, however, as he was also interfering, assertive, stubborn, determined always to get the best deal. He had the right — and insisted on it.

There was war on the outskirts of Shanghai, at the same time as trade was recovering worldwide. BBC Empire broadcasts had to alleviate fears overseas that Hong Kong might be caught in crossfire from the fighting around Shanghai! Yet, precisely because of the war, things in Hong Kong were beginning to look up — 'All public utility companies in consequence reported increased receipts.'[52] The Hong Kong & Shanghai Bank expressed a mood of 'restrained optimism' by 1938. The wharf and shipping companies, on which so much of the economy depended, benefited from a sudden influx of cargo diverted from Shanghai. Thanks to the growing population, China Light & Power could announce its first profit in years and Mr Croucher rose to praise the conservative policies of the company's management which had led to this happy state of affairs.[53] In contrast to the trauma of the mid-1920s, when turmoil on the Mainland helped inspire chaos in Hong Kong, it was outright war in China now which was to provide Hong Kong's economy with just the fillip it needed.

Amid growing instability in the region, Noel Croucher did not lose sight of the bottom line. In March 1939, he made headline impact at the annual meeting of Hong Kong Realty & Trust Company Ltd. 'Questions on Lido — Hong Kong Realty & Trust Co. Shareholder's Criticism — Wants Subsidiary Company,' screeched the *South China Morning Post*.[54] It was a point of fairness to shareholders, and accounting precision, and Noel grilled the chairman, Mr J. Fleming, remorselessly.

Noel began by saying that the written questions he had proffered before the meeting had not been answered adequately, so he was going to ask them again. He demanded detailed facts and figures about the operations of the Lido resort, its bathing facilities and restaurants. There is no doubt Noel was on top of his subject. He argued back and forth, asked why certain figures could be released to shareholders in 1936 but were now being withheld, delivering several homilies along the way.

What annoyed him and his fellow shareholders was that interest on bank loans incurred to build the Lido was being taken out of shareholder income, rather than out of the project's profits. 'It is not sound business to debit income from shares to wash out losses incurred at the Lido,' he said.

'The Shareholders want to know,' said Mr Croucher, in his sixteenth of twenty-two questions, 'whether we are making a profit on the Lido. The bathing sheds have been full and the restaurant has been packed and according to the Working Account you have a profit of $7,000. The question is, where has this money gone?'[55] He didn't get a clear answer, despite his efforts, but here was a man who refused to take any obfuscation lightly. His aggressive defence of shareholders' interests was by now a well-developed trait.

At other meetings, Noel probably met the Nemazees, the Persian trading family represented in Hong Kong since the 1860s. Mohamed Nemazee was a director of China Underwriters, a company in which Noel Croucher had a substantial shareholding.[56] Noel also knew Legislative Councillors Sir Robert Kotewall, who joined the board of China Provident by 1940, and Sir Shouson Chow, whose re-election to the board of A.S. Watson & Company in March 1940 was seconded by Noel.[57] Naturally the Ho Tungs and the Lo brothers (Man-kam and Man-wai) were also part of this business elite and thus in regular touch with Noel.

During these years, Noel began living as a part-time bachelor — his wife Simonne had taken son Richard up to school in Tsingtao and, by the late 1930s it was time to take Richard back to England for school.[58] In 1937, Noel's long-time boss and the chairman of the stock exchange, George Potts, died in Swatow. Newspaper obituaries remembered his genial personality and great longevity on the China Coast — the stories he used to tell of when he volunteered to help tackle the plague (in 1894), his action with the Hong Kong Volunteers against the Boxer Rebellion in north China, and his rowing, rugger and horse-riding pursuits. The exchange closed for the day, as did the Macao Jockey Club, and a meeting of the Coronation Committee was postponed. Noel went to the funeral, a wreath was given by 'Mr and Mrs N.V.A. Croucher', and he was on the long list of attendees which covered two full columns of small print in the next day's paper.[59]

Away from his office, Noel's favourite activity was sailing. By 1935, he was on the Sailing Committee of the Royal Hong Kong Yacht Club, and spent his weekends on the water. He was either on his own in a beautiful bay, or in a raucous party of friends — most of his closest friends were sailing friends.

Two men from that time are Robert Minnitt and Pat Sedgewick, then cadets learning the Cantonese language in Canton. Both were eager sailors. Minnitt remembers Noel well, and Sedgewick, a future director of commerce and industry and Urban Council chairman, features in old snapshots which Noel kept in his desk, decades later. The Pearl River Sailing Club was established by Minnitt and Sedgewick, but they wondered how to carry on sailing in Hong Kong in their small 'Comet' sailing dinghies. They hit on the seas around Deep Water Bay, hence the building of a matshed on Middle Island in 1937. Those were the days! Minnitt and Sedgewick once got their sailing tackle together in their rooms at the Peninsula Hotel before managing to sail the ninety miles back up to Canton in their dinghies. On moving to Hong Kong, they blithely brought their Canton boat-builder along — Ah Lung was to be custodian at Middle Island for years to come.

By 1937, Noel became Vice Commodore of the Royal Hong Kong Yacht Club. He also was on the special subcommittee set up in 1938 to find new premises for the club as the site of the current clubhouse, in North Point, was now inland. Development prospects on Kellett Island were looked into and architects Leigh and Orange were appointed. 'It was estimated that the cost of the Clubhouse would be approximately $150,000 and the Acting Commodore, Noel Croucher, had approached the Hongkong and Shanghai Banking Corporation regarding a loan which the Bank had indicated it was willing to support.'[60] Clearly the managers of the bank had faith that Noel would not let them down.

In June 1939, an Extraordinary General Meeting of the yacht club presented detailed proposals, and agreement was reached that Imperial Chemical Industries (China) Limited would use their harbour frontage for a car park and ferry steps, so as to ferry yacht club members to Kellett Island. Special mention is made in the yacht club history of one among the seven new yachts in the cruiser class: *La Cigale I*, a Sparkman and Stephens New York 32 design, built at Hong Kong Dock Company's yards, for Noel Croucher. This was the successor to the yacht Noel had bought in 1919 as war booty. Pat Sedgewick was a major competitor in his *Norena*, as was Bunny Browne, both of whom became firm friends of Noel's.

The long-awaited move to Kellett Island took place on 12 February 1940, even though war had been declared in Europe in September 1939, and even though the new buildings were not quite completed. The new yacht club premises were formally opened on 26 October 1940, by His Excellency the Acting Governor, Lt-Gen Sir E.F. Norton, but not before Noel, recently elevated to the position of Commodore, made a speech which welcomed the dignitaries, recounted some facts about the club, and even made some jokes:

> Today we have over 100 yachts and auxiliary craft, which any club may well be proud of, four bowling alleys, two squash courts and a membership of nearly 500. We hope to increase the amenities still more by the addition of bedrooms, a swimming pool and, most important of all, a causeway. These, we hope, will come in happier times...
>
> Many ladies are also unable to be with us at this ceremony, but we look forward to their return, when they will be received in the traditional manner, with open arms. (Laughter)
>
> To you, Sir [addressing Lt-Gen Sir E.F. Norton], I wish to express our deep gratitude for your kindness in coming and opening our new Club House today when there are so many calls on your time. But we feel that you have come to us with more than ordinary interest, for in the early '60s [1860s], your father, Captain Norton, was a keen and active sailing member of the Club and was one of those who did much to further the interest of boat-racing in the Colony...[61]

Noel took the Acting Governor on *La Cigale I* in the cruiser's race held as part of the opening ceremony and, happily, he won. Sir Norton referred to his usually bad experiences as a sailor: 'I have, as I say, no claim to being a yachtsman; [but] if yachting were all what has been my experience in the Commodore's yacht this afternoon, things might be different...'[62] Indicative of his closeness to the financial and banking hierarchy, Noel Croucher made a point of thanking warmly the Hong Kong & Shanghai Bank for its assistance in funding the new clubhouse, especially Sir Vandaleur Grayburn, the bank's chief manager.

But war was beginning to intervene. Most races could not be held in 1940, others had to be modified to fit with minefield restrictions. The Hong Kong Royal Naval Volunteer Reserve, which included many yacht club members, was active in regular patrol duties in the seas of the colony. Despite the clouds of war hanging over Hong Kong, there was still a lot of fun to be had, recalls Robert Minnitt.[63]

'We sailed, racing, all the time in Hong Kong — cruiser racing. *La Cigale* was one of the fleet... Noel had been sailing there of course for many years and somehow or other we just ... you know, I joined up with him and sailed with him. Noel was Vice Commodore when I got to know him well, that's before the war. He was involved in the building of the new club, on Kellet Island. ...There was also an earlier *La Cigale*, before the war, and he sold her and built this boat. It was a lovely boat, beautiful.

'And apart from racing this boat, we used to go off for weekends. Two or three boats would get together and we'd anchor somewhere, possibly off Lantau or off the New Territories somewhere, three or four boats there, and have a weekend, you see. It depended where we were, but some parts of the territory, we had rifles and we'd go shooting and if we were lucky, we'd get deer. Unfortunately I didn't get involved in a pig hunt, it was a little bit fierce I think. We used to try — there was a Chinese friend of Noel's who had some fearsome dogs, a pack of hounds, and we used to go hunting.

'We saw a tiger once ... we would go into the hills and local people would tell us where the deer or the wild boars were. Some of the wives and some girlfriends came too, and some mates and crew, which was great fun, particularly on a long weekend for a holiday or something. We had sailing races you know and I used to sail... I certainly sailed in his boat many times. Yes, he was a good sailor. Well he was a good helmsman. Tactics and so on — I wouldn't say he was so good — I did a lot of that. But it was very much a partnership. There would often be a crowd, not the same people every time.'[64]

So what did Robert Minnitt think of Noel? 'Well he was very quiet in a way. I always remember him initially as being rather quiet. But he was a very good friend. I didn't see an awful lot of him apart from sailing. I always thought he was a very nice person to know. After the war, I rather lost touch. I stopped sailing you see. I didn't know him from the business point of view so it wouldn't be fair to judge him in that way. I always found him intelligent, yes. He certainly got ahead, as it were.'[65]

At Christmas in 1940, a memorable party was held on Noel's boat, which another friend, Bunny Browne, recounted for the yacht club history. It began as a cruise with Pat Sedgewick and several others. 'After spending Christmas Eve anchored off Island House where they were entertained by the District Officer K.M.A. Barnett, the yachts sailed up to Camp Cove inside Double Haven in Mirs Bay where they enjoyed Christmas Dinner aboard *La Cigale*.

' "Here the table had been laid as if ashore with Christmas crackers at the head of each place. Ravenous, the eight of us squeezed in round the table. The meal was passed in through the galley door. Hot soup followed by roast turkey, ham, baked potatoes, brussel sprouts and creamed cauliflower. Then came the Christmas pudding with its traditional blue flickering flame and brandy sauce, mince pies for those that could take them, followed by fresh fruit, almonds and raisins. Cigarettes and cigars were then passed round with liqueurs and replete we leant back whilst the table was cleared. Then came one or two of those silly card games that are always played at such times followed by a sing song to the accompaniment of Croucher's ukelele and Kiki Chaffoi's mouth organ".

'The next day, Boxing Day, the party went ashore on a hunt for wild boar and deer in the hills of the Pat Tsin Range at the eastern end of Plover Cove. The only kill of the day was by Bunny Browne who shot a deer which was then found to have only three legs...'[66]

'We used to have really very very good parties,' recalls Robert Minnitt, referring to what sounds like the same party Bunny Browne was remembering. 'Noel's boat had an oven. We used to go out for Christmas and have a turkey, cook it on board. The trouble was, you probably had a dozen or more people so you had to have a reasonable-sized turkey. Trouble was the oven wasn't very big, so we used to have to cut the first bone off the turkey, stuff it in the oven and cook that end, and then turn it around and then cook the other end.'[67]

Such pastimes were part of a long tradition on the China Coast. In Walter Young's memorable account of yet more entertainment for the lads, he wrote: 'You can just fancy us; on a tropical night, our launch lying idly at anchor in a beautiful bay; the yellow moon as big as a balloon, the yacht heaving gently with the tide and smacking the little wavelets as they lapped her sides, patting her softly in the ribs. Now and then from the shore, or from above, the cry of a night-bird, or the distant bark of a dog, would reach us...' These boys suffered for their fun of course. Tiffin on a tablecloth in the shade of a tree — gamepie, pate de foie gras, ready-made cocktails — was served after the men had ploughed through the warm liquid mud of paddy-fields with sweat glands pouring and skin smarting under welts from insect bites.[68]

In his capacity as Commodore of the yacht club, Noel Croucher is warmly remembered by another sailing legend of Hong Kong, Patricia Loseby, then living with her mother and father in a hotel. 'We had a new manager at the Yacht Club and he didn't want [to live in] the flat at the club... Noel heard of it and suggested that the Losebys move into it. It suited us admirably. We re-decorated a bit. It was difficult at times, with the late parties, the noise. After a typhoon [everyone in] the Dragon Class would call up to see if their yachts were OK and I'd look out the window and say yes.' Noel also bought shares for Pat from time to time, whether she knew it or not — 'But he did buy me some good shares. Then he'd ask me how my mother was, and go and talk to her.'[69]

Pat's mother was famous in her own way for running an exceptional animal's home in Kowloon.[70] Emily Hahn recounted how she took her pet gibbons to stay with Mrs Loseby,[71] and Pat recalls how her mother agreed to look after several exotic beasts when the head of the Hong Kong & Kowloon Wharf and Godown Company called up one day. 'A trapper, an Englishman ... had brought five giant pandas, a golden-haired monkey with a blue nose, and some Musk deer, and I think that's about all, and he'd arrived here and then been taken into hospital, he'd contracted something in China. And they were left with these animals on the pier! Could she help...'[72]

From these recollections we learn that Noel was also a pet-lover. Pictures later in life show him with his dogs, and as far as Pat Loseby can recall, his friendship with her mother had come about at least partly through their shared love of dogs.[73] Mrs Loseby was active in charities for delinquent and disadvantaged children, which might be where Noel first encountered the ideas and plans he was to implement in the same cause. And it was Mr Francis (Frank) Loseby, a lawyer and Pat's father, who played a pivotal role in Asian history: back in 1931, he was approached by a half-Vietnamese man who had news of a travesty of justice. The victim was none other than Ho Chi Minh, then a revolutionary on the run from the French. Through determined adherence to the principle of habeas corpus, and a legal appeal process which almost reached the Privy Council, Mr Loseby saved the life of the future president of a united Vietnam. The Losebys later visited Vietnam at the personal invitation of President Ho.[74]

Back in Hong Kong, when the Losebys were living at the yacht club, Commodore Noel Croucher was more concerned about money than regional politics. At an annual general meeting of the yacht club in September 1941, Noel raised questions about its shaky financial position:

> A changeover is an awkward proceeding at any time and coming as we did into our new Clubhouse under the shadow of the war and with so many Government calls on the community for the defence of the island, it is not to be wondered that wartime conditions have had an adverse effect on the support which in happier times would

be forthcoming from members. The fact that expenditure has not been met out of current subscriptions is a matter for real concern and we cannot when renewals are needed ask our Bankers for further help.[75]

In October 1941, the new racing season opened according to plan, but was brought to an abrupt end by the invasion of Hong Kong on 8 December (the same time, over the dateline, as Japan's attack on Pearl Harbour on 7 December). 'Unaware of the fateful events which lay ahead, the Royal Hong Kong Yacht Club was hosting the annual team event between Britain and Scandinavia in "A" boats.' Bunny Browne reported: 'We had the morning race and were in the Club drinking before lunch when orders were received for all service personnel, including Volunteers, to report for duty immediately. The Clubhouse emptied, we never had our afternoon race, and that was the last I saw of the Club until after the Japanese surrender.'[76]

Thus ended the halcyon days of the 1920s and 1930s. These were Noel's high times — the years when he raised himself from runner to director, from boy to man, and from a fractured home to the penthouse balcony on which his own son now played. Then the war came, and changed everything.

'My horse "Windward", winning race, 1940.'

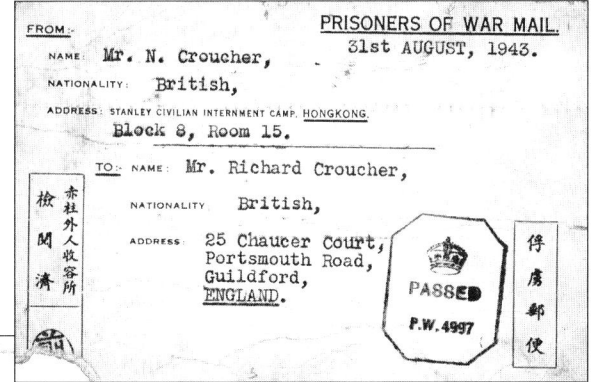

The P.O.W. Postcard.

PRISONERS OF WAR MAIL.
31st AUGUST, 1943.

FROM:-

NAME: Mr. N. Croucher,

NATIONALITY: British,

ADDRESS: STANLEY CIVILIAN INTERNMENT CAMP, HONGKONG.
Block 8, Room 15.

TO:- NAME: Mr. Richard Croucher,

NATIONALITY: British,

ADDRESS: 25 Chaucer Court,
Portsmouth Road,
Guildford,
ENGLAND.

PASSED
P.W.4997

My Dear Son,

No letter from you since August '41.
Received my first from Simonne last month
dated October 1942. You've heard that all
I possessed irretrievably lost, so must start
over again. Don't know when I'll be free
perhaps after hostilities. What are you doing?
Write and tell me all news.

Hope you will have no future regrets in
leaving school so early. Should seriously
consider continuing your studies, otherwise
you will be handicapped after the War.

I wrote Granny July.

Give my love to Mummy and Granny and
remember your responsibilities and work hard.

Your affectionate
Father.

Stanley Internment Camp, 30 August 1945.
(Courtesy of the Government of the Hong Kong SAR.)

The famous Brandy Bottle,
photographed in London, 1997.

20 Sept. '45

Notice

a meeting of members
will be held at S.C.M.P.
building, Wyndham St.,
at noon, on Saturday,
22nd Sept., 1945.

N. V. Croucher,
Commodore

Noel's priority after the war: calling a meeting
of the Royal Hong Kong Yacht Club,
20 September 1945.

Noel Croucher's rescue of the yacht club's finances, 18 February 1953.

La Cigale, *built 1897,*
bought by Noel in 1919.

Noel's second La Cigale,
designed by Sparkman & Stephens.

Noel Croucher at sea.

Life on the ocean wave — Noel and friends in Hong Kong waters.

Noel holding the Croucher Cup in May 1952 with, from left: A.G. Dalziel of Blair & Co.,
then Commodore of the RHKYC; Norman Marsh of ICI; and Gerald Carey,
assistant shipping manager at Jardine Matheson & Co.

Noel Croucher chairing the Hong Kong Stock Exchange. Francis Zimmern is second left.

George Marden.

The good old days in Hong Kong. Noel is second right.

Noel Croucher (right) with Governor David Trench (left).

Noel Croucher with Lady Hogan, wife of the then Chief Justice of Hong Kong.

Joan Scrivener, Repulse Bay Beach, 1977.

Joan wearing the beaded top which Noel sent her.

Joan Scrivener with Basil Croucher in England.

CHAPTER TEN

'ALL IS IRRETRIEVABLY LOST'

ong Kong surrendered to Japan one day after Noel Croucher's fiftieth birthday.

Considering what followed Christmas Day, 1941, for the elite in Hong Kong, it is no wonder that the years and days immediately prior to the shocking surrender have acquired a mystic glow of joy, glamour and delight in hindsight. For, in a story well documented throughout Asia, the British were not prepared for the Japanese onslaught, and anyone suggesting the need to take these opponents seriously was ridiculed. The unspoken — but largely unquestioned — idea of British supremacy was about to be shattered irrevocably.

The years 1937–41 were boom years and, economically, Hong Kong was looking ahead with hope. So, too, for Noel Croucher. From his simple beginnings, he had, by 1941, arrived. He was known as an original (but not yet an eccentric), and regarded as one of the most knowledgeable of the long-term Europeans in the colony. He was a member of the right clubs, invited almost everywhere. Like his fictional mentor in *John Halifax, Gentleman*, and his maternal grandfather Henry Stockley, he had pulled himself up by his own bootstraps into the heights of Hong Kong society and wealth.

At this stage, however, for Noel as with his business colleagues, social awareness was low. Deteriorating conditions for the masses were seen in the increase in begging on the streets of the central business district, but the common response was but a call for better policing. 'In normal circumstances it is not difficult to arrange for daily raids; the real difficulty lies in the disposal of those arrested. Women beggars, children of newspaper sellers, and boy shoe-blacks are a puzzle to police and magistrates alike. Small fines or a few days detention appear to have no deterrent effect. Heavier sentences overcrowd the prisons.'[1]

In July 1937, Japan and China had clashed at the Marco Polo Bridge in Peking and by the year's end, General Chiang Kai-shek had moved his nationalist government to Chungking after one of Japan's worst atrocities, the Nanking Massacre. By October 1938, Japanese forces had overrun Canton and within a year, the population of Hong Kong had doubled, to more than two million.

Food and beverage outlets in Hong Kong were booming. The China Provident Loan & Mortgage Company achieved exceptional earnings from the cargo dislocation caused by war on the Mainland — shareholders got a ten percent dividend and a five percent one-off bonus.[2] It became apparent that not all refugee influxes were a bad thing — many of those now arriving in Hong Kong were wealthy harbingers of industry. Increased defence expenditure was also stimulating local trade. But at a shareholders' meeting for the Hong Kong & Shanghai Bank in 1939, chairman T.E. 'Tam' Pearce warned his listeners, including Noel, not to underestimate the enemy. He observed that Japan's potential could not be ignored: 'because the country is well-disciplined, with a highly organised system of Government'.[3]

As for China, Pearce praised skilful management of the currency and financial situation, and noted that import and export of cargoes continued despite everything, 'largely due to the amazing resilience and tenacity of the Chinese farmers and traders, which enabled them to find ways and means of moving goods.'[4] The much-respected Pearce, Canton-born son of a missionary, had run the venerable J.D. Hutchison & Company and was a Dairy Farm board member and keen Jockey Club steward. He was to die in a gallant defence of the Hong Kong Electric power station at North Point.[5]

More portents of war were heard by Noel at the 1939 meeting of Douglas Steamship Company, where shareholders heard of the 'unjustifiable seizure' of a company ship, S.S. *Sagres*, by the Japanese navy. Ship and crew were released unharmed after 'inquisitorial questioning', but the incident was ominous. China Underwriters was forced to close its Canton branch during the year,[6] as was A.S. Watson & Company.[7] At the Canton Insurance Office Limited, it was noted that 'genuine trade cannot flourish under the existing conditions of unrest and uncertainty and I fear we must anticipate a further drop in income during the coming year.'[8] At Douglas Steamship Company's meeting in 1940, Noel heard how hostilities had closed the ports of Swatow, Amoy and Foochow for much of the year, and that the Sino-Japanese conflict was entirely to blame.[9]

Hong Kong society had greeted Britain's declaration of war on Germany on 3 September 1939 with patriotic, indeed alcoholic, fervour. Parties at the Gripps saw patrons singing jingoistic songs and toasts. The German Club was closed after an inventory of its bar was taken.[10]

In June 1939, as in 1917, there had been a compulsory call-up of able-bodied citizens in Britain to help in the war effort, and Hong Kong was the first overseas territory to follow suit. Conscription for active service was of British men aged eighteen to forty, while those aged forty-one to fifty-five, including Noel Croucher, were posted to one of the auxiliary defence services — Auxiliary Police, Nursing Service, Fire Service or Air Raid Precautions Department (ARP). Men over fifty-five joined Hong Kong's version of the Home Guard, the Hughesiliers, named after its first commander, the manager of Union Insurance, A.W. Hughes. Noel joined the ARP. This had started in 1938, expanded rapidly after 1939 and began building air raid shelters in June 1940.[11]

Four million sandbags were stored up, extra men trained to turn off the colony's water supply, and a quarter of a million bilingual booklets distributed, titled *The Protection of Your Home Against Air Raids*. Gas masks were made at a factory in Kowloon. The ARP director, Wing Commander A.H.S. Steele-Perkins, claimed Hong Kong could be blacked out within three minutes, to deprive the enemy of targets, but observers reported the city remained awash with light.[12]

Hong Kong at last began to sense trouble and, especially after the bombing in Shanghai, a great deal of publicity was given to air raid precautions and the construction of tunnels for shelters for the masses planned. 'I took a training course in air raid precautions and found it interesting and quite intensive. We were required to sit a three-hour paper at its completion,' recalls Jean Gittins.[13] All firms were asked to help by releasing their staff for voluntary duties. The idea was to train representatives from each firm who would then be responsible for passing on the knowledge. Classes began in December 1937. Happily, there is no record of any involvement by Noel in the 'Mimi Lau' procurement scandal.[14] In 1940, British women and children were ordered to leave, and company bosses were releasing staff for volunteer duties for one full day a week.

Despite all this earnest activity, the possibility of hordes of 'little yellow chaps' swamping an entire way of life was barely considered. Emily Hahn was in Hong Kong at the time. An American with a knowledge of China, she had astringent observations to make on Hong Kong's high society: '...they lived an ideally British sort of life. They had their golf and their races and even their hunts, when they wanted to make the effort. ...There was sailing. There was tennis; that goes without saying.

'Christmas was riotous that year [1940]... The evening ended at a typical bright young colonial party, with discreet flirtations everywhere, sleek, beautiful women and dashing young men in uniform, all being incredibly childish, so it seemed to me, and playing charades. ...We played out charades, we drank at the funny little bar, we giggled, we saw Christmas in. Half the men I remember that night, horsing around, are dead, and the girls are standing in line at Stanley [internment camp] with cup in hand, waiting for a handout of thin rice stew. Does that sound banal? It isn't. It hits me sometimes like a slap in the face.'[15]

Noel was probably at the big balls just before the outbreak of war. It was a busy social week: on Tuesday, 2 December 1941, Sir Robert and Lady Ho Tung celebrated their Diamond Jubilee with a glittering event at Gripps. 'Everyone' was there. A capacity crowd went to the races at Happy Valley where the Royal Scots band played on the turf. The Middlesex Regiment played rugby at the Cricket Club, followed by a party at the Hong Kong Hotel. The Peninsula hosted the 'Tin Hat' charity ball to raise money for Britain to buy bombers. Governor Sir Mark Young was there. It was to become, though few knew it, the *fin de siècle* event.

Noel knew war was on the way but there is no record of him speaking out about Hong Kong's unpreparedness, or of him predicting the coming debacle. On Sunday, 7 December 1941, the usual church parade of military contingents took place at a packed St. John's Cathedral. Major-General Christopher Maltby, General Officer Commanding in Hong Kong, had time to read the lesson before being called outside by a tense officer: Japanese troops had been sighted just north of Fanling. 'During the service, senior officers left in twos and threes in response to urgent whispers from orderlies and despatch raiders...'[16] Battle stations were called for 5 p.m. that day. An era was within hours of ending.

The air raid sirens were busy, but Hong Kong's air force, such as it was, was wiped out in the first five minutes of Japan's onslaught on the colony. In the days that followed, workers had to scuttle to shelters several times a day, and night. Battery Path had a shelter, which would have been the most convenient for Noel and his staff on Ice House Street. A diary written by Barbara Redwood, then a stenographer with the government, describes those tense days:

> December 8th — Scared and gloomy. I feel sure we'll have raids every night & day, & in the night much worse than in the day...

December 9th — 2 false alarms, 1 last night and 1 early this morning & six alerts throughout the morning. ...

December 10th — Went in Battery St tunnel in alarm when on way into town. It was more orderly than I had expected & quite cool... Peaceful night but 3 raids in afternoon. News is that Japs have sunk 'Prince of Wales' & 'Repulse' by bombs — hard to believe. Japs seem to be starting well...

December 11th — No raids during night, but shells are coming over now, but so far not doing much damage. ...we have apparently abandoned Kowloon & unless a miracle happens are going to be shelled to bits. There is talk that Chinese guerrillas are coming up behind the Japs & are now at Taipo, but I'm afraid to believe anything so heartening...[17]

Here we thank John Luff for his record of a story from Noel. On 14 December 1941, the day of the first Japanese 'peace mission' which the Governor rejected, a fatal tragedy occurred from which Noel had a narrow escape. Quoting Noel, Luff wrote:

' "At that time, I was living in a flat at the top of the old P & O Building, but when the shelling started, I decided it would be safer to move. After I came off duty, I had a snack at the Gloucester Hotel and decided to sleep on the ground floor of the Chartered Bank. While I was having my meal, a yachting friend joined me and asked me to accompany a party on a 'secret mission'. As I had been on duty all day and it was now after seven o'clock, I refused, explaining I was all in."

This was fortunate for Noel, for the secret mission was to escort the P & O launch, *Jeanette*, to Green Island, and to tow back to Victoria a barge laden with TNT [explosives]. Something went wrong with the security arrangements, for when the *Jeanette* was opposite Blake Pier, she was challenged by a sentry. *Jeanette* failed to reply and the sentry opened fire. The barge and its escort were blown to smithereens. Noel Croucher continues:

"I had gone along to the Chartered Bank after my meal, pulled two benches together and laid down. About eleven o'clock, I was awakened by a terrific explosion. I thought a bomb had dropped close by, but no further explosions occurred. The next day, I returned to my flat. Passing along the sea front, I noticed that every pane of plate glass had been broken. Later I heard of the tragic incident in which I might have been involved had I not just come off duty." '[18]

At least Noel's experience in World War I had given him a taste of life under fire. Detailed accounts of the battle for Hong Kong are plentiful — suffice to say that Noel made few preparations for Hong Kong's defeat, other than to lock his papers in his old Chubb safe, as he probably did every night anyway.

'From the start the position of the defenders was hopeless... British intelligence had consistently under-rated the Japanese who were well-trained, highly disciplined, efficiently handled, suitably shod for silent night work and made skilful use of artillery and air bombing.' Hong Kong's mainland fell in five days and despite determined and heroic resistance, it was all over by 25 December.[19]

As a symbol of the blow that had fallen, one of many sources of information on British dispositions in the colony turned out to be the popular Japanese barber at the Hong Kong Hotel. Mr Yamashita suddenly turned up in uniform as the top commander in Stanley Camp. He was not only an intelligence officer, but also led a syndicate of black marketeers.[20] So a man who had once cut the taipans' hair, privy to all the gossip such a position brings, now had absolute power over his former clients. Though not as feared or loathed as the Japanese Gendarmerie who later took over his post, Yamashita's rise heightened the almost farcical fall of the European elite — a fall from grace which heralded the end of colonialism throughout Asia.

ARP wardens were active on the increasingly deserted streets of Central up to and including the day of surrender and were a key source of whatever news was available. People slept where they could and, soon, those who were bunking down at the Standard Chartered Bank joined the motley crew of bankers, friends and associated dependents in the Hong Kong Bank building, which also housed the American Club, in the last days of the fighting. Given that Noel had decided to sleep on the ground floor of the Chartered Bank, according to his account of the *Jeanette* tragedy, he may well have been part of this group.[21]

The surrender on Christmas Day, 1941, was a shattering blow to Hong Kong, and the stories of survival by those both inside and outside internment camps offer a vivid patchwork of humanity under stress. Many of those people expected to be leaders or heroes were nothing of the sort. Many of those overlooked in society became, under extreme duress, leaders and heroes. Noel Croucher, of course, was a survivor.

References in letters written decades later suggest that, among Noel's personal papers at home, were extensive researches into his family history, going back centuries, all of it proving how truly English he was. There were many books, photo albums, collections of this and that — all of them lost in the orgy of looting that began as soon as homes were emptied of people. Perhaps his staff tried to save things. But the looting was not just that by marauding troops. Most Hong Kong people were embarking on a frightening period of hardship under the heel of the Japanese and, as utilities and shops folded, new sources of income and fuel were needed. Vast chunks of Hong Kong's recent past went up in flames to warm the newly destitute and to cook food. As Noel's home was in Central, his personal treasures were probably among the first to go on Hong Kong Island.

The grim new realities hit Hong Kong on 4 January 1942 when Europeans were told to bring a small bag and assemble on the military parade ground in Central. Anti-colonial Japan could not have European taipans and civil servants on the loose around town. Instead, they were to be humbled, starting with their despatch to a collection of sordid, filthy short-time hotels along Connaught Road in Central. Crammed half-a-dozen to a room, with virtually no water, food or sanitary facilities after the first day or so, Hong Kong's upper classes had a taste of their future. Alec Potts, one of Noel's stock exchange colleagues and the nephew of George Potts, was swept into Nam King Boarding House down on Des Voeux Road. There too, food was very hard to get, and the sewage situation was dire.[22]

Noel was no doubt dragged along with the rest, but may have used this time to make arrangements for survival through friends or staff. Odd groups of people were still holding out in far-flung homes on the Peak, or finding ways to avoid internment by claiming an Asian nationality through marriage (as did Emily Hahn, who claimed a Chinese husband). As far as we know, Noel was part of the pitiful march of a defeated community through Hong Kong's streets to the hovels. Sixteen days later, news of the decision to put civilians out at Stanley came as a vast relief. At least the air was good, the views beautiful and the scenery one of the firmest sources of succour to those interned there. No one knew this was the beginning of three years and eight months of callous incarceration. Historian G.B. Endacott described the Japanese occupation as 'harrowing', adding that enemy civilians were herded, like cattle, into Stanley.[23]

Yet, in the middle of all this, there was one thing which Noel did pack to take into his uncertain future — a small, much-treasured book called *The Golden Treasury*, full of extracts of the world's great poetry, edited by Francis Palgrave. Noel's choice of such a book, at such a time, shows how sensitive and cultured this barely educated broker wanted to be.[24]

Packed in the deserted buildings of St. Stephen's College, the nearby prison and related accommodation, 1,100 men, 1,000 women, 340 children and 80 infants were thrust into a wholly alien way of life. This camp at Stanley was for civilians. Military prisoners of war endured even worse conditions at camps in Kowloon. Many families were split between camps and could learn nothing of each other until after the war. Luckily, Noel's wife and son had already left Hong Kong, Richard for school in England back in 1936, and Simonne to France in 1939.

On arrival at Stanley by sea, internees were immediately forced to fend for themselves. The Americans seemed the best organised entity with a commendable tendency to work together. They buckled down to immediate cleaning up tasks whereas the British community, more divided by class, occupation and prejudice, spent too much effort and energy bickering or complaining. Not untypical of their attitude was the remark of the round British matron, who, as she watched a group of Americans repairing a store, remarked, "Isn't it fortunate that the Americans have so many members of the working class in their camp?" '[25]

Noel Croucher either chose or found himself to be in Block 8, Room 15 of St. Stephen's College — scene of some desperate last-ditch battles before Hong Kong surrendered. Dried blood caked the stairwells, walls and mattresses. Smouldering fires revealed bones and military uniforms. Toilets and drains were overflowing, the water mains were off.[26]

Block 8 held 132 prisoners of war, all of them British. Among them were many friends of Noel, including Mr and Mrs Francis and Rosa Loseby and their very young daughter, Pat. The future Lady May Ride (née Witchell) was there, a lifelong friend of Noel's. In the camp at large, Noel knew J.H. Seth, a leading chartered accountant, and J.P. Pennefather-Evans, Commissioner of Police. The Postmaster General, E.I. Wynne-Jones, was there and one wonders if Noel used the proximity to discuss his own humble past in the post office. Ben Wylie, manager of the South China Morning Post, and D.L. Newbigging of Jardine's were among those active in camp councils, as were the head of ICI, R.D. Gillespie, the acting head of Butterfield & Swire, C.C. Roberts, and chief magistrate Harold Sheldon. Committees grew like fungus — every field of human endeavour warranted one, with agenda, minutes and all bureaucratic rituals observed.

Noel lived with three others in one room: Robert Robertson, Sydney

Hampden Ross and Thomas Ramsay. They were at least of the same generation and all had business leanings.

Mr Robertson, born in Scotland in 1893, was a professor of Economics at the University of Hong Kong whose wife's address was listed as being in Sydney. (She had been evacuated.) Mr Hampden Ross, English and just two years younger than Noel, was a chartered accountant with his own firm. Mr Ramsay was the oldest and another Scotsman, born in 1882. He worked in shipping with Williamson and Company and his next of kin was, probably a sister, Mrs Murray in Glasgow.

As for Noel, his next of kin was not his wife. Instead, he listed his mother, Floss, as Mrs F. Croucher, at 29 Archers Road, Southampton. The extent to which the ignominious Alex Parker had been expunged from the family history is seen in the fact that she kept the name of Noel's real father.

Also in camp was Mr James Carson Ferguson, husband to Lillian. She, as the loyal Mrs Ferguson, was Noel's right-hand woman in his office until her death in 1966. As with too many friends and colleagues, the rigours of war and internment at Stanley caused the death of someone close to Noel. Mr Ferguson died just twelve days after British rule was re-established in Hong Kong in 1945, partly due to malnutrition. He had come to Hong Kong thirty-seven years previously and worked at Taikoo as an engineer. Although interned, he was allowed to rejoin his family on Lock Road, Kowloon, after five months — as a Eurasian, Mrs Ferguson had avoided internment.[27] Not only was Mr Ferguson a firm friend of Noel's before the war, but Noel went on to support the education of the Ferguson sons.[28]

Among other close contacts of Noel's who died at Stanley was A.L. Shields, Legislative Councillor and partner in Noel's old firm, Shewan, Tomes & Co. He died in July 1944. Charles Manners, general manager of one of Noel's favoured firms, the Hong Kong & Kowloon Wharf & Godown Company, and a former major in the Chinese Labour Corps, died in November that year, as did E.M. Hazeland, father of Noel's 'old girlfriend, Rheta Hazeland'. Mr Owen-Hughes, another prominent businessman, Legco member and company director, died in February 1945. Noel was only a few years younger than some of these men, but apparently somewhat tougher or luckier. One of many old friends was Harry Compton, a director of the Hong Kong & Shanghai Bank and boss of Sassoon's. He, too, was a fellow internee.[29]

Only a few of the many memoirs of the war mention Noel Croucher by name, suggesting that, for the most part, Noel spent his time in camp with his head down and his body relatively strong. We feel sure he talked at length with his room-mates about business, economics, Hong Kong and more. He was lucky to be with men with whom he had much in common. These might have been special friends of his, with whom he arranged to get quarters together, mirroring the bachelor's messes in which many younger men first lived on arrival in the colony, albeit in far more distressing circumstances.

His son, Richard, recalls Noel telling him how a Japanese commander in the camp had approached him for financial advice and while we cannot rule out his generosity on this front — especially if it helped ameliorate conditions — he was just as likely to have brushed off the impertinent enemy. But Noel certainly did not brush off any opportunity for a good tale to tell. The man was a born chronicler, but left the publication of such stories to others. There was the memorable moment in camp when a tiger appeared, a story best told by Noel, in the written account he gave to John Luff:

> There were many fellow internees like myself who had long been residents of the Colony, yet for various reasons, we had never met before arriving in Stanley. We formed friendships which have endured to this day. Naturally, human nature being what it is, there were profound pessimists among us who stated that the war would never end, and that we should spend the rest of our days at Stanley. They made little impression upon us. On the other hand, there were optimists who believed we should be out in a matter of a few weeks or months, at most.
>
> There were many strange incidents during those early days in Stanley, but I recall one incident which stands out from all others and enlivened the camp for a while. The coming of the warmer weather tempted some chaps to sleep outside away from the crowded rooms. One such chap took his bed outside the bungalow which had formerly been the residence of a St Stephen's school teacher. This chap said he preferred the external night cries to the snores of an overcrowded room.
>
> Very early one morning, a few of us were hanging around talking prior to commencing our daily chores when this man came up to us and said, 'There's a tiger in the camp.' We all looked at one another and thought that the worst had happened, when the chap broke in, 'I know you all think that I'm crazy, but last night, I felt the hot breath of an animal on my face, and when I looked up, I saw the head of a

tiger, its mouth was open, and it was panting. I was petrified and waited, but the tiger wandered slowly away.' We all thought that he had gone round the bend, but later, another internee reported having seen the tiger, but as no one was attacked, we took the intruder to be a large dog. Then one day we saw pug marks which some specialist identified as belonging to a tiger. The Japanese were informed and a few Indian soldiers in a prison-of-war camp in Kowloon were brought over. They soon traced the animal's progress to the Stanley Fort area, and brought it down.

There were some speculations as to where the tiger had come from, and then someone remembered there had been a circus in town at Causeway Bay. It was popular opinion that the keeper must have opened the cage and given the beast a chance to escape, before making off himself.[30]

Noel's story received wide play. In the history of the Dairy Farm Company, Nigel Cameron also quotes Noel: 'There was little enough light relief in those years... The late Noel Croucher used to tell an interesting story which might well have had a disastrous ending, but fortunately did not. George Milne confirms it ... many people [including Noel] knew that in March 1915, during the First World War, a large tiger had been found in the New Territories, it was deemed not absolutely impossible that another had reached the island. ...The carcass was taken into Victoria, and B.W. Bradbury of the Dairy Farm butchery department was taken with it out of the camp in order to skin the beast.'[31]

The overriding daily task was to find food, and the brave, endless and ingenious strategems employed to this end could fill a book.[32] Hunger consumed every waking hour and many anguished dreams. It also caused disease from dysentery, tuberculosis and pellagra, to beri-beri and infections. George Wright-Nooth recalls one never needed to cut one's fingernails — they just did not grow.[33] Before weakness and desperation took over, the organising types which appear in any community were in their element. Classes of all kinds, sports, yoga, church services and working groups filled the daylight hours. A letter from a Stanley internee to a relative reads: 'Time passes quickly, mornings occupied carpentry, repairs. Afternoons — mathematics, mechanics, electrical classes. Evenings — lectures, general subjects...'[34]

When the American contingent in camp were repatriated, six months into the internment (followed by the remaining Americans and Canadians in September 1943), they left behind their substantial library, originally from the American Club. This provided a treasure trove of reading matter for those disinclined to join the herd. Noel probably did a lot of reading in those years — he had a voracious appetite for knowledge and was a loner by instinct. A wide reading by Noel at this stage in his life helps account for the surprising depth and breadth of his knowledge and interests, considering the truncated education in his youth.

One way in which prisoners tried to survive was to trade food and cash 'under the wire'. Segregated from the rest of Hong Kong by guards, fences, guns and sheer distance, they relied on friends or former staff still alive in occupied Hong Kong for assistance. Many are the stories of loyal friends who, at great risk to themselves, brought vital foodstuffs, equipment and money to Stanley. They were themselves living in conditions of extreme hardship, forced to collaborate, steal or suffer in a city destroyed physically and emotionally. The assistance these people gave to those in camp was heroic. In some cases — such as those of the Hon. Dhun Jehangir Ruttonjee and the Hon. Dr Sir Sik Nin Chau — it resulted in their imprisonment or worse.[35]

Mrs Ferguson might have been able to help, by staying in touch with Noel in camp. Certainly someone did — because Noel was able to lend money to some of his fellow prisoners in camp. Florence Lo, who joined Croucher's office in 1968 and worked for Noel until his death, remembers Mr Croucher telling her how he collected IOUs on the scraps of paper used inside cigarette packets. Sure enough, decades after the war, Florence found a few of these IOUs, still in a back drawer in Noel's office desk.

'The simple process of writing a cheque or IOU produced ready cash and therefore food, if a middleman or agent could be found to accept it. The discount was naturally considerable because of the risk of the IOUs not being honoured. A man's word had to be accepted and the terms varied according to his standing; members of large companies of international repute had 25 yen to the pound sterling, employees of big local firms 20 yen to the pound, professional men 15 yen to the pound, and so on. ...The middlemen, Chinese and Europeans, were of course essential to the proceedings which were euphemistically regarded as commercial transactions, and they cashed in handsomely.

'To regard people goaded by starvation as being free to make commercial bargains was of course plain hypocrisy, and to turn these exceptional circumstances to commercial advantage would seem to deny the morality basic to the decencies of community life. The justification, if there is one, lies in the fact that the IOUs were generally honoured, despite the fact that the Hong Kong government after the war officially

released all individuals concerned from the letter of their engagements...
It is estimated that about six million yen passed over the wire between
October 1944, and March 1945.'[36]

The black market was one of the murkiest issues of the internment:
some traded in such a way as to alleviate hardship, save people's lives
and keep morale up, at great risk to themselves. Others, of course, used
the power they had acquired to make a fortune at the expense of others.
Naturally, many camp inmates found their assessments of people
undergoing a radical change. Many were the disillusionments following
the discovery that one's precious watch or wedding ring had been stolen
by a friend. There were stories that the former policemen of Hong Kong
now stole and stockpiled food and medicine which they hoarded until
the best price could be got. There are other stories that the police
performed a signal service to camp by managing to get their hands on
life-saving supplies.

Was Noel a black marketeer? And if so, did he use his power for the
common good? The existence of the IOUs suggests Noel was involved
to some extent, but there are no recollections of him misusing the position.
George Wright-Nooth who was in Stanley Camp too, says that as far as
he knew, Noel was not mixed up in the black market at all. 'All he was
interested in was in keeping alive — he treated a friend as a friend, a
good friend. He kept himself fit — he was quite a tough ole boy!' Wright-
Nooth stayed a friend of Noel's in post-war Hong Kong life, borrowing
some of Noel's rare old China books and sharing dinners.[37]

Robert Minnitt, sailing friend of Noel's from the late 1930s, was also
in camp. He was assistant to the Colonial Secretary of Hong Kong,
Franklin Gimson, the man who had the misfortune to arrive to take up
his post just days before the surrender to Japan. Robert Minnitt was in a
position to see and understand more of the camp's workings than many
others, and he recalls Noel as unproblematic.

'The thing is this — we hadn't any money and by various means,
various people managed to get in touch with the outside world, the rest
of Hong Kong,' recalls Mr Minnitt. 'They managed to [get money] on
credit, because you couldn't draw a cheque or cash it. So, I needed some
money because I was married in camp (to my first wife) so I was able to
get some money, Japanese military yen, worth precisely nothing at the
end of the war. Anyway I got it. And you needed it for the canteen —
you'd get bits of tea and little luxuries at vast cost. You got it, but it was
absolutely horrifying, an egg would cost about 15 pounds or something.

'You drew cheques without a payee drawer, and by various means, they would get the cheque into town, get money from somewhere, and send the money back. It came in what we called, under the wire. Totally unofficial. And we shouldn't have done it. A big risk. Very big risk. I think one or two people didn't behave very well. So far as I know, Noel, well I never heard anything against him. It was a great benefit really to be able to get money, and if one's credit was good, you could get money. Naturally you finished up with a fairly big debt on the bank in Hong Kong.[138]

Noel was probably well placed to get money in from outside the camp because, as Mr Minnitt says, 'he would have had, I presume, quite useful contacts in the Chinese part of Hong Kong. ...The Japanese gave fairly short shrift to anyone bending the rules anyway!' Indeed the risk was death.

Ethically, the question is not whether Noel lent money or not, but whether he ever insisted on repayment. The fact that a pile of IOUs were still in his desk several decades after the war suggests repayment was not something he had on his mind. Anecdotal evidence is unhelpful. Some recall bitter moments at a post-war cocktail party when a former camp inmate attacked Noel for alleged unpleasantness in camp. Many others will list the same several names of people who were indeed dastardly in camp, adding that Noel Croucher was not one of them. Croucher's former assistant recalls him expressing intense dislike for a man who had the greed and the gall to demand repayment of war debts, and he later told others that he never wanted anything to do with the fortune and philanthropic trust accumulated by another camp inmate.

'Two of the leading figures in all this wheeling and dealing were [A.G.] Dalziel and the man who skinned the tiger, butcher Bradbury. Dalziel was a businessman who did not intend to starve in Stanley. If he liked you it was possible to get a reasonable deal... Bradbury had excellent contacts outside camp and a seemingly endless supply of cash from these sources. He became one of Stanley's top usurers. His deliberate exploitation of hunger with his outrageously high interest rates made him perhaps the most despised of the internees... I am certain that there was not a single adult internee who was not involved in some form of black market deal at some stage.'[139]

Among varied activities in camp was the attempt by some businessmen to retain a sense of the normal. The minutes laboriously kept show that on 1 June 1942, a meeting of the Dairy Farm board was held inside Stanley Camp. A.L. Shields, D.L. Newbigging, J.D. Thompson and G. Milne were there, with Dodwell and Davies recorded as absent. 'The impression of reasonableness, of sane and fair compromise left by the minutes of this meeting between the (by now) ragged and dishevelled directors and managers of the two companies, says something about the courage and the (at that time) quite unfounded optimism of all concerned.'[40]

No doubt many plans were laid and ideas formulated for how life would be lived when the war was over. And occasionally, very occasionally, something would happen to perk people up — like the day the tiger was seen. But such moments were rare in the seemingly endless, virtually intolerable, incarceration.

A tragic event nearer the end of the war affected Noel more closely: 'He always kept telling that story of the day when he should have been killed. He'd been in his room and was called out to go and see the officer on the other side, and he hadn't got out of the office for more than a minute or so when it had a direct hit from a shell, and if he'd stayed in there, he'd have been dead.'[41]

American air raids directed at the Japanese took place from 1942, but from early 1945, Stanley Camp dwellers had a ringside seat in what they hoped was a final phase of war. As an internment camp, it should not have been a target, but large white crosses were not painted onto roofs until later. The military Stanley Fort was nearby, and the Japanese were shooting machine guns and anti-aircraft fire from the area, too. On 15 and 16 January 1945, dramatically close air raids took place and, tragically, fourteen civilians in camp died.

In July, two more bombs landed in camp. One fell into a lavatory where it exploded. The other landed in Noel Croucher's room. In Noel's own words, again written for John Luff, this is what happened:

> On July 25, 1945, a few minutes before noon, I was in my room with Professor Robertson, T. Ramsay, and Hampden Ross, resting after our midday meal of four ounces of rice and soya beans. I was reading a novel when I heard the sound of an approaching plane. Judging from the noise the plane was making, I would suggest that it had engine trouble. Ramsay stretched out to see the plane as it flew overhead. At the same time, I turned over in my bunk to catch a sight of the plane from the hut window. As I did so, the whole world seemed to split in two, and fragments of the roof crashed into the room which became a tangle of plaster work and dust.[42]

Noel suffered an injured shoulder from the debris and the building was quickly emptied. Among the several bombs that had fallen was a one-hundred-pound bomb which had penetrated the roof of Noel's hut.

The Japanese came along and forbade anyone to return to the building until a bomb disposal squad had dealt with the unexploded bomb. We slept in the open which was no hardship in July. Next day when the Japanese came along to deal with the bomb, it was discovered that it had come through the roof, passed through my bed, and then slithered along the floor into the next room where it rested on the floor in fragments. Had I not turned in my bed at that moment it struck, I should not have lived to tell the tale.

The next day, Colonel Nomura ordered a few of us to parade, and he called me out, told me he wanted me to answer some questions, and warned me to speak the truth. He asked, 'Was that an American plane which dropped the bomb on your roof?' I answered 'No,' and he asked me why. I told him that it must have been a Japanese plane because the Japanese had vowed that no American bomber would ever reach Hong Kong.

Naturally, Colonel Nomura was not amused. The next day, Noel was brought in for questioning again, this time with the senior Briton in camp, Franklin Gimson. They faced a Japanese general known as 'fat pig' and the bomb's provenance was again brought up. Mischievously, Noel said he could not read the markings on the bomb because he was without his glasses.

I politely asked Nomura if he would lend me his glasses. I put them on, and he exclaimed 'Read ... Read ... Read.' I read the marks out to him, and he asked 'American bomb?' I answered, 'I don't know. It must have been captured from the Americans.' At this point, Gimson interrupted and said, 'Of course it's an American bomb, Croucher.'

Croucher and Gimson were required to sign a document stating that it had indeed been an American bomb, which was obviously going to be of propaganda value to the Japanese. As they left the Japanese office, Gimson said to Croucher, 'What is the use of annoying these people? You only make it bad for everyone.' According to Luff, Croucher admitted Gimson was right and that he was being a nuisance.[43]

In another account, George Wright-Nooth's book, *Prisoner of the Turnip-Heads* — the title being a reference to the literal translation of the Cantonese slang for Japanese — reports, 'Croucher, who was bruised by flying debris, was later to claim that it [the bomb] went between his legs without touching him...'[44]

'The Japanese lost their heads as usual,' recorded John Stericker in his colourful account. 'Perhaps they were not unwise in immediately evacuating all the buildings in the neighbourhood of the bombs, but it is doubtful if any delayed action weapon ever necessitated a ten day wait... During that time many Japanese officials visited the camp to impress upon us how solicitous they were for our safety, and how vile was the so-called American plane which had deliberately bombed helpless British civilians...'[45]

Stericker also noted that Gimson, thrown into internment after barely two weeks in town, was not universally popular in his position of leadership. Many civilians felt betrayed by the government's lack of preparedness for war. 'By regarding this political undercurrent as disloyalty and, by his queer confusion between loyalty to the Crown and loyalty to the Hong Kong Government, Mr Gimson caused the interned citizens to become further aggrieved. ...The Camp expected him to come to them but he waited for the Camp to come to him.'[46]

In this bombing incident, Noel displayed his stubborn, contrary nature. He was brave enough to be cheeky and obstructive to a Japanese who had power over his life and death, and he boldly refused to budge under pressure. The flip side is there, too — his wilful bucking of the establishment, in a community as weak and fragile as Stanley then, was not likely to be helpful and could cause dangerous repercussions for others. No wonder Gimson interjected.

One can admire Croucher's brave defiance, at the same time as deploring his bull-headedness. He did not want to say what the Japanese wanted to hear, so he did not. The Japanese propaganda organ, *The Hong Kong News*, made much of how Americans were bombing their own allies in camp,[47] a victory of which Noel tried, in his own way, to deprive them. He was lucky to get away with it. Colonel Nomura was a legendary sadist and was later hung for war crimes.[48]

'There were lots of problems from the internment which dragged on after the war. But the only things from the war which I heard about Noel were positive — I mean, that he stood up to the Japs!' recalls Michael Rawlinson, who knew Noel through the Royal Society of Saint George. 'Noel should have been hungry, demoralised, bowed down. But for him to stand up to Gimson and to the Japanese would have taken guts.'[49]

Something Noel never forgot about his years as a prisoner of war was the fact that throughout the almost four years of internment, the only family member who bothered to stay in touch throughout was his mother. He never heard from his son, and heard only once from his wife in England. He was bitter on the subject for many years. Naturally, that might not have been all the fault of the individuals involved — post was a depressingly inadequate aspect of internment. Many letters sent from Stanley never left Hong Kong until after the war, if at all. Regular postal services were not allowed until April 1943 and even then, often did not make it to destination. Incoming mail was notoriously erratic and delayed.

Some people are built to cope with extreme hardship, tests of endurance and loneliness. Others, whether too spoiled in their normal lives or too weak in body or mind, found camp life unbearable. The vast majority cheated death, even if their post-war lives were never to be as whole or happy again. Some were killed by starvation, disease, accidents or atrocities. Noel Croucher not only survived — he retained physical and indeed mental health. If anything, he appeared stronger, intellectually and emotionally, after this period of enforced reflection.

In one of his letters to Joan Scrivener, written twenty years after the trials of camp, Noel treated his internment with humour and, yes, with poetry:

> I love calling to mind odd lines from the poets I had time to read years ago — I remember when I was interned carrying a heavy log of wood from the beach up to where our Camp was — it was about midnight & the moon was high. The Jap [sic] gendarme ordered us to rest as some were unable to carry on — It was unusually beautiful & I quoted something appropriate — whereupon I heard vile curses coming from another (I noticed he had picked out a small log, leaving the heavies to others) — who wanted to know what there was to see when we were starved, suffering from pellagra etc — wearing only shorts with no shoes, climbing up a rough mountain path.[50]

In such episodes, Noel confounds the stereotype of just another rich colonial. Such depths and style are worth remembering.[51]

Thanks to the memoir written by Noel Croucher for John Luff, another insight into what sort of thing stuck in Croucher's mind can be found in an episode he related from sometime in 1943:

'Mr Noel Croucher tells of a strange incident which occurred during this period,' wrote Luff. 'He says that it was his custom to watch from his window the antics of a Japanese gendarme who must, in private life, have been a school teacher. Every day he would gather the European children around him at the piano, and would lead them in singing nursery rhymes. It was strange to watch him set down his rifle, take his seat at the piano, while the children sang "Twinkle, Twinkle, little star." One day while Noel Croucher was sitting in his room, he heard cries of anguish coming from outside...'

Here Noel took over the narrative:

> We got up to see what was the matter, and saw one of the gendarmes jabbing at an internee with his bayonet. The internee was gesticulating, but the Japanese continued to prod him. We shouted at the Japanese telling him to stop, and one of our roomers who could speak Japanese asked the gendarme what was the matter.

'It appears that the Japanese authorities had issued an order that the picking up of twigs and bunches of dried grass was forbidden. This unfortunate internee had been gathering twigs to make a fire on which to boil some water.

> We had to rescue the internee and take him to the hospital. The gendarme concerned in the affair was the same chap who took the children sweets and sat down and played to them on the piano.'[52]

The impact of internment on Noel's thinking was profound, and one can only wonder where he placed himself in the scene he described:

> Nowadays, the high standard of education and welfare, all free to those who formerly one would never or seldom meet [sic!], has not succeeded in getting rid of the chips they carry on their shoulder. When they come in contact with those of a different background — you know what I mean — All this education will take time to sink in where human relationships are concerned.
>
> Being interned gave me an opportunity of seeing all classes of society in the raw. I saw among the internees those I had seen for years but never spoken to, characters of the highest standard where one would least expect it, and others with petty meannesses which were never exhibited when in a free community — well such is life.[53]

Japan admitted defeat on 14 August 1945. At last, the war was over. Internees were not let out immediately, but visitors could come in. 'The last two weeks of August were a peculiar sort of in-between period. The Japanese had surrendered, we had won the war and yet until Allied troops actually landed the Japanese retained their arms and were still nominally responsible for law and order...'[54]

A shattered remnant of Hong Kong's ruling class staggered out of Stanley into a new but decrepit world. British suzerainty over Hong Kong was re-established even before the Royal Navy steamed into Victoria Harbour on 30 August. A military administration was set up, and the Chinese flooded back into Hong Kong. Improvisation was the order of the day, the government had to buy food in bulk, trade and foreign exchange controls were introduced to conserve supplies and hard currency. There was almost nowhere to stay — over seventy percent of housing had been destroyed and people were crammed three or four into a hotel room in town.

Trials began of suspected collaborators and of Japanese war criminals. The most notorious traitor, recruited by the Japanese to infiltrate resistance groups, was George Wong. He had come to Hong Kong from neighbouring Kwangtung before the war and been employed by China Provident, Loan and Mortgage Company, of which, incidentally, Noel was a director. Wong was the first to be tried at the Supreme Court, on 1 April 1946. He was executed at Stanley Prison one hundred days later.[55]

As for the rest, 'most of the internees who came out of the camps were in poor health and were "hardly capable of great mental effort, had no power of decision, short memories, and made frequent mistakes in conversation," according to one witness.'[56] As will be seen, however, the power of decision was not something Noel lacked.

Noel Croucher thought he had little to look forward to. By now, he knew of the orgies of looting and destruction which had occurred during the war, and the dire straits in which non-interned Hong Kong people had found themselves — burning books and papers for fuel, scavenging with the rats to survive. Indeed, we know Noel believed that everything he had worked so hard for, all the wealth of property, stocks, bonds and currencies which he had accumulated over the decades, all of this, he thought, was lost for ever. For in 1943, midway through his imprisonment, he wrote to his son:

> My Dear Son,
>
> No letter from you since August '41. Received my first from Simonne last month dated October 1942. You've heard that all I possessed irretrievably lost, so must start over again. Don't know when I'll be free perhaps after hostilities. What are you doing? Write and tell me all news.
>
> Hope you will have no future regrets in leaving school so early. Should seriously consider continuing your studies, otherwise you will be handicapped after the War.

I wrote Granny July.

Give my love to Mummy and Granny and remember your responsibilities and work hard.

Your affectionate
Father.

PRISONERS OF WAR MAIL, 31st AUGUST, 1943.
From: Mr. N. Croucher, British, Block 8, Room 15.
To: Mr. Richard Croucher, British, 25 Chaucer Court, Portsmouth Road, Guildford, <u>ENGLAND</u>.[57]

There Noel Croucher stood, in 1945, with his hard times behind him, having survived death and deprivation, but his fortune had been, he assumed, 'irretrievably lost'. Throughout internment he was prey to the same fears and insecurities as everyone else and assumed the worst. He had only just reached the heights of financial success in the last years before the war. To have worked so hard for so long, he would have been depressed indeed, contemplating the long hard road ahead. Fittingly, even when he thought all was undone, he had no thought of giving up, of retiring to England, or of shirking his duties in any way. He was prepared to pick up from the beginning and start again.

In this mood of fear and determination, Noel returned to his office on Ice House Street as soon as he could. 'He had collected all his share certificates and bonds, and put them in an old tin safe in his office, and had thought to send it away, to Australia, but failed. But he had two bottles of brandy left [from his wedding present], and there was a chimney in his office, and he put one bottle up one side of the chimney and one bottle up the other side of the chimney, and then he got captured by the Japanese and taken to Stanley.

'And when he got out of Stanley he went back to his office and the first thing he saw was, the tin safe had been pushed onto the balcony, and it appeared to have a broken key in it. And he thought, oh well, they've got it, got everything. But he thought, well I'll go see about the bottle of brandy so he put his hand up one side and found a broken one. He put the hand up the other side and found the other one, its cork was blown, but the bottle was intact.[58]

'Then he went back and looked at the safe, and had it opened. And there were all his bonds, his shares, his papers, everything! And he was one of the richest men in Hong Kong — instantly.'[59]

Recalls Leslie Wright, a lawyer who knew Noel since the late 1940s: 'It was one of these ancient safes and the Japs had just pushed it onto the open balcony and left it. So he had a head start, with shares in all those companies — Hong Kong Bank, Wharf & Godown, the lot.'[60] Alongside valuable collections of stamps and coins, Noel's safe also held solid gold.

This was a defining moment for Noel Croucher. After all the privations and worries, all the expectations of a return to penury, all the chaos on the streets, he was suddenly able to pick up from where he had left off. His way ahead was clear and far, far more rosy than he had dared to hope. How his safe survived is a wonder. Perhaps the characteristic mess of his office led looters to assume the place had already been stripped. Somehow, the lock, though tried, had not failed. His safe was safe.

As for the brandy bottle which had survived the war intact in the chimney, amazingly, it survives to this day. Elizabeth and Allen Mills, friends to Noel in the 1970s in Hong Kong, heard the story of the brandy bottles from Noel at one of those odd dinner parties they enjoyed with Noel in the last years of his life. In the days following Noel's funeral, Elizabeth Mills was talking to Noel's son, Richard Croucher, and she told him the story of the brandy bottles which he had not heard before. The bottle was destined for the dustbin. The upshot was that he passed the bottle on to Mrs Mills, for safe-keeping. The label, still legible, reads: Imperial Brandy 'Grand Armée 1811 Cognac Fine Champagne'. It was the last remnant of the wedding gift from Noel's father-in-law back in 1924.

There was another lucky break for Noel, in that, among his papers which survived the war, was a pile of so-called duress notes. Their existence may be another sign that Noel engaged in some forms of commerce during the Japanese occupation, or maybe he simply bought them off others as soon as the war was over in the belief (or knowledge?) that the notes would be honoured. 'Noel would have known the Bank was bound to honour the duress notes,' says G.O.W. Stewart. 'It had to, to keep its credibility with the Chinese. Arthur Morse [the post-war Bank chairman] told me that even the British Government would have had to honour them. There was a terrific racket with Japanese currency — everybody knew the British would try to stop it — but meanwhile it earned a very high interest.'[61]

When Japan took the colony, the note-issuing banks — Hong Kong & Shanghai Bank and Standard Chartered — had been unable to destroy over HK$100 million worth of notes. A small core of European bankers were kept out of internment to work in the banks where they were supposed to be liquidating the colony's finances. At the Hong Kong & Shanghai Bank, chief manager Sir Vandaleur Grayburn (who came to a tragic end for his smuggling of money into Stanley Camp) led the bankers who first tried to burn, surreptitiously, the stock of unsigned notes.[62] Eventually, they were forced to sign the surviving notes and issue them via the Japanese, that is, under duress. It was by no means certain that these notes would be honoured as legal tender after the war, but happily for Noel and many others, they were.[63] 'People were throwing out their duress notes into a bin on Battery Path — and then the Bank said it would honour them!' remembers Marjorie Bray.[64]

It was at about this time when Noel Croucher was said to be the 'richest white man east of Suez'.[65] Though no doubt an exaggeration, this phrase summed up how far he had come. He was fifty-four and needed a rest, but had unexpected bounty in his hands. After living on watery rice, bugs and rat meat, he was probably gaunt, but he had kept his head down and, if not averse to a trade on the side, had kept his name off the list of scoundrels. And he had stayed alive. He had spent this difficult time — reading at length, occasionally stubborn with the guards — in the belief that the fortune he had made from scratch from his humble beginnings in Hampshire and Hong Kong had long gone.

What kept him on top after the war, when so many established firms and 'old guard' trades failed, was the fact that his safe was safe. How sweet those days must have been, after such privation, hunger and despair, to walk back into town, find a fortune, a remnant of normality, and be able to set to work rebuilding his life.

CHAPTER ELEVEN

POST-WAR PROGRESS

n 1945, a most extraordinary period in Hong Kong's history began. As in the turmoil of the strike and boycott of 1925–26, the community, weakened and shattered as it was by the war, pulled the basics together. Its population was a jumble of dazed, unwell people, most of them without homes, loved ones, or reason to hope. Yet, individuals from the power companies, the transportation and food supply sectors each set to work to get things moving again. Staff at companies before the war reappeared, some with miraculously preserved files of business, others ready to start again from scratch. Friends camped out at each other's places or shared hotel rooms.

Colonialism was in retreat around the world. The United States had tried to persuade Britain to hand Hong Kong back to China — at this time, the Nationalist government. Though the global conflict might have ended, turmoil on the Mainland had yet to reach its peak in the civil war between Nationalist and Communist forces. Within four years, the outcome was decided in favour of the Chinese Communist Party, dislodging most of the few foreign missionaries and traders left in China, along with hundreds of thousands of Chinese seeking a new life. Waves of people were moving to Hong Kong willy-nilly.

'Hong Kong really took off from a base of being the most looted city in the world — there wasn't a piece of wood to be seen in Hong Kong when I got back after the war from Shanghai where I'd been prisoner of war,' recalled the late Lord Lawrence Kadoorie.[1] 'And the whole city was, well, there was one cable across the harbour, there was some light in one or two buildings on this side (Hong Kong-side) and there was some light at the Peninsula Hotel, which was Japanese headquarters. But other than that there wasn't any light at all in the place. And it was black.

Rats all over the place and the complete and utter desolation you might say, on the Peak. There wasn't a single house that was habitable at all. No doors, no windows. People had left their dogs and big dogs had eaten the little dogs and become so wild that they had to get police with guns to shoot these dogs because it was so dangerous.

'And in fact when you look from that ruin it was and how it became one of the most important cities in the world, it's really, it's a miracle. But that was done largely through hard work and I think the fact that Hong Kong didn't wait to say well somebody else must pay for this. We sat down immediately, let's get busy, let's get things going. It is normal here to work hard. It's normal here to take work as something which one is given and should do and wants to do with a view to trying to climb, get higher each time, do something better. This is the point of view of the Hong Kong citizen generally and that was the main element which caused it to grow the way it has grown.'

Naturally, Noel Croucher stayed close to the action. In John Luff's book *Hong Kong Cavalcade*, specific thanks are made to Noel Croucher 'for his assistance and contribution to the chapter, "The Road to Recovery" '.[2] This recounts how Admiral Harcourt steamed into the harbour, took the Japanese surrender, and set up the British Military Administration, planned for two years back in London. Its initial actions and attitude to the local population inspired, according to Luff, new faith in Hong Kong's future. The British leaders, at least, wanted to make it clear that colonialism would be different from now on. The new administration, whatever its colour, offered stability, openness, efficiency and, most of the time, rice. Its mandate extended beyond bare necessities to the encouragement of recreation, mixed audiences at the cinema and frequent dances or parties to which Chinese were invited. (It will be seen that the military also helped Noel Croucher a lot with the yacht club's post-war renaissance.)

Hong Kong was a different town now from what it had been before the war. Members of the new military administration felt it was time for fresh blood to tackle Hong Kong, after the old colonials had had their day. 'The British Mandarinate collapsed in 1941: it has never been replaced,' observed Henry Lethbridge. He noted that Hong Kong's Chinese population had found the so-called 'new order' colonialism of the Japanese occupation to be more racialist, corrupt and arrogant than the British. This did not mean the British were welcomed with open arms by the Chinese after the war, but their focus on getting the city working again was. The experience of the British in the camps — often sharing latrines with one's social inferiors — had broken down many barriers within the community, too.[3]

Between September 1945 and some time in 1946, Noel Croucher took a trip back to England, as did most internees, to rest and recuperate and to be reunited with his family. His son Richard recalls this visit. On 30 April 1946, the civilian Governor, Mark Young, returned to Hong Kong to take up his post which had been left so ignominiously with the onset of war. War crimes trials were held, King's Theatre reopened with a backlog of Hollywood movies to show, and in the Police Force, reforms were instituted to help quash a spate of armed robberies.

If Noel was back in Hong Kong by 9 June 1946, we feel sure he would have attended the Victory Service held at St. John's Cathedral that day. On 13 June, a King's Birthday Parade was held at Happy Valley racetrack. A suspected cholera outbreak sadly deprived the lads of their fun in Wanchai, the red light district. Not until November was the district open to them.

New Year's Eve was uproarious that year. The Jardine's cannon in Causeway Bay boomed out at midnight for the first time since the war, church bells rang, pipers made their way to Gripps and elsewhere about town, and firecrackers exploded all over the place. Perhaps even more stirring to the general populace was the dramatic blasting away of the Japanese war memorial — a vast, ugly and aptly unfinished heap of concrete on Mount Cameron — on 26 February 1947. Luff claimed that the cheers of Chinese and British echoed all the way down the hills to the city of Victoria.

On Friday, 16 May 1947, Governor Mark Young made a farewell broadcast to the people of Hong Kong from the studios of ZBW, the local radio station. In this he referred to the War Memorial Fund, established on 20 February 1947, to assist those bereaved during the battle for Hong Kong and the subsequent occupation. Extracts from the first annual report of the fund in 1947 admitted the public response had been less positive than hoped. Noel Croucher was one of the earlier donors to the fund. On the list of contributions, an entry reports that 'Mr and Mrs Croucher' gave $50.[4]

Once again, Luff persuaded Noel to write down his thoughts, although it appears the published version may not be complete:

> The Military Administration before my return had already given first aid to the Colony. They saw to it that essential electricity supplies, transport and dwellings, albeit patched up, should be available.

Supplies to maintain the necessaries of life were in the meantime distributed. In August 1946, the emergency conditions had receded sufficiently for the owners of private enterprises to start taking over their properties. From then on the Colony was in a ferment of constructional and commercial activity, which has rarely slackened... Looking back, I have come to realise what a romantic story of self reliant enterprise and sheer hard work was packed into that period.[5]

One thing that did not grow immediately after the war was the trade in stocks and shares. The government suspended trading in property, stocks and shares by proclamations on 13 September and 17 November 1945. There were strong practical reasons for this — most firms had lost most if not all of their records, and much of their personnel. Many are the stories of improvisations and bold steps taken by taipans at this time, as they sought to put their companies into working order. Naturally, it would have been hard to trade in these firms so soon.

Noel Croucher, however, did not like to waste time. One of the first of many company meetings he was to attend was that held for shareholders of the South China Morning Post, on 19 September 1945.[6] As with so many of the premier companies in post-war Hong Kong, Noel could claim a part in the corporate history of the *Post* newspaper. 'There was a block of shares floating around,' before the war, remembered Guy Sayer, formerly of the Hong Kong & Shanghai Bank. 'And rather than let them get into the wrong hands — politically, it was important that newspapers were in safe hands — I think he took it on. Noel was often involved in things like that. Any big share transaction in Hong Kong, Croucher would have been involved.'[7]

Unfortunately, the legendary, big red Ledger, in which Noel recorded all his share and other transactions, has not survived. Visitors to Noel's office in earlier years remember how often a deal would be seen to be concluded only when Noel called out to his staff, 'Bring me the Ledger!', and the names and numbers would be carefully written in. Also lost are the butter ration coupons he kept after the war, according to his office boy Wong Yue-nam: 'Every Friday after the war we went to Dairy Farm with the blue ration book for a pound of butter.'[8]

Noel's first priority after the war was to stay in Hong Kong and help restore its institutions — the companies, the clubs, the stock exchange. He was probably in poor health following internment, but he was not at all short of the powers of decision.

Simultaneously, Noel Croucher was active on several different fronts.

At the same time as he was crucially involved in the Royal Hong Kong Yacht Club, he chaired the newly reunited Hong Kong Stock Exchange. At the same time as he pursued particular corporate goals (such as at the Gas Company), he began to argue with his friends and colleagues. And at the same time as he gained a reputation as a tight-fisted eccentric, he began to express his concern for the poor and disadvantaged.

Integrating all these elements into one man is not easy. Indeed, most people who knew Croucher after the war reached the easier conclusion, that he was simply a money-driven mogul. No attempt is made here to transform Noel into a better or worse person than he was. Yet by tracking the evidence of Noel's actions, on all fronts, a more rounded picture of the man can be achieved.

One of Noel's first acts after the war was to send a note to his sailing friends, on 20 September 1945, calling a meeting together in the offices of the South China Morning Post, then on Wyndham Street, Central, to discuss the future of the Royal Hong Kong Yacht Club. On 17 September 1945, when Japan formally surrendered, the club had been reopened by officers and men from HMS *Vengeance*. Noel's meeting was just four days later. (As the newspaper offices had been in use throughout the war, producing a propaganda organ, *The Hong Kong News*, under Japanese management, it was presumably one of the few buildings in usable condition straight after the war.)

'The situation was not good... The Club was heavily in debt to the Hong Kong and Shanghai Banking Corporation for the loan it had secured to build the Kellett Island premises before the War and its only liquid assets were the Members' November 1941 bar chits. These had been zealously guarded by Ah Mow, the Clubmaster. ...There were no yachts either, most of them having been sunk by the Japanese or broken up for firewood and for their lead keels and metal fittings which fetched premium prices during wartime. The few that did survive ... had been hauled ashore by their owners during the fighting in Hong Kong and laid up within the compounds of companies such as Hong Kong & Whampoa Dock Company, Hong Kong Electric and at Mackies Wharf. Boat boys had tried to protect their owners' yachts for as long as possible, but most eventually had been forced to flee...'[9]

It was decided that the armed services would use the club for recreational purposes, thus involving the Royal Navy in the restoration of the club premises. Plumbing was reconnected and the building cleaned enough to allow for its formal opening as a recreational club for officers on 2 October 1945. But the staircases were non-existent, the ballroom had no floor, and electricity and telephones were still a dream. Noel Croucher agreed to become Vice Commodore, so that the United Services Hong Kong Yacht Club could be formed with Commodore (later Admiral) Everett from the navy in charge. The first race was held on 10 March 1946, with races scheduled for Wednesday, Saturday and Sunday every week. Meanwhile, Noel continued to hold meetings of members of the original Royal Hong Kong Yacht Club, back in his own office in town.

He also took a direct hand in restoring some of the 'fittings' of his favourite club: 'In 1945 at the end of the Occupation, all existing trophies, along with everything else in the Club, were looted. Many of them ended up in the "antique" shops of Cat Street, but they were saved by Noel Croucher who scoured the shops and bought them back.

' "He bought all the silver cups that were available and put them back in the showcases in the bar," explained Gordon Dewar who joined the Yacht Club soon after the war. However, not all the trophies that he found were Yacht Club ones, so the names of their former owners were "sweated off" and a Yacht Club inscription added. "For years afterwards, members of other clubs visiting the Yacht Club would look at certain trophies and say, 'we used to have a cup like that'," added Gordon.'[10]

Step by step, the club members meeting in Noel's office were able to restore control and on 12 December 1946, Noel Croucher told an Extraordinary General Meeting of his gratitude for the Navy's great help and hard work in reviving the club. Noel's message, though similar, carried a sting in its tail, at the fortieth Annual General Meeting of the club, held on 26 September 1947:

> I should like to pay tribute to all those individual members who have during the past year assisted in the restoration or maintenance of the Club's facilities... I regret to report that never in the history of our Club has our financial position been so serious.[11]

The club counted itself lucky to have someone like Noel in charge at such a time. He knew how to handle money. 'Noel was the money-bags, he had the contacts, so he went round all the companies for help,' recalls Richard Hownam-Meek. 'I know he knew Victor Sassoon well and Sassoon was through Hong Kong sometime in those years. Noel was wooing him hard to get him to help fund the yacht club. Whenever we ran into problems on the committee, Noel would say, "Leave it to me," and it would be fixed.'[12]

'I had been a member since 1938, and resumed my membership after the war,' recalls Gerald Carey. 'We had to restore the Club, it was all in pieces. Noel contributed a lot and was very generous. He was the one person to whom all financial matters were left. And if you held any shares, he would advise you.'[13]

The club's debt to the Bank was $200,000, and, in 1948, a Rehabilitation Fund was set up which raised $100,000 in four months. The colony's leading firms and individuals were donors, including Noel Croucher. Also in 1948, Noel offered to finance the building of ten small yachts, costing $2,200 each. Amid the monthly dances, weekly club nights and special events, the yacht club became a social hub to a society just coming out of war and deprivation. It was not only a place for keen sailors, but where good times were had by all.

In these first few years after the war, Noel's private life was confused. His wife, Simonne, had returned to Hong Kong after the war, but in the course of these years, Noel and Simonne realised the relationship could not work. They probably had to wait for their old home in the P & O Building to be repaired, and so stayed at the Repulse Bay Hotel during at least part of this period. Apart from the arguments, another friend recalls that Noel bought a house in Repulse Bay after the war which he had intended to be for Simonne, but she did not want it. She left Hong Kong for good, in about 1948.[14]

With the war and its concomitant puncture to the notion of white supremacy, a new era was under way in Hong Kong. What role could the British play on an island off the coast of China in a new era of decolonisation and radical political change, when a post-war fervour for self-determination was sweeping across Asia? Governor Mark Young had thought the answer lay in democratic reforms. But his vision was overtaken by events, namely the unending stream of people pouring into Hong Kong from a China at war. On 16 October 1949, troops of the People's Liberation Army massed on the border with Hong Kong, but came no further.

China became involved in the Korean War, 1950–53, on the side of North Korea, and sent its own troops in 1951. Then the West led by a newly powerful United States of America gave full rein to its anti-communist obsession. One result was the United Nations embargo on trade with China. Once again, Hong Kong's viability was brought into question. After all, this place survived on its role as entrepôt to the Middle Kingdom. What could it do, when the Kingdom was now a People's Republic and entrepôt servicing was not allowed?

The response from Hong Kong was exciting. Smuggling along the land and sea borders was easy, but more fundamental change was on its way. Never mind all the grand ideas of legislative reform and the like — need and greed were the order of the day. Sheer necessity, exacerbated daily by the flow of refugees, forced Hong Kong into a new economic identity — that of manufacturer and exporter of its own products, rather than mere re-exporter of China's bounty. This was an entirely new approach. Political power was not in the hands of Hong Kong people, but the power of life and death was. Competition was fierce and desperate, the hours long and the pay low. Some industrialisation had existed before the war — witness Green Island Cement, for example — but the post-war frenzy was almost an industrial revolution, telescoped into a few short years. As with refugee populations anywhere, the drive is to survive, get rich and move on. Thus, modern Hong Kong was born.

'Life in Hong Kong had a feverish beat to it. Three million Chinese fighting to keep alive and grow rich in a no-holds-barred, laissez-faire jungle of energy and tumult. The purposeful crowds in the street, seen from the fifth-floor hotel window, were not like ants or any herds of animals; they were thousands of individuals, fiercely pursuing their private destinies.

'Passing among those crowds you looked into the face of a human nature as amorally predatory as praying mantises or the sharks waiting off the islands. Here the Cantonese merchant, the well-tailored Shanghai speculator and the British banker looked each other over and approved what they saw. Hong Kong was a place where a shrewd man might make a staggeringly large amount of money — and legally, too.'[15]

Noel Croucher had no trouble with Hong Kong's new identity. Such an atmosphere of ambition, drive and desperation brought out the best in him. He was now well established, an old hand, well ahead of the newcomers.

Despite the government's suspension of trading in stocks and shares, unofficial trading continued. Trade was so brisk in 1946 that the brokers had their hands full, and talks began on the desirability of combining the two pre-war exchanges, the Hong Kong Stock Exchange and the Hong Kong Share Brokers' Association. 'Government have imposed a number of restrictions which are observed by all share brokers but not completely conformed with by black market operators and a considerable number of the speculating public,' wrote the recently established journal, the *Far Eastern Economic Review*.[16]

A week later, the business community's impatience was obvious: 'Business has in fact assumed such large proportions that local brokers have their hands full and anxiously wait for the return of the recuperating or otherwise still marooned brokers. The Moratorium imposed by the Government is having increasingly less effect on share business and those interested to sell or buy shares are practically ignoring the Ordinance. It seems really absurd for the government to expect two willing persons who wish to exchange shares to obtain first of all government permission to do so. Some of the more conscientious still comply religiously with these business stifling regulations, however, the majority has become quite impatient with the unreasonable government delay. One hears among the public interested in share business some very spicy comment.'[17]

Lifting the moratorium and merging the exchanges took longer than expected. The new body, with an old name, the Hong Kong Stock Exchange, opened at last on 1 March 1947. Its chairman was none other than Noel Croucher. The moratorium on share trading was lifted only gradually, company by company, starting with the shares of the Hong Kong & Shanghai Banking Corporation on 24 June 1947. By the end of November 1948, it was finally and formally removed.

How could Noel Croucher achieve such prominence? He was now fifty-six years old and had been in Hong Kong for forty years. He was an old-timer who, unlike many friends and colleagues, was in decent health, financially and physically. And of course, he knew his fellow brokers well. The committee of the new exchange included Gilbert Harriman, P.M.N. da Silva, Choa Po-min, Ezra Abrahim, Alec Potts, J.F. Grose, Soo Pui-chen, R.A. Dastur, and C.A.L. Rickett. The broader membership included many more old friends of Noel's. Here was J.T. Bagram (nephew to Sir Paul Chater), along with the names Abraham, Ellis, Edgar, and Ellis Hayim. Horace Lo, K.B. Lee, Li Shui-pang and Francis Zimmern were there too, all from the pre-war Hong Kong Stock Exchange.[18]

From the pre-war Hong Kong Share Brokers' Association came several more names well known to Noel Croucher — A.R. Botelho, M.A. Carvalho, Lo Kin-fai, Ko Tai-tim, and Mok Ying-kie. Significantly, a leading light of the Hong Kong Share Brokers' Association was C.C. (Cyril) Blake — the man whose name first appeared on Noel Croucher's company books as able to 'sign per pro', back in 1934.[19]

The post-war Hong Kong Stock Exchange issued quotations at noon and at 3.30 p.m., Mondays to Fridays, except on Wednesdays when only the noon prices were issued, leaving Noel free to go sailing instead, if he wished. All business was conducted on a cash basis, deliveries of stocks and shares being made on the day after a deal was reached.

Francis Zimmern reminisced for the stock exchange's history: 'Clients tended to invest and hold their shares rather than speculate. However, many of the clients were directors of various companies and had no compunction about dealing in their own shares, which could be called insider trading nowadays... Brokers later on were also sometimes required to act as jobbers in order to maintain a relationship with a client by taking a position. If a client said sell 10,000 and there were only buyers for 7,500, the broker would take 2,500 himself. There were no disclosure rules, so it was possible to establish a corner in a particular share.'[20]

Little had changed since the days when Robert Shewan, George Potts and others stood accused of making a 'Corner in Ropes', except that now, trading was done according to a Board System. Exchange members would mark up on the Main Board the price at which they were prepared to buy or sell one board lot of a particular stock. Bids or offers had to be in Board Lots which varied from company to company. For example, a Board Lot of Hong Kong & Shanghai Bank shares numbered ten shares, whereas the same Board Lot for a company such as Amalgamated Rubbers was five thousand shares.[21] Having marked up a price on the Main Board, a member had to buy or sell a Board Lot to anyone in the trading hall at the price he had marked. All trading, except for Special or Odd Lots, was conducted via the Main Board, not in private.

'The Hong Kong Stock Exchange Ltd. is playing a larger part than ever in financing new ventures, and interest in its activities has considerably widened within recent years as a result of the introduction of the Board Trading System by which every deal concluded on the floor is governed by strict rules, and recorded in the closing quotations for the day.'[22]

Not everyone saw the new exchange as the seat of probity. Not for another quarter of a century would thought be given to such finer points as a take-over code, enforceable laws on insider trading and the like. A senior civil servant from that time, who prefers to remain nameless, recalls: 'I always regarded it myself as a private gambling club.' It was not always a very friendly club either. Some recollections are of a social and relaxed atmosphere on the trading floor, with brandy and cigars, dice games and Chinese chess, when trading was light.[23] But deep animosities flourished in the competition for gain, possibly explaining why some leading brokers to this day would rather not talk or think about Noel Croucher. 'A lot of brokers won't speak to each other,' notes Lord Michael Sandberg.[24]

Noel did not need to dabble every day at the exchange. 'Croucher was *above* floor trading — he had institutional business and was already a multi-millionaire, and he was busy with overseas clients,' recalls Frederic A. Silva. 'Noel believed in the Canadian and Australian markets, and I think he was huge in them. He worked in Hong Kong with Cyril C.C. Blake. And he wrote all these letters to the newspaper, signed "Little Man", "Disgruntled Investor", "Irate" and so on. He was attacking this or that director. He saw real monkey business, or injustices, and thought what was being done was wrong. And he said so.

'I don't know how exactly he made his money — probably a matter of "Buy Right, Sit Tight".'[25]

Jealousy of Noel Croucher's success and growing eminence provoked the usual complaints of dishonesty or meanness. But such judgements can be too simplistic. 'I have no knowledge of any dishonesty,' says Allen Mills, Deputy Commissioner for Securities in Hong Kong in the 1970s. 'I think he was the sort of person who could be relied on to look after you, the client. It's like the old world at Lloyds a decade ago where he was the sort of person who would make sure that in the end you came out alright if you were his client. You see, that's what his job was. I mean he was really dealing on the stock exchange to advantage. And it's like the way Lloyds used to operate. If something went wrong, you made sure you got a profit.'[26]

'What was good for Noel Croucher was good for the Stock Exchange. What was good for the Stock Exchange was good for Noel Croucher.' That's the judgement from fellow broker Francis Zimmern, neatly encapsulating the ambivalence that surrounds brokers to this day.[27] Noel had many of the right friends. He was respected at the Hong Kong Bank, and some say his long and close friendships with men in firms such as Peat Marwick & Mitchell were part of his success. He had very good sources of information somewhere.

Popular investments after the war included South African gold shares, 'until this Mandela came into the picture', commented one broker. In addition, Noel 'had some bonds, Japanese war bonds I think, they went sky high! Gold shares went very well. And he made sterling go around the world in the "switch sterling" business,' recalled Francis Zimmern.

'If you bought foreign shares in London you had to pay for them with a special sterling,' explains a former Hong Kong Bank manager,

George Stewart. 'So if one lived in London one would be paying an extra premium, while if you knew someone who lived in New York, say [or Hong Kong], one could call him and buy the shares there. But one was not supposed to do this of course.'[28]

One way around the post-war exchange controls was to move the sterling to the British colony of Hong Kong where Noel Croucher and others could invest it on one's behalf in Hong Kong shares. The shares could then be sold and the proceeds moved into other currencies. Opinion is split on whether this was strictly legal: 'It was a bit of a fiddle, let's say,' says Zimmern. 'But he was not a speculator, he was very prudent.' Hong Kong had long tolerated black markets, and was a recognised 'back door' to help out people in England. Croucher's assistant in later years remembers that 'Noel got a lot of business from these people [in Britain].' She adds: 'If there was ever any blank paper in front of Mr Croucher, he would get a pen and start doodling dollar signs.'[29]

G.O.W. Stewart, chief accountant at Hong Kong Bank after the war, remembers how useful Noel Croucher was to the bank. 'About the Telephone company — the Bank had agreed to float a one-for-one [share issue] to raise money. But no one bought into it because it was straight after the war. So I got hold of Noel and we went somewhere quiet. I said, we want to sell these shares, but we want to disguise for as long as possible the fact that it's the Bank that's selling.

'Noel said, "No problem, I'll send Mrs Ferguson over." And she would come in to my office, collect the shares and I would credit the right accounts. We got rid of quite a lot that way. I used Noel because we got a better deal with him. If I had confided in some of the other brokers — they would have blabbed it all over town. But not Noel.'

Noel was still a director of China Provident Loan & Mortgage Company, one of the companies singled out by reports at the time as a most popular buy for investors. Its premises at West Point featured godowns with a storage capacity of 160,000 tons, and plans were afoot for a modern pier. Its subsidiary, the North Point Wharves Company Limited formed in 1948, possessed the only commercial deep-water berths available to shipping on the island of Hong Kong.

The blue-chip companies of Hong Kong were almost all able to recover war losses from their reserves. As before the war, Noel's interests were in the docks, premier insurance firms, utilities and land. Not everything he touched turned to gold: 'Croucher lost a lot of money on Philippine shares. He had been very keen on the Philippines before World War II. But after the war, the shares all crashed... He said that before the war, Manila was a very modern city. But everything went bad,' recalled Noel Croucher's assistant Florence Lo.[30]

Noel chose this moment to establish another firm of his own, Commonwealth Investments Limited. Company registration records show it was formed in 1948, with N.V.A. Croucher as the chairman and it was not dissolved until after his death. This became the repository for a large part of Noel's wealth which he held in currencies such as Australian and Canadian dollars, Japanese yen, French francs and Dutch guilders. They included earnings from current accounts and fixed deposits and the dividends from a wide range of shareholdings, as well as holdings with the Hong Kong and Shanghai Bank Trustee Company.

Through Commonwealth Investments, we can see Noel's interests in the Canadian Pacific Railways, Comp. Generale D'Electricite, Nomura Securities, Mitsubishi Corporation, and Teijin Limited. Holdings in Hong Kong firms included shares in Sun Hung Kai Properties Limited, Swire Pacific, Sime Darby, Inchcape, Atlantic Richfield, ITT Corporation, Philip Morris, and Coca Cola Limited. Bond (Allied Lyons), Thorn EMI, Warner Lambert, Knight Ridder and Pacific Dunlop were also featured. Funds from a variety of banks were also held by Commonwealth Investments — the Bank of Montreal, Westpac, Lloyds, Midland, Mees & Hope N.V., and Trinkaus & Burkhardt.[31]

Noel Croucher employed Peat Marwick and Wardley Investment Services, alongside the Hong Kong & Shanghai Bank Trustee Company for most of these transactions and arrangements. And there is a note about the liquidation of an investment in Vanuatu. The papers were drawn up by premier Hong Kong law firm Johnson, Stokes and Master, and the only other shareholder of Commonwealth Investments was JSM's senior partner, Maurice Watson.

The company address was the Chartered Bank Building, and Noel's home was listed as 6 Macdonnell Road, a property he owned for many years. By all accounts, Noel moved his residence around in these years. He had been staying at the Repulse Bay Hotel, and in 1950–51, Joyce Symons recalls Noel calling up her great-uncle — a shipping broker and old friend of Noel's — Eddie H. Ray. According to her account, Noel had called up Eddie and said that Eddie was lonely! So Noel moved in, and stayed for months.[32]

Industrialisation spread in Hong Kong, helped by Shanghai emigrants in the textile business,[33] but at this time the stock exchange had little to do with it. Chinese investors raised funds from their families and banks, not the exchange. 'No attempt seems to have been made by the Stock

Exchange to attract any of this liquidity into new capital formation and trading on the stock market remained the province of the very wealthy... The market remained vulnerable to manipulation by a few major players.'[34] This was the old boys' club so often decried by those not in it. Noel was not only on the inside, but in charge.

A new man in town was to become, alongside Noel, one of the biggest players on this merry-go-round. George Marden, founder and chairman of Wheelock Marden & Company, was tough, if not ruthless, and already a legendary figure in Shanghai. Here was a man just as successful, ambitious, even abrasive, as Noel himself, a self-made man of foresight and drive. George Marden had worked in the Imperial Maritime Customs service in Canton and Shanghai, and was a fighter pilot during World War I. He established his own business in Shanghai before the war, but saw the writing on the wall and moved everything to Hong Kong just ahead of the communist advance.

At first, he and Noel shared coffee every morning, discussing the day's potential for fun and gains. These two men were so similar in many ways that they would inevitably be close friends or firm enemies. In fact, they became both.[35]

'George Marden walked into the bank one day, and saw my predecessor Arthur Morse,' recalls former Bank chairman Guy Sayer. 'Morse was desperate to lend money. Nobody wanted it! So Marden did well and bought up Shewan Tomes, Hutchison's, and more. And one of the companies he had a huge interest in was Hong Kong Gas, and of course Croucher himself had a big interest in it too.'[36]

Despite the fact that it had been been supplying gas to the colony since 1864, and despite its name, the Hong Kong and China Gas Company was based in and managed wholly from England. This waste of potential profit in Hong Kong was not to be borne, so in 1949 George Marden and Noel Croucher got together to hatch a plot to fix the gas company.

In a letter circulated to all shareholders, they proposed that the head office, and effective control, of the company be transferred from London to Hong Kong. Not only were the tax advantages obvious and the benefits to Hong Kong-based shareholders clear, but the climate in post-war Britain where utilities were in the habit of becoming nationalised, made the proposal urgent. The vehicles through which Marden and Croucher made their proposal were Wheelock Marden and Noel Croucher's Commonwealth Investments. A public company and Marden subsidiary called Allied Investors was formed, but the respective holdings of Croucher and Marden in this are unclear.

In 1954, majority control of the gas company was purchased by Wheelock Marden, which took over its management. 'Wheelocks in London had been buying [shares in the gas company] or Marden himself,' remembers Edward Lawrence of the gas company.[37] Perhaps this was when Noel got angry — had George undercut him via the London market? George Marden's son, John, recalled, 'We had the idea of selling the Gas Company's works at West Point and concentrating production in Kowloon, with a pipeline under the harbour connecting the island and mainland, and this is eventually what happened. My father felt that we could do this by buying up a certain percentage of shares of this UK-registered company, and by a change of directors.'[38]

In 1954, George Marden reported to the annual meeting of Wheelock Marden & Company that Allied Investors Corporation Ltd. had been floated successfully, 'in association with ourselves and our friends, Commonwealth Investment Ltd. for the purchase of a controlling interest in the Company supplying gas to the Colony.'[39] At the end of 1956, he said: 'Allied Investors has again operated on a subdued note, there having been no change in the position regarding their holdings in Hongkong & China Gas Co., Ltd. Together with our own holdings they constitute 55% of the Company's issued capital. We are considering a course of action designed to overcome the unfortunate impasse...'[40]

The pipeline and other modernisations were begun in the late 1950s, but the gas company's shares were not put on to the Hong Kong market until 1960. Not everyone was happy with the idea — many acrimonious board meetings took place with tension rife between the 'London group' and Hong Kong investors. 'I'd only just joined the firm, in Hong Kong, but was classified as a London boy, and so at first I was treated with a lot of suspicion,' said George Cam, of his start with the gas company in 1953.[41] 'There were lots of meetings of shareholders which the public were not allowed into, a lot of squabbles,' says Peter Vine.[42] George Marden brought in F.C. Clemo who had been with China Light and Power before the war, to pursue the Marden-Croucher goals at the gas company. George Cam worked mainly with John Marden and Douglas Clague. Other new board members included Li Fook-shu and R.C. 'Dick' Lee, the son of Lee Hysan.

Significantly, Noel Croucher was not on the board of the newly Hong

Kong-managed company. 'Noel was hurt that George did not bring Noel onto the board,' says Edward Lawrence. And the sequel was soon well known all over town — George Marden and Noel Croucher had a virulent falling-out.

Hong Kong was so small — everyone knew of the 'state of permanent animosity, punctuated by brief but violent verbal assaults... After one of these outbursts, Marden was said to have suggested that he and Croucher walk arm in arm down Ice House Street as this would start a rumour which could add a few points to the counters in which they were both known to have substantial positions.'[43]

'They had their fights and their arguments, but it was between the two of them. I was a friend of both,' recalled R.C. Lee.[44] Some suggest it was a natural spat between two powerful personalities in a split over the spoils of their joint idea.[45] Or perhaps the fact that Marden bought up the post-war Shewan, Tomes & Co. annoyed Noel as an intrusion on his old stamping ground.

The precise genesis of an argument on the scale of this one is hard to track. According to Anne and John Marden, the real story was more complex, and requires the introduction of the Royal Society Saint George to this narrative.

St. George societies were formed in the American colonies from the 1700s, as a support network for old colonialists, and a Hong Kong version was active from about the 1860s. At the turn of the century, the Royal Society of St. George was organised from London, which pre-existing groups then joined. It remains a grouping of English people dedicated to the ideal of preserving and enjoying their Englishness.[46] The St. Andrew's Society does the same thing for the Scots and the two societies vie for primacy over a certain social scene, at least in Hong Kong. Competition for precedence is fierce, not least because it was the Scots who actually built Hong Kong but it was the English who claimed to run it. Each holds an annual ball, with great fanfare, and depending on the membership at any one time, the societies also pursue charitable goals. A dearth of records leaves us unable to say when exactly Noel Croucher joined the Royal Society of St. George, but he was certainly an active member in the 1950s. So, too, was George Marden.

There came a time in the 1950s — and it is impossible to say whether this was a cause or a result of the friction at the gas company — when George Marden was about to be made president of the Royal Society of St. George. No one had any problem with the idea, except Noel, although everyone knew Noel wanted to be president, too. George Marden was widely admired, generous with money and time. There was no doubt he was qualified to lead this select cabal. And then Noel piped up — either through envy, or malice, or sheer bull-headedness. His point was outrageous: he said George Marden was not English, and so could not possibly become president of an English persons' group.

Technically, Noel might have thought he had an argument. The Marden name was first acquired as a replacement for the real family name of Gumprecht. Indeed, the Marden family is of German stock in this sense, a nasty thought just after World War II. But Noel's mistake seems almost naive. Few men were more dashing than George Marden, a man of standing in Hong Kong backed by his unquestioned pre-war status in Shanghai, who had risked his life fighting for England. There may be a longer history of Crouchers on English soil than of Gumprechts, but Noel made only himself look ridiculous. The Mardens were as German as the Windsors in Buckingham Palace, and there was little to stop people assuming Noel had an attack of something as simple as sour grapes.

George Marden's grandfather, Louis Gumprecht, went to England from Hanover in 1864 and married an Elizabeth Marden. Subsequent generations kept the Marden name, while also fighting and dying for England. 'My father got an MC fighting the Germans in World War I. And Noel had the cheek to say George was not English!' says John Marden.[47] Some saw a great deal of cachet attached to being president of the St. George Society — the balls were the biggest social events of the year. George Marden liked to organise pre-ball practices of the English dances, the Sir Roger de Coverley and the Lancers, which were almost as much fun as the ball itself. 'I suppose that was something that Noel could never have done and perhaps he did feel that he wanted to get his own back somehow.'[48]

Naturally, to be an office-bearer in the society was a good thing for an aspiring Englishman. Best of all was to become the society president for a year, able to wear the fancy medallion, to host the dinners and patronise the balls. Some members would say that attaining this social pre-eminence required wealth — all those lunches do not come cheap — but it required more than that, too. It took a certain something to make it in this circle.[49]

'I didn't like Noel particularly but he was a feature of life,' admits John Marden. 'He was reluctant to pay for a round of drinks. Basically he was honest. He was very determined in whatever he was doing.'

George Marden swept on to become president of the society. Noel Croucher was long a committee member, but he never became president.

'You would see [from the now destroyed archive] that the long-standing members wouldn't vote for Noel,' reports society member Michael Rawlinson. 'And yet he was a very generous soul. He had 7,000 shares in Hong Kong Electric and he put them down and said, that's for the society.'[50]

The society had then, and still has today, a mission to send down-and-out English people back home. Their actions carry a reminder of the earlier colonials' goal to sweep away any sign of white trash. Drunk and disorderly Englishmen were fine in the bowels of the clubs, but the destitute were 'letting the side down in front of the natives'.[51] By the mid-1990s, as Hong Kong was soon to cease being a colony and to revert to China, the society was 'gearing up to deal with a stream of the destitute and the desperate — old, unemployed and even young English men and women... And the situation after 1997 could be worse, with the society offering to be a knight in shining armour for English people facing the ignominy of deportation,' according to a local newspaper report.[52]

Noel Croucher participated actively in this welfare work of the society. Unbeknownst to most people around at the time, Noel already gave money personally to deserving individuals, or to help those who had fallen by the wayside, to leave with dignity. The practice of the St. George Society was thus an extension of what Noel already believed in. And as will soon become clear, this was just one of several major commitments Noel was to make to Hong Kong.

'Yes, now I think I shouldn't really say the name, but there was a chap who was, well, very high status in Hong Kong, who would have normally been in a private ward. He had fallen on hard times and was ill and had to go to hospital. I was the executrix of the will, so I knew he was very ill. We expected to hear of his death at any time,' remembers Pat Loseby, the lawyer and avid sailor whom Noel knew well. 'Then I heard of his death and I said, well I'll pay the hospital bill, as there was very little money and we had to keep that for the wife.

'The matron said to me, don't worry about the bill, it's already been paid, it's already been dealt with. By who? I said. She said I can't tell you. But I strongly suspect it was Noel who thought, surely with this man, whose status in Hong Kong was acknowledged, it was sad to see him in the common room. I'm sure he should be in a ward of his own to die in peace. I've always thought it was Noel who had done it — paid all the expenses, medical expenses and everything else and for help for the children. So that was one of the things and he turned up at the funeral and we managed to sort out the affairs so they had enough money to go home to England and tidy up.'[53]

Despite the gaucherie of Noel's quarrel with Marden, Noel went on to become one of the largest benefactors to the Royal Society of St. George. A trust fund in his name exists to this day, worth several million dollars, now called the Noel Croucher Shakespeare Fund with the Noel Croucher Scholarships, but first known as the Shakespeare Quater-Centenary Prize Fund.[54]

'Noel was keen on promoting the English language. The money he gave was to encourage the use of English language. But it's restricted, so we've had problems when students say they want to study Shakespeare and then they switch to engineering or something. But these are problems we're happy to have. Noel can take the credit for making us focus on charity.'[55]

The profound falling-out between Noel and a former friend was an early sign of the unhappiness ahead.

Here were all the essential conflicts in his character — his financial astuteness and good ideas, his little-known charitable instincts, his weakness on subjects of identity and standing. Certainly Noel was keen to establish his own English heritage and bona fides. Perhaps he resented his inability to rise to the top of everything he did. Seen here too is Noel's difficulty in keeping good friends, an aspect of his personality which was to lead to greater loneliness.

He achieved prominence through his position as Commodore of the Royal Hong Kong Yacht Club, but created a social disaster at the Royal Society of St. George. He was pivotal in the restoration of the stock exchange after the war, and was its chairman, at the same time as he alienated profoundly the old hongs and the business establishment. He was at the peak of wealth and influence in financial circles, but played no political or civic role.

From this time on, he enjoyed the company and counsel of a few key women friends. Yet, he became increasingly lonely and was reputed to seek more fleeting pleasures, in Macao and elsewhere. He also began to visit England occasionally, for the first time in decades, looking around for a home. But he never found one, and was to become increasingly estranged from his family and homeland.

There were to be many tangible causes of his increasing personal sense of disappointment over the years to come, but in the post-war era it also became obvious that even being immensely rich and smart was not going to propel Noel Croucher to the top of Hong Kong society.

THE QUEST OF NOEL CROUCHER

'He must have felt his position in society very much, because he was from nowhere,' comments Guy Sayer.[56] Noel was not the sort of man to play up to social snobs, and real divisions continued to exist in Hong Kong even after the war that was thought to have changed everything. This man of strong character, stubborn and determined, could not help but buck the establishment, even when his wealth might have granted him easy entry to it.

CHAPTER TWELVE

FIFTIES FUN

longside his busy working life, Noel kept up a steady stream of other activities, most notably on the ocean wave. In 1948, his long associations with Macao and with sailing bore interesting fruit following a trip he took there with his long-standing friend F. Stanley Coote, divisional manager for the Far East at Cable & Wireless. Coote was then Vice Commodore at the Royal Hong Kong Yacht Club, and, along with Mr and Mrs Drummond, formed a party with Noel aboard *La Cigale* to Macao.[1]

The trip — the first such excursion since the war — warranted almost full-page coverage in the *Noticias de Macao*, with a sketch of Noel's yacht included. Yachtsmen in Macao were trying to form their own club at the time and such inspiration from their brothers in Hong Kong was lapped up eagerly. *La Cigale* was escorted into the inner harbour and berthed overnight. 'We sincerely hope that the visits to Macao by the Hong Kong yachtsmen may become more frequent in the future and trust that Macao will have its nucleus of yachtsmen adequately trained for the purpose of interport racing,' enthused the *Noticias de Macao*.[2]

One of the trophies Noel recovered from Cat Street soon after the war became the RHKYC *La Cigale* Trophy, named after Noel's famous yacht and first presented by him in 1948 for the Macao race. *La Cigale* was the scratch boat, as it was the fastest. 'But he had a great knack of getting becalmed in front of Queen Mary Hospital. He did it time and time again,' says Hownam-Meek.[3]

Noel offered the *La Cigale* Cup to whoever won the Macao race, now back on the sailing calendar, starting on Boxing Day, 1948. This was the race Noel first won, in 1924, and almost disappeared on in 1932, so it was only fitting.

Unfortunately he did not manage to win his own trophy: 'Eight yachts crossed the line at 0700 hours on Boxing Day with *La Cigale* first boat home, 13 hours, 57 minutes later. However, she was beaten on corrected time by *Diana*... The race was so popular that another one was held at Chinese New Year with a weekend stopover in Macao where over 90 participants enjoyed the hospitality of the new Club Nautico de Macao...'[4] Bill Hancock recalls that Noel had a navigator from the Royal Navy. Noel was in the lead and doing well, but the navigator took him on the wrong side of the breakwater, so Noel could not finish!

The Hong Kong and Macao yacht clubs have been firm friends ever since. Non-sailing members travel to Macao by ferry to be part of the fun. 'On arrival in Macao, they would install themselves in the Riviero, Pousada or Bella Vista hotels and when they were not sailing, they would party.'[5] The Riviero Hotel was formerly the Macao Hotel where fifteen-year-old Noel had worked as a clerk.

These were stirring times for sailors in waters between the cosmopolitan cities of Macao and Hong Kong, and the newly communist People's Republic of China. 'I remember being out sailing with Noel in *La Cigale*, one day in 1949,' says Bill Hancock. 'We were on the western approach to Hong Kong, between Lantau and Cheung Chau [islands]. And we saw lots of what looked like barges, or converted junks, coming along. There were lots of soldiers crouched in the holds, shivering and starving. They were KMT [Nationalist] soldiers fleeing China after their officers had deserted them.'[6] Betty Boyle and Bill Hancock were both tenants of flats in the yacht club and, one thing having led to another, were the first to hold their wedding reception there in 1952. The friendship between the two men was to result in Bill naming Noel as the godfather to his son Peter, born in 1958.

Yacht club races, parties, picnics and meetings followed each other throughout the years. In 1950 a Centenary Regatta Ball, held on 25 November, heard the announcement by Noel Croucher that His Majesty King George VI had agreed to confer his patronage on the club. As Commodore, Noel had sent the request to London: 'His subjects both in the Services and among the civilian population who are members of the Club would deem it a most signal recognition of their loyalty and devotion to the Crown, which would be particularly appropriate at a time when the Colony feels itself very much on the periphery of the Empire.'[7] On announcing the honour, Noel said he and other club members were 'infused with new pride which will help us to foster that tradition of the sea which has helped to make our people what we are today.'

By this time, Noel Croucher had been Commodore of his favourite club for ten years, and it was time to hand over the reins, which he did that November to his close friend, Stanley Coote. Noel was the longest-serving Commodore in the club's history, and was made a Vice-Patron of the club.

'I have no hesitation in saying that without your wise hand at the helm in the last five post-war years we should not have been fit recipients for that great honour which has been bestowed on us and whose [royal] grant was almost solely due to your efforts,' said A. Drummond, one of Noel's sailing mates on his 1948 trip to Macao, and the speaker of a special resolution of thanks and confidence to Noel. 'Of you, Sir, it can truly be said on Kellett Island, "If you seek his memorial, look around you." '8

There were more accolades to come for Noel, for in 1953, he personally bailed out the club, with a $50,000 loan. So much drinking, eating and sailing had been going on at the club that it was able to contemplate finally ridding itself of the remaining overdraft of about $100,000 at the Hong Kong Bank.

In February 1953, after various discussions with the bank led by Noel, 'the matter had been resolved thanks to the generous terms agreed between Noel Croucher and the Chief Manager of the Bank, Sir Arthur Morse, whereby Croucher would settle the overdraft for an undisclosed sum and make a loan to the club of $50,000 to pay off the balance.'

The honorary treasurer (and Pat Loseby's cousin), Paul Chidell, spoke for the whole club: 'I must just say how very grateful we all are to you for your generosity to the Club, for the great assistance given and the interest always shown by you.'9 The club had recently completed its causeway linking Kellet Island to the island of Hong Kong, and now the club could look to the future.

Pat Loseby remembers how after races such as an Interport (racing between Hong Kong and the yacht club of Manila, for example) the crews would be invited back to Noel's place for a drink. 'He didn't seek publicity it seemed, he just did it quietly. But at the same time he did like to be noticed,' says Pat Loseby. 'One prize-winning which he attended at the yacht club, a dinner, he was sitting beside one of the members who he didn't know and who didn't know him. She told me afterwards that every time that there was a prize being presented by Croucher, he would say to somebody nearby, I gave that cup, I gave that cup. This friend of mine who wasn't sure who Noel was, said to somebody, "Who's the old geezer who's saying that he's given these cups?" We said, "Shoosh, that's Noel Croucher!"

'One occasion which was quite amusing, was when he had *La Cigale* and it was the end of the yachting series and we used to go out to what is now Discovery Bay, which of course is all ruined for sailing now. But we used to go there — nice sailing and a nice bay to anchor in. Or else we used to go to Junk Bay.

'This particular Sunday when we were going out, Noel was just ahead of us you see, sailing along. Suddenly the wind dropped and he couldn't put his engine on. Something was wrong with it. So we all offered, said could we tow him. Noel replied, "No, I don't need towing, it'll be alright!" Well in the end when we got past him, we found him hailing a sampan, or a small junk which had got an engine on it, and there was Noel being towed out of the harbour which we thought was really funny. He was too proud to have any of the yacht club doing it for him. No, we were not meant to see.

'He was a good-looking man, a big man. He had a sense of humour. He did like to do things properly. He used to worry a little bit about the yacht club, who they'd got in the hierarchy, the staff, he didn't think some people were right to do this or that. I think he'd be very much against Taking Down the Royal.[10]

'He was kind enough to lend me his boat for a weekend, sailing in the summer one year. He said, "I'm not taking it out, it sits there doing nothing. Take it out for a weekend." So I got my friends, about eight of us, we took it out, went round to Sai Kung. Took the Chinese boatboys to look after things, so all we did was sail it and then we had a party there and came back the next day, and handed the boat back and thanked him very much indeed.'[11]

Noel's dominance of the finances of the yacht club was not to everybody's liking. His generosity was acknowledged and welcomed. But whereas in the old pre-war atmosphere, having one man solely in power over a club's finances was acceptable, the post-war, new and younger membership was less happy. As some of them were also financial types, conflict was inevitable. 'We would see $10,000 spare, for example, and Noel would say, "Leave it to me". He was a wonderful one-man band. But. ...Well, words were exchanged between Noel and a man from the Bank, and a financial committee was set up. So of course Noel felt side-tracked. These were newer people, with newer ideas,' explains Richard Hownam-Meek, adding that Noel helped Hownam-Meek's son with an introduction so he could start a career in chartered accountancy.[12]

Becoming a grand old man is a process fraught with difficulties. Responsibilities can get one down, as can the jealousies and rivalries. Noel, now in his sixties, was not one who liked to let go. Perhaps, understandably, there were arguments, and often the perception that Noel was not an easy man to get along with.

But perceptions are very odd things. One crowd will say Noel got along with so-and-so, another crowd will say they loathed each other. For example, Jack McElney was a friend of Noel, and Noel shared investment advice with Jack, according to Jack's son, Brian. Yet, Jack's colleague at the doctors' surgery, Freddie Watson, maintains Jack loathed Noel deeply.[13] Another man Noel had trouble with, according to some accounts, was A.G. Dalziel, reportedly active in the black market in Stanley Camp. Opinions are divided as to whether the trade was well motivated. Dalziel's stepdaughter believes the two men were good friends.[14] When she married, Noel gave a cheque for £50, which was a lot then. Later, he also gave a grandfather clock. 'My mother always used to say Noel came out as a little boy working on a ship,' remembers Ms Bridget Corrie-Hall. 'She was very gregarious, but even she couldn't get the facts out of him!'

Others around at the time maintain Dalziel and Croucher had much in common. 'Noel did have a feud with Dalziel and he diddled with the yacht club constitution to try to prevent [A.G. Dalziel] from becoming Rear Commodore. But Dalziel had been doing a service [in Camp], getting black market goods for survival,' says Richard Hownam-Meek. 'Noel was the ancient mariner. But newer members would dodge the long raves. He was a very lonely old boy. My wife [née Shelley-Brand], she used to visit Noel a lot to talk with him, to listen to his stories. He would show his antiques. She was from a long-standing China Coast family.'[15]

'Dalziel saved lives through the black market. But he had a great contempt for those who wrote him cheques in camp but didn't honour them later on,' notes Gerald Carey. 'He was a similar character to Noel, an adventurer and subsequently a Commodore.'[16] Indeed, Carey kept a photograph of Noel, Dalziel and himself enjoying a post-race celebration together amid great conviviality.

According to Noel, sailing was perhaps his greatest joy. In letters to friends he wrote about a yacht club Interport regatta with Manila, followed by a Queen's Birthday dance, all of which was 'great fun'. A few months later, he was upset because he had strained his back again, 'just when a long weekend of horse and yacht races was beckoning.' He added that his back had persuaded him to visit a 'Chinese Bone manipulator and I think he did more harm than good...'[17]

Social life among expatriates in Hong Kong was split into sporting circles — there were the golfers, the cricketers, the sailors, the footballers and so on. The demands of time and training for the different recreations helped divide up the society, as one could not do more than one or two at a time. Noel sailed until he was in his seventies, but gradually dropped out of the racing crowd. No other hobby ever competed with sailing in his life, but he was discovering other sports.

Noel had joined the Royal Hong Kong Golf Club on 19 September 1947, when post-war rehabilitation of the desecrated greens was just beginning to show results. (He was elected a life member in 1969.)[18] In existence at Happy Valley since 1890, the club now features three eighteen-hole courses at Fanling in the New Territories, sophisticated clubhouses and facilities, and a nine-hole course at Deep Water Bay on the south side of Hong Kong Island.

Noel Croucher's name is not on the lists of organisers or captains of the golf club. Nor did he win any club championships. But he was a steady recreational golfer for years and met many friends there. G.O.W. Stewart, of the Hong Kong & Shanghai Bank, became captain of the golf club in 1952. Sir Sidney Gordon, formerly with Lowe Bingham & Mathews and now with the Kadoorie empire, was captain in 1956 and president from 1983. J.D. 'Douggie' Clague, taipan of Hutchison's, was captain in 1965. The lady captain was Mrs Shewan in 1949, Mrs Clague in 1961, and Mrs MacWhinnie in 1973. Sir Gordon MacWhinnie was captain in 1967–69. Dr Cam Gribben, one of the outstanding golf players from the 1960s on, was one of Noel's doctors.[19] Noel was close friends with lawyer Leslie Wright and they used to play golf at Fanling together: 'He never liked losing. When he played golf, if he hit a ball into the forest, he'd go and get it and throw it back onto the course — quite openly.'[20]

Noel became a regular at Deep Water Bay in his later years, rising at dawn for a round before going to work. Peter Vine, a solicitor who had known Noel since 1948, remembers Noel played golf a lot at the Shek O course as well, and an old photograph of Noel's desk shows a card from the Shek O Golf and Country Club. He was not a member there, as far as we can tell, but clearly knew many of the men from Peat Marwick and elsewhere who were members at Shek O. 'I remember he could still play thirty-six holes, in his eighties,' says Peter Vine.[21]

'Noel liked to play golf, mostly with young women,' recalled Ansie Lee Sperry, daughter of Lee Hysan. 'We once went [to Fanling] by train and after getting off at the station near the China border, rode on the back perch of a bicycle with my heavy golf bag sticking out precariously and I, sitting side-saddle with the fumes of the passing lorries asphyxiating me, was thankful to reach the Royal Fanling Golf Club. I do not remember how Noel played. I played well in those days.'[22] Another favourite golfing partner was Greta Hobbs, wife of Noel's business and Hong Kong Club friend, Jack.

Jockey Club records suggest that Noel had been a member since April 1950, even though he at least attended race meetings well before then.[23] Unfortunately we do not know who sponsored Noel's membership. What is clear is that Noel was not an avid form analyst. In 1953, one of Noel's horses, *Mainsail*, won the Somerset Plate at Happy Valley races, and he often sent pictures of himself leading in the winning horse to his relatives back in England.

But the win by *Mainsail* in 1953 was the only major one he ever achieved, even though he went on to own a total of seven horses. *Mainsail II* raced from 1954 to 1957 and *Bowsprit* ran from 1958 to 1966, with the latter the most successful horse for Noel with five wins to its credit. *Full Sail*, which raced from 1964 to 1970, never won a race but came second seven times. From 1968 to 1970, *Sandy Bay* managed just one win, whereas the griffin, *Hurricane*, raced in 1971–72 and never won anything. *Windward* (1973–77) won five times. *Topsail* (1979–) was Noel's last horse. In his letters he mentioned that it was his faithful assistant, Mrs Ferguson, who reminded him when to enter a horse in a race.

♪ ♪ ♪

If Noel had damaged his image over the gas company affair, there were many other circles in Hong Kong which enjoyed his style, sense of fun, his spectacular memory and joy in a good story. His club friends saw Noel at his most congenial, and there was no doubt he could turn on the charm whenever he wished to. Tall, straight-backed, elegantly turned out, he sported flowers in his buttonholes and a large coloured handkerchief in his top pocket — cheerful, good-tempered, courteous, affable ... 'scandal touched him not', said Brian Johnson. His attendance at cocktail parties usually ended with a 'Must Dash Old Boy!' and the promise of a lift home from somebody. 'A little prudish, he strongly disapproved of mini skirts and see-through dresses,' said Johnson.[24]

Ansie Lee and her husband Hank Sperry lived in Hong Kong after they left Shanghai in 1949, and remember their friendship with Noel from those times: 'From those years, we knew Noel and liked him tremendously. We belonged to the same church, St. John's Cathedral, and we sailed separately in our own yachts. Ours was built in Hong Kong of teak and we christened her *Princess*. He had a beauty and preferred to sail alone but we had good times listening to him talk of the old days when we rendezvoused in some cove. ...Noel also had a bad back, and his cure for it was always the same. He would disappear from social life for weeks and weeks, lying in bed. He told Henry it always did the trick and sooner or later, he would appear, paler but able to walk, dapper as always and standing as straight as ever.... I always thought of Noel as a straight-laced Englishman.'[25]

'When cruising, Noel would invite us aboard for drinks. Great hospitality, but he wasn't over-powering. There was no fireworks or flamboyance about Noel, no shouting or swearing. He was very placid, easy-going, orderly, quiet. He had no eccentricities,' remembers Bunny Browne. 'He loaned *La Cigale* to us with its two boatboys — we had a glorious week.'[26]

'I was very fond of Noel. He was a very great friend,' said Bill Hancock. Bill worked in insurance in Hong Kong and his wife Betty was employed at the local office of MI5. They were keen sailors, too.[27] 'I was on the club committee in 1945 and Jim [Jim Boyle, Betty Hancock's brother] was too. I had hundreds of meetings with Noel. He was not tight-fisted at all, I never heard that. I remember once at a yacht club committee meeting, he was fed up when whisky and soda went up 5 cents — but that was natural!

'One very pleasant memory was when my mother came to Hong Kong. It was a lovely day and Noel invited us up to his house, and produced a bottle of champagne. That was the sort of thing he did — very generous, friendly. He did things like that.

'Mind you, there was one chap, I won't name him, who wore a military cross. Noel said he hadn't earned it — and he was right. Noel sort-of found things out like that.' Jim Boyle used to drink with the legendary Australian journalist Richard Hughes and others at Hong Kong's Foreign Correspondents' Club, in a group calling themselves Alcoholics Synonymous. Once or twice Noel turned up at these esoteric gatherings. 'I never saw Noel the worse for wear. He would drink, but never lost his dignity,' notes Bill Hancock.

Even when a friend was concerned about Noel's blood alcohol level, Noel managed a riposte marked by quirky wit. Lawyer Brian Tisdall recounts a memorable incident in which he admits Noel had the last laugh:

'I was at the Hong Kong Club one evening and saw Noel — he always ate garoupa done in a special way, it was known as Croucher's Garoupa. He was obviously pretty drunk at about 9 p.m. I said, "Uncle Noel, where are you going, you're too drunk to drive. I'll take you home." Well, Noel put his fists up at that, he wanted to make a fight out of it. So I let him go. I got my own car and told my driver to follow him, which we did all the way from St. John's Cathedral up to Magazine Gap Road. He was all over the road!

'Eventually we got to the end of Mt Cameron Road and I told him, "You're a disgrace!", and went on home to Stanley. When I got home, my wife was up and said, "Are you OK?" I said, "Yes of course, why ever not?" And she said, "Well Uncle Noel just called to tell me that YOU were very drunk!" It shows a certain kind of style, doesn't it!'[28]

Throughout these years of business, Noel was supported in his office by a loyal, but small, staff. Mrs Lillian Ferguson was Noel's right-hand woman, 'a plump, bespectacled, good-natured middle-aged lady.'[29] Noel often professed himself to be wholly reliant on her. She organised not only his office life but the rest of his commitments as well. Then there was Emily Fox-Fernandez — 'Emily said he was strict but fair,' says Joyce Symons, a leading educationalist in Hong Kong.[30] Sadly, Emily Fox-Fernandez died just three weeks before research for this book began. Florence Lo, who now works for The Croucher Foundation along with Rosetta Chung, did not start working for Noel Croucher until 1968. In addition, Noel had an amah at home, a boatboy and son at the yacht club, and an office boy, called Wong Yue-nam.

Mr Wong has nothing but praise for Noel Croucher. He started working in Noel's office at the age of nineteen, in 1949, and was still there, literally, at Noel's death.

'Mrs Ferguson put an advertisement in the paper in 1949,' says Wong Yue-nam. 'And through some friends I got an introduction and so went to the office to meet Mr Croucher. He asked me if I knew any English, and I didn't know any at all, but he saw that I was very clean and well-educated. I was from a good Canton family, so he offered me $120 a year and said that if I did the job well I would get $150, which was a lot.'[31]

Mr Wong's duties were to carry messages, deliver papers and do whatever odd jobs were around. But after three years, young Wong told Mr Croucher that he wanted to quit so he could go back to school. 'I told him it was nothing to do with money, I just wanted to learn more.

'Well, Mr Croucher said he wanted me to have an education, and not to worry. So for ten nights a month I went to night school, learning English. He gave me the money for the school fees, and when I stopped going to the classes, he said I could keep the extra money for myself.'

Mr Croucher always gave Mr Wong a gift of money whenever Wong visited his family back in his home town in China. 'He would give me a $500 gift for my mother — when my wages were only $280!! After thirteen years of this, I refused to take his money for my trips home any more, because it was too generous.' Wong was very generous in his own way, too. He refused to leave the office at night for so long as Noel was there. He never left Mr Croucher on his own — for thirty-one years. Meanwhile, Noel approached his friends in the Li family to seek help in finding a cheap flat for Wong and his family — where he still lives to this day.

'Mr Croucher always said he would take care of me. He said, "I will take care of my Boy." And if he had visitors, he would even introduce me. He would send me to the [Hong Kong & Shanghai] Bank sometimes, with messages for the top men. And he said I had to give them to these important men personally. Well, it was very unusual for the Boy to see the top people. Mr Croucher seemed to think that, well he could see the top men, so why not his staff!'

It is tempting to think that this is just how a much younger Noel might have first made the acquaintance of many of the top business names.

Mr Wong was not always delivering messages. Every autumn he had to deliver white camelias, plucked from Noel's garden, and give them to people like Sir Arthur Morse, chairman of the Hong Kong Bank. Noel was famous for his fresh buttonholes. He grew both camelias and gardenias at his house on the Peak, wearing a bloom of one or the other without fail. And every Friday, Wong collected food from the Hong Kong Club kitchens which was destined for the supper bowls of Noel's cat and dogs.

Through Mr Wong, an endearing picture of Noel can be built up. Wong remembers Noel's afternoon naps on the big covered balcony of his office on Ice House Street, and Noel's habit of asking Wong to take the daily newspaper back to the news-vendor downstairs every day after Noel had read it. The idea was that the vendor could then resell the newspaper and make more money. He also gave money to the newspaper seller from time to time, for a treat at the races. Noel liked taking people under his wing, and his staff remember Noel's patronage of a disabled artist, whose paintings cluttered up the office for years. No one can remember the artist's name, but Wong believes Mr Croucher arranged for him to sell his paintings through a hotel boutique and tried in vain to persuade the artist to study abroad.

Wong carried out increasingly sensitive tasks for Noel. He delivered all the share certificates and helped Mrs Ferguson carry her work home at night as well. One day, Wong recalls, Mr Croucher got out an old-fashioned rattan briefcase, gave it to Wong and asked him to go to Kowloon Tong. There he met a particular man who put a packet into the briefcase, and Wong duly carried the bag back to the office. Once there, Mr Croucher opened it, and Wong was astounded to see a large pile of cash. Apparently, it was in return for some share certificates.

Mr Croucher liked to reward honesty around him. 'One time I was to go to a foreign exchange dealer and buy some pounds sterling for Mr Croucher,' remembers Wong Yue-nam. 'So I went to the forex counter and gave over the cash for the sterling, and the dealer gave me the change. But I saw the dealer had given me $600 too much change by mistake. I went back and told Mr Croucher about the mistake and Mr Croucher said I should take the $600 back to the dealer so he wouldn't be out of pocket. Then he thanked me a lot for spotting the mistake, and then he gave me $600, for my honesty! Out of his own pocket.'[32]

Noel put in long hours, from about eight in the morning until eight at night. Often, after trading hours at the exchange were over, he put in a game of dice at the Hong Kong Club while Wong waited. On Wednesdays there was no afternoon trading, so there was sailing, and every Saturday too, and sometimes the horses at Happy Valley. The largest bet Wong can recall Noel ever making at the races was $10, and Noel always told his staff of the evils of gambling. Every Friday, Noel would lunch at the Red Room in the old Hong Kong Club. And whenever new members joined the stock exchange, they went to talk with Noel Croucher first.

Noel's style as a boss was patriarchal. Cheung Kam-chuen's father, Cheung Loo, was Noel's 'Boat-Boy' for two decades. Cheung junior remembers helping out on the weekends. 'Mr Croucher didn't give much money — but he introduced my brother and I to the Hong Kong & China Gas Company,' he reported.[33] Cheung Kam-chuen still works for the gas company. 'He told us of his poor background, and you could see he was very much against any waste. For example, if an employee had bought expensive sunglasses, he would tell them off for wasting money. If Mr Croucher ever threw anything out, it would be completely used up.'

Cheung remembers Noel's habit, at least in the later years, of sailing alone and dropping anchor in isolated bays. 'If someone else came in, he would leave that beach to find another to be in, on his own. And when he was alone, he would read, walk around and fish. He would have a fishing line off the boat when we were moving and was very proud of his catch — he would eat it, and share it at the Club.' Cheung remembers having to copy out the Chinese inscription on the gravestone at Shek Kwu Wan, which had long fascinated Noel.

The standard tale is that Noel never wanted a chauffeur as it was wasteful to pay someone to sit around doing nothing all day, but Wong remembers it differently. Noel did employ a chauffeur, but this driver unfortunately got involved in extracurricular activities such as robbery and gambling and fled Hong Kong by skipping bail. 'Mr Croucher never had another chauffeur after that,' says Wong.

Visitors were in and out of the office much of the time, the door was always open. Wong adds that students came by to get Noel's signature on sponsorship forms for scholarships. 'Lots came to see Mr Croucher, asking for favours.' A friend of Noel's, Richard Stoneman, agrees: 'He was helping students before he set up the foundation. He sponsored many young people.'[34]

Throughout the first decade or so after the war, Noel Croucher made very few overseas trips. Judging by various letters, he visited England and saw his brother Basil, in or around 1956.[35] He also went in 1962/63, on a P & O liner, *Arcadia*. But before that, Noel made a major improvement to his home life. Though he could not attain the peak of social respectability — in St. George Society, at the top firms — he did finally make it permanently to the Peak. His wife was firmly settled in Eaton Square in London by this time, his son now worked in London, and Noel had little inclination to leave Hong Kong.

So he bought a house at 22 Mount Cameron Road, the Peak, in 1953. It had a view stretching across the south of Hong Kong, over Aberdeen and Lamma to the horizon. It is one of the quietest residential areas of the Peak to this day, although sadly, Noel's house has been replaced by a pink condominium development. It was, whether he realised it then or not, the place where he was to live for the rest of his life, and a place which gave him much joy. Noel's house-warming party is still remembered by many.

'I knew him of course — everyone did. We met socially occasionally and I have outstanding memories of a wonderful party he gave at the housewarming of his new abode, where all Hong Kong was gathered on his most splendid lawn,' writes Norma Rasmussen.[36]

'He bought it from a man called Ott, who apparently made his fortune, so Noel told me, by selling arms to both sides during the troubles in China in the 1930s,' reports Ian MacCallum. 'It was an interesting house. It was quite large but it only had one bedroom. So Noel never had to entertain [house guests]. It had a huge lounge, huge dining room, one bedroom and very large servants' quarters.'[37]

The unusual layout of Noel's house provoked amusement and comment in later years. People assumed it had been deliberate on Noel's part to exclude the possibility of house guests, but his subsequent actions were to disprove this. What he did instead was no less controversial, as he built a garden bungalow in the grounds, unfortunately without first securing planning permission.

Wynne Ward, one of the few English people born and bred in Hong Kong and still here, remembers Noel asked for help in furnishing the garden hut. 'He told me not to be too expensive and only to buy things second-hand. So I did, I went round the sales and of course to Lammert's auction rooms. But he still needed curtains. He said he couldn't spend any more money, so I said I happened to have a big roll of material. I had it made up for him, and he was thrilled to bits.

'There were wine cellars deep under the house and they gave me the creeps! Full of spiders and roaches. But he had a wonderful collection of old snuff boxes, coins and a Penny Black stamp. My daughters thought he was fascinating. He was a very nice man, good company.'[38]

The house became a repository for Noel's collections of all kinds of mementoes from a rich and varied life. It was also the site of many happy parties. 'Noel used to give Boxing Day parties and we all drank Black Velvet — a wonderful China Coast cocktail [of Guinness and champagne],' recalls Anne Sorby, née Burrows. An avid student of Chinese language and culture, she had worked in Kunming during the war and joined the administration in Hong Kong after that. When she married Terence Sorby, a future Director of Commerce & Industry, Noel came to the wedding reception held at the home of Sir Lindsay and Lady May Ride. This was the Vice Chancellor's lodge at the University of Hong Kong. 'Noel probably knew Terence's parents before the war. Terence had a great regard for him,' recalls Anne Sorby.[39]

In Noel's house was a wide range of fascinating objects. (They were not all *objets d'art*.) 'The contents of his office, and his home — you've no idea! Paintings, books, stamps, coins,... There were people spilling out of China and they brought their things. Croucher was the chap they went to because he had the resources.'[40]

Many were the times when Noel told the story of a man from Nanking, who had fled around 1949, carrying a horde of precious and beautiful stamps:

> You will have a lot to do but please take your time and don't spoil the Sheet of Stamps. I bet there is not another about. When Chairman Mao took over, the assistant Commissioner of Posts in Nanking left for Hong Kong. He did not want to join Chiang Kai-shek. He left for Indonesia. I met him through mutual friends and lent him money on some valuable pieces of porcelain. He died and did not repay me the loan...[41]

Noel spent some time trying to trace the proper values of the stamps, enlisting the help of one or two friends in England. His efforts to sell and profit from such collections appear half-hearted, however. Rather, the impression is that he was proud to own such exceptional things.

> Catalogue value of stamps is always on the low side, but the 200 you have of Sun Yat Sen would fetch much more as they are one piece... I have a lot of stamps all nicely put under transparent paper. I am thinking of taking out a page or two and sending them to you to find out what they would fetch at Auction, and also what commission one has to pay... Other Stamps: the £5 Orange 1865; the Penny Black issued but not put into circulation and the Republic of France...[42]

Among Noel's personal effects was a list of Chinese imperial statues, ivory and jade carvings, a set of eighteen named Buddhas, the name of Japanese sculptor Takaaki, and jewellery ranging from watches, rings, brooches, earrings, cuff links and bracelets to jade pendants. He was not a learned connoisseur, and though had accrued enough money to buy up the world's greatest art, he bought instead a mass of pictures by obscure painters and hoarded odds and ends of Victorian silverwork. He had the wherewithal and the aspirations to learn about his world, its history and culture — but he lacked the grounding to know just where to look.

No wonder he loved his books so much. Some of these were extremely rare and valuable. *China Monuments, Sacred and Profane* was compiled by Athanasius Kircherus of the Society of Jesus and published in Amsterdam circa 1664. Kircherus' name also cropped up in records Noel owned of the ambassadorial travels of Peter de Goyer and Jacob de Keyzer, from 1655.[43] The frontispiece shows an emissary of the East India Company sent to the Grand Tartar Cham. De Goyer and de Keyzer went from Canton to Peking and this account is, not surprisingly, fascinating. Along the way, the ambassadors were entertained by the Governor of Nanking, a Tartar, whose wife was described by the travellers as a 'bold virago' who 'drew out our swords, discharged our pistols, which much delighted her.'[44]

Noel was a keen reader of books such as Norton-Kyshe's *History of the Courts of Hong Kong*. His collection included books on European philosophy, History Club publications, the history of the Anglican Church in Hong Kong, books on Machiavelli and Cellini, on the development of Chinese art, and even a well-thumbed copy of *How to Minimise Death Duties*.[45] Teresa Price of Lammert's Auctioneers remembers Noel had sketches and books about George Chinnery, 'marvellous books', including *MacCartney's Embassy to China*, a two-volume illustrated history of the Chinese Empire, four volumes of *China Illustrated*, and prints of drawings by Thomas Allom (1843).[46]

Noel was reputed to use the library at the Hong Kong Club a lot, but liked to keep copies of special books himself. When a friend was ill, he recommended a course of reading of books by Danielle Varé (1880–1956), who wrote books such as *The Last of the Empresses, Passing from the Old China to New* (1938), and *The Maker of Heavenly Trousers* (1937). 'I used to borrow books from him, his old China books. And if I mistreated a book, I had to have it repaired,' says George Wright-Nooth.[47] In Noel's letters to his son, he often discussed books:

> I got the names of a few of André Maurois Books — but the ones I wanted are not included, As you are fond of reading as I am — I'm reading again Orwell's '1984' and Huxley's 'Brave New World', & 'Science Liberty & Peace'. Maurois's book 'Call No Man Happy' is one of the many...

> You told me you are very interested in Books... I have a Persian friend who is anxious to buy Bertholds Laufer's Book 'Sino-Iranica' a fascinating compendium of China's debt to Persian Civilisation... I've read Aurel Stein's book — most interesting — Alexander the Great marched as far as Bhutan North India in 387 BC and made certain excavations, found sealed scripts in containers sealed with Greek seals...[48]

Noel encouraged his son to read Thackeray, Dickens and Fellimore Cooper. He owned *Dostoevsky*, and Abbe Huc's *Travels in China*. He sent many books from the Everyman Library series to son Richard. Noel had a curious inquiring mind but, according to his son, was shy of exposing it, fearing ridicule if he ever showed his sensitive side to the world. Noel's music collection was dominated by Bach, Brahms, Beethoven and opera. Whatever the outside world thought of him, Noel was a thoughtful and cultured — as well as a powerful — man.

CHAPTER THIRTEEN

PUBLIC AND PRIVATE LIVES

ollowing the effective end to his marriage in the late 1940s, Noel settled into a rounded, active life in his lovely home on the Peak. However, this was not enough for Noel. Unbeknownst to most people at the time, and despite all the tackiness of his spats with Marden and others, Noel Croucher had begun his private involvement in some of Hong Kong's neediest causes.

The most surprising thing about Noel is that at the same time as he was aggressive, competitive, jealous and controversial in business, and the 'old hand' at his favourite clubs, Noel was also deeply sensitive to the traumas around him in Hong Kong.[1] Until now, Noel had acted as any other affable businessman would — helping his clubs, making money, sailing and socialising. But from the beginning of the 1950s, he displayed a powerful social conscience.

That all these activities were happening at the same time as each other is important — so many have thought Noel Croucher only gave money away in his last years for no better reason than that he was disappointed in his family. The facts, inconvenient though they are, show that Noel looked out early on and saw things beyond his small circle of privilege. And he did not like what he saw.

'There are beggars everywhere, who make the avoidance of thought difficult at my age,' wrote F.D. Ommanney, an academic who lived in Hong Kong at the time. 'They are not only in the streets ... they come to your office and to your house with long, elaborately prepared hard-luck stories. Soon you begin to feel that everyone in Hong Kong is after you. You develop a callous crust and a harsh manner to keep at bay the armies of the needy, the poor, and the down-and-out. You feel, if you feel at all, that you are surrounded by a great, dark ocean of human misery and unhappiness.'

Ommanney admits that in the midst of the squalor, a few 'charitable organisations and kind-hearted individuals swim bravely against the tide of want and misery.'[2] Funnily enough, Noel Croucher was one of them.

One morning in about 1951, Noel sat reading the local paper as usual. There was a report about destitute children on the streets of Hong Kong. Noel sat up and read it through again. This speech reminded him of what he saw every day on his way to work — the fact that hundreds of young children were without homes, schools or work, and were camping out in desperate straits on the streets of Hong Kong. Many orphans were arrested by Hong Kong police and shipped back to China, often to be left stranded at the border.

Noel immediately offered to pay for a home for these children and by so doing met taxi-company owner Chan Nam-cheong. How much Noel gave overall is open to doubt, but several sources say the first gift was at least $150,000. Chan was an exceptional man who had built an impressive commercial and philanthropic empire in Hong Kong. His businesses ranged from restaurants and supermarkets to property, cinemas and grocery shops. Meanwhile, Bishop Ronald Owen Hall, known as 'R.O.' and the recognised 'Conscience of Hong Kong', was the zealous Bishop of Hong Kong from 1932 to 1966 and founder of much of the post-war social welfare infrastructure. Bishop Hall offered Chan the site of his garage, where Ice House Street joins Lower Albert Road, for a children's home and school.

The Juvenile Care Centre was soon looking after eight hundred boys, two hundred of them boarders and the rest coming to school by day. In the mornings they received primary education, in the afternoons they learned a trade. Noel Croucher, among others, used his contacts to benefit his cause. Soon the Jockey Club was donating regularly and the Governor's wife, Lady Grantham, became interested. Noel also used his stock exchange savvy, distributing share allocations to this and other needy organisations.

Marjorie Bray, born in Hong Kong, remembers the early years of the Juvenile Care Centre, a cause she has been involved with for twenty-five years. 'After the war, orphans and children were roaming the streets, committing petty crimes, stealing hubcaps and so on. And Noel decided to scoop up these children off the streets. He joined up with two Chinese, who were not related, Mr Chan Nam-cheong and Mrs Winnie Chan Fung-chow (née Mok). They got together with the bishop and built the building that is still standing there. It was called the Boys' Home, and then it took in girls as well.'[3]

The boys' home had started in 1948 as the Shaukeiwan Children's Camp. 'The primary aim of the Centre at that time was to provide a home for orphans and the homeless and also for those who had inadvertently erred and been discharged from the juvenile courts, to provide them with care, shelter, education, handicraft training and the chance to be brought up as useful citizens,' states the Juvenile Care Centre's brief history.[4] It must be recalled that not until 1958, well after a rash of disasters in crowded housing areas caused by overcrowding or bad weather, and well after destitution was noticed in Hong Kong, did the Juvenile Care Centre receive its first funding assistance from the government.

The premises in Central which Noel funded were opened by the Governor, Sir Alexander Grantham, on 13 April 1953. The foundation stone was laid by Mr Croucher in 1952. Mr Croucher was one of the centre's honorary presidents, from September 1953 until his death in 1980.

Nowadays, the needs have altered but by no means have they gone away. Despite, or because of, Hong Kong's increasing prosperity, children now need residential care for the treatment of personality disorders, behavioural problems, or 'exposure to moral danger'. The Juvenile Care Centre thrives to this day, in new premises in Pokfulam. Priority is accorded to maladjusted children for residential care. If of school age, the children, both residents and day students, can attend the Chan Nam Cheong Memorial School of the centre. Unfortunately, Noel Croucher died before he could make one of his promises to the JCC come true. He had apparently pledged a new $3 million donation, but it was not written down in time and thus could not be acted on.

'Some time after that, the same people set up the Stanley Sea School,' said Mrs Bray. The then Commissioner of Prisons, Cuthbert James Norman, was one of those involved. Although Noel is not known to have contributed directly to this, he did help build a retreat at Tai Tam Bay for the Sea Scouts in the late 1960s.[5] John Marden, son of Noel's friend and foe George, was the first chairman of the Sea Scouts and worked well with Noel in arranging the money.[6]

The 1950s were desperate years for most in Hong Kong. Indeed, hundreds of thousands of people were living in unstable slums perched on hillsides, without electricity, water or basic drainage. On Christmas Day, 1953, the horrific fire at one such squatter area at Shep Kip Mei made fifty thousand homeless. More fires occurred in 1954, and still more people continued to arrive. At a time when sheer survival was under threat, sophisticated health and childcare services were virtually non-existent.

Those who had already become involved, through such projects as the Juvenile Care Centre, were natural candidates to come to the rescue again. So the Society for the Relief of Disabled Children was born, and plans laid for a children's hospital at Sandy Bay. Noel Croucher helped make it happen. An active committee, comprising individuals such as former legislator and businessman Jimmy MacGregor, also put in much time and effort for Sandy Bay.[7]

Sandy Bay became, with Noel's donations, a pioneering centre providing free medical, surgical, rehabilitation and education facilities for the disabled children of Hong Kong. The Columban Sisters were involved almost from the beginning, due to their experience at the Ruttonjee Sanatorium for tuberculosis victims, and Sister Barbara O'Sullivan, now at the Catholic Diocese Centre in Hong Kong, joined Sandy Bay in 1967.[8]

Professor A.R. Hodgson innovated a treatment for spinal tuberculosis in children after his arrival to lecture in orthopaedics at the University of Hong Kong in 1951. He made a vital contribution to orthopaedics in Hong Kong. He was also a firm friend of Noel Croucher. Jenny Hodgson, the professor's daughter, recalls: 'Noel was just non-establishment. Noel was "different". So was my Dad. He didn't conform either, he didn't say the right thing at the right time.'[9]

The idea was that by centralising the treatment of children with orthopaedic ailments, a close study of the genesis of the diseases and research into treatments could be carried out, as well as the provision of much-needed care to the victims of spinal tuberculosis. Children were discharged from hospitals due to a shortage of beds but still needed convalescent care. When it began, Sandy Bay was the largest such hospital in the world and the first of its kind in Southeast Asia.

Clarifying exactly who gave what to which part of Sandy Bay is difficult. Some former members of the committees involved maintain Noel Croucher talked about the hospital but never gave a cent. Others are sure his role was pivotal. Records are scanty, and changes in patronage and management since Noel Croucher's time have sadly muddied the waters of recollection.

An official history of the society and the hospital reports that in November 1956, the convalescent home, with fifty beds, was opened by Lady Grantham. 'Funds for this building were donated primarily by one of Hong Kong's leading citizens,' it reads. In 1962, the Convalescent

Home Extension was opened, thanks to a grant of land by the government 'and a generous donation from a member of the Society [for the Relief of Disabled Children]'. In 1968, the Children's Orthopaedic Hospital was opened, and in February 1970, Her Royal Highness the Duchess of Kent visited Sandy Bay and agreed that it might be named after her. In 1975, 'with the promise of a few big donations' the society decided to build a five-storey extension (opened by Lady MacLehose on 6 October 1975.)[10]

Luckily, a newspaper clipping kept by Noel, and discovered in the mess of his desk after his death, refers specifically to his role at Sandy Bay. Under a picture of children playing in a swimming pool at the hospital, it announced the opening by Lady Trench of the new wing of the Sandy Bay Convalescent Home for Children 'yesterday'. The story reads:

> The new six-storey building was built on a $1 million donation from Mr N.V.A. Croucher, vice president of the Society for the Relief of Disabled Children. Mr Croucher was also the donor of the main building, built in 1956. There are a total of 106 beds in the home, all occupied. The new wing consists of two wards with a total of 56 beds on the ground floor. Built on an area of 100,000 square feet, the new wing also contains two classrooms, a swimming pool and a playroom...[11]

Another piece of paper left lying around by Noel is part of a brochure from the Sandy Bay Children's Orthopaedic Hospital and Convalescent Home. Again, it is undated, but must be from before the name change in 1970. This lists Noel as president, with the patron the Governor's wife, Lady Trench. One of the vice-presidents at this point was Chan Nam-cheong, another was Hari Harilela, and leading the executive committee was Mrs J.A.H. Saunders (wife of the then Hong Kong Bank taipan).

'I was told Noel had donated enough to build two wards at Sandy Bay,' says Brian Tisdall, a lawyer who was chairman of Sandy Bay from November 1975 to January 1986. 'Noel gave HK$150,000 for Wards 1 and 2 at Sandy Bay, circa 1968. As far as I know, he never gave another brass penny. There was a plaque on the wall, naming Croucher I believe. He would have *raised* money for them though, as well as giving his own.'[12]

Lord Michael Sandberg of the Hong Kong & Shanghai Bank remembers that Noel was a 'great patron' of Sandy Bay, but that Noel 'didn't like it to be publicised', as he didn't want his post to be inundated with begging letters. 'I think he was, like many of us, two persons in one. I think he was generous in many ways and bloody mean in others.'[13]

There were a myriad of ways in which someone in Noel's position could help out a cause such as Sandy Bay. Peter Vine's wife, Aida Agabeg, was chairman of the Choral Group which produced operas in Hong Kong and also raised money for good causes. 'Croucher used to help out. He did it for four or five of Aida's productions, not by giving money, but by putting up the money before there was any income from ticket sales,' says Peter Vine. 'He would put up the money for the expenses of costumes, production costs, the booking and paying for the hall and all that. This was extremely helpful.' Noel's costs were later reimbursed, and the profits from the concerts went to Sandy Bay. 'I think Noel did give a lot, but he was always afraid people would get after him and make his life a misery.'[14]

Now known as the Duchess of Kent Children's Hospital, it is administered by the Hospital Authority, and the portraits of Noel Croucher, among others, no longer take pride of place. Some things remain clear, however: Noel was indeed generous and he did not simply throw money at worthy-sounding causes and then forget about it. His involvement at Sandy Bay, as at the Juvenile Care Centre, was personal and consistent.

'I remember him sitting on the window sill of my office with his leg up, and talking. He knew so much about early Hong Kong,' recalls Sister Barbara. 'He loved the children and was a very warm, honest and decent person. Noel never missed a meeting or a Christmas Day. He always arrived with a bunch of camelias from his own garden, for me — Gorgeous! And whenever anything was happening Noel would ring up to see if we were alright. He even came down to Sandy Bay during a typhoon.'[15]

Noel often brought individual gifts for the children. He would pick up and hug the children, and enjoyed playing with them. He gave sweets and practical toys at Christmas and, by all accounts, when with the children, he was very human.

Another recipient of Noel's charity was the Alice Ho Miu-ling Nethersole Hospital, which grew out of the Alice Memorial Hospital, founded by Sir Kai Ho Kai. A lawyer and a brilliant doctor, Ho Kai was keen to bring progressive health care to Hong Kong. Donations were also forthcoming from the London Missionary Society and from Mr E.R. Belilios. The project played a vital role in bringing about Chinese and British cooperation in health work.

Richard Stoneman was treasurer of what became the Alice Ho Miu-ling Nethersole Hospital. 'Noel established a fund for them and we managed the fund. It got bigger and bigger, it got up to $10 million which was a lot of money in those days. In their accounts from the late 1970s, it should show the Croucher monies as "Special Reserve Fund". He didn't want his own name on it. He had a genuine feeling for the hard-done-by. He did virtually everything anonymously. A generous person.'[16]

Brian Johnson confirms Noel gave a lot, often in the form of shares and their income. 'He was extremely generous where children and the sick were concerned. He was a generous benefactor of the Alice Ho Miu Ling Nethersole Hospital where he helped to set up the first intensive care and intensive burns units in Hong Kong... I was told that he also maintained a number of Chinese orphans in a house in Kennedy Road and that he paid for their further education where appropriate. I always had the impression that he skirted publicity for his good deeds...'[17]

An old carbon copy which Noel kept in his desk until his death is clearly the draft of a speech which he gave to a nurses' graduation ceremony at Nethersole Hospital. He noted that nursing demands 'special qualities among them being cheerfulness, patience, thoughtfulness, anticipation of the wishes of those in your charge, and these cannot be acquired, one is born with them... The Nethersole has an enviable reputation in the community and its good name lies, to a great extent, in the hands of its Matron and Nurses...'

One of the many ideas Noel came up with was that of a hospital in Iran. 'Noel wanted to set up a teaching hospital in Iran, I've no idea why. I think he was trying to find something to remember himself by,' reported the late Bernard Mellor. 'I told him I knew a Hong Kong man, a Persian, who had done that, had set up a teaching hospital in Iran, namely Nemazee, who died many years ago. Nemazee carried the Shah, paid his bills, for years. Nemazee was a DBS [Diocesan Boys' School] boy who made good. He made a helluva lot of money.

'I was astonished when Noel came up with the same idea. Maybe Croucher was a friend of Nemazee's, maybe Croucher was thinking of adding to Nemazee's hospital? I don't know.'[18] Noel's office assistant Florence Lo believes Noel was a trustee for the Nemazee scholarships, or perhaps this is the 'friend' Noel Croucher mentioned once in a letter, who had given him a power of attorney.

Nemazees were in Hong Kong since the 1860s. In 1897, Haji Mohamed Hassan Nemazee became involved in import and export, manufacturing and land (he bought Prince's Building in 1923 but foreclosed in 1926). His son, Mhd Mehdi Nemazee (1903–67) is buried in Hong Kong's Muslim Cemetery, and his son was Kazim. It is not clear if this strand is the same Nemazee family which was involved in then-legal opium in Macao.[19] Perhaps Noel was inspired by the Nemazee philanthropy as described in the *South China Morning Post*:

'The Nemazee family, which is still represented in this Colony, have conferred a great boon both upon their native city of Shiraz and on their country [Iran]. They have established, as a perpetual religious trust, one of the most scientifically modern medical centres in the world and, side by side with it, the only great pure water system in the whole of Iran except for the British-built system at Abadan...

'The two inter-dependent undertakings are part of the remarkable philanthropic enterprises of Haj Mohamed Nemazee, the former shipping magnate here... Mr Nemazee spent about US$6,500,000... A nursing school is attached and a Shirazi trader in India, inspired by the Nemazee philanthropies, has given a 50-bed eye hospital.'[20]

The Cheshire Home in Stanley might have benefited from Croucher largesse. Noel also became a life member of the Hong Kong Society for the Protection of Children. The society has no record of any particular donation from Noel[21] but executive committee member Betty Forsgate confirms Noel must have been on the committee or even chairman, to have become a life member of the society.[22] This society is one of Hong Kong's oldest such institutions, established in 1926 to provide day care for underprivileged children who would otherwise be left alone or in danger. It was formally registered in 1929, with the Hon. Sir Shouson Chow, as chairman. Noel knew Sir Shouson through business and mutual friends. Re-formed after the war, the society set up many new clinics and day care centres in the 1950s.

Hong Kong in the fifties was torn between the unremitting pressures of massive migration from China with all its related demands, and Hong Kong's cultural and political commitment to laissez-faire. Hong Kong was not only a capitalist paradise to those Mainlanders arriving at the border every day. It was also the epitome of Adam Smith's doctrine of the invisible hand to such an extent that the existence of any 'hand' at all was in doubt. Fans of doctrinaire economic individualism were vastly impressed. The law of the jungle prevailed. A harsh and haphazard way of life for anyone without an aggressive edge to their personality — no wonder Noel felt at home.

No wonder, however, that Noel also saw in the desperation around him some reminder of his own difficult youth. On the one hand, Noel's moneymaking drive could find full play in a town where everything needed to be built from scratch again, where new people, skills, and fortunes were arriving at the border every day, and where he knew the game of old, the contacts of old, and could steal a march on the newcomers.

On the other hand, Noel's love of poetry, his compassion, his concern for others — this now began to find its fullest expression. He was already a benefactor, to the Royal Hong Kong Yacht Club and to the Royal Society of St. George, among others. But the Juvenile Care Centre and other children's charities comprised a key facet of Noel Croucher — an interest for which there is no explanation other than Noel's genuine concern for his fellow man, and a deep-felt commitment to Hong Kong. 'Noel did a lot of good by stealth,' recalls Sir John Cowperthwaite, Financial Secretary to Hong Kong, 1961 to 1971.[23]

It was Sir John who institutionalised what was later called Hong Kong's doctrine of 'positive non-interventionism': 'In the long run, the aggregate of decisions by individual businessmen, exercising individual judgement in a free economy, even if often mistaken, is less likely to do harm than the centralised decisions of a government, and certainly the harm is likely to be counteracted faster.'[24]

Such a doctrine could be expected to have found favour with Noel Croucher. But unlike most millionaire tycoons, then and now, Noel retained a knowledge, deep within, of what it was like to be poor. He felt he had missed out, especially in education, and he now set about helping others to have the opportunities which he had lacked. Moreover, we must conclude Noel's philanthropic instincts to be real, as he spent an increasing amount of his time on welfare work and got very little public acclaim in return. Perhaps it suited him to have people think he was mean — it stopped a steady stream of supplicants from lining up at his door. Noel simply confined his generosity to what he saw to be deserving causes.

Noel also believed that such concern for others was his duty. He was strongly opposed to ideas such as the welfare state or trade unionism, and had no time for anyone not prepared to work hard on their own behalf. He knew capitalism was a system which was often abused, but believed individuals were required to do their best in an imperfect world. Though rebellious in the context of company board meetings, Noel was not out to change the system. But he refused to be blinded by his wealth, shut off inside a charmed circle of privilege.

I'm not a kill joy by any means — but on the afternoon I gave away to 500 waifs their Xmas presents — a paper bag containing a tooth brush, a face towel, an apple, sweets, a small toy, costing about a shilling — they had nothing like it before. I had a sherry before lunch at a friend's house and the wife who had just arrived to spend Xmas with her husband was wearing a lovely dress. She said it cost her £150 (They are nouveau riche) and I remarked that my Xmas party to the kids only came to one third of the price of her dress and would she like to give me something — not a sous. Some people are devoid of all feelings of sympathy and compassion, but they seem to prosper nevertheless. There will be a great awakening, but perhaps not in my time.[25]

We should not be surprised at what may seem to be contradictions in his character — Noel was human like anyone else. He believed he had a right to make money and pursue recreation as he wished. He also believed, just as strongly, that with his wealth came responsibilities. Perhaps, the war and internment heightened his sensitivities on this score. His old-fashioned values — his aversion to debt, insistence on hard work, his belief that everyone should do their best for the community — all this came to the fore after the war.

Croucher, Noel Victor Amor, J.P., Director, China Underwriters Ltd.; British; Unofficial Justice of the Peace; Sole Proprietor and Manager, Croucher & Co.; Director, China Provident Loan & Mortgage Co., Ltd., Sandakan Light & Power Co., Ltd., North Point Wharves Ltd.; Hon. President (permanent), Hong Kong Juvenile Care Centre; Vice President, Children's Playground; Committee Member, The Society for the Relief of Disabled Children; Vice Patron, Royal Hong Kong Yacht Club; member, Hong Kong Stock Exchange; Chairman, Kelly & Walsh Ltd.

Address: Croucher & Co., 2 Holland House, 7th Fl., 9 Queen's Road, Central, Hong Kong.[26]

Noel's public life is neatly encapsulated by his entry in the *Who's Who*. But his true prominence in the world of commerce is only hinted at. Any major business event from the 1950s onwards can be assumed to feature some input from Noel. When Swire, or more particularly the Taikoo Dockyard and Engineering Company of Hong Kong, went public in April 1959, it was Noel's Croucher & Company which underwrote the shares offer.[27]

There was a rash of new listings at this time. Among the biggest were the listings of Kowloon Motor Bus in 1961, and China Motor Bus in 1962. Noel played a significant role in each. Both issues were prompted by the need of companies for new capital to invest in keeping up with demand — tens of thousands of new migrants continued to swell Hong Kong's population. In 1961, Jardine Matheson offered 900,000 shares, the price of which rose ninety-two percent on the first day of trade. The response to the issue was so great that it drained the banking system of funds and the Hong Kong Bank was forced to feed money into the system to allow settlement of inter-bank call loans.'[28]

Noel's involvement with China Underwriters is remembered by Jose Olbes who, after the war, was president of Insular Life Insurance Company, then part of the Ayala commercial empire in the Philippines. 'Right after the war, we at Insular Life decided to expand into Southeast Asia — we had only one branch office then, in Honolulu,' says Jose Olbes from his home in Spain. 'We found out that the people in Hong Kong were trying to sell China Underwriters, so we bought it. And I kept most of the people who were already there on the board.'[29]

The board under Olbes thus included Sir Sik-nin Chau, Li Fook-wo, Leo d'Almada, and Noel Croucher. 'We kept Noel Croucher because he was so helpful in many ways, on the stock exchange for example, and he was very rich. He had power,' said Jose Olbes.

A charming gentleman of business, Jose Olbes visited Hong Kong throughout these dealings and, as a highly educated Filipino, has a helpful perspective on what he found among his Hong Kong colleagues. 'They brought their outside problems into the board. When the Mardens or some people like that, invited me to the Hong Kong Club for dinner, they wouldn't invite Noel. And Sir Sik-nin wouldn't come anyway because this club had not accepted him as a member [because he was Chinese]... Noel never took me out to dinner but invited me to his home which was much nicer. He had a lot of lovely things in that house.'

Less in the limelight were companies such as booksellers Kelly & Walsh, of which Noel was chairman at this time. Established in 1885, the firm comprised Kelly, an Irish printer, and Walsh, a Scots bookseller and publisher. It once boasted branches in Shanghai, Singapore, Hankow and Japan, with printing presses in Shanghai and Singapore.[30] Early newspapers invariably featured a box advertisement from Kelly & Walsh, advertising its titles on offer.

Noel Croucher kept his hand in with several smaller investment vehicles, such as Caroline & Company Limited, with nominal capital of $1 million, subscribed to by a collection of Hong Kong Club members, and 'Noel Victor Amor Croucher, Holland House, Hongkong, Stock Broker.'[31]

Noel's old habit of making a nuisance of himself at company meetings had not abated. Brian Tisdall remembers how he met Noel: 'I did a column for the *South China Morning Post* and when checking on a story I got in touch with Noel Croucher. He then put $100 worth of shares in my name so that I could go to the AGM of a company called Kowloon Development. Noel had a very suspicious mind, but usually with justification.

'Well, Tang Shui-kin was at the meeting and the question Noel wanted me to ask was, How could the directors of the company justify their expensive launch. Tang replied that they were always on the lookout for development opportunities in the outlying islands. So Noel was stymied on that one.'[32]

Noel was obviously dealing in everything, not just in stocks and shares but in property as well, sometimes acting as a real estate broker or middleman. 'And if he needed finance, he could always go to the [Hong Kong & Shanghai] Bank.'[33]

'He said he'd bought and sold every building in Central one time or another. Telegraph House, for example, he says that was bought and sold several times with his help,' remembers Duncan Graham, a man who has the dubious honour to be the only man ever to join Noel in business, albeit not for long.[34] Noel bought several houses on the Peak and, when the owner of 6 Macdonnell Road died in the 1950s, he bought the property and redeveloped it.

The famous Ledger, now lost, recorded each share he had ever bought, when and for how much, and the records went back at least five decades. His favourite buys were utilities, mining and bank shares. 'He had lots and lots of Hong Kong Bank shares, and an enormous quantity of gold, real gold. I heard of a stack of gold ingots in a vault somewhere in a bank in Canada. I do remember the physical gold,' says Duncan Graham. Noel was friendly with the Shanghainese brokers, and with Sir Joseph Ho Tung and Ho Shai Lai. He was also a big fan of the Bank of East Asia. At the same time he kept in close touch with historian G.B. Endacott, who used to come to the office to talk a lot with Noel.

Noel was well known as an aggressive competitor and operator. 'He was an activist shareholder. He was a prominent shareholder in Indo-

China Shipping Company, for example, which was part of Jardine, and I was with Jardine. Noel would pump me and then ask sticky questions at board meetings. He knew everything, had contacts everywhere, He was no fool,' avers Richard Hownam-Meek.[35] Brian Johnson, formerly of Peat Marwick, recalls Noel being 'worked up' about a shares reorganisation of Indo-China stock by Jardine. 'He said it was robbery ... and ruffled many feathers.'[36]

When the Hong Kong & Shanghai Bank, which assumes some functions of a central bank, needed to know anything about the market, it was Noel they turned to for advice. 'As I understand it,' ruminates Allen Mills, 'he was still, even right up until virtually the end, one of the brokers of the Hong Kong & Shanghai Bank, one of those people who was summoned to discuss with the chairman the situation any particular morning — like Mok Ying-kie.'[37]

'In the late 1950s, I was in charge of the securities department at the Bank,' says Guy Sayer, of the Hong Kong & Shanghai Bank. 'In those days people didn't deal directly at the exchange, they tended to buy and sell their shares through the Bank. We were big players on the market, sometimes on behalf of customers, sometimes on behalf of the Bank itself. So brokers liked to keep in touch with us.

'They all came to see me every morning — Croucher, Potts, Zimmern, they all came round. I had a counter in the old Bank, and we'd talk about what's going on, just to keep in touch. I had to parcel the work out — it was very difficult, the Bank was so powerful. But of course it was worth their while to keep in touch with the Bank. Noel knew what was going on.

'Noel was the most influential broker, no question about that. He had the money and the resources. And he knew what he was doing, a very shrewd operator. In business, he was a hard man, fair but strong. We used to take his advice. He knew the market extremely well. He knew how to deal, and was very careful about his money. That is the way to get rich.'[38]

Peter Vine was a senior partner at Hong Kong's leading law firm, Deacons, for forty years. He says the firm's stockbroking business usually went to either Noel Croucher or Alec Potts. And he remembers Noel's help in securing the listing of a company called Local Property & Printing Company. The stock exchange committee had refused to list the company, seemingly because of some personality clashes. 'So I rounded up Noel to suggest means to get the company listed as cheaply as possible, and we found a convenient side door. Noel said we should allot the whole lot to him, at two percent lower, and he would get the other committee members to buy off him at one percent lower. So he got us a cheap quotation, and he got himself a tidy profit.'

We should also remember that those days of doing business in Hong Kong allowed a great deal of latitude to the colony's leading businessmen: 'Being on the board of directors of a company in those days was regarded as an opportunity to get a bid in before the general public. It was not considered wrong to take advantage of information — no one took any notice.'[39]

Noel dined from time to time with former senior partner of Wilkinson & Grist, Peter Griffiths, and lawyer Leslie Wright. 'Noel would talk of the background of all the big Chinese families, the Lis, the Laus, the Lees, the lot. He knew all the original companies from when they were first listed, and he was well known to them all. He knew everything about the antecedents of the big families, he was always at cocktail parties with them.'[40]

But there were some curious gaps in Noel Croucher's knowledge. Brian Tisdall recalls a dinner at Noel's house one evening, when good friends Jack and Greta Hobbs were there. 'Someone mentioned the P/E ratio [price/earnings ratio]. And Noel piped up and said, "What's a P/E ratio?"!' He was also reputed to be unable to read a balance sheet.[41] Noel's entire lifetime of moneymaking had been achieved by a mind wholly untrammelled by economic theory.

♪ ♪ ♪

This position of canny, wise old man of affairs gave Noel immense power, a power which he was not averse to exercising.

In the late 1950s, Noel created a stir through his brinkmanship with a stalwart of the elite old China Coast companies. The Union Insurance Society of Canton prided itself on its lineage back to the early days of trade, founded in Canton in 1835 by British merchants aligned with venerable Dent & Company and moved to Hong Kong in 1842. Its managers hailed from the right schools and breeding grounds in the City of London, and its board mirrored, on a smaller scale, that of the Hong Kong & Shanghai Bank.

Noel Croucher had his eye on Union Insurance and decided it was time to accumulate a significant holding in the firm. He had been at the company's meetings before the war and was well acquainted with its assets and prospects. He built up a strong interest in its stock and thought, not unnaturally, that sooner or later he should be asked to join the board.

Nigel Rigg joined Union Insurance in 1951, but was not based in Hong Kong until 1960. He remembers the consternation caused by Noel's request that he be invited onto the board in about 1958–59.

'Croucher owned about thirty percent of Union Insurance — I think it was held on behalf of the Little Sisters of the Poor and he had power of attorney over their accounts. (Many religious groups owned shares and he controlled them.) Well, he said, "I can control the company, let me onto the board." But the rest of the board said they would all resign if he became a director!'[42] So Union Insurance turned him down.

Noel Croucher — chairman of the Hong Kong Stock Exchange, Commodore of the Royal Hong Kong Yacht Club, horse-owner, respected Hong Kong Bank client and Stanley Camp survivor — all this was not enough to get him into what its incumbents thought was the inner sanctum of the Hong Kong elite.

Noel Croucher, boy-clerk turned millionaire, was not going to take the snub lightly. He went to London, found a buyer, and arranged the take-over of Union Insurance by the Guardian Assurance group of London.

'He was not a popular character among the old established hongs,' recalls Nigel Rigg with circumspection. A large part of the problem was class, of course. 'I think it probably played a big part — Noel had a dubious background.

'The shareholders were delighted, but inside the company of course there was disappointment at the loss of independence. Someone at the time said, "If only the Bank or someone had told us [about the take-over threat from Noel], then we would have bought it all up and kept it from him." The board was absolutely furious! But Noel had done a good deal. We were more upset that other substantial investors allowed it to go ahead. Noel definitely got his own back.'

Lord Sandberg, then on his way to becoming chairman of the Hong Kong & Shanghai Bank, remembers the Union Insurance saga well. 'I recall he'd built up a large holding... And he thought that his holding entitled him to a seat on the board, which I think it probably did. But the directors of Union Insurance in their wisdom — or lack of it — refused to allow him a seat on the board so he then engineered a take-over! I can't think of another like that. That was outstanding!'

To many such as Sandberg, Noel's riposte to Union Insurance displayed a certain style. As for the old hong, 'Well, it was too late. They weren't a very big company but they were quite important in the pecking order in Hong Kong and they got their comeuppance,' Sandberg remembers. 'I think they were damn silly to turn down his request. I don't know how they did it. I wasn't involved in the machinations. But they were stupid not to use his experience.' Asked if Noel had overreached himself, presuming above his station, by demanding a place on the insurance firm's board, Sandberg says, 'Oh God no, no, no, no.

'I think he had a long memory and I think he probably wouldn't forgive slights like that. But I always had a good relationship with him although he was old enough to be my, certainly my father if not my grandfather. He was switched on. Obviously he made mistakes in the market as well as successes, but his successes far overwhelm his mistakes. He was just a smart cookie. A sort of one-man research unit I guess.'[43]

George Stewart of Hong Kong Bank happened to be in Toronto at the time, returning to Hong Kong from Britain. He saw an announcement of the take-over of Union Insurance by Guardian in a Toronto newspaper. 'I went to the Union Insurance office there,' recounts G.O.W. Stewart, 'and the man there was very excited but knew nothing about it. I later discovered Noel had organised this and I said to Noel, I hope you're not going to go too far in this...

'I said we [Hong Kong Bank] and Union Society were very similar institutions, we had started the same way. So I hoped Noel was not going to try to take us over! We were always aware that Hong Kong Bank could be taken over, we had to be careful. Well, Noel said, "Oh no, don't worry, you're different. The Bank is well managed."

'The point here,' Mr Stewart continues, 'is that Noel was very important to the Bank. It was much better to have him as a friend than as an enemy.'[44]

But such realities were never enough to get Noel onto the board of the Bank either. Certainly in post-war times, businesses, including the Bank, were more likely to find worthy recipients of the honour among the increasingly wealthy and powerful Chinese of Hong Kong, or others with a productive range of contacts. 'We wouldn't want anybody quite like him on the board of the bank,' adds another former Hong Kong Bank staff member.

As for the Union Insurance Society of Canton, its official history makes no mention of Noel Croucher. Their account of the saga is concise:

'In 1960 the Society took a step which seems to have been forced on it by the need for far larger resources, to cope with what was an expanding business world. A revolution in transport and travel had taken place, first among the transatlantic countries, and then to encompass the developing nations in a few short years. The Society merged in that year with the Guardian Assurance group of London, but continued to operate under its own name and those of its subsidiaries, and to maintain its old links with clients.[45]

❧ ❧ ❧

Far away from these corporate sagas is an aspect of Noel's life which few people knew about, and which many would have misunderstood anyway. In 1956, Noel met a woman who was to become a trusted confidante for years to come. Her name is Joan Scrivener. She was a friend to Basil and Inez Croucher back in England, Basil being Noel Croucher's brother. The brothers had seen little of each other over the years. But it was only natural that when the young attractive Joan went to Hong Kong on a trip to attend a girlfriend's wedding, she took family greetings to a man called Noel Croucher.

Here began a genuine friendship which occasionally looked as if it might veer into something deeper, which was marked throughout by great trust and liking on both sides. Here also began a correspondence of incredible regularity, with letters going back and forth several times a month, for twenty-three years. Thanks to the generosity of Joan Scrivener, we gain an unparalleled insight into the life, loves and thoughts of Noel Croucher.[46]

On that first trip of hers to Hong Kong, Joan stayed first with her girlfriend and eventually at Noel's place, all with the utmost propriety. There is little doubt — and can be no surprise — that Noel greatly enjoyed the company of this messenger from home, this bright, thirty-seven-year-old unflappable young woman. In an envelope containing a few photographs, left behind after Noel's death, several are of Joan Scrivener.

Noel wrote of the water shortages, the typhoons, the social conditions, his daily life, building a picture of a full life, experienced sometimes with real depression and at others with his very quirky sense of humour. His writing shows how weighty a man Noel Croucher was. Whatever his competitors in Hong Kong said of him, Noel was a man who cared about serious matters, about culture as well as business, and for others as well as himself.

This friendship with Joan lasted to Noel's death, despite the large age gap between the two. Joan is the nearest Noel got to having a true 'family' friend, someone he could trust and confide in. And the strength of that bond highlights how few other people Noel ever let into his personal sphere.

He revealed himself to Joan as a warm, humorous and fascinating man. He loved pets, he loved his home, the views, his sailing, the weather. And he genuinely meant well in his philanthropy. Frequently, he referred to being 'tied down doing unremunerative work which gives me pleasure'. In these letters is found the clearest statement of Noel's convictions about philanthropy:

> All this is very rewarding and is some compensation, but I believe I'm doing the right thing in the community and the country will be all the better. Those with the brains and the keenness to work should be encouraged and money or the lack of it should not be an impediment.[47]

Noel firmly believed in the value of education, and he certainly had his views on wealth well organised. He was not bemused by his money — he wanted to use it wisely and well. His notions of natural justice were such that he felt money, or the lack of it, should never get in the way of people fulfilling their potential and contributing to society.

Noel also revealed himself as a romantic. We had a hint of this already in his love for poetry and appreciation of beauty. Here with Joan was a rare opportunity for this side of him to come out. The time he spent with her was a rare treat, while the letters were a lifeline for him to a saner world. His search for a home in England had begun. So, too, had his bitterness about events within his immediate family which, sadly, was to dog him for years.

That Noel actually writes about how 'unremunerative work' gives him such pleasure will surprise some readers. At last, with these letters, there is evidence of the depth and breadth of this complex man. Here was one who, for whatever reason, hid these bright lights under a bushel of gruff, Scrooge-like tendencies. The money-grabbing rascal some of his Hong Kong acquaintances saw, was but a part of the whole man.

Film stars and money men — Noel Croucher is third from right. On his right is John Hunt of Peat Marwick accountants. Next is Li Fook-shu, father of David Li Kwok-po, of the Bank of East Asia. On the couch at right is Li Lihua, a famous actress.

Noel Croucher with Frank Sinatra. Sinatra made several trips to Hong Kong in the 1960s. In 1962 he gave three charity concerts at City Hall in aid of the Sandy Bay Children's Home, among other child-care causes.

Chan Nam-cheong,
Hong Kong Bank's Mr Turner,
and Noel Croucher.

Noel Croucher (second left) with golfing friends at Fanling.

At Sandy Bay: Chan Nam-cheong and Noel Croucher stand at the left with, slightly hidden, Professor John Hodgson. In the centre is Governor Alexander Grantham, and far right is Mr Turner. Third from right is the first matron, Mrs Watson.

Ceremony held to rename Sandy Bay hospital the Duchess of Kent Children's Orthopaedic Hospital, 17 December 1970. From left: Sister Barbara O'Sullivan, an unidentified supporter, Noel Croucher, Lady Trench, Dr Gerald Choa – Director of Medical Health Services, Mrs Saunders and Mr King.

The children of Sandy Bay with Noel Croucher and a visiting U.S. Congressman, 1962.

Noel Croucher at a Christmas Party at the Juvenile Care Centre.

Noel Croucher.

Richard Croucher, 1980.

St. John's Cathedral Hong Kong, showing the window Noel Croucher donated.

Detail of the East Window, St. John's Cathedral.

Noel Croucher at home with his dog.

Noel Croucher at home, 22 Mount Cameron Road, the Peak.

Noel Croucher's office, 1979/80.
(*Thanks to the* South China Morning Post.)

The cabinet full of company files in Noel Croucher's office, 9 Ice House Street.

Lady May Ride.

Trustees of The Croucher Foundation. From left: Lord Lewis, Lord Butterfield, Noel Croucher (in portrait), Ian MacCallum, Lord Todd, and Rayson Huang.

Trustees of The Croucher Foundation with Anson Chan, then Chief Secretary of Hong Kong, 20 March 1997.

South China Morning Post, *June 1981, when the old Hong Kong Club Building on Jackson Road was being pulled down.*

CHAPTER FOURTEEN

END OF AN ERA

I strove with none, for none was worth my strife

Nature I loved and next to nature art

I warmed both hands before the fire of life

It sinks — and I am ready to depart.[1]

n 1960, Noel was one year short of seventy. It is not surprising that at this age he seemed to be trying to make sense of his life, to inject some meaning into his activities, and to cope with increasing loneliness and fears of infirmity. In fact, Noel had a fantastic constitution and good health, and was to remain active around town for another twenty years. The trouble was that Noel began growing old in full view of his colleagues, competitors, friends and enemies, in small and unforgiving Hong Kong.

A Hong Kong Chinese millionaire could expect to have a full support system of family and culture around him as all those irritations and frustrations of age creep up on him. Expatriates who never go 'home' are different. They are already mild freaks, because no matter how long they have lived in Hong Kong they are still foreigners (and always will be). If they are lucky, they may have a spouse with whom to share the changes. It is very rare for them to have children or grandchildren around them — younger generations usually move on. The isolation is compounded by the feeling, for many permanent expatriates, that they have nowhere to go 'home' to.

Unless one has kept and nourished friends and connections elsewhere, the adjustment from Hong Kong back to a village or suburb one barely knows in a country on the other side of the world which is theoretically one's own — well, that is too much to face for many expatriates, and a recipe for unhappiness, too. The privilege and wealth of these foreigners are easy to see, yet so is the cost they pay in terms of emotional comfort, even identity.

In Noel's case, he had no spouse or family around him. His status in Hong Kong business circles was, if anything, a disadvantage, as it kept him in the public eye. It meant that many harboured grudges against him, or enjoyed a good joke at the bar at his expense. Added to these practical disadvantages was Noel's temperament.

He just did not know when to stop. All his life he had been driven to achieve, to get ahead, to make money, 'to make it'. He could not conceive of not working, no matter how rich he was. And this, in itself, was a sign of nuttiness in Hong Kong — here was a man richer than anyone, who chose not to flaunt his wealth! And his immense worldly success had never been matched by the same degree of personal happiness — except perhaps when he sailed and *La Cigale* was 'going like a bomb' in the harbour which he knew from his youth.

Noel Croucher was beginning to progress, if that is the word, from a position as an original, a fascinating millionaire yachtsman, to that of an eccentric. As he went about his business, sailed and went to the horse races, invested globally and enjoyed a very few old friends, Noel became more lonely and, to the outside world, more weird.

The image of eccentricity was nurtured by the rebellious aspect of Noel's character. He had never been shy to say what he thought, at the risk of upsetting others, because he had that blend of conviction and idealism that produces stubbornness and contrariness. He could be didactic, self-righteous, overbearing — yet this was mostly because he firmly believed he was right, not because he wanted to alienate everyone. Indeed, he was aware that many people thought he was tight-fisted and mean, but was surprised when a person took offence at something he said.

'He said to me once, "Do you think I'm mean?",' recalled Wynne Ward. 'I said, well, you're not mean to other people, you're not mean to charities, but you're jolly mean to yourself! You're so proud to tell me your shoes are thirty years old!' Noel also told Wynne he was 'dead from the neck down'. In other words, she was safe from any improper advances. 'He was himself. Noel was Noel. Noel was a nice man actually, he was eccentric. I didn't really see much of him until he was quite old.'[2]

In June 1961, Noel Croucher resigned his chairmanship of the Hong Kong Stock Exchange.

> The fantastic events on the Hongkong Stock Exchange are perturbing a number of people. The price for a seat in the Exchange has now risen to about HK$220,000 — more than four times what it fetched at the beginning of the year ... (one of the senior stockbrokers in the Colony was reminiscing to me the other day that he paid $1,000 for his seat when he first joined many decades ago). ...The sixty members of the Exchange are now almost all Chinese.
>
> Mr. N.V. A. Croucher, the veteran broker who got the Exchange going again after the last war, negotiated for its building and is the 'grand old man' of the local share market, resigned recently... His rare brand of good-humoured and racy directness will be missed.[3]

Alec Potts' second wife, Rosie Potts, joined the exchange a decade later and sees nothing strange in this changing of the guard. 'I think nobody voted for him — that's why he resigned. Noel was not friendly with anybody, and you've got to be friendly at the exchange. He had nobody to go to the exchange for him any more and he wouldn't pay the staff to write on the board. We [Chinese brokers] felt sorry for him.' Noel was not even that friendly with George Potts' nephew, Alec. 'He used the same tailor as Alec, Luk Hing Wing. But Alec and Noel never saw much of each other, they were competitors.'[4]

Though little realised at the time, the argument between Noel Croucher and George Marden in the 1950s was the beginning of the end for Noel. It was by no means the first or last time Noel had an argument about business matters, not at all. But it became a lacerated sore for Noel. He mishandled it, and this put firmly in the public domain the fact that Noel had trouble keeping his friends.

The larger message was that Noel's time was passing. The society in which he had taken his early steps to riches had now changed irrevocably. He could not expect to remain at the top of a small clique in Hong Kong finance. The intrusion of someone like George Marden was the writing on the wall. Later revolutions in the stock exchange coupled with the rise of new Chinese tycoons, such as Li Ka-shing and Lee Shau-kee, were to alter profoundly the particular old boys' club in which Noel had made his home.

Noel Croucher had made his way to wealth and prominence in pre-war Hong Kong. He had achieved most social and financial goals by

1941. Then the war came. As a harbinger of the depths of change, there appeared the breezy new men, ready to apply Shanghai style to slumbering, provincial Hong Kong. Pre-war Shanghai was home to racy nightclubs, outrageous style and cosmopolitan pizzazz, whereas British Hong Kong closed down each night at 11 p.m. with 'God save the King' on the radio. Once the war was over, Noel felt it was time to enjoy old hand status. Chairing the exchange, leading the yacht club, enjoying his home on the Peak — all this was only what he deserved, one can argue, after his decades of striving against the odds.

Then, men like George Marden came to town, throwing money around the market, scooping up every old firm they could find. The perception at the time among an older guard of financiers was that men such as Marden were scary. He was changing the rules of the game which had suited the old guard at the exchange very well to date. No wonder Noel's nose was put out of joint.

'Mind you, Marden came into Hong Kong and did a terrific job,' recalls Hong Kong Bank's Guy Sayer. 'Hong Kong was a mess, everybody was leaving, and he put a lot of money in. George Marden was very active in the market, the whole time buying up companies. And his offices were right underneath the stock exchange. I think Noel felt probably that his influence had been affected by George. So I think there was a bit of competition going on.

'I think the Marden thing was very significant. And if you're into making money you begin to suspect everyone. It's the same with all people who make money. You don't know if people are your friends or your enemies.'5

Sometimes, people would be looking at what shares were for sale, and then Noel Croucher would walk in and whistle, and say, 'I'll take those, I'll take the lot!' People would scramble around, asking what was going on there, and so on. He could not actually manipulate the market, but he was by far the biggest potential dealer in the market. He knew it and he enjoyed those moments.

Noel Croucher, now fabulously wealthy, still wanted to feel he was Hong Kong Bank's broker. Having built up an ego over the years, he wanted yet more. This is difficult in one's seventies or eighties. 'His biggest friend was the Bank, as much as anything, I think it really was,' says Guy Sayer. 'He was good to have a chat with about whatever was going on. Then just as he is going out the door, he'd say, "What about giving me more business?" I'd say, "Noel you're rich as hell! Get out of here!" Then we'd laugh about it.'

Noel the showman was threatened by George Marden, and George's interests were everywhere: 'He was always buying and selling companies, and Croucher, well, I don't think he entirely approved actually of the way Marden operated — there were pretty odd things going on, by today's standards you probably wouldn't get away with it. In many ways Croucher was very upright you see.'[6]

'George Marden was a bit of an old rogue too you know,' explained Leslie Wright. 'A charming rogue, well-educated, got an MC in the war and all that. And he had this mellifluous voice. I remember him making an appeal for the Red Cross on the radio one time, in this lovely voice.'[7] By contrast, Francis Zimmern remembers Noel as a bull in a china shop, who, though very normal in the early days, went sour in his last years. 'There was no reason — he had more money than the rest of us.'[8]

But perhaps there were some reasons for Noel appearing increasingly out of tune with his world. Eugene Yourieff remembers the early days of Hong Kong, pre-war, when his office was the Captain's Bar, everyone met at the Gripps, and men went to the Cosmo Club, the only place which stayed open past 11 p.m. Lots of business was conducted over coffee at the Hong Kong Club. People dressed in linen and carried baskets to work containing a change of clothes, made necessary by the weather in the days before air conditioning. They could dive into the harbour for a dip in central Hong Kong. Time did not matter, lunch was two hours long. One also had to be careful because the town was so small — everyone knew you and heard everything.

In this world, Mr Yourieff feels that Noel never wholly felt at home. 'He felt people looked down on him. Noel had a chip on his shoulder.' Those who saw (and see) themselves as the China Coast aristocracy were not only widely known as taipans, managing large firms with a proud lineage in trade, but they also played rugby or cricket and shared school memories. Noel lacked such props.[9]

Jose Olbes retains a sad picture of Noel. 'Noel had a lot of power in Hong Kong, but he was not, or he felt he was not, on good terms with the rest of the community, or he felt that way. They thought he was not up to their level. We talked, and I tried to cheer him up — he didn't like being on his own in Hong Kong, he felt his family should be there...

'He was quite powerful but you could sense it — he resented the fact that "they" didn't accept him despite his wealth. He was bitter about life in general. I liked him but I sense he was not a happy man.'[10]

The rivalry between George and Noel was at first good-natured but ever-present, according to George's daughter-in-law, Anne Marden. Many others attest to the strong friendship as the two men plotted their incursions into high finance. George and Noel were contemporaries. Both were ambitious, both had a knack for making money, and both lived their lives on the China Coast.

But George had yet another advantage over Noel, the significance of which would only increase over the years. Whereas George married well and had a son who followed in his business footsteps, Noel had no one to follow him. His son never made a home in Hong Kong and Noel could never bring himself to hand over the reins anyway. Noel would have liked to be a taipan, but remained a one-man band. 'Noel seemed to play with a straight bat. But he always seemed a second-hand merchant somehow. He never made it to the top bracket. I'm not sure why.'[11]

Though no longer chairman, Noel remained on the stock exchange committee. In some ways it helped that George Marden left Hong Kong in 1959, though he revisited on and off for years. Marden's departure heralded, at last, the listing of the gas company in Hong Kong, and, in 1964, the entry of Noel Croucher onto its board. Richard C. Lee, Noel's good friend, became chairman of the board. Eddie Lawrence of the gas company remembers Noel as 'a decent chap. But it was always difficult to leave his office — he liked to chat, he was a lonely man. He knew so much about people, he had so much knowledge, he could have put on paper so much of interest. He told stories, stories about corruption at pre-war Shewan Tomes for example, which were fascinating.

'There was an awful lot of speculation about Noel... He had no steady girlfriend — it would have been all over town if he had! And he was very set in his ways. Noel was not cantankerous but he was very hard to dissuade, and it was very, very hard to get him to change his mind. He had a lot of character.'[12]

Alongside the suggestions that Noel's lack of the proper breeding kept him out of the top circles, was the fact that Noel was a broker. He made money out of other people's money and either was not interested or lacked the vision to conjure up long-term creations. He was not directly engaged in producing new ideas or products and was not interested in major infrastructure projects unless he saw a short-term profit.

'Noel, as a financial man who knew the stock exchange, was very valuable to us,' says George Cam, also of the gas company. 'He could advise on rights issues and the like. But he was very much a short-term financial man. Gas is a long-term investment, you can't expect your money back within five years. I battled with him over putting a gas main out to Repulse Bay, and Noel said there'd be no return so he didn't want it — it was a case of the utility ethic versus the shareholders' ethic.' George Cam's other recollection is of Noel scooping up the free pens and paper from board meetings.[13]

In his social life, Noel achieved a more benign image. He was the ancient mariner, the man with fascinating stories to tell. In 1963, the Royal Hong Kong Yacht Club threw a party to mark the fiftieth anniversary of Noel Croucher's membership of the club. Few others could claim such an honour. Noel gave an oil painting of Captain Kellett's junk to the club to mark the occasion. And despite some nerves, he also gave a speech.

'He was a great man, but he was a shy person. He didn't want to get up and speak at the fiftieth anniversary,' remembers Pat Loseby. 'But he liked having it, he liked inviting people and having a party. He rang me up and said, was he supposed to make a speech and I said, "Yes, you are." He said, "I don't like making speeches." So I told him, "Don't make a long one! Just say thank you." Then of course he gets to his feet — he had something to tell you all the time — and he made a long speech then.'[14] Someone else there that night was Joy Dickinson and she too remembers the speech: 'He was unprepared, he had no notes or anything, but he rambled on and it was incredibly interesting. We were glued! I can't remember what it was about, probably the early days of the club and so on.'[15]

The year before, Noel had been on one of his rare trips 'home' to England. Through the Hong Kong Club, he was a member of the Junior Carlton in Pall Mall, so that after one night staying at his wife's place in Eaton Square, he had somewhere else to stay. He began looking for an English home at this point, but was also tangled in the affairs of his immediate family. His son's family life was difficult, Noel thought, and, typically for a self-made man of his generation, he just could not understand the way his son Richard went about things. That Richard chose to retire before he turned fifty, and seemed to live well regardless, was galling to Noel who saw work as a duty and life as a mountain to be climbed.

Noel became embroiled, as the years went by, in a most unfortunate quarrel with his son, and anyone he talked to about it was shocked at the depth of anger and frustration displayed. Of course, money (and a disputed loan or gift) came into it, as well as different perceptions about the meaning of life. Noel also tried to influence the upbringing of his grandchildren. At its best, this was a genial patriarch, putting money aside for the young ones' futures, and expressing concern for their education and values. At its worst, here was a manipulative and interfering old man, using his money to try to run other people's lives.

Throughout these years, Noel, the frustrated patriarch, paid out thousands of pounds — for some in his family, the house he had bought for them, the schooling fees for the grandchildren and much more besides. He also set up very generous trusts in his offspring's names. Several Hong Kong friends recall dissuading him from attempting legal action against his son.

None of this will surprise anyone in a family of strong personalities. The particular dynamic facing the second generation, the sons of the self-made man, must also not be forgotten. Wherever fault lay in all these arguments, there is no doubt that great pain was caused all around.

The more important point, for our understanding of Noel Croucher, is that Noel dearly wished for a large and happy family. He had never had one himself. And he dearly wished that this family should have the education and opportunities to make something decent of their lives. He had never had much of that either.

In between the rows and disappointments, the outbursts of generosity and the revitalising of his business contacts in London, Noel also found time to buy shoes from Lock and suits from Saville Row. From his Index Book, we learn he was familiar with the florists Blakes of Chelsea, the stock and share brokers W.N. Middleton & Company, the shirtmakers Turnbull & Asser on Jermyn Street, Robinson & Cleaver department store on Regent Street, and Truslove & Hanson — booksellers, book binders, court and heraldic stationers and engravers.[16]

Bill and Betty Hancock met Noel by chance as he returned from this trip, in 1963: 'We decided to do something different, to sail back to Hong Kong from Trieste. And we met Noel on the train from Paris to Trieste!' recalls Bill Hancock. 'We had an amah and two kids with us, Noel was alone. The captain of the ship was nervous — it was the first time he'd taken passengers, and there were wars everywhere. It was not like a cruise ship, it was full of people going back to work. We shared a table in the dining room with Noel. The first port was supposed to be Aden, but there was war there so we had to go on to Djibouti instead. Our second port of call was supposed to be Karachi, but there was a war there, so we went to Bombay... And then we got to Jakarta and soldiers with tommy guns came on board. When we got to Singapore it felt like civilisation...'[17]

Once back in Hong Kong, Noel was returning to what one civil servant described as a decade in which 'it was just one damn thing after another'. If the watchword for the fifties had been survival, it was now security or stability. A city cannot live by improvisation for ever, and the people of Hong Kong wanted more. The mood was not helped by months on end of droughts which caused water rationing to be introduced. In 1962, an unprecedented mass exodus was underway from southern China into Hong Kong, a result of real famine mixed in with politics.

Nor did the rash of other disasters help. In the mid-1960s, there were runs on several local banks, causing the demise of two Chinese banks. In 1965, the Hong Kong government had to import British sterling banknotes because local banknotes could not be printed fast enough to satisfy the demand. (They were never used.) In 1966, a massive storm created a deluge which made Magazine Gap a raging torrent and 2,000 people lost their homes. The year 1966 was the year of the Star Ferry riots, and in April 1967, Hong Kong was rocked by riots, partly caused by the excessive enthusiasm of the Cultural Revolution in China.

Noel's perspective on these events can be guessed at with the help of his letters. In a cryptic reference to the Star Ferry riots, he wrote:

> Things are quiet here again and have returned to normal, but for how long I don't know. What made things worse was the very bad hooligan elements that took advantage of the situation. ...Trouble here is very annoying and interferes with our peaceful way of life and if it goes on I'm afraid business is bound to suffer — but it is not anything like as bad as the Home Press would have you believe.[18]

> Things are quiet here and except for a few bomb throwing or planting, are normal. The bombs are not actually bombs but small tins of explosives that make a big noise but do little or no damage... Things are a bit worrying here after the Peking Legation being ravaged. But apparently there is no authority with power in China and if it goes on like this the whole country will be one big mess...[19]

In fact, riots, bombs, skirmishes and fifty-one deaths occurred over six months until, as eyewitness Robin Hutcheon records, 'the fever passed to leave the red sun glowering over the border in an angry, sullen, brooding silence. ...The Cultural Revolution is today seen as the wild aberration of an aging Mao Tse-tung and his rabid supporters, but in Hong Kong it was a call to the people to make their commitment at every level of society. And they did so with a unanimity which was surprising in the way it snowballed in favour of the Government in the course of a few short weeks.'[20]

Another indication of what Noel thought about such things comes from one clipping from *The Star* newspaper (founded by Graham Jenkins in 1965, now defunct). A column entitled 'Expat's Point of View, with Noel Croucher' featured the topic, 'Give Legco Wider Powers'. Unfortunately the date of the clipping is illegible, but here is a rare example of Noel's political views:

> The responsibilities of Government have expanded beyond anyone's expectations, but here in Hongkong the machinery of Government is outdated and is not necessarily suited to present conditions. The problems have become too complex and Hongkong too important to be controlled by a few Government officials.
>
> We have in our community people who are in a position to give Government the advice they need on their lack of efficiency in government departments, but they find it necessary to bring out efficiency experts at the cost of several million dollars...
>
> We have a Legislative Council of businessmen and yet their recommendations are so often overridden by senior Government people. Everyone knows this but nothing is done about it.
>
> We are about to spend $5,000 million on Mass Transport, though it will be nearer $10,000 million when completed. To commit Hongkong to this expense now is madness. We still have 400,000 to 500,000 people living in huts on the hillsides without sanitation and water. There are nearly two million under the age of 15, thousands unable to go to a free school, hundreds queuing up for medical attention and hundreds of thousands living below the poverty line.
>
> There are about 60,000–70,000 leaving school every year, most of them looking for jobs. In the next few years unless we are very careful there will be mass unemployment followed by civil disturbances.
>
> I would like to see a petition drawn up calling on the Secretary of State to expand the size and powers of the Legislative Council.

The column carries a brief note at the bottom: 'Noel Croucher is a member of the Hong Kong Stock Exchange. He has lived in Hong Kong since 1910.'

An important point from this opinion piece by Noel Croucher is his apparent concern for people at the other end of the social and financial scale to himself. How many brokers generally concern themselves with the thousands living without electricity on the hillsides? Noel was also concerned about the costs of government business, and his comment about locally available advice sounds as if he believed Government should have been consulting him!

From his letters, we know Noel strongly disapproved of phenomena such as trade unions, strikes and the alleged 'self-indulgence' of 'the workers'. In Hong Kong, however, he had no need to harangue the workers to be more competitive. Instead, he advocated democracy as the answer to the abuses of government.

Noel's continuing commitment to welfare work kept him active throughout the last two decades of his life. As can be expected, Noel did not casually throw money at the major institutionalised causes. His was a personal, sometimes maverick, approach. He followed his nose, responding with sensitivity to the needs he saw around him. With many of these charitable activities, it is hard to know exactly when and how Noel got involved. Records are scanty, and Noel seemingly chose to keep most of these good deeds quietly anonymous.

In one case, we do not know exactly what Noel gave,[21] but we know that in 1961, he sent a 'generous donation' to the University Library at Cambridge, England.[22] Among the papers left behind at his death, Noel had kept what appears to be a segment of a letter, from an unnamed librarian of Cambridge University:

> 10th November, 1961.
>
> Dear Mr Croucher,
>
> I write to thank you most warmly for the generous donation you have sent to our funds. I propose to pay for a particular book with this, and to put a donor's label inside it bearing your name...

Several years later, Noel helped to save a rare edition of a mediaeval manuscript at the Cambridge University Library. These are important examples of the breadth of Noel's philanthropic instincts, and of his deep love for books — he believed that culture and heritage were important, and gave freely in their name.

The story of this second donation begins with Noel's habit of reading the London *Times* (and *Financial Times*). In 1966, *The Times* highlighted the plight of a vital piece of literary heritage.[23] Volumes one to nine of William Caxton's translation of Ovid's *Metamorphoses* of 1480 were sold privately to an American bookseller, and an export ban on the work was to run out in three weeks' time. The newspaper pleaded with readers to help, and so donors in England and around the world sent cheques to help keep the precious work in England. Judging by a letter Noel wrote to his son years later, Noel was one of those donors:

> I happened to help in saving Chaucer's translation of The Ovid, which was going to be sold to an American — as a John Croucher about 1400 was the founder of a Library at Cambridge University College. I for sentimental reasons [also] subscribed for a number of books to be published at £100 a time. This was done and the manuscript remained at Cambridge.[24]

As was not unusual at this time of his life, Noel muddled up a few of the names — he means Caxton's, not Chaucer's, translation of the Ovid. Librarians agree this is a common mistake. As for the mysterious John Croucher, he did exist, but he did not found a library. Instead, he gave Cambridge University Library a very fine MS/manuscript of Boethius' *De consolatione philosophiae*, accompanied by a translation into English, by Chaucer, some time between 1429 and 1454.[25]

Cambridge University's Biographical Register records that a John Crowcher [sic] was a fellow of Gonville Hall in 1407–08 and eventually became dean of Chichester Cathedral. His donation of the Chaucer translation is listed, as is his gift of a window to the dining hall of his college.[26] Quite how or why Noel had come across this John Crowcher of the Middle Ages, we do not know. Perhaps a family story had percolated through generations and become attached to Noel's branch of Crouchers. Noel seems to be following consciously in the footsteps of John, through this contribution to the saving of a precious manuscript.

As for the mediaeval Crowcher's donation of a window, it was something else Noel was to copy.

Noel Croucher had long been active at St. John's Cathedral in Hong Kong, and was a council member for years. The first listing of his name on the Cathedral Council was in April 1955. A lasting reminder of Noel's enthusiasm for his church can be seen by any passer-by today. The East Window, a stained glass rendition of five lancets grouped under the Agnus Dei symbol, shows Christ on the cross outside the walls of Jerusalem with the sun of Resurrection behind him.

A cathedral history reports: 'Dedicated in September 1956 to all who suffered and died in Hong Kong during the Japanese occupation, it was the gift of the late Noel Croucher.'[27] The window was designed and constructed in England by Joseph Edward Nuttgens and transported in crates to Hong Kong. Special steel frames from a Chester workshop were used in an effort to withstand typhoons.

'After many years of thought and discussions a beautiful East Window is now in place; I myself am delighted with it, and as far as I can gather general opinion is favourable, unless people are being very kind,' enthused the Dean. 'One comment I think sums up the improvement the window has made: "the Cathedral has become again a place where it is possible to say one's prayers at odd moments during the week". The beauty of the East Window has made other windows look desperately naked... We are most grateful to Mr Croucher for his gift, and to Mr Nuttgens, artist and craftsman for his skill.'[28]

The North Window, dedicated in 1959 to all who lost their lives at sea in the two world wars, was the gift of an anonymous donor, who was probably Noel Croucher. A note about the new stained glass window, in the *St. John's Review* of October 1958, reads: 'We are most grateful to the anonymous donor, not only for this wonderful gift, but also for his unfailing regularity at worship every Sunday, for his quiet and humble goodness and the constant regular help he gives to so many friends when they need it, unobtrusively and without anyone except possibly the clergy knowing anything about it.'

Noel's interests in the cathedral were varied and his role wide-ranging. It so happened, for example, that he had kept a publication dating from 1870 titled *The Royal Visit* which made possible the printing of an article about the 1869 visit of His Royal Highness, Alfred, Duke of Edinburgh, to Hong Kong, in the *St. John's Review* of November 1958. On his visit, the Duke of Edinburgh had laid a special stone under the East Window. Noel's name also cropped up in *St. John's Review* as he was thanked for his gifts of flowers for the cathedral compound.

The Very Revd John W. Foster, now of North Yorkshire, arrived in Hong Kong in 1957 to be a chaplain at the cathedral, before becoming Dean until his retirement in 1973. He sees Noel Croucher as a 'good and generous man'. He remembers the parlous state of welfare provision in Hong Kong after World War II, and the partnership role which the church played alongside the government. To the churches fell much of the burden of providing social services — from schools, clinics and vocational training centres to children's creches, clubs and even a cooperative fish market. 'All these provisions had to be financed. Generous financial assistance from churches overseas was forthcoming but a great deal of local money was also required. There was an immense job to be done and Noel Croucher was one of the local benefactors who gave generously to enable those projects to be established.'[29]

The Revd Foster recalls that when it became time to build the New Hall, a public appeal was launched: 'The Appeal Fund remained open for some time, but eventually Noel Croucher asked how much money was still required. He then gave a cheque to complete the appeal and the hall was built...

'One of the responsibilities of the Cathedral was to bring together people from the wide range of nationalities living in Hong Kong so that there could be an active social interchange in the community. Indeed this was a great success. It was achieved largely by the Cathedral clergy holding sherry and other parties in their homes, and especially at the Dean's house, where people from all interests could be introduced to other members of the community. From time to time, two cases of sherry would arrive on the doorstep with Noel's compliments...

'One evening, my wife mentioned the booming stock market and said that she wished she had money to buy some shares. Noel said that if she would care to entrust him with whatever money she had available, however small, he would invest it for her. She only had a very small sum but she gave that to him. In a month or so he sent her a cheque far beyond the money she had given, saying that her investment had prospered. The amount she had given him was so small I have always thought that it was Noel who had "prospered" the investment personally, but my wife was so delighted with her profit.

'...He was a man who would help to build a school or a cathedral hall or donate a church window or a case of sherry or "encourage" a woman's small investment, and if you didn't happen to know he would not have told you. Thinking back, I think he was a lonely man...'[30]

Long-standing members of St. John's congregation regard Noel Croucher as a grand old man of the cathedral. After his death, the then Dean, The Very Revd Stephen Sidebotham, wrote to Noel's friend Joan Scrivener:

'...We have definitely decided now to call part of the Cathedral Endowment Fund, *which Noel himself established at the time with an anonymous gift*, the "Noel Croucher Fund", which will certainly be a suitable memorial to him and his long years of association with the Cathedral, not only in worship but also as our financial adviser.'[31]

The joke people like to tell about this is that whatever Noel did for the church, he won back through the perk of a free car park in the cathedral grounds. A tree-shaded, off-street parking spot in central Hong Kong was and is a rare treat!

☙ ☙ ☙

And all the while, Noel Croucher kept writing letters to Joan Scrivener. He was concerned about his family — that his son had remarried and that Richard's first wife was also remarrying, what was to be done with the children (Amanda and Nicholas) and so on. A major bone of contention was a house at no. 25 Radnor Walk in London, which Noel had bought in the hopes his grandchildren would be brought up there, but the marital changes forced new arrangements. He bought a country cottage for the grandchildren's holidays. When his brother Basil died, he helped the widow, Inez. He had her cottage redecorated, the hot water put on, paid for a woman to come in and help, and gave Inez a new TV.

Noel talked about his health and daily joys in Hong Kong. Among the celebrities he was proud to say he had met on the social rounds were Jack Hawkins, Peter O'Toole, Greer Garson, Gina Lollobrigida and the New Zealand Olympic running sensation Peter Snell. He referred especially to Joan Fontaine:

> She was born in Japan and wanted to revisit the place. Just travelling alone and left by plane for England to relatives de Havilland, who live somewhere in Surrey. She is very very natural and completely unspoilt. We went around on our own. She introduced me to the twist which I gave up after a few turns. She adored my bungalow and the dogs.[32]

Another typical reference is: 'I had dinner last night with Lord and Lady Sainsbury — grocer shops — on their way through from New Zealand. A very nice couple, quite unpretentious. He imports about 1 1/2 million lambs from NZ every year...'[33]

Noel displayed an understandable pride in his charitable achievements, and referred to the visit of Princess Alexandra: 'I was presented to her. She wanted to know how long I had been here and if I was going home again...'[34] He saw no clash between the recounting of his private woes, alongside those of the Chinese masses: 'Did I tell you about the Typhoon we had. I lost about 50 trees and half my roof. I had a place where the street sleepers and others slept, about 400, and it was [so] blown about and damaged that the government ordered it to be demolished...'[35] Frequently, Noel worried about the weather, particularly the water rationing and the sight of 'stoic' Chinese queuing at public taps.

Noel enjoyed risqué comments or jokes, or veiled allusions to being in the company of women. But he did not overstep a line drawn by his old-fashioned sense of propriety and the fact that he was still a married man with a public position to uphold. He saw Joan as a 'lady' so kept his tone light and amusing.[36]

Surprisingly, Noel wrote often about his personal beliefs and values, his views on education, what really mattered in the world, and how to solve inequities and injustices. In such discursions, he consistently put matters of personal faith and friendship ahead of financial gain. On the subject of educating the young, Noel had firm ideas, and was pleased a grandchild was going to a school —

> where tuition is along the lines I like, where religion is not forgotten, and charity towards all is remembered. This is what is lacking in our world today. Browning said God is in his heaven and all is well with the world, but *he is not* to an ever growing number. Don't run away with the idea I am sermonising, I'm not. If only the headlines in our kindergarten copy books were faithfully followed, the world would not be in such a mess.[37]

Noel's letters also give an insight into the expatriate dilemma: where is home? Noel's ambivalence about where to live and his ruminations on how ghastly the weather is in England, strike a chord for many. So, too, does his awareness of how his long life in the East had changed him:

> I wonder what picture you saw of me at Inez's. I came across one I had taken in the first war in uniform and after being in the East so long and getting a lot of England knocked out of me. The girls said I was different to the homeside Englishman, and I suppose I was. As a matter of fact, we who have been abroad so much are a lot more attractive — not so much nowadays as years ago. What with travel speed, T.V. etc we all seem to be going into the melting pot...[38]

> What a novel could be written of the characters and their background and secret affairs. The only one who has had a normal existence is myself and if I had never come East and [had] remarried in England, worked in a family concern far removed — I would never have found myself encumbered with so many hangers-on, but [would have] retired to a country cottage with plenty of woodland and a stream near by. Yet I doubt I would want to forego the experience between the years.[39]

Indeed not. He knew that by living in Hong Kong for so long, he had garnered opportunities he could not have found anywhere else.

> I have an immensely wealthy Spanish friend in Manila, who with his friends has built the most exclusive Golf Club in Spain, with residences for members. Bobby Jones designed the Course and from the brochure it is lovely. Several thousands of acres. And if I were living in England I doubt I would meet these people, but here I am one of the Directors of their Hong Kong Company...[40]

At the same time as knowing how special his life in Hong Kong was, it was also in these years that he came the closest to packing up and going away, especially when his faithful office assistant Mrs Ferguson died in 1966. She had worked for Noel for twenty years. She did everything for Noel — entered his horses for races, saw that his yacht was slipped when it should be and even kept track of his spending, as well as running his business. Her death probably explains Noel's various lapses in years to come, such as the fact that he left his cherished yacht to rot. Her steady presence and loyalty also encouraged an early outburst of philanthropy on Noel's part — he claimed in a letter that he paid for Mrs Ferguson's children's education and was very pleased at how well they had turned out.[41]

But as he argued it out in his letters to Joan, he clearly found it impossible to leave his Hong Kong life, despite the loneliness.

> You ask what is keeping me in Hong Kong and this is something I'm asking myself all the time and my family are asking me. Well, I'm involved in so many matters — companies operating in Canada, Australia, South Africa, a Hong Kong Hospital, welfare centres. And though I know one is not indispensable I have never left anything undone which should be done, and there is much, apart from business, and this has its problems. For instance last year's troubles with the riots etc, many thousands of strikers left and now want their jobs back, having sat outside their Manager's office singing Mao's songs...[42]

Noel Croucher's daily life of dinners and welfare commitments, golf and gripes, as described in his own voice in his letters to Joan, was less exotic, perhaps, than the legends would have us believe. But his writings have the advantage of bringing us into the reality of his world.

CHAPTER FIFTEEN

FAR-FLUNG FRIENDS

o matter what others thought of Noel Croucher and his supposedly obscure beginnings, Noel never derided his roots. Instead, he attributed his values to '...my forebears, who were old fashioned with some ideas of right and wrong.'[1] Perhaps no one asked Noel to intervene in the affairs of his offspring in England, but many individuals and welfare groups in Hong Kong did. This may have been part of the appeal of charitable work — Noel felt needed and important as he single-handedly made many good things possible for others. Yet, Noel seems to have actually cared that young people in Hong Kong had homes, health care and the right educational opportunities, and he was prepared to spend a lot of his time as well as money, making sure that they did. Increasingly, he seemed motivated less by a sense of pleasure than of duty. He was not necessarily happy with his life, but saw no way to change it.

The impression is of a man who, though once driven by an urge to become rich and powerful, now wished for more intangible things — such as the love of his family or of the right woman. Now entering his eighties, Noel spent his time keeping in touch with old friends, and making connections with his own past through the few people remaining who might be able to share it. Most of his external commitments — in business, at his sports clubs — were carried on by sheer force of habit. With a lifelong companion, a person's rough edges or peculiarities of behaviour are often smoothed out. In Noel's case, his individualism only became more marked. If not lunching in the Red Room at the Hong Kong Club, relaxing at the yacht club or playing golf, or at a welfare or business meeting, Noel was writing letters.

In the early 1970s, Noel's files included a handful of letters he exchanged with the office of Madame Chiang Kai-shek in Taiwan. It was only natural that Noel would be concerned about the bad health and finances of the dependents of a past good friend — the forgotten victims of the life and politics of the China Coast. For these letters were about the increasing ill health and difficulties faced by the wife and daughter of Noel Croucher's old friend, W.H. Donald. Donald was one of those amazing figures on the Coast — an Australian newsman who arrived early this century to join the *Hong Kong Telegraph* office only to become seduced by the politics of the Middle Kingdom. He was so committed to the Nationalist cause that he was to serve as adviser to Sun Yat-sen and Chiang Kai-shek.[2]

Decades later, when Noel Croucher heard of the desperate circumstances in which W.H. Donald's widow Mary and daughter, Muriel, were living in California, Noel became the conduit for money from Madame Chiang to the two women. One of the letters shows he told Donald's widow that 'I met you and W.H. at the beginning of this century' and had kept in touch with W.H. up to the last war, often sailing together in Hong Kong...'[3] The existence of W.H. Donald's wife and daughter was barely known to most of his China acquaintances — but Noel knew more than others.[4]

The surviving correspondence shows that in November 1970, Madame Chiang's secretary, K.C. Yu, wrote to Noel Croucher, thanking him for letting the Chiang office know about Mrs and Miss Donald, and forwarding a cheque of US$2,500 to each. 'Their Excellencies the President and Madame regret to learn of the ill health of the late Mr Donald's dependents... For your information, Her Excellency has also informed Marshal Chang Hsueh Liang of the Donalds' present predicament. As Marshal Chang was a very close friend of the late Mr Donald, I am sure you will be hearing from Marshal Chang shortly.'[5]

There is a slim chance Noel might have met Donald in and around Macao during the years 1908–11, as Donald was there at the time. But it is more likely the two men had met at the yacht club in Hong Kong. Throughout his years of travel and politicking in China, 'Don' would pop back to Hong Kong waters whenever he could. By 1935, he was having a yacht built for him in Hong Kong, the *Mei Hwa*, and might well have asked the then Commodore of the yacht club, N.V.A. Croucher, to keep an eye on the process. (The yacht was built at the Hong Kong & Whampoa Dock Company then run by Edward Cock, a firm in which Noel maintained a lifelong interest and investment.)

The two would have enjoyed each other's company — both were blunt men with underlays of surprising subtlety. Besides, Donald had 'become a sort of oracle. He knew the causes and reason behind any event'.[6] Noel's greatest asset in business was his in-depth knowledge of the Coast, of the market and of the people. It may be that he gleaned some of this knowledge from Donald. In 1919, Donald was interested in a proposed engineering project in Hong Kong, and acted as mediator between Canton and British and American investors in the railways.[7] In the 1920s, Donald was running the Bureau of Economic Information in Beijing. 'Don' and Noel also had strong mutual friends, such as Ansie Lee Sperry, daughter of Lee Hysan.

The letters do not suggest Noel Croucher had any personal connection with the Chiangs — his tone is respectfully polite, not intimate or friendly. On the contrary, in a letter he wrote to Mrs Mary Donald, he described his efforts to get a letter through to the Generalissimo:

> Though I tried in many ways to make contact and to make sure of his getting my letter it was almost impossible and then you wrote and said not to trouble, but I still waited for an opportunity and then a Chinese friend of long standing in transit [sic] contact with someone close to H.E. Chiang Kai-shek's secretariat took a letter for me.[8]

Muriel Donald, daughter of W.H., was uncomfortable about approaching the Chiangs for help, even though her mother was dying and she herself was suffering from cancer: 'You see, Noel, I have always felt that my Father's association with the Chiangs was his life and his business, and really had nothing to do with us. We have always managed to get by, though rather slimly in the past few years due to illness.'[9] This letter also suggests that Noel's initial contact with the Chiangs on behalf of the Donalds was prompted by the widowed Mrs Donald in a moment of stress. The money arranged through Noel Croucher helped get a new bed and wheelchair for the elder Mrs Donald, to pay off the mortgage on their property and a long list of unpaid bills.

'What more can I say good friend, other than you have my deepest thanks,' wrote Muriel Donald to Noel Croucher.

It is not clear whether Noel sent any of his own money to the Donald women, separately to what he arranged through the Chiangs. The correspondence simply shows a man with a long memory and a sense of compassion to those who were in some way victims of life on the Coast.

Dr Diana Siu, a successful medical practitioner in Prince's Building, Central, is yet another example of Noel's secret philanthropy. Back in 1970, she had finished school near the top of her class, but, if she was to pursue her dream of becoming a doctor, she needed to get a scholarship or two. Her father had died when she was eleven, and her mother had to work hard in order to support Diana's education. This was exactly the sort of person Noel liked to help — one who had proven her brains and determination and needed only some extra help to make a real success. Many times, in his letters to Joan Scrivener, Noel looked back happily on his ability to help in such situations. He was almost as proud as if the recipient had been his own offspring, and liked to mention the Diana who had become a doctor. He also liked to help professions which he thought added to the greater good of the community, and medicine was clearly in this category.

In a letter by Noel to his son Richard, he referred to his satisfaction at being able to help people such as Diana Siu:

> I've recently been told that a very poor girl who studied at a Government school, whose Father died — her mother became a factory worker and lived in a single room 20' x 20' with her two daughters paying 3 1/2 £ a month rent — the daughter preferred to study medicine and she came to see me giving me the news she was a Doctor with honours — after 8 years. A friend of mine gave a few scholarships to the HK University and I had his Power of Attorney and gave one to this girl. She passed with honours and is now spending a year in our leading hospital. She came to thank me for what I had done for her.[10]

It is not clear from Noel's letter if he is referring specifically to Diana Siu here, but indeed, she did visit Noel Croucher to express thanks. 'I actually went to thank both Mr Fung Ping-fan, and Noel Croucher, for their help with scholarships. I went to the seventh floor of Holland House each year,' Dr Siu remembers. 'Mr Croucher was different — he would spend time asking me how I was getting along. He seemed interested, very down-to-earth, very approachable. He was fatherly. When I finished University, I went to him again to thank him.'[11]

Two years later, Dr Siu was married and sent an invitation to Noel Croucher. He responded by offering her a choice of cash or a diamond ring for a wedding present. 'And to my surprise, he even attended my wedding! I knew very little about him, but from what he told me, he came to Hong Kong as a messenger boy in a stockbroker's company, so he had started at the bottom. I owe him a lot.'

Similarly, if someone he knew had wasted an opportunity or wasted money, Noel lamented the waste in his private letters, usually adding, 'it might have been spent on young children from poor families, who had the intelligence and keenness to learn and to be a credit to the community...'[12] Many times, the example he used was that of Dr Siu.

'I think Noel had an interest in young people, to help them,' says Rayson Huang, former vice-chancellor at the University of Hong Kong, and later a trustee of The Croucher Foundation. 'I understand he used to give young people a few hundred pounds, to study in Australia, or to study in the UK. If they were coming back and were short of money, he said, "Well, take a few hundred pounds, forget it, take it and don't worry about it!" That sort of thing you see. All the time he was helping young people. And imagine him giving away money like that when he would be careful about a taxi fare!'[13]

A major commitment which Noel took on in his later years was the Ebenezer School and Home for the Blind (now Visually Impaired). Noel was an active supporter of this pioneering body from 1975 until his death in 1980, giving 'generous sums on a regular basis'.[14] Founded in 1897 by Hildeshiemer Blindenmission in Germany, the Hong Kong branch serves specifically Chinese children. Located on Pokfulam Road, it is not far from the Sandy Bay/Duchess of Kent Children's Hospital which Noel visited regularly.

The evidence, as usual, is hard to find, but two letters remaining in Croucher's files together prove that in August 1978, Noel's trust funds at the Hong Kong Bank donated $1,004,663.29 to the Ebenezer project. In the letter to Noel from the bank, informing him that the money had reached its destination, this payment is described as 'Your Third Settlement'.[15] The way this donation was made, through Noel's trusts at the bank, is a good example of his clandestine philanthropy. The odd-figured amount implies it comprised earnings from a share allocation or similar. It also shows that as far as the Ebenezer staff knew at the time, the donation was entirely anonymous.

The director of Ebenezer then was Keith Marshall, and he thought the mystery donor was Noel: 'He called me up, introduced himself, and said he was very interested in the work of the school and as he did support other charities, would I be willing to talk to him. That continued for a considerable amount of time, about six months. He would call, usually on a Saturday morning, and would address me as Doctor Marshall, I don't know why, and I kept saying, "No, no, I'm a Mister."

'He was always very interested in what we called Special Programmes, not just handing money over for running expenses. He asked me if there was something special I would be interested in. So I talked to him about the Special Programmes — mainly orientation and mobility training, teaching children how to travel independently... We also had a programme of integrated education — when our children left our school they'd had only nine years of schooling, so I said this is crazy, especially for kids who are particularly bright. I approached St. Paul's [Boys' School] and later St. Stephen's [Girls' School]. Two boys from St. Paul's went through and got degrees at University. They set the tone.

'He used to ask me a lot of questions about these things. In the end, he sort of intimated to me that he would be willing to support them. As far as I can remember, I can't think of any other donors on that scale. When the big donations came in, he was the only person we could link it to. But you see this is the only contact I ever had with him — I never met him, I only talked with him on the phone. I often invited him to visit the school, but he never came around. A very strange sort of relationship.'

Keith Marshall recalls that this mystery donor on the phone sounded elderly and often repeated himself. Noel would talk for a long time, as if he was lonely, but Keith Marshall expected nothing to come of it. 'When I asked if he'd like to be acknowledged for his donation he said, "Oh no, don't worry about that." He was very non-committal.'[16]

Noel Croucher was apparently fascinated by the fact that a fellow expatriate was doing what to him seemed very unusual work — being an English principal of a school for blind Chinese children, founded by a German mission. It is indeed often forgotten that many in Hong Kong are not motivated by money, but to Noel, it seemed rather odd.

Keith Marshall's wife studied at the University of Hong Kong, so had already heard of another aspect of Noel's philanthropy — his support of several student bursaries for many years. These were first proposed as Royal Society of St. George Bursaries, as Noel made the money available from the Shakespeare Fund, which he had already established.[17] But alongside literary interests which Noel hoped to encourage, he also funded General Bursaries through which any undergraduates could apply for help to study their subject of choice. In 1980, after his death, the total was increased to cover ten studentships to be awarded on the basis of financial need.

Noel Croucher also took his duties as a Justice of the Peace very seriously. He often referred to this commitment in his letters, such as in this letter to his son:

> Our Commissioner of Police is a close friend of mine and you may
> know that HKong is a Drug centre. ...We have about 3,500 gaolbirds

in our Prisons & 55% are there for being involved in Drugs. Being a Justice of the Peace my duty is to visit them now and again.[18]

In August 1971, Typhoon Rose left a hundred dead. Two months later, the Jumbo floating restaurant caught fire, leaving thirty-four workers dead. In January 1972, the famous Cunard liner, *Queen Elizabeth*, just purchased by C.Y. Tung, strangely burned and sank at her moorings in the harbour. In June that year, a record rainfall and deluge wiped out the squatter area in Sau Mau Ping, killing seventy-one. The dramatic and tragic collapse of an apartment block on Kotewall Road in Mid-levels left sixty-seven dead. Meanwhile, China was opening up as it recovered from the Red Guards. Illegal immigrants were surging across the border and Hong Kong's population exceeded five million before the end of the decade.

From the early 1970s there was a share boom, attracting almost everyone from housewives to labourers and policemen. Tycoons made fortunes and a succession of companies went public, but 'small wage-earners watched their savings vanish in Hong Kong's greatest paper chase. It ended when the Hang Seng Index reached a peak of 1774, and months later sagged to 150.' Long queues formed around Central as people lined up to get new company prospectuses. One firm hired the Old Hall at St. John's Cathedral for a rights issue, so the *South China Morning Post* headline that day was 'Oh come all ye faithful...'[19]

These were years of radical change on the financial scene. The Hang Seng Index of stocks and shares on the Hong Kong Stock Exchange, though dating from 1964, was only made public in the aftermath of the 1966–67 disturbances, and a subscribers' broadcast service was introduced to the stock exchange. But, as the official history notes: 'One of the criticisms of the Stock Exchange was that it had remained the preserve of, and subject to the whims of a few wealthy people. In addition, it had failed to attract the great liquidity of the Hong Kong people into the formation of new capital or equity holding by keeping the par values of shares high. It had also remained something of a closed shop with membership restricted to 60 under the terms of its original constitution.'[20]

That constitution had been drawn up with Noel Croucher's input back in 1947, when he became chairman of a newly unified post-war exchange. Clearly the winds of change were catching up with him. The city of Hong Kong was now home to about five million people, with money and dreams of their own. By all accounts, Noel was slow to accept the need to evolve. He was a dyed-in-the-wool traditionalist in business and knew the advantages of a monopolistic position. He had already resigned his chairmanship of the exchange, but he was soon to see the vast masses sweep in a new era at the once exclusive hall of trade.

Malcolm Surry remembers that the stock exchange in those days was a club wherein its members made money, 'like shooting at fish in a barrel. And then the great unwashed got involved. Of course the old exchange was reluctant to admit new members. It was a colonial club.'[21]

Francis Zimmern, a member of the exchange since the beginning of Noel's chairmanship, reported that Ronald Li Fook-shiu had approached Noel in the mid-1960s suggesting membership should be increased to eighty, adding that Noel apparently rejected the idea. Alexander Potts, Noel's successor as chairman, may also have rejected it.[22] Debate was joined. Some brokers were unconcerned about the prospect of more exchanges in Hong Kong. Others, such as Noel, were less sanguine, predicting a 'mess' which would be harmful to the public interest.

'Noel felt that the stock exchange should never have allowed the setting up of other exchanges. The Hong Kong Stock Exchange should have accommodated the new people,' recalls Duncan Graham, who worked in Noel's office in the early 1970s.[23] Indeed, we can see Noel's point of view from a letter to Joan:

> I've never been so busy for ages — the state of the Stock Exchanges is such that Government has appointed an Advisory Committee to look into matters. Their first recommendation is for the 4 Stock Exchanges to have the same hours and to close 3 afternoons a week to catch up.
>
> I warned Government several times in the last 2 years what would happen if they permitted several stock exchanges to open, but this was ignored. The Chinese Exchanges are nothing else but gambling dens...[24]

Li went ahead and founded the Far East Exchange in 1969. It succeeded beyond anyone's expectations, and helped to transform Hong Kong from a domestic to an international market. It also admitted female members for the first time. Increasing prosperity among the Chinese led to the entry of thousands into the local stock market. It was followed by the appearance of the Kam Ngan Stock Exchange in 1971 and the Kowloon Stock Exchange in 1972. 'Membership at one of the three new exchanges was seen as virtually a licence to print money.'[25] The next year, 1973, was a roller-coaster year — it began with an incredible boom and ended with an incredible bust, only to fall further in 1974. Meanwhile, a new Securities Ordinance was made law and a Securities Commission established as watchdog. Many more regulations followed, the overheated market was cooled, a take-over code introduced, and finally, the exchanges were unified in law by 1980, and in practice by 1986.

Noel participated in the broking scene well into the 1970s. In 1972 he played a key role in the first contested take-over bid in Hong Kong, the take-over of independent Dairy Farm by the Jardine-backed Hongkong Land. This was a dramatic event in Hong Kong corporate history. The two venerable firms hired special advisers and those board members with interests in both camps had to stand back. The battle and the bargaining were played out through a series of full-page advertisements in the newspapers, until Hongkong Land could announce they had acquired a majority of Dairy Farm's shares.

Noel had been active at shareholders' meetings for both Dairy Farm and Hongkong Land for many years, and he had the kind of contacts which enabled him to still claim a pivotal role.[26]

In 1975, Noel again played a key role. This time it was the turn of Hong Kong & China Gas to feel the heat of Hong Kong Electric's advances. In a reminder of past battles between Noel and George Marden, this time it was George's son, John Marden, who was leading the HK Electric take-over attempt on the gas company. The gas company board was chaired by Richard C. Lee, and the company resolved to fight the take-over.

'Hong Kong Electric made what appeared to be a good offer to take over Hong Kong & China Gas,' recalls Malcolm Surry. 'But Croucher organised a group of shareholders to reject and fight off the take-over. He was on the phone to me, huffing and puffing about how the bid from HK Electric was not good enough, and that it would be rebuffed. I just thought he was an old buffer... But he was right. The take-over bid was rebuffed. In fact, it was handsomely beaten off.'[27]

Noel Croucher is recorded in the minutes of board meetings of the gas company during those fraught days: 'Mr Croucher stated that he considered the take-over bid was not in the interests of shareholders.'[28] Board members, shareholders and a selection of happy Towngas customers all agreed, and Hong Kong Electric's offer was aborted.

The jubilant gas company board wanted HK Electric to admit how few shares it had accepted during the battle. This exchange gives us a delightful insight into Noel's way of doing business: 'Mr Croucher commented that he had arranged for a spectator to be at the offices of Peat, Marwick, Mitchell & Company, and that on most days very few acceptances had been handed in. On the last day about 30 persons had attended, but he thought that only approximately 40,000 shares had been handed over.'[29] Once again it is obvious that a key to success was Noel Croucher's innovative intelligence, and his intelligence systems.

Noel remained on the stock exchange council but was not active in the exchange on a daily basis in the 1970s. Francis Zimmern recalls Noel around this time as someone who 'didn't fit in, in Hong Kong, no. He was against all the changes here.'[30] By the time Hong Kong's regulatory bodies were suggesting new codes of practice nearer the end of the decade, Noel wrote a letter to his son Richard: 'Things are not so good in my business — as stockbroking is absolutely dead. Many brokers are closing shop.'[31]

The new market conditions in Hong Kong, following Ronald Li's unleashing of revolutionary notions on the unsuspecting old guard, attracted a different type of customer. Most notable in the early 1970s was the arrival of Slater Walker, an English financier fresh from Singapore where he had already acquired and stripped a famous old firm, the tiger balm lotion manufacturers, Haw Par Brothers International. After Slater Walker's arrival in Hong Kong, Noel wrote to his son: 'There is so much going on which has cost small investors big losses like Slater Walker for instance & many others...'[32]

Noel may have been more exercised by the Slater Walker saga than the comment suggests. In his letters to Joan Scrivener, Noel Croucher asked Joan in England to post — anonymously — certain packets of information to the English satirical magazine, *Private Eye*. On 30 October 1976, he wrote: 'Please send to, "Slicker", Private Eye, 34 Greek Street, W1. I am sending them some information anonymously as though it comes from London.' A few days later he wrote again: 'I sent you a letter yesterday asking you to address the enclosure to Private Eye. It is about some "monkey business" going on with some HK firm which they mentioned in a previous issue and I am giving them some more information, but don't want them to think it is from HK, or who the sender is.'[33] Looking at the magazine at the relevant times, the major story from Hong Kong which it covered was that of Slater Walker. It appears, but cannot be proven, that Noel was a source for the critical coverage given by *Private Eye* to the controversy.[34]

This was not a man who had lost his propensity for outrage at impropriety and dishonesty. Even in the last years of his life he was going out of his way to expose wrongdoing, as he saw it.

The rapidly growing market heralded the arrival of merchant banks, which could underwrite and handle new issues on the market, such as Rothschild's. Running the office was one Stuart Ross, who was initially a friend of Noel's. Noel placed some of his wealth with Rothschild's, and thought of leaving his fortune in a trust to be managed by them after his death. He is on record in board minutes from the HK & China Gas Company, as arguing, in vain, for the appointment of Rothschild's for extra assistance during the attempted HK Electric take-over bid. Unfortunately, the relationship came to an end after Ross absconded, and it was discovered that he had misappropriated client funds.[35]

In just the last year or two before Noel's death in 1980, he was to see the most significant trend of changing ownership yet. The top handful of established hongs — major firms — one by one were absorbed by a few emerging Hong Kong Chinese tycoons. 'Operators see a realignment of ownership shaping up, with local property interests buying into established foreign concerns like Wheelocks,' reported the *Far Eastern Economic Review*.[36] The first company Noel ever expressed interest in, back in 1911 — the Green Island Cement Company — was now chaired by the leader of this new breed of investor, Li Ka-shing. His flagship, Cheung Kong Holdings, also acquired twenty-two percent of Hutchison Whampoa from the Hong Kong & Shanghai Bank.

Noel's time was passing. His dominance of the market was over, and his friends and colleagues were passing away around him. It is tempting to interpret this changing of the guard as purely a political transition — Hong Kong was shaking off its colonial past and racing to meet a new future. Men such as Noel had had their day, and new entrepreneurs were ready to scoop up the pickings. This march of history cannot be denied.

But Noel's own transition, from market leader to bystander, was mainly a product of age. Had Noel had another twenty years in him, we feel sure he would have dived into the new financial realities — whatever their ilk — as he had dived in almost seventy years before.

In this last decade of Noel's life, he displayed, once again, his difficult personality. He dearly wished to have someone to carry on his business — otherwise, all this work over so many decades would add up to nothing in the end. So Noel looked around him for a potential partner, perhaps even an heir. His relationship with his son was still difficult and Richard was busy with his own life elsewhere. Several close friends from this time remember Noel fretting about what would happen to his business when he died. His relationship with his son was to improve later anyway. In the meantime, Noel offered a place in his office to a young man of business called Duncan Graham, in June 1970. 'I was at Peat Marwick and looked after a few of his companies,' remembers Duncan Graham.[37] But the working relationship was short-lived and, according to Duncan Graham, foundered on a remarkable absent-mindedness of Noel's, by November 1971.

We cannot know Noel's views of the situation, but Duncan Graham reports that it was just very hard to be sure what Noel meant at any one point: 'Noel had a very bad short-term memory. We used to have arguments about things that had already been discussed and agreed.' Given Noel's age, this is perhaps understandable — or was he just a grumpy old man who hated to let go of anything which might be to his advantage?

Problems would arise when a share allocation, which Noel said he didn't want to take up, was taken up by Graham. If Graham's clients did well with those shares, Noel would be outraged, and would deny he had ever allowed Graham to place the lot in the first place. 'He wouldn't want them, then I'd place them with clients, and then he'd want them. But apart from incidents like that, he was a very amiable old chap. There was lots of talk in the office, he told wonderful old stories.

'We didn't have a falling-out *per se*. It was just, it was not an ongoing friendship. Noel would say — "Damn that Duncan Graham, I gave him a wonderful opportunity!" I told him that I had decided to get out of broking, which I did.'

♪ ♪ ♪

The Noel Croucher who Duncan Graham remembers was an enigma, a man who was wealthy but penny-pinching, friendly but gruff, and a quirky yet gracious host. This older Noel was someone who had a lot of misunderstandings with people close to him. Also in these years, anecdotes are told about Noel's enjoyment of the occasional night on the tiles. Some friends recall seeing him at this or that bar in Wanchai, the red-light district. The sightings were irregular and he was not one of the famous characters of the nightclub belt.

More public was Noel's determination that the old Hong Kong Club building should be preserved. In many ways he was the archetype of the old guard, a noted mascot about the Hong Kong Club, a known character, with his lapel blooms, his tall stories, his eccentricities. He died just in time to avoid seeing his clubhouse of decades replaced by an office block. The structure's poor foundations, built on rubble, seemed to move every time building works occurred nearby. It was demolished in 1981.

Yet still, Noel seemed to rub some people up the wrong way. One observer from the 1960s has anonymously put his finger on the nub of it: 'Noel was not accepted by the real establishment. Among the old China hands there was very much a class thing — in the cricket club we had so many "Blues" we could beat England. One would have thought a man of his standing should have been on the Legislative Council or something — but there was no sign of that.'

There was also an assumption that because Noel was so rich, he must have been a crook. Anyone choosing to believe that modern Hong Kong is relatively uncorrupt sees pre-war, colonial Hong Kong as a different entity. 'At least he must have cut corners to make the sort of money he did,' says former Chief Secretary Sir Jack Cater. 'But probably so did everyone. With these big-money people, certainly pre-war, it would probably not have occurred to them that this might be less than honest. Given the circumstances of the China Coast, they would see nothing wrong with it. I think today we work by different rules...'[38]

Setting aside for the moment Pierre-Joseph Proudhon's notion that property is theft, we should also note that it is in the nature of old money to look down on new. The assumption that people like Noel did not get rich honestly could itself be a form of snobbery, a sign of an inability to accept the *nouveau riche*. Civil servants and some professionals resent those able to make a fortune even while they cherish their more sanctified position in the social hierarchy.[39]

Joyce Symons, headmistress of Diocesan Girls' School, knew Noel and Hong Kong well. 'I've never heard of any dishonesty attached to Noel. There were opportunities of course. But if you aspire to join, the only route is money.'[40]

Noel was beginning to feel his age, paying frequent visits to a doctor only to find he was perfectly well, and he was beginning to feel shut out of a changing city and economic scene. He was looking for a home in England and not finding one. He had been hoping for a rich family life through his offspring, an arena for his patriarchal instincts, and he was not finding one. And still, there were one or two peaks he could not climb.

It may not be surprising that a clique which had watched him argue with George Marden and finesse the take-over of Union Insurance, was not one likely to be well disposed towards him. The popular conception of Noel Croucher was that of a crusty old miser sitting up on the Peak, counting his money, and an amusing eccentric on a good day.

🍂 🍂 🍂

It is from this period of Noel's life that so many wacky stories stem, about Noel's alleged eccentricities.

'Noel had an enormous capacity for telling stories of old Hong Kong. And he had a very interesting way of telling them!' according to Peter Vine. 'The stories were all memorised, recorded in his brain. They were word-perfect. If he was interrupted, he would always repeat the last four or five words from before he was interrupted, like putting the needle back in the groove, and then he would carry on.' The stories were often of scandals in the old days, corruption at the big firms, stock exchange happenings, and all about the old families of Hong Kong.[41]

'He was a compulsive talker and on occasions when he found himself doing battle with one or other of similarly long-winded members in the Hong Kong Club, the conversational cut and thrust was quite diverting,' remembered his old friend Arnold Graham.[42]

Noel told stories all through his life — to the Chinese 'coolies' in World War I and to the captive audiences at a bar, some featuring himself, but not all. In this way are legends created. But in addition, many people have enjoyed telling stories about Noel. Many cannot be proved and most tellings of them conflict with each other. But key legends from this time include that of the slab of meat Noel apparently bought from the closing down sale of Cold Storage Ltd., which he fed to his guests for years. Anyone dining at Noel's house had a funny story to tell — about the meat, the small portions, the archaic or macabre touches.

'I remember it incredibly well because it was one of those extraordinary evenings, ingrained on my psyche,' says Elizabeth Mills of a dinner at Noel's house. 'There was one lamp in the drawing room. And Noel sat in his armchair and yelled: "Amah!" This incredibly frail, ancient, androgynous being walked into the room, or should I say hobbled into the room and says "Yes masser!" He says, "Is dinner ready?" She replied, "I ask cook!", and yelled, "Cook!" And in came yet another absolutely frail, ancient old crone. "Is dinner ready?" "Yes masser!"

'And Noel got up, he took his handkerchief out of his pocket, turned off the lamp, removed the light bulb, and took it with him into the dining room, where he put it into the only lamp in the dining room, and turned the light on again! Absolutely amazing.' Allen Mills, who was there too, confirms Noel did indeed move the light bulb. 'But I think it was just a rather incompetent household.'[43]

Noel had a passion for old-time music-hall and his favourite song from this Victorian genre of mass entertainment was 'Happy Days Are Here Again'. One is reminded of the Noel who played his ukelele on the deck of *La Cigale* on those great sailing trips of pre-war times. 'He was incredibly gallant,' Elizabeth Mills adds. 'He did have this marvellous ability to make a girl feel like she was probably the most important person in his life. He really was extremely enchanting and he loved to be surrounded by fun young people who weren't at all intimidated by Noel's venerability. He was a very secretive man, he only wanted people to know a little bit of his life... No one ever got a full picture.'

It was the late 1970s when the Mills met Noel Croucher. 'I thought he was a typically colonial personality,' laughs Allen Mills. 'But a source of useful information. I was told very clearly by James Selwyn [the Securities Commissioner] that I was going to meet a very eccentric person. And I met a very eccentric person. I like eccentric people. He had ceased to be important in the market, but could still irritate those who were.'[44]

Peter Vine also remembers a dinner at Noel's house: 'He took a lot of time telling me he wasn't paying anything for what we were eating. He was actually proud of it. The meat came from New Zealand (he said he was an honorary adviser to the Meat Marketing Board there), the fruit was from somewhere else and the wine was a gift...'[45] Noel was said to have bought a whole side of a cow, which lasted three or four years.

'We bought our house on the Peak from a retired Chief Government Architect,' recalls Judy Green. 'He had arrived in Hong Kong in the late 1920s and left in the early '60s. He had been a sailing friend of NC in the old days but had rather lost touch by the time he left. NC used to keep an office in the same building as ours — 9 Ice House Street — and one morning in the lift he congratulated us on having bought our house (I've no idea how he knew as the man we bought it from had returned to Vancouver the day after shaking on the deal and had dropped dead within a week). [Noel said] "You know, of course, that Feltham promised me a 5% commission on the sale if it went through, don't you?" We laughed good humouredly but he was deadly serious and stalked out of the lift in a huff! I think that was about the last time we had a chance to talk to him as we moved offices and he became something of a recluse.'[46]

Even in his later years, Noel Croucher was to feel somehow intimidated or overawed by some of the bigwigs around him. A secretary at the Hong Kong & Shanghai Bank, Joy Dickinson, recalls that at some meetings at the bank, Noel would take her aside and say, 'Don't sit me next to those brainy people — I wouldn't know what to say!' Ms Dickinson remembers Noel as a man who was really a leading figure in society — but he didn't seem to feel it inside.[47]

Noel was reputed to grow one finger nail very long, so that he could cheat at Liar's Dice games in the Hong Kong Club; he apparently went to the Furama Hotel bread shop just on closing time every afternoon, to get the two dollars off the price of bread because it was not morning-fresh; he allegedly would go to extraordinary lengths to avoid picking up a lunch or drinks bill. People remember the way he travelled by bus, back when buses were without air conditioning, and the seats were bamboo slats, not cushions. Yet, he would astound visitors to his Dickensian office by opening the door of his massive old safe. Out tumbled piles of gold coins — a sack of them — Mexican florins, sovereigns, golden eagles and more.

Yet, there are other memories of Noel Croucher.

R.C. Lee, the impressive and fascinating friend and colleague, said: 'Noel Croucher was noted for his honesty. That's how he made so much money. He was honest.' Dick Lee also recalled Noel's interest in the Marco Polo Club — an association aimed at bringing Chinese and foreigners together. 'His main aim was to make the foreigners learn more about the Chinese,' said Lee.[48]

Gerald Carey recalled that the last time he went to see Noel for a chat was on a visit in about 1970: 'I had a Yacht Club blazer which was getting tatty. Noel said, "Give it to me, I'll get a tailor to fix it." It was ready the next day! With a new lining. And I still have the blazer, thanks to Noel.'[49]

Noel also expected a lot from others. Sir Jack Cater, Hong Kong's Chief Secretary from 1978 to 1981, remembers the day when Noel came to his office, at the height of a quarrel over the legality of the bungalow which Noel had built in the garden of his home. 'He came to complain about the then director of public works [David McDonald]. What had happened was that Noel had built a garden hut. He had started to build it so his granddaughter [Amanda] could stay. He did it without seeking planning permission. And he asked me to overrule David McDonald!

'He felt he was so wealthy and prominent that people should do what he told them to do. He was nice, but told me frankly how awful government was and so on. I said I supported my public works department. He told me I would suffer, that unless I approved [of the garden hut] then he, Noel, would take steps against me! He was the only one who ever did that to me when I was Chief Secretary.'[50]

The stories of Noel's irascibility go on and on. The important thing to remember is that Noel was entering his eighties, alone.

Throughout these last years of Noel's life, letters have survived which he wrote to his son, Richard, as well as to his good friend Joan Scrivener. In them we can see what Noel thought of his own life, his dreams and fears. Through them, Noel reveals an often unhappy state of mind. Joan Scrivener's mother dropped a line to Noel (in February 1972), in which she writes, perceptively, 'You would be happier if you were not so rich.'

Noel never went so far as to agree with her, but it is clear his wealth could not buy him happiness. He seemed to admit that lavishing money on his offspring had probably done them a disservice. (For example: 'Had I not sent you to a Public School and let you fend for yourself you would probably have done better.') Referring to Gerald Parker (his half-brother) as 'my brother', he mentions that Gerald was taking a last look at the home county: 'I would like to do the same but there is nothing for me to do if I came home, and it is very expensive — I have no hobbies and I would hate having nothing to do...'

Noel also displays his strong interest in books, literature, history and antiquarian treasures, sharing his reading tastes with his son. As for England, he wrote that 'the old Country is passing away.' He railed against those 'bringing the Capitalist system into disrepute,' and wished all the moderates would get together to kick out the extremists (the latter apparently including trade unionists).[51] And he wrote of his 'big losses in South African Gold Mines, like others', and again ponders how his son could retire at fifty while he, Noel, was still working at the age of eighty-four.[52] Sometimes he signed his letters 'Taipan'.

Discussing one person who had had the benefit of expensive education, he described it all as a waste because the person 'lacks art, literature, music, and purpose in life', and was 'of no value to the community'. He also writes, 'I am in my 84th year and may go into orbit any time now... I want to get my affairs tidied up.'

Encapsulating Noel's view of the world is the Christmas card which Noel sent out in 1974. It is in the pile of letters Noel wrote to his son in those years, which Richard Croucher kindly contributed to this book. These letters show a Noel Croucher interested in arts and learning, in his family, and in adding up the sum of his life. His curiosity extended well beyond the bounds of mere business.

Christmas Greetings, 1974
Dear Richard...

I don't think the times warrant the usual Xmas Card so I thought of something different, more in keeping at my time of life — You remember I wrote you many years ago about a text I read on a successful man's desk (a man of integrity) — 'I am becoming what I will be'...

> The life of man is a long march through the night, surrounded by invisible foes, tortured by weariness and pain, towards a goal that few can hope to reach and none may tarry long. One by one as they march, our comrades vanish from our sight seized by the silent orders of Omnipotent Death. Very brief is the time in which we can help them in which their misery or happiness is decided. Be it ours to shed sunshine in their path to lighten their sorrows, by the balm of sympathy to give them the real joy of untiring affection. Be it ours to feel that where they suffered, where they failed, no deed of ours was the cause.

Excerpt from 'A Free Man's Worship' by Bertrand Russell.

Noel Croucher. X'mas 1974.

22 January ?1976
Dear Richard...

I am not a poor man. My only regret is that I have no assets to leave which the community could be proud of... One of these days you will hear many things about me after I have passed on and my one regret is that I will leave nobody behind to follow in my footsteps. ...One man I admire was the Govt [servant] or Parliamentarian who got mixed up with a call girl some years ago — he left official life & devoted himself to welfare work — I cannot recall his name...

You probably know I've been and am the senior J.P. here and visit the Prisons to report and I have seen so much of what the Drug

addicts have come to. We have a small Island where they are put —
many dying a slow death...

7 March ??
Dear Richard...

I listen to the BBC as often as I can. I'm a poor sleeper and at 2 a.m. I
hear all the News from London. Politics, finance — in fact everything
of importance — In fact one can get VOA Germany Moscow Ethiopia
South Africa and numerous other places & it's worth keeping awake
for. I heard a particular good record & wrote to the BBC for particulars
as I want to get a Cassette. ...

4 July 1977
Dear Richard...

Do the work that's nearest
Though its dull at whiles
Helping when you meet them
Lame dogs over stiles.

Noel's letters to Joan Scrivener from the late 1960s on, are similarly
redolent of a passing era. Noel was aware of his mortality by now, yet
could not relax into a leisured old age. He watched gloomily as the world
as he knew it came increasingly under threat — his old friends were
dying, the British empire was folding, the weather at 'home' depressed
him, as did the endless strikes and economic woes of England. He
expounded on the state of the world, the threat of growing competition
from Japan, and the hard times ahead. The bright spot, he felt, was
Richard's second wife, Penny Croucher, and the daughter she had with
Richard, Camilla. They visited Hong Kong in 1977, after which Noel
wrote that he had great respect for Penny, and high hopes for Camilla.
(That Penny did not accept any money from Noel no doubt helped form
this view.)

In 1977, Joan Scrivener came out to Hong Kong again to visit Noel,
and the letters from that period are the happiest, most human expressions
by Noel in decades. Most of the rest of the letters, however, are full of
references to the ups and downs surrounding Noel's property at no. 25
Radnor Walk, Chelsea. Joan, at Noel's request, worked hard on fixing
the house up, redecorating it, buying furniture and fittings, in a largely
unpaid labour, for many months. He was very pleased with her tireless
efforts on the house and said so often: 'Many thanks for your help Joan
— I can't tell you how much I appreciate it. Love, N.'[53]

Noel also shared his personal worries with Joan, along with his dreams of England, his daily life in Hong Kong, and his many pungent observations and jokes. He occasionally sent her a gift, such as a tailor-made outfit in new fabrics, in the earnest hope that she would like it. When a mutual friend was about to visit Italy, he joked she should wear 'tin panties', in protection against Italian men. He also joked about needing a housekeeper, and advised Joan to buy shares — in Borneo Petroleum Syndicate, De La Rue or Plessey, for example.

Joan was a rare friend to Noel in those years, albeit long-distance. Clearly, too, Noel remained an old-fashioned guy. There was a moment during or after Joan's visit in 1977 when Noel seemed to wish for a lot more of Joan, but he never quite spelled out his obvious desire for a companion. Both Joan and Noel seemed to hedge and fudge any question about the future of their relationship until it was too late. Ambivalence was allowed to drift into inaction. Of course, Noel was still a married man, so there would have been few options for Joan had she chosen to act on the oblique phrases and obvious loneliness of her correspondent. Had this situation arisen now, among a younger generation, a solution might have been easier to find. But Joan also had her own life in England and an ailing mother to care for. The tragedy in Noel's life is that he failed to tackle his emotional needs until it was too late.

One of the most extraordinary legends of all about Noel Croucher is another of those stories which might almost be true, but which in fact is not. At least three separate sources believe that Noel Croucher lived under an assumed name in Cannes, France, during the 1970s. They describe a man who might well be Noel — an Englishman of aristocratic bearing, who kept a pile of old *Financial Times* in a corner of his flat and who threw bohemian parties. He was known to all as Guy Puckle. The impression was that Guy had fallen on hard times and was escaping unwelcome legal attentions in Hong Kong.

One day the British-French community staged a parade in Cannes which featured, among other things, a float depicting 'England'. Guy Puckle was asked to play the part of the English gentleman, which he did, and the photographs of the dressed-up participants of that parade show a man who could almost be Noel. During the parade, Guy Puckle turned to his companions and said, 'This is very appropriate you know, because I used to be an actor. My real name was Noel Croucher, but so many confused me with Noel Coward that I changed my name to Guy Puckle.'

There is no way this can in fact be our Noel Croucher, as we know he was alive and well in Hong Kong throughout these years. The evidence of his Hong Kong life is too overwhelming. The sting in the tail of this tale, however, is that our first news of the alleged double life came from a name and address found in Noel Croucher's personal Index Book — Lady Emma Henderson. Some connection there must have been. A separate source (Mrs Dorothy Chamade) has photographs of the man she knew as Guy Puckle, actually on the parade in question, and there is a resemblance to Noel.

Perhaps the real Guy Puckle had been through Hong Kong or otherwise knew of Noel Croucher and decided to make a play on names and appearances to his friends in Cannes. It is interesting to note that he wanted to associate himself with Noel. Perhaps the two men did have things in common and time has muddled the memories.

At the least, the story tells us how mysterious Noel either was, or was thought to be. Many people who knew him could believe all manner of things about him — just as a previous generation of relatives could easily believe Noel's mother, Floss, had swept into a royal reception with feathered hat and lorgnette flying.

.

CHAPTER SIXTEEN

THE LEGACY

 e would, I truly believe, have heartily endorsed Dr Johnson's assertion to the effect that there are few more innocent ways for a man to be employed than in making money.'[1]

Wanted —
God give us men. The time demands.
Strong minds, great hearts, true faith,
and willing hands. Men whom the lust of office
does not kill. Men whom the spoils of office
cannot buy. Men who possess opinions and a
will. Men who have honour, men who will
not lie. Men who can stand before a demagogue,
And dam his treacherous flatteries without
winking. Tall men, sun-crowned, who live
above the fog. In public duty and in private
thinking.[2]

'Noel and his extraordinary career encapsulate the good and the bad of British colonial times.'[3]

Knowing he had little time left, Noel finally began to consider ways for his wealth to live on beyond him. The result was the formation of The Croucher Foundation, a well-funded organisation which pays for bright Hong Kong people to pursue postgraduate research in science, medicine and technology.

A portrait of the older Noel Croucher hangs in the boardroom at The Croucher Foundation offices in Kowloon, where leaders of various professions meet to decide how best Noel's wishes can be fulfilled with his money. Some of the people around the table are from families which provided Noel with some of his earliest friends in business, such as Chief Justice Andrew Li, from the Bank of East Asia family. The man who succeeded Noel's close friend Philip Griffiths as senior partner at Wilkinson & Grist solicitors, Ian MacCallum, is there. So, until recently, was the former chairman of the Hong Kong & Shanghai Bank, Lord Sandberg. Several positions are held by leading academics — the sort of men Noel always admired and envied for their learning. Thus, the elite in business and academia pays respect to the memory of the former post office clerk.

Given Noel's sense of humour, this gift of The Croucher Foundation was perhaps his way of having the last laugh on all those around him who disliked or despised him. But the idea of The Croucher Foundation began in tears.

At first Noel's idea was to establish a charitable trust at a bank and leave the trust managers in charge. But of course that idea soon palled on a man who was patently unable to delegate. He kept looking for ways to make an impact on issues he believed in, at the same time as he wanted to keep costs down. As an indication of his early thoughts on the issue, he wrote to Joan Scrivener in 1977:

> Dear Joan,...
>
> My intention is to establish a Foundation, as Dr Joseph Needham, Master of Gonville[4] College, Cambridge suggests — to exchange students from China with ours — only a few. The rest will be for Science, medicine, especially for those students who need financial help. I get so muddle headed over this and I don't want to put Trustees who employ Directors, Financial Advisors etc who make a living out of it. Naturally there are expenses. The other day a well dressed man and wife came into the office, they are collecting for the very aged etc. I asked about the institution they represented and for whom they were collecting as we had many in H.K. He said they were collecting for Africa, India, and the UK. He handed me a Book of Information. I noticed about 20% of what was collected was spent on getting it, and this man and his wife were travelling around and wasting money in Hong Kong. ...[5]

Almost a year passed before Noel got any closer to his goals, and then only because he cried. Lady May Ride was a long-standing friend of Noel's. As May Witchell, she had worked at the University of Hong Kong before the Pacific War, was interned at Stanley (as was Noel), and married the war hero and University Vice-Chancellor Sir Lindsay Ride after the war. One day in 1978, May Ride dropped by Noel's office on Ice House Street, as she often did, to see how Noel was getting along. To her surprise, she found Noel with his head in his hands, in tears. Asking him what the matter was, she heard this globally envied financier lament that he did not know what to do with his money! If he left it to a large bank in a trust, well, anything might happen — his life work could disappear with anyone but himself in charge of it. What to do?

'I said, why don't you set up a foundation?' recounts Lady Ride.[6] 'He said, "What's a foundation?" His actual words — "What's a foundation?" '

May Ride explained that interest on invested capital would keep the foundation going, forever, and that Noel could specify what goals he wanted met with his own money. 'And people will be educated which I know is something you have great admiration for as you had no education yourself,' recounts May Ride. 'He said, "My God, I never heard of this!" — his exact words, you see?'

May Ride and her husband were friendly with a visiting examiner in chemistry (and later, Council Member of the Congregation of the Chinese University), Lord Alexander Todd of Trumpington, who was soon due to visit Hong Kong again. May offered to introduce the two men. 'Noel looked at me and said, "He's a lord?" I said, "Well, what's the difference?" He said, "I've never met a lord in my life May!" I said, "He's only a human being! Go and talk to him. I'll write to him and you go and talk to him. Lord Todd was from the Nuffield Foundation — he will tell you how to set up a foundation."

'He looked at me and said, "Do you really mean it?" I said, "Yes, I do." I said, "You will have a foundation for ever." '

And so it came to pass. May Ride introduced Noel Croucher to Lord Todd in a letter dated 13 June 1978, and the two men, so different in many ways, began to build The Croucher Foundation.

Alex Todd was a tall Scots scientist who won the Nobel Prize in Chemistry in 1957.[7] He was president of the Royal Society for many years, the Master of Christ's College, Cambridge, and experienced in the ways of funding education through his work for the Nuffield Foundation and many others. Lord Todd was also a Master of the Salters' Company of the City of London, a wealthy mediaeval guild founded back when the salt trade and the salting of meat was vital. This guild had approached Lord Todd to find useful ways to spend their funds on the development of science — after all, mediaeval salters were akin to the chemists of today. Lord Todd had also been visiting Hong Kong since 1957. Most important of all, Lord Todd was a man of strong principle and blunt honesty.

Noel had been looking — for years — for a man he could trust. He liked negotiating his work in finance with the needs of his welfare committees, and he already gave money to specific scholarship funds, such as the Noel Croucher Shakespeare Fund at the Royal Society of St. George. He began wondering about arrangements such as the Rhodes scholarships, or the money offered each year by Swire's and Jardine's for scholarships at Oxbridge. He had also asked around about how others did it, such as the Vanderbilts, the Fords and other like names. The conversation with Lady May Ride cleared his way ahead.

He talked with many friends about how to start a trust. 'His object was to promote youngsters in China and to get them to learn about English literature,' recalled one of them. Wynne Ward remembers Noel searching for a few years for a worthy cause, such as hospitals and schools. Noel had already set aside money for his offspring. Besides, there was more money than he seemed to know what to do with, and, Noel was not a trusting person. He continually feared people approaching him for hand-outs, and felt often cheated in his personal relationships the minute that money raised its ugly head. Noel enjoyed the company of people who did not give a damn about his wealth. But he had yet to find a man he could trust, and trust enough to leave his wealth with.

Lord Todd, with the weight of his learning, his standing in academic circles, and his absolute disinterest in the money, was the answer to Noel's tears. He was soon writing to Joan: 'I am very glad to say I have come to some arrangement with my Trustees and that is a load off my shoulders.'[8]

'Noel had talked with May Ride about the fact that he'd been trying to find an honest man in Hong Kong and had failed,' said the late Lord Todd. 'Everybody he got hold of wanted to get something out of it, something for themselves, and did she know anybody who was straight, above-board and wouldn't take that view and she apparently said it was me. Whereupon he got in touch with me, a long letter from him, a long rather rambling letter of course, and in it he said he would like to make me his sole executor and trustee. Now I wrote and told him I couldn't do that because I had little experience of that kind of thing and I didn't think I would like to handle the amounts of money he was talking about.'[9]

Unbeknownst to Lord Todd, a disinterest in money was the way to Noel's heart.

As talks progressed, Lord Todd's early ideas focused on how Christ's College Cambridge (where he was Master) could use the Croucher money. He suggested several research studentships with any excess funds going to Christ's College's other educational needs. Noel took several months to reply to this tentative beginning. On 9 October 1978, he wrote to Lord Todd:

> I have been meaning to write to you long before this and to thank you for your letter of June 23 regarding the financing of Chinese Students. I had this in mind some years ago but thought the time was rather premature and so did Dr Needham[10] who passes through Hong Kong now and again. But the situation has changed for the better and I wanted to do this.
>
> My idea is to help students irrespective of Nationality. You say where the need is greatest particularly favouring research students and I entirely agree with you... I will be greatly honoured if you would also be a Trustee as what you wrote in your letter is very much what I have in mind and heart.
>
> I had a letter from Mr Peter Burbridge who is raising funds to support the scholarly work of Dr Needham. I received this after I mentioned my intention of establishing a Charitable Trust to Dr Needham, but I do not wish to do this.
>
> Yours sincerely,
> N. Croucher.
>
> P.S. The amount is between £10–15 million. The investments are in first class securities in Canada, Australia. In South Africa there is about £2 million in gold shares.

Noel's intentions were not yet clear but he had begun trying to tackle the problem of what to do with his money. Indeed, so had other people, as the reference to Dr Needham's work reveals. But Noel wanted to do something special, other than support a cause already well established such as Needham's work on the history of Chinese science. Lord Todd later recalled how amazed he was that Noel, in this postscript, seemed uncertain about the amount of money involved. In fact, it was nearer £20 million.[11]

Lord and Lady Todd were planning a trip out to Hong Kong, for late

January 1979, and Noel was planning dinner with Lady Ride in attendance.[12] This was the dinner which was first meant to be at Noel's house, but which Noel prevailed upon Michael Sandberg, the Hong Kong Bank chairman, to host at his house instead. Lord Sandberg has a funny story about how Noel made his approach:

'Noel said he was going to invite Lord Todd to dinner, and would I like to come. I said, "Yes, thank you very much." So having established that I was free on that night, he then rings me two days later and says, "Well you know I've been thinking about it — Lord Todd's a very influential and important man and I'm in a very humble house, why don't we hold the dinner in your flat?!" So that was agreed. We had a very congenial dinner in my flat. It must have saved him all of five bob.'[13]

During that trip, Lord Todd and Ian MacCallum had lunch with Noel Croucher at the Hong Kong Club on 23 January 1979. 'My first impressions of him were favourable,' recalled Lord Todd. 'He was getting a bit woolly. But that apart he was fine, he had the right sort of ideas.

'We left it that day that the old man wouldn't agree to anything the lawyers said,' said Lord Todd. 'But he agreed with me to set up The Croucher Foundation. He didn't give it that name but it was a fund anyhow, to be operated by me. I think this was largely because he knew I had been a Nuffield trustee for some time and knew something about the orderly handling of these things. So after a bit of palaver, I agreed... Well, what he did that day was in effect turn over the handling of any money that came from his will, to me!'

The conversations between these two men, both tall and blunt-speaking, and both distinguished, albeit in very different fields, were a new experience for both of them. Lord Todd secretly felt Noel Croucher must have been crooked to have become so rich, while Noel was no doubt impressed but puzzled by the fact that Lord Todd really did not want the money, nor did he want to be a trustee or executor for such a large amount. Such matters were not intrinsically fascinating to a precise Scots scientist at Cambridge.

'He said he couldn't help that,' recalled Lord Todd of Noel Croucher. 'But when he died he wanted me to take charge of his money and use it in accordance with what he wanted — to support promising young Hong Kong people in the world of science to go abroad and get experience. And they've all got to come back here and work for Hong Kong. He was most interested in Hong Kong youngsters who might become really first-class scientists.'[14]

Lady May Ride, meanwhile, was keeping an eye on things from the sidelines. 'All of Hong Kong was laughing their backsides off, saying, the silly old man wants to set up a foundation and of course it will never happen you see — which made me laugh!'

In fixing on Lord Todd, Noel Croucher was indeed securing a wealth of relevant experience. The Nuffield Foundation was set up by a man who was first a bicycle repairer. William Richard Morris Nuffield (1877–1963) went on to pioneer the mass production of cheap cars such as the Morris, and he used part of his vast fortune to benefit hospitals, charities and Oxford University before establishing the greatly respected Nuffield Foundation in 1943.[15] The Nuffield remit is the 'advancement of health and social well-being'. Within Britain it funds medical, biological, physical and social research. It also offers scholarships throughout the Commonwealth. The Croucher Foundation initially established a unit in the offices of the Nuffield Foundation in London, before setting up on its own in Cambridge, in addition to the head office in Hong Kong.[16]

'I'll tell you what Noel wanted,' said Lord Todd. 'He wanted his money to be used to help really able Hong Kong youth, to do a good job for Hong Kong. That's what he was really interested in. Very specifically, it was the Hong Kong people he had in mind. I mean I don't think Noel was ever a sort of, what we call a general do-gooder, or person who thought his money should be used as a sort of general fund, no. He had specific ideas of what he wanted done with it.'

Once all this was clear, speedy progress was called for. Lord Todd next wrote, 'I think as we are none of us getting any younger the thing to do now is to get the basic trust deed drawn up and signed.'[17] He had to repeat his urgings but by the time he was back in Hong Kong in October, Noel was ready for lunch at the Hong Kong Club with Lord Todd, and a meeting on the next Saturday morning with Ian MacCallum, before taking Lord and Lady Todd to the races. It seems Noel also took time to introduce the Todds to the joys of the local Mark Six sweepstake as he had to report that Lord Todd had not, after all, won that jackpot. In another sense, he had, of course, as by 3 December 1979, the deed establishing The Croucher Foundation was legally complete.

On 21 November, Lord Butterfield had cabled Lord Todd: 'Noel Ian Rayson And I Signed Documents At Simple Ceremony Here Last Evening Many Congratulations and Deepest Thanks.' Lord Todd promptly affixed his signature, adding: 'I do feel that you are doing something really great and I would again assure you that it will be my constant endeavour to see that the Foundation operates in accordance with your wishes.'[18] As for the lawyer Ian MacCallum, he went home that night to tell his wife

Wendy: 'This is probably the best day's work I have done in all my life.'[19]

The first meeting of trustees took place in Noel's office in Holland House on 28 January 1980, following another lunch between Noel and Lord Todd at the Hong Kong Club. By now, the goals had been refined. Noel wanted scholarships to enable young Hong Kong Chinese of outstanding ability in the fields of science, technology or medicine to be able to develop their talents further by postgraduate research and study in Britain and the Commonwealth. (He was against sending students to the United States as too many might stay there, and he felt overseas Chinese had enough resources to hand. He clearly believed Britain was a less tempting prospect to the young.)

The priority accorded to science subjects was not set in stone, but Noel did express to Lord Todd his aversion to the field of sociology, viewing social science in general with suspicion. Noel remained averse to any 'waste' of his money on constructing buildings, but nurturing institutions so they might reach international standards of education and research was important to him. He allowed for the possibility of exchange visits by senior scholars from overseas, and for the funding of research in Hong Kong institutions of higher learning. He also, with great foresight, empowered his trustees to promote contacts and joint research projects between higher educational bodies of Hong Kong and China.

The last letter written by Lord Todd, before Noel's death, was full of cheer:

Dear Noel,

My wife and I greatly enjoyed being with you again in Hong Kong; I really do wish it were possible to get some of your reminiscences down on paper for they are not only interesting but are in some cases of considerable historical interest. We must talk about the possibility again some time.

I thought we made considerable progress at our meeting and I hope you felt so too...[20]

Plans were made for a next meeting in mid-April 1980 and in Lord Todd's note, he says there should be time both for various bits of business, 'and perhaps also to fit in some racing at Shatin...' But there was no time for any of it, as Noel died on 6 March 1980. Lord Todd and the trustees had only just made it — The Croucher Foundation came into being with barely weeks to spare.

'Well Noel was very glad that day, and the next evening I had a whole group up to the Vice-Chancellor's lodge at Hong Kong University,' recalls Rayson Huang. 'So we had a party. That night I could see Noel was very happy. He had quite a few drinks and he was very happy. It was a job done at last. You see, you know, you decide to do something and it hangs around and finally you do it, execute it, lawyers, all the trustees and whoever. We had a very nice party and I was glad to see Noel so happy. Done at last. Just in the nick of time. I could see how happy he was. He felt he was doing the right thing.'[21]

What motivated Noel Croucher to set up his foundation? Some who are called philanthropists are eager to give, in the hope of worldly rewards — witness the competition in some circles for awards such as a Queen's Honour, or similar. Was Noel perhaps wishing his name-plate could be graced by an MBE or OBE?

According to many who knew him, Noel was genuinely uninterested in such a prospect. There is a story that he was 'offered a gong by Grantham', that is, an award by the Governor of Hong Kong 1947–57, but that he had turned it down. His contact with Government House was long-established — Sir Robert Black, Colonial Secretary in 1952–55 and Governor for 1958–64, remembers Noel as an engaging character, entertaining as a retailer of Hong Kong life, and one who was involved in unostentatious charitable work.[22] Noel was invited to balls at Government House, such as the one for the visit by the Duke of Windsor. Says a dear friend to Noel in his later years: 'He could have been knighted, he could even have bought it. But he shunned such things.'

'To have got an honour, Noel would have had to make public how much money he was giving away, and he didn't like doing that,' comments Ian MacCallum. 'Also, he had a big run-in with the then government after Sir Paul Chater died [in 1926]. Sir Paul left his collection, the Chater Collection, to "the people of Hong Kong". That was how it was in the will. And the government said, "Oh that means us." Noel was furious and said, "No, it was meant to be for the public." So I know he had a great row with the government after Sir Paul died over the disposal of the Chater Collection.'[23]

Characteristically, Noel seemed to prefer actions to florid words or honours. He would have been deeply pleased to hear the reaction of men he respected greatly, such as former Governor of Hong Kong, Lord Murray MacLehose: 'I knew and liked and respected him ... he was obviously pretty successful and his Foundation was a magnificent contribution to young people in Hong Kong.'[24]

If not motivated by the thought of rewards from the State, then was Noel's generosity a dramatic sign of his frustrations with his family? A close friend to Noel knows it was not like that. 'He put charity up there as very important. It was not only the disappointment with his family, but a genuine commitment to charity,' she says. Also in the discussions towards forming the foundation, one of the prospective trustees had asked Noel, 'What about your son?' Noel's reply was that he wished his son well but believed more money would harm him.

As it happens, Noel's son Richard admits freely he did not need the money, and now, through his own charitable foundation, is following in his father's footsteps. The Gemini Trust, for which Lords Sandberg and Butterfield are also trustees, also funds education for young people. Following the research for this book, it now offers scholarships for bright students from Noel's home town of Eastleigh, Hampshire, to enable them to go to Southampton University. Named the Noel Croucher Scholarships, they were launched in Eastleigh on 28 April 1998, with the help of local historian Gordon Cox, and the mayor of Eastleigh, Godfrey Olson. 'I think the suggestion was that Richard and his father didn't get on very well and I don't think that's really true. They had a regard for each other,' says Lord Sandberg.

Noel's decision to establish The Croucher Foundation was not some kind of distempered freak, born of revenge or thwarted goodness. It was an idea considered by Noel for years in the abstract, and for months in detail. Here was a very determined man, with the full right to do as he wished with his fortune. After due consideration, an educational foundation was the answer.

The late Lord Lawrence Kadoorie, whose forebears had founded the brokerage where young Noel Croucher had learned his trade, was another man who gave a great deal to Hong Kong through charitable activities, not least being the Kadoorie Farm. He once expressed his view about why rich and powerful people should give money to others: 'I think there is an obligation on the more wealthy and better-off in the community to return a portion of what they've earned. I think they owe it to the place in which they are. You can't just take everything, squeeze it all out of the place as you go and that's the end of it. You must think of doing something for the people. I think that is of tremendous importance.'[25]

That May Ride played a pivotal part in setting up the foundation is appropriate because she, too, cares deeply about education. She was in a position whereby she could demystify aspects of the University of Hong Kong and the people involved for Noel, and make sure momentum was not lost. 'To me, I think education is the hope of this world. Without education, you don't have the ability to think. I don't care if computers are running the world — what kind of people are there going to be? Anyone can press buttons, but how many people can think? It gives me the willies to think what the future's going to be.'

'Noel would always say he was not well educated. But he was very keen on encouraging others,' recalls another close friend of Noel's. 'He had a wonderful brain for figures. He was truly honest and kind, and was always keen on education, that people should have a chance for higher education. And he wanted to give something back to Hong Kong.'[26]

It is no accident that Noel developed this commitment to the idea of education. Any discussion of Victorian values will focus on the role of education, not only in securing upward mobility, but in the march of progress. Free trade, self-improvement, perseverance in face of difficulty, and the central importance of family were all essential Victorian values. Liberty, education, thrift, enterprise — these are the ideals of the age into which Noel Croucher was born and bred.[27]

Victorians believed strongly in 'free trade', in entrepreneurial exploits, and indeed, in empire. We also know that the Victorian era featured gross injustices, mass poverty and depredation, and a brutality in the market-place which the coddled post-war generations of this century can barely imagine. At the same time as hundreds of thousands of workers in northern England were losing their health and lives to the onset of the machine, dumpy Queen Victoria was ecstatically enjoying the delights of bourgeois suburbia down on the Isle of Wight. Individuals such as William Lovett lived in penury so as to pay for more schools in the land, at the same time as it was accepted that men such as 'Rajah' Brooke had a right to rule a vast terrain peopled by 'natives' on Borneo.

Not only does Noel's kind of philanthropy alongside his enterprising spirit suggest a Victorian frame of mind. So, too, does his chaste but cherishing attitude towards Joan Scrivener and other ladies. If he was raunchy on the side, that, too, is part of the Victorian package. Women were either idealised or debased, virgins or whores, there was no in-between. And though different rules applied to each group, nonetheless, rules did apply. Many of the puzzles about Noel Croucher's character can be answered if we see him as a product of the age.

Signing the deed to establish The Croucher Foundation was the biggest step Noel Croucher had taken to enshrine his beliefs about education and the purpose of wealth. As he wrote to Joan Scrivener of his wish to put his affairs in order, Noel spent his last years doing just that. Having finalised the foundation, he finally turned his attention to his relationship with his family.

Just three months before he was to die, as he pondered on what really mattered in life after all, Noel dared a rapprochement with his son.

He sent a telegram to Richard Croucher in London and, delightfully, received one back soon after. The wording of both is indicative of two strong yet humorous personalities who, no matter how much they might have annoyed each other, could not yet deny they loved each other too. With these words, Noel tidied his life up, prompting a reconciliation which would last beyond the grave.

> **THE RECONCILIATION CABLE, 31 DECEMBER 1979**
> I WAS 88 X'MAS EVE AND CAN'T LAST MUCH LONGER SO WISH TO LEAVE IN PEACE AND SO MY COMPANY THERFFORE HAS INSTRUCTED THEIR SOLICITORS TO WITHDRAW ALL PROCEEDINGS REGARDING UNPAID RENT RADNOR WALK I HAVE PAID IT AND OTHER CLAIMS AND YOU CAN START THE NEW YEAR HELPING OTHERS I HOPE YOU APPROVE AMANDAS ENGAGEMENT WRITE YOUR ACTIVITIES ALSO FULLY REGARDING PENNY AND WISHING YOU EVERY HAPPINESS AND PROSPERITY
>
> YOUR FATHER NOEL CROUCHER.

> **THE REPLY, 3 JANUARY 1980**
> THE INNOCENT MUCH APPRECIATES YOUR PARDON AND RECIPROCATES STOP 88 AND STILL BATTING STRONGLY STOP SO BANISH ALL THOUGHTS ABOUT LEAVING STOP LIKE OLD MAN RIVER YOU JUST KEEP ROLLING ALONG STOP WRITING
>
> RICHARD

There was yet time for a few letters between Noel and his son, and Noel lost no time in joking, 'man-to-man': 'You also hoped I would continue batting but I lost my middle stump some years ago...'[28] Noel still wanted to involve himself in family affairs, and particularly wanted to know how his youngest grandchild, Camilla, was getting on. He asked about Richard's life and wrote, 'Now be open and frank...' He still could not get over the fact that his son could retire before him: 'unless you have a hobby to keep you busy, life becomes wearisome...'[29]

Most significantly, although in practical terms he was too late, Noel made clear that he had indeed put past arguments with his son behind him: 'I'm making my will & I don't want to leave my son out of it irrespective of what he has. ...Well I've written enough for Sunday morning. Now remember; be frank and tell me everything. You won't regret it. All the Best. Old Man River.'[30]

A few days later: 'I wrote you a few days ago. Reply as much as you can — there should be nothing between us Now. Old Man River.'[31] In his last letter, of 18 February 1980, he was still joking around with his son's name. Whereas in the bad days he had sometimes addressed Richard as 'Dear R. Supwards', now it was: 'Dear Richard III...'

Noel's last letters show that another long-running saga — that over his house at no. 25 Radnor Walk in London — was finally ended with the sale of the house in January 1980. On 8 February that year, less than a month before his death, he was making jokes about an idea he had for buying up lottery tickets in England. Then the all-too-short correspondence, inspired by one cable, was ended by another:

CABLE TO RICHARD, 6 MARCH 1980
MR NOEL CROUCHER HAS PASSED AWAY PEACEFULLY
CROUCHER AND COMPANY.

Unfortunately, there was one thing which Noel failed to sort out before he died — his will. Many are the times he wrote in letters or told friends in Hong Kong that he meant to change his will, and his comment to Richard was obviously part of a general rethinking which he left too little time to complete. After The Croucher Foundation deed was drawn up, Noel's lawyer, Ian MacCallum, tried to persuade Noel to update the will to take the new circumstances into account. Noel never did. 'I said to Noel, we need a will, so we did the will, and in fact after we set up the trust, he broke with Rothschild's, and I said, "Look, you know, we need to change the will now and put in new executors." He said, "Well, I want to change some of the beneficiaries as well."

'You know, it was one of these things. I kept nudging Noel, saying, "Look Noel, we need to change this will. Now we've got your trust set up we need to put that specifically into the will, and change the trustees." He'd say, "Yes, yes, and I've got some other legacies I want to think about and I'll come back to you." So he died with a will that was not what he wanted. He hadn't got around to changing it.'[32]

The result has been some confusion about exactly what Noel's intentions were regarding the funding of 'charities in my name'. But at least he did leave bequests to his amah, his cook, his office boy and his assistant. His half-brother, Gerald Parker, received a healthy bequest, whereas the amount left to Noel's wife had to be updated and enlarged. A small amount also went to a Chinese woman of San Francisco, whose name has not cropped up elsewhere.[33]

It took four years after the death of Noel Croucher for probate to be granted. At one stage it looked as if some family members might contest the will, even though they were already benefiting from trusts set up in Noel's lifetime. Some charitable bodies had been made verbal promises of which there was no sign in the will. Some relatives had wondered but not asked if they would receive anything — none, bar his half-brother and his wife, did.

At the subsequent auction of Noel's home and effects (in 1984), some friends bought up blocks of his most personal possessions to save them from the public maw. Many others retain mementoes of Noel's life on the China Coast. Lady May Ride said, 'I remember the last time we had a dinner party in Noel's house — it was absolutely like old times, everything the way it used to be years ago.'[34] Brian McElney, formerly a lawyer with Johnson Stokes & Master and founder of the Museum of East Asian Art in Bath, remembers the day Noel took him into a drying cupboard at Noel's house to show him four imperial Ming lacquer bowls. Unfortunately, they were falling apart.

He also remembers the auction held by Lammert & Brothers where there were two silver gravy boats dated as being from 1903. McElney was convinced they dated from 1743 instead and secured a great bargain by buying them both for $6,000.[35] Noel might have minded missing out on the bargain, but would have been pleased at his silver finding a home with a family which he knew.

Another old connection which followed through to the auction of Noel's effects was his friendship with the Jebsen family. Hans Michael Jebsen is the current taipan of Jebsen & Company, the shippers and traders with China. His own strong sense of history is displayed in his replica

China Coast mansion on Middle Gap Road on the Peak. His father, Hans Jacob Jebsen, had been a friend of Noel's, and his name was in Noel's Contacts Book. 'My father liked and admired Noel,' remembers the younger Jebsen.

'But I had a more morbid relationship with Noel, as it was mostly after his death. I was house-hunting at the time and was curious about Noel's house and so was shown around it by the amah. It was eerie. There was a peculiar mixture of Hollywood-type fake antiques in this very 1930s colonial atmosphere. There were few valuable things in the whole place. I bought up his entire wardrobe as I thought it was very sad all his personal items had to be on display like that. There were top hats, walking sticks and about thirty pairs of suede shoes! There was a lot of 1930s gear, hardly used, sharkskin suits, even some shoe trees initialled with "N.C." [for Noel Croucher]...[136]

A full camphor chest was found to be full of classical music cassettes, a lot of it religious. The books were mostly history, not novels. H.M. Jebsen also picked up Noel's office furniture which included a tall cabinet with about sixty small shelves. Each shelf was labelled with a different company name — Hongkong Land, Wharf & Godown, the Telephone Company and so on. Unfortunately, all the files that had once been in the shelves had disappeared. Jebsen also collected some of Noel's silver pieces which now fit well with the historical ambience of the Jebsen home. They include a foot-long ebony and silver stick, a Victorian silver box with a royal crest on it, a silver cigar box and a Russian silver bowl decorated with a silver scarf-like design across it.

'There wasn't anything of great value,' recalls Ian MacCallum of the auction. 'The house suffered from damp anyhow. Noel had a grand piano which I never saw him play, but you could see that was suffering from damp too.'

For the rest, there are the memories — of a brash, pushy rascal on the one hand, and of the generous man who gave gold coins to children on their birthdays and left his fortune to Hong Kong.

Unwittingly, Noel had still one more legend to create — that of how he died. For he passed away in no ordinary way. About a week before he was to die, he was in Canossa Hospital for a minor stroke. He had called his office boy, Wong Yue-nam, up to the hospital to apologise that he felt he had little time left to change his will. Mr Wong told him not to worry and that anyway, Mr Croucher was not likely to go so soon.

Within days of his discharge from hospital, Noel was due for a check-up with his doctors at Anderson & Partners in Prince's Building. But he had been caught in the rain and was wet when he got to his own office. He asked Mr Wong to put on the electric fire until it was time to go to the doctor. 'Time's up!' said Mr Croucher. Then 'Nam' took his boss on a short cut through the Landmark shopping centre. Noel was not at all well. He said to Wong, 'Nam, ask for the nurse, quick quick quick!' As Croucher and Wong stood at the reception in the doctor's surgery, Noel asked his Boy why there were so many people around. When it was his turn to see the doctor, he stood up, walked to the corner of the corridor and that was the last that Wong Yue-nam ever saw of him.

'After about five minutes, someone said, "Call the doctor!", and they asked who was with the gweilo.[37] I asked them what was the matter and the nurse told me Mr Croucher was dead. Then the doctor came and said he was very sorry, Mr Croucher was dead,' recalled Wong Yue-nam. 'I was very unhappy, surprised and very sad. I had tears in my eyes and couldn't see anything any more.'[38]

Noel Croucher had become such a larger-than-life figure that, despite his eighty-eight years, his death was still a surprise. It became, inevitably, the occasion for yet more legend, especially about how exactly Noel had been caught in the rain on his way to work that day.

'The day he died, he walked in the pouring rain to catch a bus, so he was soaking wet by time he got to the office,' reports Lady May Ride. 'He collapsed. Now that was meanness to himself, wasn't it? His office boy, he's an absolute darling, he was there.'[39]

'I was so surprised,' says Florence Lo. 'Every afternoon Mr Croucher used to have a siesta on the balcony. I always thought it would happen then, and I used to keep an eye on him. I was sad when he died. He was my boss for so long and he would take care of me if I asked him. He would help with my problems.'[40]

Everyone remembers the story. Why would a multimillionaire want to catch the no. 15 bus to get to work? Some friends recall offering him a lift to town that fateful day. But stubborn old Croucher saw no reason to change his habit of decades. He had never relaxed into his role as a wealthy man. He was able to afford every pleasure but somehow forgot his own. It was the final irony in a life full of such quirks. Perhaps, this is what is meant by eccentricity?

'Yes, I think so,' considers Ian MacCallum. 'The day he died, he wasn't feeling well in the morning. It was absolutely pouring down that day. In the end he decided he was going to go down to the office anyhow. The amah said, "Take the car because it's raining." "Oh no," said Noel. He walked from his house to Stubbs Road to get the no. 15 bus. And he had to wait at the bus stop, so by the time he got downtown he was absolutely soaked and freezing. And then he felt so bad, he decided he would actually go round to the doctor, and I gather had this heart attack in the waiting room.[41]

The *South China Morning Post* wrote: 'It was the day of the huge thunderstorm two Thursdays ago and the billionaire stockbroker and businessman ignored the warnings and marched off into the rain to make the half-mile walk down Mount Cameron Road where he stood patiently waiting to catch a bus. He had discharged himself from hospital only six days earlier.' Kevin Sinclair also reported that when Noel discharged himself from hospital before the fateful day, he had gone down to the Hong Kong Club to join a sing-along of his favourite old music-hall songs. It was a special pub night function which went on until well after midnight. Noel apparently said the next day that he felt much better, and that the music-hall had done him a world of good.[42]

Strangely enough, there was a notorious figure in the history of the Isle of Wight who, in the early 1600s, did something very similar to Noel Croucher, also of the Isle of Wight. Robert Brackley lived in Newport on the Isle but one night found himself stranded on the mainland, with no ferry boats available to take him home. So he slept in a church porch, to save the money required to stay at an inn. So he caught pneumonia and died worth a small fortune, the richest man in town.[43]

According to Noel's assistant, Florence Lo, Noel actually had a business appointment with the up-and-coming property tycoon Li Ka-shing on the day he died. Florence Lo remembers calling Li's secretary to cancel the meeting.[44] Had it occurred such a meeting would have reeked with historical symbolism. Here could have been an icon of the old guard meeting the leader of the new.

Li Ka-shing and Lee Shau-kee were among several new tycoons who shared with Noel the drive to overcome a lack of education and to indulge in philanthropy, while amassing vast fortunes. But the differences are instructive. Li Ka-shing, with his dramatic incursions into the world of firms once held solely by the British, symbolises the evolution of the Hong Kong business scene. In the past, connections with Britain were the key. Through Li, many learned that now it was connections with the Mainland and a vision of Hong Kong in China's orbit that mattered more. Thus, through his death, Noel missed a date with the future.

The funeral was held, of course, at St. John's Cathedral, under the stained glass window Noel had donated. Noel's regular place of worship was packed with people for the occasion. Then Governor Sir (now Lord) Murray MacLehose led the mourners, who included Hong Kong's top names in business, the civil service, philanthropy and the best clubs. Many of them might have shunned or disliked the man in life, but were ready to line up in black at his death. The Dean, The Very Revd Stephen Sidebotham, noted it was impossible to sum up Noel's life in a short eulogy. He described Noel as 'something of a gadfly to the last.'[45]

The pallbearers gave an impressive cross-section of Noel's interests and contacts. There was R.C. 'Dick' Lee, son of Noel's friend Lee Hysan and a close friend and colleague of Noel's through the gas company. There was F.S. Li, of the Bank of East Asia family, and Dr Douglas Laing, Jockey Club steward and good friend of Noel's. The son of Chan Nam-cheong, with whom Noel began his post-war philanthropy, was there. So, too, were (Lord) Michael Sandberg, chairman of the Hong Kong Bank, and last but not least, Noel's son, Richard Croucher.

Lady May Ride was one of the mourners in the cathedral that day. She was there with Mordia Ho Tung (née O'Shea), a daughter-in-law of Sir Robert Ho Tung, and with Daisy Li-Tebbutt, another dear friend of Noel's. These ladies appreciated the presence of Noel's special friends and pallbearers, but were also amused to see the self-styled aristocracy of Hong Kong in full attendance at Noel's passing.

'Mordia turned to me and said, "Noel must be laughing! These people would never even have passed the time of day with Noel, but they all turn up at his funeral! What absolute hypocrites," ' recalls Lady Ride. 'And she was absolutely right, you can quote that. Noel would have been laughing his head off at this church packed with people who would never even pass the time of day with him. They had all turned up and why, because he was made of money, that's why. They were all hypocrites.'[46]

One last story must be told about Noel Croucher. A question had arisen over just how to dispose of Noel's mortal remains, as the original idea of a mausoleum near the church had to be ruled out — the ground was so soft it was feared it would sink. Noel's son Richard took the decision in favour of cremation.

'I spread the ashes all over Hong Kong — some in Ice House Street, some at the Yacht Club, in his office, at the Jockey Club, and in the garden at his house. I took the rest back to England.'[47] Unbeknownst to Richard, his action was to have a sequel. Jack Hobbs, a long-standing friend of Noel's,[48] went up to Noel's house after the death to keep an eye on things. He found the lawn untidily overgrown and questioned the staff about why they had not mowed it.

They replied, 'If we cut the lawn we might cut Mr Croucher!' Jack Hobbs then told the staff: 'If you're sitting here and getting your monthly pay and not cutting the grass, he'll be a bloody sight more angry!' Thus the grass was cut.

♪ ♪ ♪

In the course of this remarkable life, Noel Croucher was part of all that Hong Kong went through as it clawed its way up from an accidental outpost of empire into a thriving city-state. He lived through the fires and typhoons, the blockades and riots, the smells of war in China, vast waves of refugees and of money from fallen Shanghai. He was part of the rebuilding of Hong Kong and part of its emergence into a global finance centre. He helped build the companies that built the homes and ferries and wharfs and telephone lines. He helped start the charities that kept children off the streets and helped build Hong Kong's brain trust among its young. He sailed Hong Kong's waters, played its golf fields, bought and sold its properties, and met its most famous visitors. To the end, his life was focused on Hong Kong. And he did all this from a poor and difficult start, against that wall of colonial snobbery, and despite his obvious weaknesses.

Noel Croucher became frustrated and irritated about most things in the early 1970s, the visions, the possibilities, the friendships, the good old days — all were passing. There is no room these days for men like Noel Croucher as colonial.

But now, as always, Hong Kong plays host to people just like Noel, the edgy young person determined to get ahead, that stuff which is the essence of refugee towns. So it is that the story of Noel Croucher is a story of Hong Kong. And Noel, whether he likes it or not, provides an excellent example of that kind of person who, had he spent his life in the small town in Hampshire where he was born, would probably never have achieved what he did. Abroad, he could traverse those boundaries of class which would have held him down at home.

Born into the Victorian era, Noel spent his formative years on the China Coast, the home of thoroughgoing capitalism where free trade and the merchant class were supreme. Here was a continuation of the free traders' ideal and in Hong Kong it could flourish to an extent not possible in a traditional society. The mercantile spirit bloomed in Hong Kong as in a greenhouse.

At first, it seems appropriate that Croucher died when he did — it is argued by some that his era, if defined as 'colonial', was passing, and his time was therefore past. But if his particular milieu was not so much colonial as mercantile, then few could say the mercantile era of Hong Kong has passed.

If Noel were alive now, he would still be trading, meeting a wide range of business contacts, and supporting any cause which he felt would advance the well-being of Hong Kong. A stickler for convention he would still flout many. He would be dapper, well-dressed, a striking figure of a man, charming the ladies at will. He made money then the same way many make money now — parlaying information, keeping secrets, organising take-overs, buying futures, speculating in currencies, investing in growing markets.

Great theories could be built around men such as Croucher, as front-line imperialists, pirates and exploiters, or indulged spoiled brats of Peak society. But Noel was much more simple than this. He just believed in hard work and due reward, in having goals and working towards them, in working first and playing later. The shame is that he did not fit in more of the play.

Noel's vision of Hong Kong easily encompassed the fading away of the British colonial, and the presence of a Chinese population to whom Hong Kong — not China or Britain — is home. He could see new generations of Hong Kong people growing up knowing no other, and he worked out what they would need to get ahead.

As to why he felt like this, he might well have reasoned it all out intellectually. But it is more likely that he simply felt these things, because Hong Kong was his home too. It was the only true home he ever had.

LETTERS TO
JOAN SCRIVENER

ote: The letters have been edited for ease of reading. This required frequent corrections of grammar, and insertion of punctuation, along with cuts of repetitions and the occasionally slanderous remark. Care has been taken throughout to preserve Noel's own voice and meaning.

17 January 1957

Dear Joan... You might have stayed on here, with the 'watchman' sleeping outside your door. You were occasionally given to apologising for being a trouble — well I'm used to trouble, but of a different kind, and this was a most refreshing change. I certainly enjoyed our trip to Macao and am glad you made up your mind on this last day of the year to do something you might remember when other things have been forgotten... I'm in my room writing with the cat looking up in expectation of being combed and brushed. You certainly started something — but she is looking ever so much better for your careful brushing... The best thing you did in Hongkong was to take my advice — there were one or two other things I could have advised you on which you may not have acted on at once, but later possibly. But your ship was steaming away through Lyeemun Pass and then it was too late...

11 March 1957

Dear Joan... I had a robbery too. While I was out sailing over the weekend a thief entered my bedroom window and stole the contents of my locked drawer in the dressing table — silver bowls, candelabra, clothes —

amounting to £600. I got £400 from the Insurance which the late owner of the house had transferred to me without my knowledge so I was lucky. This happened at 4 a.m. and the police were down in 20 minutes taking finger-prints etc, but so far nothing has been recovered. A chopper was left on my bed which didn't induce the sound sleep I generally have when I return from sailing...

My house is slowly looking less bare. The Dining Room will look very nice. During the cold weather — it got perishing cold after you left — I put the fire on and you remember how big it is — filled it with logs and by jove it was lovely sitting in front of it. I had to ring up a friend or two for them to see how lovely it looked...

I would like to come home for a couple of months — but I've come to the age when I'm tied down doing unremunerative work which gives me pleasure. Lady Lenox Boyd was here recently and made a special visit to me in hospital. All the tiny patients were looking as well as they could, lying in their beds in plaster casts, cheerful as ever — in such circumstances it is amazing and is a tonic for others. From all reports, which are very flattering, it is considered the best equipped and run of all the others in HK.

The weather has not been kind lately as far as sailing goes, but I did have a nice weekend, alone, on some faraway island beach and fasted for 48 hours — except for oranges.

15 March 1957

Dear Joan... this enormous grate is lovely to sit in front of — just having a sherry or two, a nice dinner, and after dinner smoke, puts me in mind of home...

19 May 1957

Dear Joan... The rain has been pelting down for the last few days and water restrictions are off — so the patient poor are no longer queuing alongside street water taps with their kerosene tins. When we had excessive rains before we hadn't enough reservoirs, now the newest one is complete there will still be a lot going to waste... I've got a large size French Poodle (puppy), white colour, coming along and it will suit the colour scheme with Samy [the cat]. Can you picture them lying alongside on my Blue Peking Carpet...

3 July 1957

Dear Joan... I've had a very hectic time recently ... the abnormal rains did an enormous amount of damage and a heavy landslide completely blocked the entrance to the Children's Convalescent Home. This put the kitchen out of action. A big boulder weighing many tons rolled down the hillside and by the Grace of God stopped by the side of the wall leading to a ward. Had it continued it would have gone clean through to the sea. Thank God it stopped...

My poodle puppy is the cleverest and most intelligent dog I've ever set eyes on. He is just six weeks old and knows already his place outside.

I came back yesterday after 3 days out in *La Cigale*. It was hot but evenings were cool and swimming was just grand. I tried to get a shark but no success...

28 September 1957

Dear Joan... Tomorrow is Saturday and the weather looks bad as we have just had Typhoon Gloria, so I am going to Macao instead of sailing. The last time was on New Year's eve with you, and after the Chinese Cabaret we walked back to the Bela Vista Hotel — you leading me on as I did not know the way. We had been to a Chinese Cabaret, it was moonlight, and I took you in my arms and gave you a kiss — only one — it might have been more, and then we walked back up the 15th century little road to our hotel and I saw you next morning. It might have been different...

❧ ❧ ❧

New Year's Day, 1958

Dear Joan... One year ago we were in Macao and I would have much loved to have gone over again. As it was I spent it alone. Last night I was about to do it again, when somebody phoned and said they were waiting for me at the Yacht Club where the usual New Year dance was on. So I dressed and went forth, didn't dance a step, and felt bored stiff... My place is looking nice and I don't like going out, but love people coming to see me.

My back is still troubling me. I'm out of the cast as it made the pain worse. Someone suggested I should have a nurse to look after me but I'm not that far gone — but it certainly gave me an idea.

I've been in my house a year and time has just rushed away...

P.S. By the way next time you wire, 'Croucher Hong Kong' is sufficient.

12 March 1958

Dear Joan... My French Poodle has been stolen and although I offered a big reward and put it across the Radio and newspapers I had no reply. It was certainly not eaten as Chinese only like Chinese dogs. My house is looking as nice as ever and I've had a few parties which some say are the best they've had. I'm glad your Mother is in better health...

I want to come home sometime this year to have my back looked at but don't know if I can make it. Things are not so good with the credit squeeze. Marchwood's house, you mentioned, interests me, have you any particulars — price, area etc, is it within easy reach of the town, London? I'd like to see the place where my Daughter-in-law is living and get a small place in the Country, but she is Chelsea-minded. I knew Marchwood when he was George Penny, a stockbroker in Singapore. He had 2 brothers. He came out as an officer in the P & O, fine looking, and well dressed, made a fortune in 1910...

27 April 1958

Dear Joan... It was thoughtful to send me particulars of Marchwood's House which is on the market. 'Twill be a pity if it is pulled down and flattened over... I knew Marchwood when he was Lionel [sic] Penny, a stockbroker in Fraser & Co in Singapore. There were 3 brothers [sic] he was an officer in the P & O and stopped over in Singapore and decided to stay on and made a fortune in the Rubber boom especially, came home, entered politics, and known as the best dressed man in the House.

I've seen many attractive houses in Country Life but from this end it's risky to buy, one doesn't know if government will develop close by. You find yourself with other people's kitchen gardens with clothes hanging up to dry blocking your favourite view...

I went to a Charity Ball last night in support of my Hospital for Children and at the end of a dance, a chap collapsed with a heart attack and died. No one knew until afterwards, they were told he had fainted.

I'm sitting on my verandah before going away for the weekend in my boat. It's one of the loveliest days and the flowers are blooming and there's a solitary bird chirping away in a nearby tree which is in full bloom with red blossoms. I told you my Poodle was stolen, and my Persian cat has disappeared, probably bitten by a snake and went out into the wood and died. Yesterday the Airedale [terrier dog] disappeared, but this morning the police reported it had been picked up by another dog owner. So Tim came back this morning looking sorry for himself, tail between his legs. I know it's going to be lovely sailing as the breeze is just getting up. I'd love to catch a big tunny [large marine fish] just to top everything. My daughter-in-law is holidaying with friends in Italy. I'd love to be home [England] if the weather was like today. Motoring through the west countryside at one's own sweet will.

I've been preoccupied with some company litigation which necessitated bringing an eminent counsel out from Home. We proved our case and all is well. Then another outstanding matter of some 3 years standing is about to be settled so there is a possibility of a short holiday, but who knows...

15 June 1958

Dear Joan... At last your much travelled book has arrived and I have read some of the verses and like it very much...

Things here are progressing, but yesterday we experienced torrential rain, traffic disorganised, Chinese buildings collapse, about 15 dead and thousands homeless — if one can call a few bits of wood nailed together with a tin roof a home...

I have all the worries that it's possible to have — but they will soon disappear like a flock of birds passing overhead. I wanted to get home this year but just couldn't make it...

14 July 1958

Dear Joan... I've just got your letter which is most amusing, asking if my wife was back as according to 'Howells' whom I don't know, she is. They probably saw my picture taken at a Charity Do, sitting next to a grey-haired lady, Mrs Goldsach. Her husband is a prominent businessman and I met them for the first time. The Chinese photographer asked some 'wag' who was in the party, and next day Mr and Mrs Croucher was [sic] in the picture. There were plenty of telephone calls next morning from old residents to me and also to Mr Goldsach. I thought it might reach Mrs Croucher's ears, but so far I've heard nothing.

My son and daughter-in-law are going to be divorced — most distressing — but there it is. I do more swimming now than before as it is best for my back. 'Twas a lovely weekend I spent on my own, sailing... If Mrs Croucher was within 1,000 miles I'd never enjoy this and probably be a nervous wreck...

17 November 1958

Dear Joan... Things here are indeed quiet — I've all the worry of my family and the impending divorce. I would like to get home next spring but it depends on the situation out here. Have you ever been to New Zealand? I read in one of their papers that 20,000 well-to-do bachelors are looking for wives from England...

♪ ♪ ♪

8 August 1959

Dear Joan... I'm sorry to hear you've been hospitalised... What on earth were you doing to allow a cabinet to fall on your bosom. Had you told me it was a lovesick swain who had lain his head on it, I could understand it. But to bring in a cabinet as an alibi demands a little imagination, and cabinets being what they are can't say anything. Next time, keep clear of cabinets, and try something more sympathetic and to your liking. These things generally happen when you feel it's great to be alive and fit — sure enough something disturbs that sense of well being.

I am well and enjoying my boat...

♪ ♪ ♪

10 August 1960

Dear Joan... You are probably fast asleep while here it is very early morning, 6.30, and I'm having my tea and watching the dogs play on the lawn. It is usually very lovely to look out into the hills and beyond to glimpses of the sea, but today the Peak is shrouded in clouds and it's raining. I received the snapshot thank you ... my brother seems to be all ears and chin. He had a holiday for the purpose of looking up some old records. I lost a lot during the war and want to get them together again. We come from around West Sussex and in East Dene Church are several Crouchers buried, and I asked him to go and see if the inscriptions are still legible. Should you ever come across any very old books of Sussex records, let me know. I collect old books and archives. Recently a bookseller at home wrote and said he had a volume written by a Jesuit recording his journey to Peking in 1650, it was in Latin, rather bulky. It was in the possession of some villager. I gave him what he asked though I felt I was getting a bargain. I wanted to come home this year ever so much but with one thing and another cropping up, I couldn't. My domestic affairs worsen...

On the other hand my secretary [Mrs Ferguson] who lost her husband during the internment has 2 boys, 2 girls. The boys worked hard at the University and one is a Doctor and gone to Australia, a girl has become a teacher also gone to Australia and the eldest boy is studying electronics and Rolls Royce have sent him to Canada, Sweden, and want him to join them. All this is very rewarding and is some compensation, but I believe I'm doing the right thing in the community and the country will be all the better. Those with the brains and the keenness to work should be encouraged and money or the lack of it should not be an impediment.

1 May 1961

Dear Joan... I owe you several letters and I've been meaning to sit down and tell you how nice it is to hear from you. It was sad losing my brother. I think he may have lasted longer had he had the operation when the trouble started and then going down to his sister's funeral in his poor state of health did not help. My sister I had not seen for 35 years and never really wanted to, but with Basil we had become closer as the years passed though it was many years since I saw him — before 1956 when I was home last. During our life I don't suppose we were together 10 years from childhood on and my meetings with Inez [Basil's wife] could be counted on one hand. So really it was not as if we had been in close contact for a long time. Inez will miss him a lot...

31 May 1961

Dear Joan... You gave me more information about my late Brother's family or domestic affairs than I have ever had...

My grandchildren are simply charming in their photographs. They both go to Lady Eden's school but Amanda is leaving soon and will go to a very nice school — Radcliffe, Lymington, Hampshire, only for girls, where tuition is along the lines I like, where religion is not forgotten, and charity towards all is remembered. This is what is lacking in our world today. Browning said God is in his heaven and all is well with the world, but *he is not* to an ever growing number. Don't run away with the idea I am sermonising, I'm not. If only the headlines in our kindergarten copy books were faithfully followed, the world would not be in such a mess.

16 June 1961

Dear Joan... My memory seemingly is not so good this morning (6.30 am) — I had a late night — Chinese Celebration, and unlike the usual Chinese Dinner where the guests all go home when there is nothing more to eat, this one hung on and on. The Europeans kept looking at each other with strained faces until someone made a move, and I got home at once. I didn't want to go as I'm a bit off colour, the weather has been most depressing and I thought I'd have my blood pressure checked as I do about twice a year. No change, still 114 and pulse 62...

...I only wanted one [picture] of myself and family and my Grandfather Stockley who had a white beard... What you might do is to look up all your maps and find where the village or hamlet of LUDSHOT was located. It is or was not far from Selbourne and some Crouchers lived there.

16 November 1961

Dear Joan... I wonder what picture you saw of me at Inez's. I came across one I had taken in the first war in uniform and after being in the East so long and getting a lot of England knocked out of me. The girls said I was different to the homeside Englishman, and I suppose I was. As a matter of fact, we who have been abroad so much are a lot more attractive — not so much nowadays as years ago. What with travel speed, T.V. etc we all seem to be going into the melting pot...

All the millions spent [in England] on Education seem to have no effect. Workers on the continent produce at least one third more than our people. When we are in the Common Market there will be a big change if this continues and we will find ourselves in trouble and it will be entirely due to the workers. But I think something must be done to curb this wild speculation in shares and property and people must not be allowed to get away with these expense accounts which are abused.

I haven't got my guest house or room yet. The Chinese have a way of arranging things — one bed space serves two people. The person who has a day job sleeps at night and the one who is on night shift uses it during the day. If they are men there is no overlapping taking place but you know how unpunctual women can be. I am going out to a Chinese dinner tonight for my sins. I have a duty to perform. Princess Alexandra had a great time here. I was presented to her. She wanted to know how long I had been here and if I was going home again. She would have opened the new wing of my hospital, but it could not be got ready in time. It is going to be a fine building, altogether 110 beds, Physiotherapy, Hydrotherapy, Operating theatre etc. Love, N.

9 January 1962

Dear Joan... I thought of going away in my boat over the holidays and giving up the invitations [from those] who took compassion on some of us who lived alone. But I went to Church on Xmas, and went and saw my new wing to the hospital and had my Dinner alone — New Year's Eve the same. I felt for the first time happy to do so. In younger days I thought I'd be missing something, and usually was the party.

But with all mothers of refugees on either side of us I felt I'd be better, thinking of these — I'm not a kill joy by any means — but on the afternoon I gave away to 500 waifs their Xmas presents — a paper bag containing a tooth brush, a face towel, an apple, sweets, a small toy, costing about a shilling — they had nothing like it before.

I had a sherry before lunch at a friend's house and the wife who had just arrived to spend Xmas with her husband was wearing a lovely dress. She said it cost her £150 (They are nouveau riche) and I remarked that my Xmas party to the kids only came to one third of the price of her dress and would she like to give me something — not a sous. Some people are devoid of all feelings of sympathy and compassion, but they seem to prosper nevertheless. There will be a great awakening, but perhaps not in my time.

1 March 1962

Dear Joan... Here it never dropped under 46° [Fahrenheit] and it was so nice to put on a log fire and look into it. In my time of life I'm wondering how many there are ahead for me:

I strove with none, for none was worth my strife
Nature I loved and next to nature art
I warmed both hands before the fire of life
It sinks — and I am ready to depart.

8 June 1962

Dear Joan... We have had a lot of publicity recently over the Refugees. Much was exaggerated and things are normal again. You can deny these people are starving — it is complete nonsense, American propaganda. It is true food is short and without any variety at all, and rationed — but to say the refugees are leaving because they are starving is nonsense. These people come from the mainland and have their relations in Hongkong. Our population is 1/2 million — 1/2 of this number were born on the mainland and they are trying to get some of their relations into the Colony where it is cheaper to feed them than by sending food parcels — when they arrive here they soon get jobs. The trouble is we are very over-crowded and cannot handle a big sudden influx.

We have had a very dry winter and water is short, we can only have four hours a day and the wretched Chinese queue up in hundreds at the water hydrants with their Kerosene Tins to collect their ration. I hear you have had a cold spell lately...

[Re Joan working as a cartographer] I'm expecting to see you heading a column marching on Parliament carrying a Banner — 'Not another line without an extra dime'.

Did I tell you Margot Fonteyn gave a couple of performances at the New City Hall. I didn't go. The good seats were 4 guineas, no orchestra and the corps de Ballet amounted to 6 others. Two pianos in accompaniment. This was the reason I didn't go. I'm surprised she agreed to dance at all. Another very charming star also visited Hongkong — Joan Fontaine, the movie actress. She was born in Japan and wanted to revisit the place. Just travelling alone and left by plane for England to relatives, de Havilland, who live somewhere in Surrey. She is very very natural and completely unspoilt. We went around on our own. She introduced me to the twist which I gave up after a few turns. She adored my bungalow and the dogs. How is your mother... I've got a list of Crouchers registered at East Dene and Singleton from 1550 — about 60 of them...

16 October 1962

Dear Joan... Well you may be surprised to hear my son has married again, 3 months ago. I heard from a third party... I am just opening up to you Joan some of the worries which beset me [to see] what you think of them and your reaction.

Did I tell you about the Typhoon we had. I lost about 50 trees and half my roof. I've never experienced a worse one. It hit my place and the immediate surroundings worse than any other. 75/7,500 [?] were homeless — but our organisations are ready for all kinds of emergencies and soon fixed them up. I had a place where the street sleepers and others slept, about 400, and it was [so] blown about and damaged that the government ordered it to be demolished. This meant clearing out the families and putting them on the hillside in rude wooden huts. The Chinese take everything in their stride and have enduring patience and face any disaster like most orientals with stoicism.

28 December 1962

Dear Joan... the horrid English climate. I shudder when I am lying on the beach to hear about smog, coldest day for many years, Paris record cold for 83 years etc. And then I ask myself why go home and put up with it. Millions of people are getting more and more than ever dreamed of a few years ago in the way of material comforts and yet go on striking for more. The trouble is being half educated or not having the intelligence to understand the first principles of living and doing an honest day's work.

I read recently of the demand for £10 a week extra pay for the men who erect steel structures for buildings and the employers are offering £4. These men get £40 a week already. By way of comparison we are erecting two luxury hotels, each 26 storeys, one with 900 rooms and the other 500. The men doing the same jobs get no more than £20 a month — which is good and it costs them about £3 a month for food which they consider ample. They work 8 hours a day, no more. If they choose to do a few hours work elsewhere it's their business.

We have no unemployment nor welfare state, and no one goes hungry. 5,000 were out of work one day from a Textile mill and were absorbed elsewhere within a few days. There is no demarcation of labour as in England where hundreds will down tools because metaphorically speaking a man is asked to turn on the gas instead of the electric light. Until the Trade Union Leaders assert their authority [presumably, against the workers] we [England] will be unable to compete and things will get worse. The abuses of Capitalism are slowly being righted but Trade Unionism is holding the community to ransom, and it remains to be seen what Labour will do if it takes office. I think MacMillan has had a more difficult time than any other Prime Minister and has done well.

♪ ♪ ♪

9 February 1963

Dear Joan... I wouldn't be surprised if we don't get a cold spell — though it is about 40 years [since] there was a thin frost near the Peak Flagstaff.

27 February 1963

Dear Joan... Spring is here again, but the water problem is a worry. Macao has had no rain for 4 months — HKong about the same. The reservoirs are dangerously low and the water supply is for only 4 hours a day... God knows what will happen if the Rains failed to come with our population of nearly 4 million.

8 March 1963

Dear Joan... I noticed in The Times, March 5, last page, 'Croucher's Farm', advertised for sale, by Hamptons. It is near Battle, Crowhurst. The solicitors — 3 High St, Newhaven. Is this the place you kindly sent me a photograph of I wonder? It is a XVI Century Cottage Residence, fully modernised, 1 1/2 acre. I'd love to know more about it, if it is an attractive place, not near any ribbon development, suitable for the grandchildren, I'd be interested. If you are not too far away, could you run over one day and give me your opinion and find from the Solicitors what they are asking for it — for goodness sake *don't mention my name as the price will go up*. I wonder if a Croucher is living in it. I've seen so many lovely cottages with gardens that it would be better to have the [grand] children there than in Chelsea.... This cottage is to be auctioned on April 24. I have in mind to buy a big place later on and put a man in to run it and make it worth his while...

Here the water situation is worse than ever. No rain for 4 months and the Kowloon Reservoir is absolutely empty. The Chinese on the other side of the border give us about 25 million gallons a day which helps a lot, but they too are experiencing a bad spell and may have to reduce this as the river is pretty low...

21 March 1963

Dear Joan... What a mess the country [England] is in. Who will win the next Election — if we change it will be a case of out of the frying pan into the fire...

By the way you know my son is in the property business and he saw the advertisement about Croucher's Farm and sent me a Brochure from Hamptons and is going to see it. They want 8,500 for it and from the particulars it is two cottages joined... So I am not interested. I'm sorry if you went to any trouble.

28 April 1963

Dear Joan... I'm making a very great effort to get home this year, but I've been doing the same thing for years, but I'm still here — whether I'll be able to do so remains to be seen. If I do make it, I'll come by boat as I hate flying.

10 May 1963

Dear Joan... We are still without rain, not a drop in 6 months and I expect the taps will be on for 2 hours every other day. What tricks nature can play on us. I cannot imagine what we would do if we had no rain when the reservoirs ran dry. There would be an exodus to Canton of the Chinese and Hongkong would become deserted.

I saw Alexandra's wedding on T.V., what a well matched pair, and what a contrast to Margaret and Snowden. Her carrying on with Townsend wasn't a good example to the young was it.

9 August 1963, postmarked London

Address: Langham 4142, 3 Mansfield St, W1.

Dear Joan... I arrived home a short while ago and have been busy with family affairs. I won't be here long I'm afraid. Have you a telephone ... address your letters to Junior Carlton Club as I'm only at the above address for lunch... I will ask my son to motor me down very soon. I wish I could drive but I won't take a chance. Must get a chauffeuress. Yours, Noel.

25 September 1963, postmarked London

Address: Junior Carlton Club, Pall Mall, SW1.

Dear Joan... I'm sorry having made a mess of my arrangements which upset you. You've no idea of the places I've been looking at houses, one day 220 miles — with no results. I'm booking my air passage and expect to leave very early in October... In the last two days I've been with my London solicitors, who are not satisfied with the legal documents drawn up in HKong. Then a co-director arrived yesterday from HKong who is here on some Trade Mission. I've got to such a state that I'll be ready to get back and have a holiday. My domestic affairs are no better either...

Unknown date

Sorry I have not seen you before taking off tomorrow... I hope to return sometime in May...

Fancy my paying £350 for the picture from an Italian Nobleman, introduced to me by a very highly respected Italian Father in HK, and for Sotheby's to value it at £20. Should I have a sale in my house in HK I'm sure I'd get my money back. But I haven't the nerve to include it.

7 October 1963, just back from England

Dear Joan... I arrived here on Sunday afternoon, very tiring but smooth. Had a wonderful view of Mt Everest.

I certainly had a hell of a fortnight before I left, what with solicitors, draft copies of this and that, changing of wills and settlements, due to new family address — and in the end coming back with very little done. If I come to Europe next year I've a good mind to give England a wide berth and go elsewhere. I found my house in perfect order and my dogs all happy to see me again...

14 November 1963

Dear Joan... I have been catching up with a lot of work since my return. My secretary who has married children in Australia, Canada and Scotland wants to visit them as she hasn't had a holiday for 10 years so I'll have to get a temporary makeshift. Always a nuisance.

14 December 1963

Dear Joan... We have a movie team here of stars filming Lord Jim — Jack Hawkins, Pete Toole, Askin? Kirmeorff? and others.

I am meeting Greer Garson tomorrow at the Races. She is travelling around with her American Husband. She must be getting on for 50.

❧ ❧ ❧

27 February 1964

Dear Joan... Very much occupied lately with visitors passing through. Meeting [Gina] Lollobrigida tomorrow evening, who will be making a picture here I expect. Several big stars have recently been here and their opinion is that HKong is a tip top place for film making...

8 April 1964

Dear Joan... We are still without rain. Life's tempo is getting more and more hotted up. What with old friends returning — farewell tiffins and dinners and cocktail parties which make one very tired — the Chairman of my Hospital at Sandy Bay had a heart attack and will be laid up for 2 months, and he ran the whole place. Now this is added to my list of troubles. I can hardly believe my holiday was about a year ago...

The Yacht Race to Manila — 600 miles for my Challenge Cup — finished last week. It took the winner 4 1/2 days. Now, how are you keeping? ...

If one is to believe the papers, there won't be honeymoons in the future. All the curiosity of marriage will be found out before leaving school. Teenagers want to step out Now, because tomorrow never may come.

7 May 1964

Dear Joan... My domestic trouble is unchanged. What a novel could be written of the characters and their background and secret affairs. The only one who has had a normal existence is myself and if I had never come East and [had] remarried in England, worked in a family concern far removed — I would never have found myself encumbered with so many hangers-on, but [would have] retired to a country cottage with plenty of woodland and a stream near by. Yet I doubt I would want to forego the experience between the years.

10 September 1964

Dear Joan... Typhoon Ruby last weekend was a bad one but in my place it was not so bad as 'Wanda' which was the worst I've experienced. Now today another is on its way, 'Sally', with winds much stronger. At 11 o'clock this morning, the Radio warned all to go home and prepare for the blow. So I've been sitting here since noon, with everything fastened down, all pictures, curios, taken down and put away. Last week, 'Ruby' found me unable to get home until it was over. I ordered my car but it stalled outside the Hilton Hotel, near the Cricket Ground. Telephone poles were buckled in two, but casualties were small, about 50 dead...

I wish I could chuck my business up — but if I did, what would there be for me to do besides my own affairs [and] welfare matters. And I cannot see myself giving all this up.

I've had some delightful sailing weekends, perfect conditions.

The Olympic Torch arrived here en route to Japan. It was taken from Kai Tak [airport] by several relays of runners to the Kowloon Pier where it was handed to a Yacht Club member who is racing his boat in the Olympics. [Alan Stevens, with Bill Hancock, one of the crew for the 1964 Japan Olympics. See Gillian Chambers, pp. 118–9.] He crossed the harbour aboard a launch, standing at the bow with the Torch held high. I in my boat and 3 others provided the escort across the harbour, where it was taken to the City Hall where the Governor received it. Unfortunately a typhoon was expected and next day 'Ruby' came along, so the Torch was delayed for a day but eventually was taken across the harbour, again escorted.

This is the kind of weather one likes to be marooned with pleasant company — if you savvy what I mean.

5 October 1964

Dear Joan... What on earth is Daphne talking about me having a housekeeper. I suppose she thought my house could not be so nicely kept without one, but she doesn't know what good house boys can do, from cooking to flower arrangements.

27 October 1964

Dear Joan... I'm just off to have lunch with the New Zealand Olympic runners, Snell, etc., who are passing through on their way home. Our women runners were marvellous — the mother of a small child winning the long jump and a record as well, shows what they can do. [Ann Packer of Britain won the 800m in 1964. Peter Snell of New Zealand broke records to win Olympic gold in the 800m in 1960, and gold in the 800m and 1,500m in 1964.]

♪ ♪ ♪

4 February 1965

Dear Joan... Chinese New Year, February 2, has come and gone, and to us who have seen so many, I'm glad. According to custom, all outstanding debts must be paid by the previous day and years ago, the incidence of fires was very high as Insurance Companies would often save the face of those who were unable to meet them. All employees get an extra month's pay as according to Chinese calendar there are 13 months in the year. All servants leave for at least two days, so I remain to look after the house as bad characters often take this opportunity of seeing if anybody is home. Not all householders do this, but I do. Everybody puts on their best clothes and those who want to save face borrow them for the occasion or take them out of the pawn shop where they have been during the year.

5 March 1965

Dear Joan... I have so much to do these days instead of having less, that I find little time to do the things I would like to do. The HK Bank is now holding its 100-year [anniversary] and 2 weeks of dinners, cocktail parties etc, and on the top of all this the usual visitors passing through. Things would continue the same, or better — if I dropped everything — but I just can't.

I realise now that what I need is a good secretary to do all my letters, welfare work, and the other activities I'm engaged in. So that I could just give her or him my ideas and sign the letters. I'm a very poor letter writer but I evidently size up matters pretty well — while many good correspondents would and do make a hash of things.

I'm feeling very well, but am told by my friends I should take things easy and go home every year. I'm urged to go to N.Z., Australia, Canada, and yet I'm happy to some extent in staying on here...

14 April 1965

Dear Joan... After 16 years my good cook has left me — to start a shop — and it is difficult to get another...

26 April 1965

Dear Joan... I went to have a small operation and was in Hospital for 10 days and lost 10 lbs — so if you want to lose weight come out and go into the same Hospital — it doesn't matter if you are ill or not, you lose a pound a day. I was there over Easter and feel a bit weak and sore, but I'll soon be myself again.

24 October 1965, on return from a trip to London

Dear Joan... There is quite a change for the worse in HKong. Thousands of empty flats where before there was a shortage, and property values have gone down 50% which is very serious. As a matter of fact one doesn't know what the values are.

I expected to find my two dogs waiting for me (nobody else) but when I got to Singapore a letter from Mrs Ferguson told me that Toby, the big white Poodle, had died of cancer in the stomach a week previously. This upset me very much indeed as for the last 7 years he was always with me. In the early morning when I had my tea, 6.30, he would sit around and for the last two years with his sooty coloured son, and at lunch, and on my return, they would both be waiting expectantly, wagging their tails. Well I suppose it is as well he died before I got back as it would have upset me terribly.

On the whole, my two months in England were not so happy. My family almost drove me round the bend and I'm seriously thinking of reducing my association with them.

5 January 1966?

Dear Joan... I kept out of Hospital and gave up all Xmas and New Year Parties and gave my back a rest. I needed somebody to rub it but couldn't find anyone...

I had two telegrams from my son — asking me to let bygones be bygones...

If you were here I'd give you a kiss. Now I come to think of it, I never have kissed you have I? ...

4 February 1966

Dear Joan... Thanks for sending me the sad news of Inez's passing. Although at one time it looked as if she would pull through it requires great reserves of strength to sustain an operation at her age ... but 'Inshallah' as the Arabs say, God's will...

I had a letter from Richard's second wife Penny, and a photo of the baby girl, now 3... One thing about her, she is my daughter-in-law, and she has never troubled me in any way or behaved dishonestly.

18 March 1966

Dear Joan... Have you seen the cottage I bought near Hastings for the grandchildren...

30 April 1966

Dear Joan... After being with me for 20 years, the embodiment of all the best in all secretaries, Mrs Ferguson, has had a stroke, and never recovered. I was speaking to her two hours before it happened. She is irreplaceable — looked after my office affairs, home, servants, reminded me to enter my horses for the Races, collected rent, in fact did everything. I had intended to take things easy for some time, and this has made me make up my mind. I am giving up my Stockbroking business, and [will] keep a few directorships and go easy. I'll probably take another sea trip...

12 May 1966

Dear Joan... Did I tell you my secretary for over 20 years, Mrs Ferguson, died from a stroke, and I simply do not know which way to turn. Her two sons flew out for the funeral. She was the embodiment of all good secretaries. I knew very little of her private affairs and her sons knew less. It took days to find a will and she had a bundle of papers with shares worth about £10,000. She was my office. She did everything — entered my horses for the Races, saw my yacht was slipped when it should be and restricted my spending also.

Her children are well educated — one son a Doctor, the other an electronic engineer and the daughter a teacher. The boys had a good education and finished with University degrees. They do not know I paid for their education. Their father died during the Japanese occupation and she was left with 4 children aged 10 to 14. It is so gratifying to see what fine citizens they are...

I've definitely decided to retire from the Stock Exchange Business, when I get straightened out...

6 June 1966

Dear Joan... I have a new secretary [the late Emily Fox-Fernandez] who is 58. She will be as good as Mrs Ferguson in a little time which is a load off my mind, but I have so much to tidy up...

4 July 1966

Dear Joan... Have you been down to Greywings [cottage]? Marguerite [his son's first wife] sent in some snaps which give a good idea of the place. It is very done up inside and out and the children are thrilled with the prospect of spending the summer holidays there. It is not very far away from the Cliffs, which slowly fall into the sea...

We had a terrific deluge a couple of weeks ago. I got home on Saturday when it started to rain and couldn't leave until the following Thursday and then had to go down a hill path as all the main roads to the Peak were impassable. Enormous landslides brought about by the rain, Killed at least 100, and made 7,000 homeless. I had no telephone. Gas, Electricity, Water — all broken. Helicopters took food supplies to the Peak. My Cook and Gardener and Driver were out and couldn't get back, so there I was incommunicado. A police officer made his way to our area to ask if we wanted anything. There was nothing I wanted but something to boil the water and it was ridiculous to ask for that. The Inspector said, 'God, I wish they were all like you.' The heaviest fall in one hour was 6 1/2 inches. My Jaguar was in the garage but the Rover was outside and the water came just above the axle when the rain subsided. It [the car] started immediately. Large apartment houses of 15 to 20 storeys were evacuated as the torrents of rain washed the earth away in places. At North Point, on the way to Tai Koo, a fall of land covered 70 cars and lorries and you could sail a boat on the Racecourse. One of the streets resembled a river taking everything with it — cars, stalls.

Fortunately, I was unable to get out and my place is safe, but I'm afraid if we get more rains and a typhoon there will be further collapses. Some people refuse to return to their homes as they look unsafe. Good for you you were not here...

I hope your mother is well and you are still looking for Ludshot, near Selbourne. Love, N.

31 August 1966

Dear Joan... [Re Amanda's birthday] I sent her a present to be opened at the Party, it was a gold bracelet with Chinese charms — maybe it was a bit old for her just now, but on special occasions she can wear it...

I've spent about £1,200 on repairs to Greywings and now more is wanted...

I hope your mother is keeping well and not worrying about her shares — they will all come back in about 18 months if not before. But times are going to get tough. The workers have been having too good a time for too long and not producing enough to pay for it.

4 October 1966?

Dear Joan... I can't make out your recipe for Ratatouille. What are courgettes? And what proportions? It looks good on paper but I'd rather have them on my tummy...

I wanted so much to come home this year but I'm up to my neck in all kinds of things which I can't shake off. I made several discretionary Trusts some years ago when R and M married and had children. With the changes I have had to change them, and then his second wife has children and Inez dies, and my own affairs are muddled up too. I should like to be like your mother — have a house, and an income, with no worry. I've got stuff all over the world, which I am gradually putting into a Trust.

My house has been redecorated and I gave a cocktail party — the first one for 7 years, of 80 people. It was a lovely evening, but too hot to be on the lawn. The sky was beautiful with the distant Peak and hills stretched out. My guests left one by one, and I was left alone.

23 April 1967

Dear Joan... I've just been reading about Mde Callas the opera singer and the Greek ship owners. She could write a book and how it would sell...

26 May 1967

Dear Joan... [Re riots in Hong Kong] Things are quiet here again and have returned to normal, but for how long I don't know. What made things worse was the very bad hooligan elements that took advantage of the situation.

14 July 1967

Dear Joan... Trouble here is very annoying and interferes with our peaceful way of life and if it goes on I'm afraid business is bound to suffer — but it is not anything like as bad as the Home Press would have you believe.

2 August 1967

Dear Joan... Just a line to say how pleased I am to hear the beaded blouse has arrived and that you like it. I got your picture of yourself and Mother.

Things are quiet here and except for a few bomb throwing or planting, are normal. The bombs are not actually bombs but small tins of explosives that make a big noise but do little or no damage.

10 August 1967

Dear Joan... [Re no. 25 Radnor Walk's wallpaper] I have seen at Government House which has lately been redecorated... It's an enormous place, as big as my house here [sic], and if I had a dozen concubines they could each have their own place. I must tell you of a very old Chinese friend who died some years ago. As you know, concubinage is recognised in China and this chap had about 14 all living in the same house and his wife also. His bedroom was fitted up beautifully with Chinese and Foreign furniture. By his bed he had a bell indicator to all parts of the house and a telephone also to each room of the concubines and if he felt like enjoying the company of a particular one she was there to answer the bell or telephone. This is true, and it was a very happy household.

24 August 1967

Dear Joan... Things are a bit worrying here after the Peking Legation being ravaged. But apparently there is no authority with power in China and if it goes on like this the whole country will be one big mess.

31 October 1967

Dear Joan... I've mislaid your measurements and I've seen lovely creations at the Hong Kong Exhibition, they are being sold here. Buyers from all over the world have arrived to buy. It may surprise you to know that some of the newest fashions shown in Paris and Bond Street are made here with expert guidance. I'm going to have a look myself and see what new things there are. A Fashion Designer from Paris is here with models and another from Los Angeles...

Believe it or not, it is now 5.30 am. I don't sleep very well so am off to golf and back at 9 am.

23 November 1967

Dear Joan... Amusing to hear I'm leaving my money to Simonne — most of it has gone with the riots and devaluation. One cannot sell property here...

28 December 1967

Dear Joan... Fortunately — I sprained my back a week before Xmas and cancelled all my engagements and stayed at home, mostly in bed as it was rather painful. But parties are so exhausting.

22 January 1968

Dear Joan... You are a busy girl and now the containerisation is keeping you busy. [Joan now worked for the Port of London Authority.] I am Chairman of a Wharf Company and the other Shipping companies with wharfs, like Holts, are all going into the matter and reporting. Hong Kong is somewhat different to other big ports... If you have any material on the matter of containerisation which has been published, will you send it out as there may be information we haven't got yet.

10 February 1968

Dear Joan... I was very disappointed not coming home but I'm very conscious of my responsibilities and Sandy Bay Hospital New Wing was held up owing to a number of various reasons and I was kept here. You will see from the brochures my contribution to Hong Kong. I built and donated the Care Centre where 120 kids are boarded and another 400 attend for school. The 1st and 2nd Wing of Sandy Bay I also built with 100 beds. The last Wing was paid largely by outside help and it is now the most modern in this part of the world, including Japan, Australia. I could not leave with this trouble.

5 March 1968

Dear Joan... You may not believe it and wonder why I do this but this morning I was up as usual, 5.30, teed off at Deep Water Bay at 6.15, arrived home, had breakfast, met a Government official JP, and together left Queen's Pier in a Fast Police Launch to visit one of our prisons on Lantao Island. Took 1 hour, 20 minutes each way. We listen to the prisoners' complaints if they have any and inspect the place. I got back to the office at 2.30, no lunch, reading office letters and answering yours — and I suppose I'll leave at 6.30. Why should I do all this is what everybody asks me when I might be going places. I'd like to know also.

5 April 1968

Dear Joan... The Big Yacht Race from HK to Manila, 650 miles, starts at 4 o'clock this afternoon. The Governor is starting the race and I'm going with him. There are 17 yachts, from Japan, Australia, Manila, Guam. The Challenge Cup is a beautiful piece of silver, given by me.

12 June 1968

Dear Joan... I'm glad you like my photographs — show them to a housekeeper (36–26–34). She might be willing to work for nothing!!! especially with a word of recommendation from you!!!

13 July 1968

Dear Joan... You ask what is keeping me in Hong Kong and this is something I'm asking myself all the time and my family are asking me.

Well, I'm involved in so many matters — companies operating in Canada, Australia, South Africa, and a Hong Kong Hospital, welfare centres. And though I know one is not indispensable I have never left anything undone which should be done, and there is much, apart from business, and this has its problems. For instance last year's troubles [in Hong Kong] with the riots etc, many thousands of strikers left and now want their jobs back, having sat outside their Manager's office singing Mao's songs...

8/9 August 1968

Dear Joan... I have an immensely wealthy Spanish friend in Manila, who with his friends has built the most exclusive Golf Club in Spain, with residences for members. Bobby Jones designed the Course and from the brochure it is lovely. Several thousands of acres. And if I were living in England I doubt I would meet these people, but here I am one of the Directors of their Hong Kong Company... I had a letter from Moller who has built a small block of flats in Mansfield Street next to his house, and he has offered me one complete with help...

5 October 1968

Dear Joan... I did intend to make a quick trip, but several business takeovers were being negotiated, not by me, but I was involved...

17 November 1969

Dear Joan... I'm terribly busy as there is a boom on, but mostly Chinese speculators, not foreign...

9 July 1970

Dear Joan... There is nothing more delightful [than] to meet good old friends but I'm afraid I've lost my capacity for enjoying myself...

14 October 1970

Dear Joan... I met with a slight accident recently. It had been raining very hard and I slipped and gave my head a bang against my heavy garden gate. I did not feel it at the time and went to the office the same as usual. But in the afternoon somebody came in and said, 'what did you do to your eye'. I looked in the mirror and evidently I had broken some blood vessels and right underneath the right eye was a mass of broken blood and an enormous black eye... I went to the doctor and had an X-ray, but nothing. But I had a heavy head and stayed in hospital for a week, just resting. I'm alright except I was a bit giddy when I started to walk.

30 November 1970

Dear Joan... I'm in hospital again and lucky to be alive. The accident I had two months ago resulted in a brain cell being damaged and it took two months for the blood to move around to another part which incapacitated my left hand. I was on the way back from Golf when I noticed my right hand was doing all the steering and when I got home I found my left hand could not pick up anything, so went to hospital right away and had an operation to remove some blood cells. I've been in Hospital, where I am now, for nearly 3 weeks... You should be here to look after me. The doctor says I've been working too hard. Love, N. [In a later letter he refers to this illness as a stroke.]

21 December 1970

Dear Joan... My hand and arm is quite normal and I'm resting at home and have no inclination to take a walk — I just sit around doing nothing...

8 April 1971

Dear Joan... I told you about my accident in my previous letters. I'm nearly 100% but have a continuous buzz in my head, which is annoying. I only hear it when all else is quiet, otherwise I don't as there is too much noise going on outside my office...

30 June 1971

Dear Joan... I really am up to my eyes in work and although my doctors (2) say I should take a complete rest I simply can't find the time. Besides my business, I am involved in several welfare matters, Hospital, Juvenile Care Centre (300 kids going to school instead of reformatory) and being President and Chairman, and the committees won't do anything on their own and always get after me. A new addition to the Hospital is now being planned, and after leaving office at 6, I go to a meeting of the executive committee to discuss it. Then the Yacht Club is having the Race to Manila next year and about 18 yachts from Japan, Malaysia. Australia and Hong Kong will compete. I gave the Challenge Cup and I'm Vice Patron of the Club, after being Commodore for many years, Her Majesty being Patron. I feel really worn out... I feel fed up with everything... I forgot to tell you my shoulder is giving me a lot of pain and I have had to give up golf, which depresses me, as I played nearly every morning from 6.30 to 8.30....

You are the only one I can open up to, and I got your letter today and am glad you are feeling better for your holiday...

4 July 1971

Dear Joan... Many thanks for your help Joan — I can't tell you how much I appreciate it. Love, N.

16 August 1971

Dear Joan... Even if you were not helping me with my problems, I'd like to send you something...

20 September 1971

Dear Joan... I like your remark that I won't see you in your dress from the new production of Othello, in London. Desdemona is strangled in the nude by Othello. There is some controversy about this as in those days female parts were taken by young men — and throughout Shakespeare's plays there is nothing mentioned about nude women. I think the producer of the play now running is looking for success financially...

22 January 1972

Dear Joan... We don't like to see a place with so many happy years with fond recollections be changed — for money means nothing compared with this. I sold a lovely house next to mine, to the Dutch Government the Xmas before last, nearly an acre. Property has gone up enormously — believe it or not I'm selling a small vacant piece of land to a Chinese. It's barren, the sea is in front, about 150 feet, and impossible to walk on the beach because of rocks and filth, you can't even land on it. But the Chinese believes it will go up in value — it was bought many years ago by me at $5 a square foot and sold for $150...

30 May 1972

Dear Joan... I met some friends from the Bahamas recently and they said the place is soon going to be run by the local inhabitants, same as Bermuda and other places in the Caribbean. What the world is coming to God knows. England doesn't set a good example from what is going on. These Unions are holding the community up to ransom by their strikes and blackmailing methods. Even their Union Bosses are ignored. They are ruining the Country and I honestly believe England has had it and we are on the decline...

3 July 1972

Dear Joan... You see the great social change taking place. The working man is much better educated than his father and wants more of the cake — but he wants to work less hours and, what is more, produce less. You have heard of the heavy rains we have had. Apartments on the hillside collapsed, the rubble falling on to others below, over 100 bodies of the tenants have so far been recovered — many thousands homeless for the time being...

I have never been so busy as now. I realise I want to do everything myself and now I cannot as there is too much. The Radio has just announced a Typhoon Warning and I must go home...

20 November 1972

Dear Joan... I've lost 3 very old and dear friends in one week — 2 from cancer, the other heart, all English and all around 70. It makes me wonder how much longer I've got. So far I'm quite well, but working too hard and not sleeping well. My friends say I should have a concubine, but it's too late I'm afraid. I haven't heard from my wife for nearly a year...

28 May 1973

Dear Joan... Some movies were shown here by a private club in the City Hall where nothing was left to the imagination. It was a Jugo Slav Film — sexual intercourse and nothing else, two of my friends who are members told me. I am writing to Government, not to allow our City Hall to be used for this. I don't know how a young couple would feel if they were invited, not knowing what film was being shown. I'm no prude, but there are limits. Now I hear Lord L, and Lord J, have resigned because of their call girl affair. What is the fuss about. They are men, and it is a private matter... Very soon all Members of Parliament will have to wear a Chastity Belt...

22 June 1973

Dear Joan... I've never been so busy for ages — the state of the Stock Exchange is such that Government has appointed an Advisory Committee to look into matters. Their first recommendation is for the 4 Stock Exchanges to have the same hours and to close 3 afternoons a week to catch up.

I warned Government several times in the last 2 years what would happen if they permitted several stock exchanges to open, but this was ignored. The Chinese Exchanges are nothing else but gambling dens...

8 September 1973

Dear Joan... I've a terribly bad cold, the first for many years, I don't know where I caught it. I'm told to stay at home, but what's the use, I might as well come to the office. There are, I believe, package tours to Hong Kong, but the place is so expensive now and has lost all its charm. I was only the other day speaking to an old friend and he said, 'I feel like chucking everything up and clearing out...'

Bribery, Rape, Robbery with Violence by young thugs is increasing every day and I don't think we can stop it. We have 4 1/4 million population and 41% are under the age of 15 years. In a few years 600,000 will be looking for jobs and there may not be any. Over crowding, where 500,000 are living in huts on the hillsides — it's very depressing. And the Central District is packed with Cars, Buses, Lorries, four abreast, making it impossible to move along the road.

My son unexpectedly visited Hong Kong for 10 days. He stayed at the YMCA...

24 January 1974

Dear Joan... This is Chinese New Year Day. As you know they are a sensible people and go by the Lunar Year — 13 months. This way all employees receive an extra month's pay at this time. I received your nice long letter recalling the time you came out here — I can't remember the year, but do the other events... Why is it so many men want to go the very limit with women, more so today than ever. I don't believe it ever, or very seldom, makes for enduring happiness. When all this sex is satisfied, one looks for something more in the way of character and companionship.

Things are pretty bad in England's green and pleasant land. People have had it too good for too long and they must tighten their belt. I think the Miners have a dirty job and should get a bit more — but they chose to be a miner in the first place. These men are the sons of those who fought in the first War and saved England. In the last war a different lot won the Battle of Britain in the Air and at Dunkirk, and it looks as if they did this to make England safe for the Communists....

21 May 1974

Dear Joan... When you were here the Flat where you stayed has gone up 6 to 8 times in rent. Rice, the staple food for the Chinese, was 20 cents a pound, now ten times as much, my servants wages five times. But the income of those who pay out hasn't gone up so much, and taxes are higher. On the top of all this, property has declined and shares have flopped. The index last year was 1,700, now 300...

I am keeping well thank goodness, but am very occupied with unremunerative work — as most of the Stock Exchange members have no business and pass the time playing cards...

31 May 1974

Dear Joan... I often look back and recall the many girls I met and thought how wonderful it was at the time — and then love's young dream would end. I had very very few experiences, and often wonder if I could have been happy with any of them, but I don't think so. And I suppose you too may have had similar experiences.

Things are changing and home life as I knew it is unknown to most of the present generation. Calling on friends' houses where a half a dozen would sing, play the piano or violin, all good and jolly fun.

I had a good voice and had about 2 years with an Italian singing master, Maestro Galluzzi. [Professor A. Galluzzi was a music teacher in Hong Kong, at least in the years 1913, 1918 and 1919.] I'm wandering, sorry.

My trouble was that I had responsibilities and had to keep very busy to meet them. After many many years I got married which I soon realised was a mistake, and you know the result of having a son ... his wife and two children for 20 years — they are grown up and must go their own way...

1 June 1974

Dear Joan... I received an invitation to meet Lord Aldington at a lunch party on June 11th. I don't know why except that I have been Chairman of a Company which handles Containers. In fact I joined the Board 46 years ago. We were the first to handle Containers, and our biggest customer is the United States Line. We have just agreed to purchase from HK Government about 40 acres on which to build an extra three berths. You know what is going on in the PLA [Port of London Authority]. As he is the chairman I thought you might have some questions ... and I could put them to him...

1 July 1974

Dear Joan... When you wrote your last letter I thought you were in a nostalgic mood as you were reminiscing about events of long ago and like myself wondering if our life would be any better, happier is a better word, if we had taken decisions which seemed to be alright at the time, but there was that something which stopped us from doing so. Future events have I think as far as I'm concerned proved to be right. Looking back, as we all do, we have had love affairs, passionate for a while, and thought the object of our love was meant for us and no one else — and we lived in dreamland until we came back to earth. Look how miserable one would be if we had succumbed to love at first sight, or a little later. Well, enough of this...

2 August 1974

Dear Joan... I am interested in the hamlet Ludshot and you may remember years ago when you were a cartographer you could not find any trace of the place. Well, several hundred years ago a man by the name of Croucher was fined so many stacks of wheat for some offence committed in Ludshot, and I believe there is some reference in Selbourne Abbey in fact to Croucher.

I think most of us like to know where we come from especially in this day and age. I know we all come from this part of Sussex and Isle of Wight, and in those days the population of England was about 3 to 4 million, if that many. I have an old relation who loves looking up the family tree and several years ago I read in an Australian Paper a reference to N. Croucher! — so I wrote to him saying he would probably be surprised to see on the back of the letter my name — same initial as his. We exchanged a few letters. I was Commodore of The Royal Hong Kong Yacht Club and he was Commodore of Southport Yacht Club, Surfers' Paradise and he sent me a picture of his lovely yacht. I asked how he came to be in Australia and where did his forebears come from. He was a squadron leader in the Air Force during the War, and his Grandfather came from Shanklin on the Isle of Wight, and he gave his name. Well, this old lady looked up the records which she obtained from Church Registrars, and found that his Grandfather and my Grandfather were brothers — without any doubt.

Well, sometime later he and his wife and daughter took a trip to Japan, Malaysia and H.K. and we met — and still write to each other. Then another from the same family went to Canada and the son is connected with the airline company.

We must have come from France originally as Croix means Cross and in the old Village there was ??? on His X, and this was known as Peace of the X. Crowchere — interesting...

16 December 1974

Dear Joan... Things are so topsy turvy these days and we are experiencing the worst slump in our history. Good shares like Telephones, from 135 in 1973 to 9 1/2 today, and HK Land, from 60 to 3 1/2, to mention one or two.

I don't like Xmas and New Year. I get depressed and usually I am alone for my birthday, Xmas Eve, and New Year's Eve. I sent you a Xmas Card, not the usual kind but something which means something, you can read over once or twice. ['The life of man is a long march ... was the cause.' Excerpt from *A Free Man's Worship* by Bertrand Russell.]

I am keeping very well, but at this time I feel the loss of 5 very old friends who passed away during the last month, 3 within 2 weeks. I had a letter from a friend of mine who lived here before the War, her family too. She married a Naval Officer who quite unexpectedly inherited a Peerage — Lord Ashbourne, distant relation. Well she [i.e. Rheta Hazeland] wrote and said her Mother was a little deaf and had just had her 104th Birthday...

21 March 1975

Dear Joan... I am well but can't sleep, generally wake up at 2 a.m. and doze off after an hour and wake up at 5, make my tea and read and then at 6 leave for the Golf Course and tee off at 6.30, returning at 8 a.m. After several sleepless nights I get over tired and then having a lot of little matters which must be attended to — welfare principally — my brain gets tired. I need something to keep me in bed — what do you recommend!

I wish the Dockers could be shut out and all ships on their way to London be diverted elsewhere, and those laid up must wait until the Dockers see sense. It's a pity we couldn't send 100,000 Chinese Dockers over — they would do twice the work in half the time. During the 1st World War, China sent 100,000 over to France to work. On one occasion, some barges had to be emptied, all the same size and contents — flour bags each 100 lbs — alongside a canal next to each other, the same number of workmen to each barge moving the Flour from barge into Railway trucks. Some Chinese would carry 2 sacks on their shoulders, occasionally 3, the majority only 1 bag. We promised when a barge was emptied they needn't work any longer. The same conditions in every respect were given to the men from London Docks (all in Khaki). They took nearly twice as long, none carrying more than one bag, and just sauntering across to put one bag into the train. This is true in every detail. And sometime later the Major in the Transport Depot came over and saw for himself. Of course one couldn't bring Chinese labourers to England but if we only could, what an example. Love, N.

12 August 1975

Dear Joan... I feel awfully tired these days and yet continue to work though there is no reason to do so...

3 October 1975

Dear Joan... There is more and more unhappiness where the pursuit of money is concerned and the love of it increases and so many go through life with this in mind...

♪ ♪ ♪

5 February 1976

Dear Joan... [Re money] It might have been spent on young children from poor families, who had the intelligence and keenness to learn and to be a credit to the community. I don't know if I told you but the daughter of a very poor family (Chinese) was strongly recommended for her outstanding achievements at school. Her father was dead, and her mother a factory worker. She had a younger sister who went to the same school (free) — all she wanted was a chance. I interviewed her, [she was] poorly dressed, all living in one room, 20' x 20'. I arranged for her to go to a better school and after a few years she studied medicine — this was 8 years ago. She finished up and passed with honours and was now a Doctor, and had to spend a year at the largest Govt hospital. She comes to see me now and again to thank me....

This Joan is why I think money is wasted... Capitalism is not utilised as it should be.

31 May 1976

Dear Joan... It is good to be kept busy... I have no hobbies of any kind which I could spend my leisure on — and if I was not involved in my business which is not [worth?] mentioning, but principally Welfare Matters, I'd go crazy. The thing I feel most is living alone. I've got my Cook, Gardener and Washwoman. And I go out sailing and Golf — but they are all newcomers...

16 August 1976

Dear Joan... I seem to be on the go all the time and feel I must be doing something or else I'll get ill. I've had a bad cold lately. I get one every few years just for 8 or 9 days, regularly, and I often wonder why it is...

...You could get one of these cheap flights. But I'm not the same Noel you remember. Time changes. But you could put up with me for a week or two... If you want to find out more about cheap flights, call at 15 Wardour Street, W1, Chinese Social Club. I am a member, HK82744 — it is really English. Love, N.

7 September 1976

Dear Joan... We have had the heaviest rains for many many years, 18 inches in one day and nearly 20 another. A landslide demolished some Chinese flats, killing about 18 people. One very very sad [case] happened where a man and his wife were alright, but all their 5 children were buried and found dead — the eldest was 8. She [the wife] didn't want any more children and was treated to prevent it. The local doctors say something may possibly be done to enable her to have children...

2 November 1976

Dear Joan... I sent you a letter yesterday asking you to address the enclosure to Private Eye. It is about some 'monkey business' going on with some HK firm which they mentioned in a previous issue and I am giving them some more information, but don't want them to think it is from HK, or who the sender is...

England has seen better days, and like other Empires — Spain, Portugal, Roman, France — we have had it. In the early part of the last century we supplied the undeveloped world with nearly everything. Even in the U.S.A. we practically owned the Railways, supplied South America with everything in exchange for medicines(?), but now all those countries supply their own needs. Japan, even 80 years ago, were not making Motor Cars, now they are shipping them all over the World and improving their workmanship. [In England] A couple of hundred door makers in Leyland go on strike and 5,000 are laid off. This doesn't happen in Japan or most other places, and now Japan wants to assemble cars in England, cheaper than Leylands. Then we have about 1–2 million coloured workers and they get looked after like our own people...

17 February 1977

Dear Joan... You could come out for a fortnight and sleep between nice embroidered linen sheets, something like table cloths, and they would keep you awake admiring them — unless something else did...

29 March 1977

Dear Joan... I sent you a telegram just now to come after the 23rd April, anytime. I hope this will suit you. April 23rd is St. George's Day and I am a senior member of the Society (oldest). We lay a wreath on the Cenotaph at 8.30 a.m. then go to the Cemetery, then go to the Cathedral...

15 May 1977, after Joan's visit to Hong Kong

Dear Joan... In a way I'm sorry I built the bungalow, what with the leaves disturbing you and the Frogs and the dogs scratching at your door and spiders, and you getting up for the Amah. I'll have to change this next time and take the Bungalow and you take my room. But you must lend me your torch.

I miss you very much and wonder why you did not come out more often. After all, once in 20 years is a life time, and there is no fun in the Boneyard.

You will have a lot to do but please take your time and don't spoil the Sheet of Stamps. I bet there is not another about. When Chairman Mao took over, the assistant Commissioner of Posts in Nanking left for Hong Kong, he did not want to join Chiang Kai-shek [or the Communists]. He left for Indonesia. I met him through mutual friends and lent him money on some valuable pieces of porcelain. He died and did not repay me the loan...

19 May 1977

Dear Joan... When I spoke about you not being here for 20 years, I forgot I was home in 1965, so it was only 12 years since we last met. In the letter you wrote after you got home, you wrote —

'There is one part of your letter I do not quite understand.'

I'm trying to remember what it might be. So please remind me next time.

Love, Plus? Noel.

26 May 1977

Dear Joan... I'm terribly bored (tired?) these days. There is so much to do and I just do nothing about it. I've read your letters over again because you mention having told others of your trip out here and living in the Bungalow and we were close friends...

Love, Noel. X.

27 May 1977

Dear Joan... My intention is to establish a Foundation, as Dr Joseph Needham, Master of Gonville College, Cambridge suggests — to exchange students from China with ours — only a few. The rest will be for Science, medicine, especially for those students who need financial help. I get so muddle headed over this and I don't want to put Trustees who employ Directors, Financial Advisors etc who make a living out of it. Naturally there are expenses. The other day a well dressed man and wife came into the office, they are collecting for the very aged etc. I asked about the institution they represented and for whom they were collecting as we had many in H.K. He said they were collecting for Africa, India, and the UK. He handed me a Book of Information. I noticed about 20% of what was collected was spent on getting it, and this man and his wife were travelling around and wasting money in Hong Kong, expensive hotel etc...

Catalogue value of stamps is always on the low side, but the 200 you have of Sun Yat Sen would fetch much more as they are one piece... I have a lot of stamps all nicely put under transparent paper. I am thinking of taking out a page or two and sending them to you to find out what they would fetch at Auction, and also what commission one has to pay...

In your first letter you wrote of something I mentioned that you did not understand and I asked you what it was but you haven't referred to it — Pourquoi — Don't let my letters lie around, I know you won't, but just in case. I miss you very much.

31 May 1977

Dear Joan... When I get a letter from you I must reply to it right away and drop everything I'm doing. I suppose I feel closer to you, that's why...

13 June 1977

Dear Joan... I played Golf yesterday in a competition. It was about the hottest day of the year and it took 4 1/4 hours to play 18 holes. I almost gave up but managed to finish. The temperature was close on 100° with a blazing sun. You certainly did your stuff at the Function... When are you due for another holiday? As you wrote your letter after returning from the Lunch I appreciated it all the more. Love, N.

1 July 1977

Dear Joan... We are experiencing the driest season on record and water is being rationed so many hours a day. The Radio asks us to have a shower instead of a bath and save ten times the amount of water. My garden will suffer if this goes on but fortunately there is a small pool on the hill opposite the Bungalow and I had a pipeline put in and so far there is a supply for the time being. When it rains, only a little, the pool fills. Your Frogs kept you awake and you kept me awake!!! Love, N.

1 August 1977

Dear Joan... Today is August Bank Holiday and I am working in my office endeavouring to sort out many matters connected with my family... I get such a feeling of relief when I write to you...

I'm wondering if the funny sensation I had [after swallowing] was a cockroach...

You know Penny and her daughter Camilla came out...

12 September 1977

Dear Joan... I have had one letter from Penny, for whom I have respect, since she came out here...

23 September 1977

Dear Joan... I'm feeling very well. Up at 4.45 am, played a round of golf. In the office at 8.30, with stacks of letters...

27 September 1977

Dear Joan... I am very very busy doing all kinds of things for others. Such as Hospital meetings, Juvenile Care Centre and then business meetings, then 2 visitors one after the other. Rothschild came out and I had lunch with him.

27 October 1977

Dear Joan... I don't know if I'm coming or going. I'm simply pestered by the many concerns I'm associated with that I have no time to attend to my own affairs... I get so little time for Golf unless I get up at the unearthly hour of 4.45 am and tee off at 5.40 and home by 7.30 then have breakfast etc and in the office at 9. It is now 4.45 pm and I have to go to the Cathedral as we are having Michaelmas Fair on Saturday, an annual event. It has been pouring with rain this afternoon and all the Stalls are on the Lawn outside the Cathedral — it looks as if the rain will continue. This morning when I arrived there were 5 envelopes, very bulky, all from separate institutions — SPCA, 3 Chinese Hospitals, mentally handicapped children, Blind Home — each one containing 250 tickets for a Raffle and I'm asked to sell them. I just have to take them and send a cheque. I've never won anything yet... I wish I could get away to some place for a holiday...

5 December 1977

Dear Joan... I wish I could relax. Try as I will I've got to go on and on. I had to go to a meeting the other evening and crossing the road which is half dug up in connection with the Cross Harbour subway, slipped against an iron post, but did not fall down, and it badly twisted my leg just below the knee. So I am unable to play golf for a few days...

3 January 1978

Dear Joan... the Xmas card was in aid of Sandy Bay Hospital and it was a picture of Hong Kong 1855... I must say I have been inundated with work. Giving presents to the poor children at Juvenile Care Centre, then going to Duchess of Kent Hospital on Xmas Day, and on top of this I scratched my leg below the knee cap, very small but I must have poisoned it. That was just over a month ago. I had to give up golf and see the doctor, and had a big lump where the scratch was as big as the yolk of an egg and the doctor had to lance it twice and take out blood. The leg was sore and the skin around the ankle became all blue. It is nearly alright.

10 January 1978

Dear Joan... on December 25 I sent an urgent business cable to London and as my office was closed I could not get my [cheque-book?] or money. I explained to the Clerk who did not know who I was that I had an account with them. He was not satisfied. It happened that I was replying to a cable I had received and showed it to him, and also my identity card. I am so well known here that I was surprised at this questioning. Then I went to collect a cable that was waiting for me, with this trouble maker, and he appeared to be satisfied — but the telegram has not been received...

6/10 April 1978

Dear Joan... I mentioned yesterday that I had sent something by Sea Mail which you will like. There is also something which you like which I can't even send by Air Mail...

8 April 1978

Dear Joan... I had a letter from Mimi Compton, an old friend, she had a son, a friend of my son Richard...

4 June 1978

Dear Joan,

My half brother in Canada has a daughter. She and her husband are coming out in June ... they are strangers...

I'm glad you can take care of yourself when you come as you did before — and will not expect me to change my routine.

Mrs Mimi Compton, whose son married one of the Ranks, Pat, is living on the Isle of Man with her daughter Suzette who supports her. She is in hospital with a broken hip and needs financial help. I wrote and asked if some of the Companies her husband was connected with could help. Her husband was head of Sassoons and was interned with me for 4 years. He died soon after release and her gratuity has all gone. He was Director of the HK Bank also.

I'm also having trouble with my Trustees...

I enclose memos from Stanley Gibbons. I don't know how much the Black 1d got and the £5 Orange...

This Sunday morning I should be out but I'm in the office trying to clear up accumulation of matters connected with business and welfare...

12 June 1978

Dear Joan... Another headache — [Re prospective visitors to Hong Kong] I've got an idea they think I have money, but why should they come, I've never seen them before...

19 June 1978

Dear Joan... I am very glad to say I have come to some arrangement with my Trustees and that is a load off my shoulders.

9 August 1978

Dear Joan... We have had a Typhoon, coming and recurring. About 50 were lost and everything was at a standstill for nearly 5 days. I hope you are still thinking of going up to Lantao Monastery to see the friendly monks who are waiting for you!!

I'm fed up with family matters...

20 August 1978

Dear Joan... I have just received the parcel containing the 6 lots of Silver Jubilee Coins. They look very good, but each lot costs about £13 1/2, the postage was £3 1/2. It wasn't worth the trouble. The large silver piece has no monetary value on it but I suppose a collector doesn't mind...

2 September 1978

Dear Joan... What you wrote about Mimi Compton is very interesting and from the letters I get from Suzette, makes it rather confusing. Here are the facts. Harry Compton was Manager of Sassoons in 1918 and married Mimi about 1924. She had 2 children, Ronnie and Suzette. Harry was interned by the Japs with me in 1941, and released in 1945, and re-formed Sassoons. Then after a few months he retired to England and died. I cannot remember the exact date... This is all very interesting...

15 September 1978

Dear Joan... I have been very anxious about a property deal I'm putting through and also the trouble with Amanda and Nicholas...

2 October 1978

Dear Joan... I hope your Mother is keeping well. I haven't much to say just now as I'm busier than ever. The Cathedral (I'm on the Committee) is having Michaelmas Fair and thinking of additional quarters for a new chaplain. I feel like chucking it at times. LOVE XX N.

19 October 1978

Dear Joan... Excuse this hasty note, but I got your letter about the Lord Mayor's Banquet and the sleeveless top, beaded, etc, you wanted to wear with the dress. This was 3 days ago and I at once got in touch with 2 ladies I know and gave them the piece of coloured pattern, bust measurement 38″ and exactly what you wrote... I will be very disappointed if what you want can't be got. One of the ladies is very up to date in fashion and I will ask her for an alternative, and send it in time. If by good fortune they do find something beaded all the better, then the extra one will do for next year...

21 October 1978

Dear Joan... I'm sending by Air Mail the sleeveless top you asked me to get for you. Whether it will meet with your approval I don't know but I had 2 lady friends looking all over town...

15 December 1978

Dear Joan... Xmas is coming soon and I'll be glad when the holidays are over. I'm fed up with all these family troubles — not of my own making except I shouldn't have married...

25 January 1979

Dear Joan... Lord and Lady A Todd arrived here and I had lunch with them. I did not know what an important person he is — F.R.S. O.M. Nobel Prize Winner...

I am having so much trouble with some land I've sold. It was vacant and squatters built matsheds on it and occupied the place and I cannot get rid of them. There are 11 families. What with this and a dozen other matters, I am at my Wit's end. I had no Xmas card from my wife. Now a crowd has just come in — the squatters representatives to discuss with me what they can do as it is Chinese New Year on the 28th, so excuse short note — Love, N.

2 March 1979

Dear Joan... I am having trouble with my Cook. He is 75 and wants to leave and it is impossible to find a good one if I want to entertain. My amah can make my breakfast which is usually porridge and fruit. I have lunch in the Club and a small snack at dinner. I would very much like you to come out for a couple of weeks, but I'd worry without a cook...

8 March 1979

Dear Joan... I am very very busy doing things for several Welfare Bodies. That's the trouble of being a long resident. New ones want to know what happened 50 years ago. Anyhow it keeps me busy. I have just sacked my gardener who was hopeless.

16 April 1979

Dear Joan... As for myself I'm getting fed up. The Hong Kong $ has never been so low. A few years ago a £ was worth 8 1/2, you could buy £1, now it is 10. If I want to send money home from H.K. it is 10, last year 8 1/2...

8 May 1979

Dear Joan... I've been and am very very busy and thank goodness I am keeping well. A very old friend came with me to the Races. The next day he had lunch, he went to the reading room in the Club as usual, was found dead, heart attack. I was a Pall Bearer. I received a letter back from another old friend, with 'deceased' written across it.

16 October 1979

Dear Joan... I don't know if I am coming or going, I am so busy. Lord Todd, President of the Royal Society, Order of Merit, Nobel Prize Winner and a lot of other distinctions, has been here for a week and left this morning. I have had to do something for him. I got your letter and you mention about coming out... I don't know if I told you that my little place where you slept is an illegal structure according to the Government and if you do come out it may not be standing... If you do come I would like to see you. Come by all means but I can't give you much time as I told you... Love, N.

15 November 1979

Dear Joan... You have probably read about the thousands of refugees coming from Vietnam which I am trying to do something for. I get very little sleep...

CHAPTER ONE

1. Letter dated 2 August 1971 from Noel Croucher to a relative of his, Betsy Treadgold.

2. Interview with Dr Deanna Lee Rudgard at the offices of Lee Hysan Estate Company, one Hysan Avenue, Hong Kong, on 18 November 1996.

3. 'It was in his private life that Mr Croucher presented a mystery to even his closest associates.' ('Top Stockbroker Noel Croucher Dies', *South China Morning Post*, 7 March 1980.) Also 'Eccentric Emperor...', *South China Morning Post*, 16 March 1980.

4. Ward Lock & Co. Ltd., pp. 95–6.

5. Lytton Strachey, 1971, pp. 116–7.

6. There were many Huguenots in the Southampton area, with the greatest flood of emigration from France by Protestants of all classes after Louis XIV revoked the Edict of Nantes on 18 October 1685. (Email from Angela Trevor on 11 October 1997.) One relative to Noel Croucher, Jennifer Kang, has compiled a family tree which starts with a Huguenot Croucher arriving in England in the 1600s. A study on the origins of the name suggests it derives from the word 'crouche', meaning a roadside cross and hence the priests at roadside churches who 'bowed to the cross'. The French Crouchard families are also thought to be linked. ('Conjectural Analysis', commissioned by the Croucher family in June 1986.)

7. Indeed, he could not, perhaps because another reference he made to a potential forebear, a John Crowcher [sic], was dean of Chichester Cathedral. (Letter dated 31 May 1969 from Noel Croucher to Revd Alan Daniels, Yarmouth, with thanks to Beryl Daniels.) Nor was it clear how this fit with the Huguenot idea.

8. Doris Croucher has a fine view of the castle from her window. Her late husband descended from Robert Croucher (1825–91), a brother of Noel's grandfather, John.

9. 'There was a background ... of piracy and privateering under foreign flags ... also abundant native talent... These people might on occasions be regarded either as criminals or as benefactors.' (Jack and Johanna Jones, pp. 74–5.)

10. And of Crouchers Ltd., the removal contractors featured in Donald A. Parr, 1994, p. 64.

11. A railway to nearby Ventnor was not opened until 1900. See P.E. Jarratt, pp. 34, 38.

12. P.E. Jarratt, p. 4.

13. E.F. Laidlaw, p. 47.

14. Gordon Croucher married Hilda Ethel Cropp, whose surviving daughter from this marriage is Ruby Doris Webb, née Croucher.

15. With thanks to Gordon Daubney Cox, and his book, *Eastleigh*, p. 25.

16. Kathleen Clarke, p. 26.

17. From Dr Gavin G.S. Bowie. No page numbers.

18. 'It seems that the Stockley fortunes were somewhat better in the early 18th century than they were in later years, though with evidence of wills from all generations but one, they were at least educated to a greater degree than the common throng.' (Email from Angela Trevor on 4 October 1997.)

19. Henry Stockley's second wife, Frances Amor, née Oakley, brought two stepdaughters, Sarah and Florence Amor, and produced one more daughter (at the age of forty-seven), Muriel Everlyn Amor Stockley. It is interesting to note that Noel was christened Noel Victor, but later added the name Amor. It comes not from his mother, but from Floss' stepmother's first husband. 'Perhaps Floss was close to her step-mother since she was only 6 years old when her own mother, Elizabeth Cartwright, died.' (Email from Angela Trevor on 23 September 1997.)

20. Letter dated 2 August 1971 to Betsy Treadgold, Muriel Stockley's daughter. Noel referred to a Mr Shepherd who he thought had a large farm outside Eastleigh. The Shepherd name comes into Noel's family tree on the other side — a great-uncle of Noel's, Robert Croucher, married Amelia Shepherd. These Crouchers and Shepherds owned warehouses in Newport on the Isle of Wight. The Shepherds are still in the carrying business and one Robert Shepherd has written a book, *Newport Remembers*.

21. Census Returns, 1841, 1851, 1861, 1871, 1881, 1891.

22. Interview with Betsy Treadgold in Devon on 16 March 1997.

23. Letter dated 2 August 1971 to Betsy Treadgold. It also recounts that Henry Stockley's brother, Ephraim, 'ran away to sea and I believe was on the ship that took Dr Livingston to Africa in about 1856 or thereabouts and had to help carry supplies'.

24. Interview with Betsy Treadgold in Devon on 16 March 1997.

25. Interview with Betsy Treadgold in Devon on 16 March 1997. Perhaps the wedding reception story referred to the marriage of Queen Victoria's daughter, HRH Princess Beatrice on 23 July 1885, on the Isle of Wight? (Jack and Johanna Jones, p. 122.)

26. The grandparents of Floss' late husband had lived on Pyle Street in the 1860s and this Croucher home in Newport, Isle of Wight, may still have existed in the 1890s.

27. Interview with Betsy Treadgold in Devon on 16 March 1997.

28. *Eastleigh Weekly News*, 15 December 1916, provided by Gordon Cox.

29. Total destitution was unlikely. The Woking Homes for railway widows had no Croucher staying in the 1890s, and what records survive from workhouses or children's homes in the area show no sign of a young Noel as resident.

30. Betsy Treadgold, whose father, Frederick William Lording Hood, was a well-known teacher at Chamberlayne Road (now Norwood) School in Eastleigh, thinks Noel grew up in Southampton as Floss was not likely to have stayed close to home. 'I am inclined to think that Floss might have been living in Southampton either before, and certainly after her [first] husband died. She would be very difficult to find in [the] 1891 [Census] as Southampton was quite a large city by this time. (Email from Angela Trevor on 23 September 1997.)

31. The story about meeting Lord Alfred Tennyson is much the same. Both are unprovable, yet both the Queen and the poet were there. (Various interviews, and with his former assistant, Florence Lo, Hong Kong, 6 June 1996.)

32. See Bibliography for details.

33. Mrs Craik, p. 26.

34. The book inscription was recounted to the author by Noel Croucher's son Richard in the course of conversations in 1996–97.

35. Gordon Marsden, p. 2.

36. The family's address was Belmont, 272 Shirley Road, Southampton. Floss and Alex had married from 60 Portland Place, most probably a lodging house. (Letter dated 13 November 1996 from Joanna Smith, archivist, Southampton City Council.)

37. 'Now here's my mother's wedding. I wonder if Floss gave a present. All the presents are listed... Miss Annie Stockley — silver jam dish. Miss E. Stockley — silver butter dish... I don't remember any of them. They're all Stockleys. Oh yes, Mr and Mrs A.V. Parker! What did they give? A silver teapot.' (Interview with Betsy Treadgold in Devon on 16 March 1997.)

38. Letter dated 2 August 1971 to Betsy Treadgold.

39. Letters from and phone calls with Ruby Doris Webb at Shirley, Southampton, in 1997. She is Noel Croucher's eldest niece, and says that when Floss went to Hong Kong, Ruby Doris' father (i.e. Noel's oldest brother) helped pay her way.

CHAPTER TWO

1. From Rudyard Kipling.

2. Veronica (pseudonym), p. 40.

3. Daily newspapers of the times did list arrivals in the colony, such as Sir and Lady this, with native servant, or Mr and Mrs so-and-so of New York. And one can peruse the adjacent hotel guest lists to see where they stayed. But, tellingly, such lists were not race-based as expected for an imperial outpost, but class-based — names appeared only of those travelling in first class. As for the rest, they were merely numbered, as in 273 Chinese, or 6 Europeans 'in steerage'. Shipping lists held by the Public Records Office at Kew, England, are more comprehensive but offer no sign of the Croucher-Stockley names. Perhaps the family, or at least the mysterious stepfather, worked the passage out? Crew lists are held by the Maritime History Archive at the Memorial University of Newfoundland in Canada. Searches there also produced no trace. Crew lists for every five years, held for some reason by the National Maritime Museum in Greenwich, London, could not help. Registers of seamen were discontinued between 1857 and 1918.

4. Noel Croucher joined in 1928, according to a Club Members' List of January 1977. 'The Hong Kong Club's success made it an artificially created status-conferrer, playing a regulatory role on the behaviour of the self-created upper class gentlemen. To belong to the club was to be a member of this class.' (W.K. Chan, p. 37.) See also W.K. Chan, pp. 35–40.

5. This address was on the top of a letter from Noel's brother Basil in Hong Kong to his other brother 'Gordon' Wallace Oliver back in Southampton, kept by Gordon's daughter, now Mrs Webb.

6. Eric Cumine, p. 29. Ethel's house was not demolished until 1980. Austin Coates recalled that Noel loved all the Ethel Morrison stories, as found, for example, in Austin Coates, 1977, pp. 114–5.

7. With thanks to Carl T. Smith, phone call on 25 October 1997.

8. Henry J. Lethbridge, 1978, p. 210. Chapter VIII was reprinted as 'Condition of the European Working Class in Nineteenth Century Hong Kong' in *Journal of the Hong Kong Branch of the Royal Asiatic Society,* 1975, pp. 88–112.

9. Henry J. Lethbridge, 1978, pp. 163–88.

10. W.K. Chan, p. 15.

11. G.H. Gompertz, p. 35.

12. See W.K. Chan and Henry J. Lethbridge, among others. In 1901, the population of 300,660 included about 10,000 non-Chinese civilians. By 1911, a total population of about 500,000 included about 12,000 non-Chinese civilians. (G.B. Endacott, 1964, p. 276.) 'The hierarchy of government officials and leading taipans created a miniature replica of social life in Britain, the struggle for status being much intensified by the smallness of the expatriate community...' (Colin Crisswell, p. 104.) See also Henry J. Lethbridge, 1978, pp. 181–4; and W.K. Chan, pp. 33–4: 'In other words, status divisions served the latent function of maintaining the European social system ... [this] was an unintended consequence; the pursuit for status was a deliberate process of a socially ascendant group artificially creating an upper class out of itself.'

13. Geoffrey Robley Sayer, 1975, pp. 90–1. In fact the Lammerts, as auctioneers, were not particularly upper-class, but they qualified as an old name.

14. W.K. Chan, p. 24. Chapter Two of this book provides a helpful account of the complex relationships between the merchants and other expatriates.

15. James William Norton-Kyshe, p. 540.

16. Henry J. Lethbridge, 1978, p. 170.

17. Henry J. Lethbridge, 1978, p. 171.

18. In the beginning these were 'mostly composed of discharged soldiers' and by no means up to snuff. See James William Norton-Kyshe, Volume 1, pp. 125–6, 279. As to how they plundered where they pleased, see Volume 1, pp. 401–2; Volume 2, pp. 60–2, 496–502.

19. Attempts to find Alex Parker's regiment have been unsuccessful. Of all the regiments in Hong Kong at the time (Royal Garrison Artillery, Royal Engineers, Army Service Corps, Army Ordnance Corps, Army Pay Corps, Royal Army Medical Corps, and the Nottingham & Derbyshire Regiment), the most likely would have been what is now called the Royal Logistics Corps which, alas, has no record of him. (Letter dated 12 August 1997 from Ms K. Walker of the Royal Logistic Corps Museum, Camberley, Surrey.) Henry J. Lethbridge, 1978, says many Public Works Department overseers were former Royal

Engineers, but this hardly fits with Parker's past as an actor, nor do the Royal Engineers have any record of Parker. (Letter dated 19 November 1997 from Maggie Magnusan, Royal Engineers Library, Kent.) Searches for any discharge of Alex Parker from the military have been unproductive, as have searches of lists of army widows and their pensions. In the words of a researcher at Kew, 'this negative search means that any service record has not been saved, and does not necessarily mean that Alex Parker did not serve in the British army.' (Letter dated 11 March 1997 from Tim Hughes, Kew.)

20. Hong Kong Government Civil Lists and Blue Books, 1905–08. It is possible that Alex Parker was recruited from London and shipped out by the government, although the Hong Kong Government records him as 'appointed by the Governor...' If hired locally, he could have arrived in Hong Kong on his own or with the military, members of which preferred to get their discharge in Hong Kong where there was a chance of a job. 'The Civil List record of his Date of Appointment as 1 August 1905 refers to his appointment as 2nd class Overseer,' explained Norman Miners in a letter dated 17 July 1997. 'Date of First Appointment to the Colonial Government [1 April 1905] would normally mean that he was already employed by the colonial government in a lowlier post for four months before promotion to 2nd class Overseer. I suppose that it could refer to the interval between appointment in London and the passage by sea....'

21. Henry J. Lethbridge, 1978, p. 194.

22. 'Henry Thomas Jackman (1874–1928), Engineer, Public Works Department, Hong Kong' by Stephen Selby, *Journal of the Hong Kong Branch of the Royal Asiatic Society* 26 (1986), pp. 46–54.

23. G.H. Gompertz, p. 26.

24. Interviews, with Florence Lo, The Croucher Foundation, Hong Kong, on 6 June 1996 in Hong Kong, and with Dr Douglas Payne on 9 July 1996 in Cambridge.

25. Isabella L. Bird, 1983, pp. 30, 36.

26. G.H. Gompertz, pp. 22–3. Gompertz was born and bred in Hong Kong, his father being a Colonial Service Cadet, Magistrate, Puisne Judge of the Supreme Court and occasionally Acting Chief Justice. Gompertz junior was schooled in England and returned to Hong Kong in the service of Jardine Matheson & Company Limited from 1924. His combined background of colonial service and commerce give him an astute eye on his milieu, that of expatriates on the China Coast.

27. Geoffrey Robley Sayer, p. 72. With thanks to G.R. Sayer's son, Guy Sayer, for the gift of a copy.

28. The original Hong Kong Club, planned in the earliest days of the colony in 1845, was opened on 26 May 1846.

29. 'I had better point out that the dollar referred to was a Mexican coin of silver, so do not run away with the idea that the Club dues were light.' (John Luff, 1968 — Noel Croucher is listed in the Acknowledgements, pp. 4–5.)

30. *The Directory & Chronicle for China, Japan, Corea, Indo-China, Straits Settlements, Malay States, Siam, Netherlands, India, Borneo, the Philippines etc.*

31. Norman Miners, p. 81. Also, see *HK Hansard*, 21 February 1918, pp. 3–4, and CO 129/434, p. 394.

32. G.B. Endacott, 1958, p. 279.

33. Norman Miners, p. 99, and his letter dated 17 July 1997 to the author.

34. Blanket searches throughout the counties of England for the birth and death of Alex Parker are ongoing, albeit in vain. If he died in Hong Kong, there is no record of that either: St. John's burial records from 1892 to May 1918 are missing and searches of Hong Kong government records from 1908 to 1929 have been fruitless. His son with Floss, Gerald Parker, later settled in Canada, but has since died and Gerald's three daughters have been impossible to trace.

35. If a Western woman was let down by her husband, she would have had little option but to become a prostitute — 'the common destiny of many European women deserted, abandoned or widowed, whose husbands or protectors were, or had been, policemen, turnkeys, inspectors, overseers, or employed in similar occupations...' (Henry J. Lethbridge, 1978, p. 198.) There were no jobs available for uneducated European women and, apart from work in mission schools, few for the educated.

36. *South China Morning Post*, 16 March 1980.

37. Interview with Eugene Yourieff on 17 February 1997. This is indeed possible but cannot be confirmed. In 1890 the Government Central School for Girls (later renamed Belilios Public School) was founded on Old Bailey Street (next to her father's Police Station) to provide 'an ordinary middle-class English education' to the daughters of Chinese, European and Indian residents of Hong Kong. It also took in the occasional boy. Another friend believes Noel spoke of school in Hong Kong: 'Was he in the Cathedral school? I think he told me he sang in the choir.' (Interview with Guy Sayer in London on 3 March 1997.)

38. See Chapter Eleven of this book.

39. Mrs Craik, pp. 97, 145.

40. Letter dated 5 March 1965 by Noel Croucher to Joan Scrivener.

41. Interview with Peter Vine on 26 February 1997.

42. Letter dated 27 September 1996 from Frederic A. Silva. Interview with Silva on 28 October 1996.

43. Interview with Jimmy MacGregor, OBE, ISO, JP, former Legislative Councillor in Hong Kong, on 23 January 1997.

CHAPTER THREE

1. First verse, *Sonnet to Macao*, Sir John Bowring, Governor of Hong Kong, 1854–59.

2. Much of this chapter relies on research conducted by the venerable Carl T. Smith. There were no direct sailings from Europe to Macao, not even from Lisbon. Anyone wanting to reach Macao had to go first to Hong Kong or Canton.

3. *The Hong Kong Guide*, Kelly & Walsh, 1893. Reprinted in 1982 by Oxford University Press, Hong Kong, with Introduction by H.J. Lethbridge, p. 131.

4. People with roots or homes in Macao prefer to call themselves Filhos Macao. See Frederic A. Silva, 1996, p. 27.

5. Simon Kent's *Ferry to Hong Kong*, a novel later made into a film, depicts the desperate fate of a man condemned to ply the ferry between Hong Kong and Macao for the rest of his life, as punishment for being drunk and disorderly in a Hong Kong bar.

6. *The Hong Kong Guide*, p. 132.

7. The other two: Hotel Sanataria de Boa Vista, Rua Tanque Mainato, managed by F.J. Marques; Oriental Hotel, 73 Praia Grande, managed by Jayme dos Santos.

8. 'The Decline & Glory of Macao's Hotels' by Maria do Rosário Lopes, in 'Macao Special 96' by the Macao Government Media Bureau, 1996, pp. 164–77.

9. *Special 96*, p. 164.

10. R.D. Cremer, p. 79.

11. *The Directory and Chronicle for China, Japan, Corea, Indo-China, Straits Settlements, Malay States, Siam, Netherlands, India, Borneo, the Philippines etc.*, 1906–08 editions.

12. It is possible that Sir Paul Chater was related to this Jordan, as he was to the Jordans of Hong Kong.

13. AHM/Administracao Civil/Processo, 17 February 1913, found in the Archivo Historico de Macao by Carl T. Smith.

14. *Daily Press*, 3 July 1903.

15. With thanks to Carl T. Smith.

16. 'Rickshaws and Limousines' by Pedro Dá Mesquita, in *Special 96*, pp. 194–215. See especially pp. 197, 201.

17. Noel Croucher became a shareholder of Green Island Cement Company and followed the firm closely throughout his life. See Chapter Six of this book.

18. In fact, it was 1825. See Austin Coates, 1966, p. 147.

19. Susanna Hoe, pp. 5, 9–10.

20. See Lindsay and May Ride.

21. Lindsay and May Ride, pp. 47, 163–4.

22. Letter dated 28 September 1957 from Noel Croucher to Joan Scrivener.

23. Noel was curious about history in the area. His papers also include notes on the burial of a ship captain's wife, at Shek Kwu Chau. See 'The European Grave on Shek Kwu Chau, Hong Kong' by J. Moore, in *Journal of the Hong Kong Branch of the Royal Asiatic Society* 14 (1974), pp. 186–7.

24. Interview with Teresa Price, Lammert Brothers, Hong Kong, 1996.

25. Another friend, F.S. Coote of Cable & Wireless Co. in Hong Kong, apparently shared weekend trips to Macao with Noel Croucher in the 1950s and 1960s.

26. Letter dated 28 March 1957 from Noel Croucher to Joan Scrivener.

27. Interview with G.O.W. Stewart in the Cotswolds on 20 March 1997.

28. Letter dated 28 March 1957 from Noel Croucher to Joan Scrivener.

29. Interview with Lady May Ride in Bournemouth on 18 July 1996.

30. With thanks to the Carl T. Smith Collection.

31. Eunice Price, pp. 14, 18.

32. Eunice Price, pp. 22, 26.

33. Eunice Price, p. 39.

34. Eunice Price, p. 101.

35. The Civil List of 1907, p. J54.

36. Or did some Crouchers go to Australia? Later correspondence by Noel with a vaguely related Norman Croucher in Australia led them to swap pictures when each was a Royal Hong Kong Yacht Club Commodore.

37. Interview with Noel Croucher's former assistant, Florence Lo, on 6 June 1996.

38. Earl Albert Selle, p. 27. A new biography of Donald is in progress, by Frank Bren.

CHAPTER FOUR

1. Chapter XLIII: Sir Catchick Paul Chater, CMG, LLD, The 'Grand Old Man' of Hong Kong, in Mesrovb Jacob Seth, 1983, pp. 550–60. With thanks to Carl T. Smith.

2. Chapter XLIII: Sir Catchick Paul Chater, CMG, LLD, The 'Grand Old Man' of Hong Kong, in Mesrovb Jacob Seth, 1983, pp. 550–60.

3. Solomon Bard, p. 95.

4. *China Mail*, 27 May 1926.

5. Article by T.P. O'Connor, M.P., in *Sunday Times*, September 1924, quoted by Mesrovb Jacob Seth, 1983, pp. 553–4.

6. Arnold Wright, 1990, p. 108.

7. The Chater Collection remains famous to this day but alas, the only remnant of it in its entirety is the catalogue by James Orange, itself a rare book of great value — with thanks to Wendy MacCallum for showing her copy to the author. Most of the collection was destroyed in World War II, with the remainder, about eighty items, now held by the Hong Kong Museum of Art.

8. Recounted in Michael and Mun Him Wise, p. 194.

9. The house was bequeathed to Sir Paul's widow but she apparently left Hong Kong in 1927. In 1935 it became Admiralty House, home to the Naval Commander-in-chief of the China Squadron. The house survived Japanese occupation during World War II, but soon suffered from fire and dereliction, and was demolished in 1953. See Peter Wesley-Smith's 'Note on Marble Hall' in *Journal of the Hong Kong Branch of the Royal Asiatic Society* 18 (June 1979).

10. Letter dated 21 March 1990 from Austin Coates to Susanna Hoe. In this letter, Austin Coates also described Croucher's relationship to Chater, as the fellow 'student' of Sir Robert Ho Tung. (See p. 37 of this book.) I am deeply grateful to Ms Hoe for her kind permission to quote from this letter.

11. *China Mail*, 28 May 1926.

12. See succeeding chapters for a description of kerbstone broking in Hong Kong.

13. Eric Cumine, p. 56.

14. Interview with Ian MacCallum on 2 July 1996.

15. Austin Coates, 1980, pp. 156–7.

16. Interview with Florence Lo in Hong Kong on 6 June 1996.

17. Russell & Company was founded in 1818 in China, to trade mainly in opium. Its Hong Kong branch was opened in 1850 and by 1859 it had expanded

into financial services, and ran a steamer between Canton and Hong Kong. Among those associated with the firm was William C. Hunter, the sole American trader to learn Chinese. His *Fan Kwae at Canton* was reprinted as *An American in Canton 1825–44* in 1994. Russell & Co. worked with Baring Brothers of London and with Jamsetjee Jeejebhoy in India. Registered subsidiaries included Hong Kong Rope Manufacturing Co. and Shanghai Steam Navigation Co. Shanghai Steam wanted access to godowns for storing their goods, other than those controlled by the two largest firms of the day, Dent's and Jardine's. It thus precipitated Dent's demise and, with Jardine's, accumulated most of Dent's assets. Unfortunately for Russell & Co., Shanghai Steam became so important that its sale in 1876 (to the Chinese government-backed China Merchants' Steam Navigation Company) spelled the beginning of the end for Russell & Co.

18. Walter Feldwick, pp. 550–1.

19. Austin Coates, 1980, p. 135.

20. Published in *South China Morning Post*, 14 February 1931.

21. Solomon Bard, p. 77.

22. The name Tomes reappears in Noel Croucher's Contacts Book of 1977, but no response from the addresses listed was forthcoming.

23. Henry J. Lethbridge, p. 141 and note 28 on p. 156.

24. Shiona Airlie, p. 54.

25. Shiona Airlie, pp. 56–7.

26. 'Late Mr R.G. Shewan, Reminiscences by an Old Friend of a Fine Character', *South China Morning Post*, 17 February 1934.

27. Colin Crisswell, p. 191, and Nigel Cameron, 1979, p. 12.

28. Frank H.H. King, Volume I, pp. 462–6, Volume II, pp. 22–6.

29. 'Late Mr R.G. Shewan, Reminiscences by an Old Friend of a Fine Character', *South China Morning Post*, 17 February 1934.

30. *South China Morning Post*, 27 March 1911.

31. In 1930, Shewan, Tomes & Co. Ltd. relinquished their thirty-five-year-long General Managership of Green Island Cement Co. See *Far Eastern Economic Review*, 27 May 1954. See also R.D. Cremer, pp. 81–2.

32. Austin Coates, 1980, pp. 134–5.

33. 'The "Corner" in Ropes, The History of the "Corner" together with a Report of the Sensational Trial, Potts v. Rustomjee' reprinted from the *Hong Kong Telegraph*, 16 July 1889.

34. 'Fifty Years in Hong Kong, Mr R.G. Shewan's Long Association', *South China Morning Post*, 14 February 1931.

35. 'Fifty Years in Hong Kong, Mr R.G. Shewan's Long Association', *South China Morning Post*, 14 February 1931.

36. Solomon Bard, p. 77.

37. 'Late Mr R.G. Shewan, Reminiscences by an Old Friend of a Fine Character', *South China Morning Post*, 17 February 1934.

38. *South China Morning Post*, 23 September 1967. Wheelock Marden & Co. was itself absorbed into Hutchison Whampoa Ltd. Group in the 1980s.

CHAPTER FIVE

1. Norman Miners, p. 2.

2. Interview with Duncan Graham in Hong Kong on 4 September 1996.

3. With thanks to Charlotte Havilland of Swire Group Public Affairs. Consideration was given to the possibility of a transcription mistake, but Mr J.W. Crouch is shorter than his colleagues in the 1912 photograph. Noel Croucher was usually taller than others.

4. Thanks to the Carl T. Smith Collection.

5. Ministry of Defence, United Kingdom. Letter dated 28 November 1996 from K. Welbourne: 'Served in Hong Kong Volunteer Corps Artillery Section for 4 years as a Gunner. Appointed to a Temporary Commission as Temporary 2nd Lieutenant, 14/05/17.'

6. Gillian Chambers, 1993, pp. 120, 153.

7. Thanks to Jason Wordie, historian and former Royal Hong Kong Defence Corps member.

8. Gillian Chambers, pp. 41–3.

9. Letter dated 17 January 1957 from Noel Croucher to Joan Scrivener.

10. Letter dated 8 August 1959 from Noel Croucher to Joan Scrivener.

11. Interviews, with Eugene Yourieff on 17 February 1997, and R. Hownam-Meek on 21 April 1997.

12. Letter dated 16 July 1958 from Noel Croucher to Joan Scrivener.

13. Letter dated 19 February 1976 to W.H. Adgey-Edgar.

14. Letter to the Editor, signed Arnold Graham, *South China Morning Post*, soon after Noel's death, saying that Noel went to Miyajima 'circa 1913'.

15. Interview with Revd John Chynchen in August 1996.

16. 'English Arrogance' by Sir Charles Wentworth Dilke, in Barbara-Sue White, 1996, p. 70.

17. G.H. Gompertz, p. 43.

18. G.H. Gompertz, p. 56.

CHAPTER SIX

1. George Hayim, p. 3. Years later, when war came to Shanghai, 'father had started a refugee camp for Hitler's victims who had landed penniless in Shanghai. The austere Aunt Maisie, who had become very fond of me, ran the organisation. Father was busy with a brewery he had floated for Jardine Matheson, called Ewo...' (George Hayim, p. 61.)

2. Austin Coates, 1994, p. 159.

3. Ellis Hayim was son of Joseph and Hannah, and brother to Albert and Maisie.

4. With thanks to Carl T. Smith and his Collection.

5. Solomon Bard, pp. 94–5.

6. Colin Crisswell, pp. 137, 187–8, 190, 195.

7. Mrs Lipton Hutton Potts, widow of late Lipton, died on 10 February 1914, according to next day's *Hong Kong Telegraph*. She died at what was presumably her own family's home at Rossborough Park, Harrow-on-the-Hill.

8. Obituary, *South China Morning Post*, 29 June 1918.

9. John Graham, p. 11.

10. Interview with Jack Yuan Potts at Liss, Hampshire, 11–13 March 1997.

11. Source is the *Daily Press*, via the Carl T. Smith Collection.

12. A Notice of a Change of Name to this effect, by Ellis Kadoorie, appeared in *China Mail*, 10 May 1901 — the Carl T. Smith Collection. This Kelly had no connection with the bookshop and publishers Kelly & Walsh.

13. *Daily Press*, 1 April 1890.

14. Jury lists; and re R.M. Potts' death, see *Daily Press*, 18 August 1902.

15. Robin Hutcheon, 1983, p. 19.

16. *Daily Press*, 2 April 1906.

17. Prince's Building was built in 1904 by Leigh and Orange, for Mody and Chater. (Nigel Cameron, 1979, p. 67.)

18. The Carl T. Smith Collection.

19. Interview with Jack Yuan Potts at Liss, Hampshire, 11–13 March 1997.

20. Jack Potts loved cars and was an East End mechanic before his father put him into Cornhill insurance company. Jack joined the Hong Kong Royal Naval Volunteer Reserve and served on *HMS Cornflower* before World War II.

21. The Carl T. Smith Collection.

22. Harry Odell, born in Cairo in 1894, was the son of a cigarette manufacturer and was taken to Shanghai as a child. He worked briefly for the British American Tobacco Company at Hankow, before going to sea as a stoker aged eighteen, fighting in World War I, and returning to Hong Kong in 1921. He joined trading firm Getz & Company but left to become a stockbroker, to later diversify into film and entertainment. See advertisement 'Harry Odell says...' in Robin Hutcheon, 1983, p. 120.

23. Ellen Field, p. 209.

24. Emily Hahn, 1944, p. 275.

25. *South China Morning Post*, 17 August 1964.

26. Letter dated 24 September 1997 from Jack Potts.

27. Austin Coates, 1994, p. 146.

28. *South China Morning Post*, 27 March 1911.

29. *South China Morning Post*, 28 April 1913 and 12 April 1915.

30. Letter dated 5 March 1997 from Ho Shai Lai, Hong Kong, to the author.

31. John Graham, p. 32.

32. See Stock Exchange of Hong Kong. The first companies registered were Hong Kong Hotel Company (2 March 1866), Hong Kong Fire Insurance Company Ltd. (11 April 1866), and Hong Kong & Whampoa Dock Company (11 October 1866). The Hong Kong and Shanghai Banking Corporation had been incorporated earlier under a special ordinance.

33. 'Early Days of the Exchange', opening article in *Hong Kong Stock Exchange Yearbook*, 1985. As the Hong Kong Club was then on Queen's Road, the gutter referred to is on Queen's Road between Wyndham and Ice House streets.

34. Walter H. Young, pp. 18–9, 108, 171.

35. Walter H. Young, pp. 125–7, 219. Without delving into the intricacies of Mr Young's plot, it is interesting to note that on repairing to Macao in pursuit of a forger, he 'snatched a couple of hours' sleep in Hing Kee's Hotel', thus placing his narrative before 1903 as we know that this is the year when Hing Kee's became the Macao Hotel, source of employ a few years later for Noel. See Chapter Three of this book.

36. Papers laid before the Legislative Council, 1890–91, HK S L51 SL, 21 July 1890.

37. Papers laid before the Legislative Council, 1890–91, HK S L51 SL, 21 July 1890.

38. Papers laid before the Legislative Council, 1890–91, HK S L51 SL, 19 June 1891.

39. Walter H. Young, pp. 144–5. 'These "niñas de salon" were all perfumed with the sickly-sweet odour of the apple-blossom, a scent which stuck to one's clothes for days. After being in contact ... it was never safe to go to the Club until we were fumigated, for fear of unkind remarks. It is a compromising perfume in China, and has broken up many a happy home.' (Walter H. Young, pp. 148–9.)

40. Walter H. Young, p. 171.

41. Walter H. Young, pp. 169–70. 'Honourable Soapy Jim' must be J.J. Keswick of Jardine Matheson who introduced the bill.

42. Once in business on his own, Noel's office was in Holland House, Ice House Street. The exchange operated first on the site of Holland House and later in part of the David Sassoon and Co. godowns. Part of this lot was later purchased by the exchange, to build the Stock Exchange Building at 10 Ice House Street in 1934. Holland House was part of what is now Number 9 Queen's Road Central.

43. 'The Hong Kong Stock Exchange', *Hong Kong Tatler,* January 1979, p. 26.

44. 'The Hong Kong Stock Exchange', *Hong Kong Tatler,* January 1979, p. 27.

45. What we might call corruption now, was seen by some as a stabilising factor in colonial life then: 'It was one form of accommodation between two disparate sets of people — Chinese and European — and was both a natural outgrowth of behaviour institutionalised in traditional Chinese society and of the expectations and motivations of Europeans.' (Henry Lethbridge, 1978, pp. 16–8.)

CHAPTER SEVEN

1. Daryl Klein, p. xi.

2. In May 1916, for example, Noel was at Indo-China Steam Navigation Co.'s Annual General Meeting; in 1917, at Hong Kong Bank's and Hong Kong & Whampoa Dock Co.'s meetings.

3. Nancy Nash, pp. 18–9.

4. Re Germans in Hong Kong in World War I, see Michael and Mun Him Wise, pp. 190–1.

5. See Michael Summerskill, p. 80. With thanks to his son for the gift of a copy of this very useful work.

6. Michael Summerskill, p. 1.

7. Michael Summerskill, p. 54.

8. Michael Summerskill, p. 47.

9. Michael Summerskill, p. 56.

10. Michael Summerskill, see Chapter Ten.

11. Michael Summerskill, p. 86. See also Harley Farnsworth MacNair, pp. 235–8.

12. 'The "Coolie" Killing Fields' by Danny Buckland in *The Independent* newspaper, London, 28 June 1997, p. 18.

13. B. Manico Gull, pp. 125–35.

14. Noel Croucher's typescript of these recollections was in his desk when he died. It has been edited for clarity only.

15. In fact, Noel was referring to Reginald F. Johnston. He was in the Weihaiwei administration, but beneath the Commissioner, James Stewart Lockhart.

16. That is, the Canadian Pacific Railway-owned ship, *Empress of Asia*.

17. See Michael Summerskill, pp. 116–7, 122, for the use Summerskill made of these reminiscences, albeit without specific credit to Noel Croucher.

18. Emphasis added.

19. Letter dated 28 November 1996 from Mrs K. Welbourne, for Departmental Record Officer, Ministry of Defence in Hayes, Middlesex.

20. 'He decided he ought to join up and do something in the war and he was aggrieved when all they did for him was to offer him charge of a Chinese labour battalion. He didn't go into the war to look after "coolies". He went into the war with the idea of taking part in it.' (Interview with Lord Todd, 9–10 July 1996.)

21. Interview with Bill and Betty Hancock on 20 July 1996.

22. Michael Summerskill, p. 124.

23. Michael Summerskill, Chapter 15, especially p. 155.

24. Michael Summerskill, pp. 144–8.

25. Letter dated 21 March 1975 from Noel Croucher to Joan Scrivener.

26. Daryl Klein, pp. viii–ix.

27. Daryl Klein, p. 57.

28. Michael Summerskill, p. 8.

29. *The Times*, 28 December 1917.

30. Daryl Klein, p. 12.

31. Daryl Klein, pp. 58–9.

32. Daryl Klein, pp. 71–2.

33. Daryl Klein, p. 145.

34. Daryl Klein, pp. 4, 7, 31.

35. See Michael Summerskill, Chapter 11.

36. Daryl Klein, pp. 36, 197.

37. Martin Gilbert, p. 311.

38. Daryl Klein, p. 31.

39. Daryl Klein, p. 63.

40. Lloyd George quoted by Martin Gilbert, p. 360.

41. Facsimile dated 24 March 1997, and subsequent conversations.

42. 'My Dear Edgar': letter dated 19 November 1976 from Noel Croucher to W.H. Adgey-Edgar.

43. See Shiona Airlie.

44. Dated 11 October 1977. The correspondence included an aerogramme from Noel to Adgey-Edgar signed 'Yours, No. 53 Co - CLC'.

45. Martin Gilbert, p. 414.

CHAPTER EIGHT

1. Letter from Noel Croucher to a friend, 1977.

2. Gillian Chambers, p. 42.

3. 'Mafoo' is the China Coast term for 'groom'.

4. Letter dated 6 September 1997 from Ansie Lee Sperry.

5. *South China Morning Post*, 26 February 1917. The top names of Hong Kong business: S.H. Dodwell, taipan of the leading hong, Dodwell and Company, likewise P.H. Holyoak of Reiss and Company. Sir Robert Ho Tung was there with his brothers Ho Kom Tong and Ho Fook, and nephews Ho Wing and Ho Leung. So, too, were T.E. 'Tam' Pearce and H.R.B. Hancock, George Potts, Hormusjee Mody and Ellis Kadoorie, and H.M.H. Nemazee, a Persian trader whose family became friends and fellow philanthropists to Noel in later years. Files, made available by Dr Elizabeth Sinn, were compiled as part of a project funded by The Japan Foundation, entitled 'Materials on Hong Kong Companies'.

6. Austin Coates, 1980, p. xii.

7. Noel's attendance at company meetings included:
   China Light and Power Company (1919);

Hong Kong, Canton and Macao Steamboat Company Limited; China Sugar Refining Company Limited (1921);

Green Island Cement Company; Hong Kong Hotel Company; Hong Kong & Whampoa Dock Company (1922);

China Sugar Refining Company; Hong Kong Fire Insurance Company Limited; Canton Insurance Office Limited; and Hong Kong Hotels — which now controlled the leading hotels in both North and South China (1923);

Hong Kong Fire Insurance Company Limited (1924).

— *South China Morning Post*, 30 April 1923 and 24 March 1924.

8. *South China Morning Post*, 21 March 1921.

9. *South China Morning Post*, 11 February 1924.

10. *South China Morning Post*, 14 February 1923.

11. John Graham, pp. 190–2 — extract from *South China Morning Post*, 2 June 1924. Other signs of status included the lists of pew-holders at St. John's Cathedral. There is no sign of Noel Croucher on these lists, and the practice of allotting the seats was abolished in 1929. (Hong Kong Public Records Office Ref: HKMS 47.)

12. See Arnold Wright, p. 111.

13. Letter dated 27 February 1978 from Noel Croucher to Joan Scrivener.

14. 'Young European women are still in short supply... Not all Europeans engage in this chase: many acquire what is known locally as "yellow fever" — a permanent condition only curable, in a few cases, by marriage. They justify their choice on a number of grounds: that, simply there are more Chinese girls to select from; or that Chinese girls look younger longer, carry less avoirdupois and are more feminine.' (Henry Lethbridge, 1968, pp. 276–9.)

15. Austin Coates, 1977, pp. 114–5.

16. Letter dated 7 March (year unclear) to Richard Croucher. A Magnificat is a song of praise, or canticle, deriving from early Byzantine hymns. Noel Croucher was most probably referring to the great Magnificat by Johann Sebastian Bach written for five-part chorus and orchestra. See Donald Jay Grout, pp. 14, 433.

17. Letter dated 16 October 1962 from Noel Croucher to Joan Scrivener.

18. Jean Gittins, 1969, p. 46.

19. Letter dated 18 December ?1967 to Joan Scrivener.

20. Letter dated 28 December 1967 to Joan Scrivener. Sir Robert Jones was indeed a renowned British orthopaedic surgeon, 1858–1933. (*Webster's Biographical Dictionary*, p. 792.)

21. Interview with Allen and Elizabeth Mills in London on 16 July 1996.

22. Letter from Noel Croucher to a friend, 1977.

23. Letter dated 6 May 1977 to Joan Scrivener.

24. Interview with Allen and Elizabeth Mills in London on 16 July 1996.

25. Interview with Allen and Elizabeth Mills in London on 16 July 1996.

26. Other correspondence shows he got at least one letter from his wife during World War II.

27. Letter from Noel Croucher to a friend, 1977.

28. Jury lists show Noel Croucher's address as the Hong Kong Hotel, 1916–17 and 1920–25. But birth records reveal the Peak tenancy.

29. 'From 1918 the Executive Council decided all applications... Only one Chinese was granted permission to live on the Peak between 1918 and 1941: Mme Chiang Kai-shek. A similar system was set up to create a European reservation in part of Cheung Chau in 1919, but a few Chinese were permitted by the Executive Council to live there in the 1930s.' (Norman Miners, pp. 54–5.) Sir Robert Ho Tung, a Eurasian, was another exception, and built the impressive Ho Tung Gardens on the Peak.

30. Only at the Helena May Library, 35 Garden Road, Hong Kong. With thanks to Marjorie Bray, who referred the author to this work, and, to the Helena May.

31. Henry J. Lethbridge, 1968, pp. 174–5.

32. Letter dated 7 February ?1973 from Noel Croucher to son Richard. A letter of 1974 refers to a future Financial Secretary: 'John Brembridge who knew you at school is the manager of the Biggest Company in Hong Kong & Director of all the best Companies.'

33. *South China Morning Post*, 29 December 1924. 'Joss' here means luck.

34. *South China Morning Post*, 29 December 1924.

35. P.C. Potts was brother of George Potts and colleague at Benjamin & Potts.

36. 'People said his wife was very common...' (Jack Potts, 11–12 March 1997.)

37. Interview with Diane de Precourt in Amberley, Sussex, on 19 March 1997. Noel continued to send Christmas cards to Mrs de Precourt for decades, which was why her name was in his 1977 Index Book.

38. Alec Hutton Potts' son, Peter, went to school in Tsingtao. (Paul Gillingham, p. 127.)

39. This could not be substantiated. It may have been the Gloucester Hotel.

40. Thanks to Frank Bren, we found the following entries in the Index to Foreign Office Correspondence listings: Croucher, N.A. Certificate of British

Nationality, 1939 (T15792/T16712/T16204/29/378); and Croucher, N.A. Renunciation of French Allegiance, 1940 (T5206/30/378). These suggest Noel had to clarify Simonne's right to British nationality. Document copies were unobtainable.

41. 'Your Mother wrote — quite nice to begin with for a change until she met somebody at a party who on being introduced to her said, "Are you married to that awful man in HKong" — Your Mother took the trouble of writing this to me ... well ... better than writing it in her usual large handwriting on a Post Card for all to see. I sent it back to her.' (Letter from Noel Croucher to son Richard, circa 1974.)

42. See F.M. Grafton. Also *Freemasonry in Northern China 1913–1937* and P.J. Rich.

43. Thanks are due to the curators of the District Grand Lodge of Hong Kong and the Far East, the United Grand Lodge of England, the Grand Lodge of Ancient, Free and Accepted Masons of Scotland, and the Grand Lodge of A.F. and A Masons of Ireland. Correspondence, 1996–97.

44. Letter in late 1967 to Joan Scrivener. He was referring to Elinor Glyn, 1864–1943, a writer of romantic novels who went to Hollywood in the twenties to see her books glamourised on the screen. One of her books, *Three Weeks,* written in 1907 was regarded as somewhat risque. Anna Pavlova, 1881–1931, was the famous Russian-born and -trained ballerina. Pearl White, 1889–1938, was an American film actress who retired to France in 1924. Joan Fontaine is another film star. (*Webster's Biographical Encyclopaedia.*)

45. Letter dated 30 May 1972 to Joan Scrivener.

46. John Luff, 1968, pp. 58–60.

47. Letter dated 4 January 1976 to Joan Scrivener.

48. Letter dated 4 November 1975 to Noel Croucher from Sir Robert Neville. Interestingly, the other letter to Noel was addressed simply 'Hong Kong', and it reached Noel Croucher's office.

49. Charles Higham, p. 62.

50. The future Duke and Duchess of Windsor stayed friends with Sir Victor and his cousin Sir Philip Sassoon. In London in the 1930s, they socialised together at Park Lane, and on the Sassoons' vast estate, Trent Park. See Charles Higham, pp. 124–5.

51. Of various 'singsong' houses, 'the only one ... which admitted foreign women was in Repulse Bay. As the visitor entered, a smiling male slave in a blue cotton robe would appear...' (Charles Higham, p. 65.)

52. See W.K. Chan, pp. 161–6.

53. W.K. Chan, pp. 166–91.

54. Paul Gillingham, Chapter Five, especially p. 38.

55. Formerly Cafe Weissman, but changed to a less teutonic version circa World War I.

56. By now, Noel had left the Regiment, although his personal papers include HKVDC dinner invitations (for example, 'Dowbiggin's Trophy Dinner, Hunter's Arms, April 26, 1930') and a Christmas card photograph of the Corps in 1860 and 1930.

57. Hong Kong General Chamber of Commerce, Annual Report, 1925, pp. 20–2. Not until late 1927 was the 'acute' China situation said to improve.

58. *South China Morning Post*, 20 February 1925.

59. Paul Gillingham, p. 44.

60. Interview with Florence Lo in Hong Kong in June 1996.

61. Paul Gillingham, pp. 48–9.

62. See Henry J. Lethbridge, 1978, pp. 19–26. For a detailed, albeit jingoistic, account of the 1925 strike, see the Annual Report of the Hong Kong General Chamber of Commerce for 1925.

63. Henry J. Lethbridge, 1978, pp. 24–5. Lethbridge's observation seems timelessly apt.

64. Robin Barrie and Gretchen Tricker, pp. 45–6.

65. *South China Morning Post*, 31 May 1926. At the March 1926 Hong Kong and Whampoa Dock Co. meeting, shareholders demanded an investigation into cutting costs and debts. Noel Croucher was there and would no doubt have been in support of such moves.

66. *South China Morning Post*, 31 March 1927.

67. *China Mail*, 28 May 1926.

68. In 1976, the record was ten hours, thirty-seven minutes, twenty-eight seconds. (Gillian Chambers, p. 156.) By the 1990s, the trip took four hours.

69. 'On the proposition of Mr A. Keith, seconded by Mr A.P. Samy, the appointments of Messrs P.M. Hodgson, N.V. Croucher and S.M. Churn to the Board of Directors were confirmed.' Sir Robert Ho Tung was a director. ('China Provident ... Pay Off Godown Debt', *South China Morning Post*, 7 February 1928.)

70. On 19 July 1927, Noel Croucher bought property at 501–61 Canton Road/ Wai Ching St./Kowloon Marine Lot 49. (The Carl T. Smith Collection.)

71. 'Directors' Fees, Criticised at Tug and Lighter Meeting', *South China Morning Post*, 28 June 1928.

72. *South China Morning Post,* 1 May 1928.

73. *China Mail,* 30 April 1928. Ansie Lee Sperry says newspaper reports were not accurate. Her version: 'Father had not yet entered the club which was on the 3rd floor of the building; was shot at three times and a waiter from the club rushed down, and raced after the assailant with Father still clutching to the wall of the covered walkway ... when other members found him, he was already dead.' (Email on 19 August 1998.)

74. Interview with Ansie Lee Sperry and Hank Sperry on 30 October 1997. Also, letter dated 6 September 1997 from Ansie Lee Sperry, and fax dated 1 September 1997: 'I was fascinated to hear Noel tell of the time of that very tragic death when Noel was also about to have tiffin... I believe Noel told us he alerted the police.'

75. *South China Morning Post,* 2 May 1928.

76. Letter dated 6 September 1997 from Ansie Lee Sperry.

77. See Chapter Eleven of this book.

78. Interview with J.S. Lee on 18 November 1996 and with F.A. Silva on 28 October 1996.

79. The Hong Kong Club List of Members, January 1977, kindly provided by former club chairman, G.R. 'Ronnie' Ross, of Deacon & Company.

80. That is between Wyndham and D'Aguilar streets. The club claims it started in 1844. W.K. Chan and Henry Lethbridge both say it opened in 1846.

81. Eric Cumine, pp. 96–7.

82. 'The Hong Kong Club', by Neville Chesney, in the *Hong Kong Tatler* magazine, April 1977.

83. W.K. Chan, p. 36.

84. Noel did not join the club until he had been in business for seventeen years. Compare this to the arrival of Ferdinand Gerald Nigel, who arrived in Hong Kong in the 1930s to work for the law firm Johnson Stokes & Masters. 'And they made me join the Hong Kong Club, said it was a term of my contract that I should apply for membership within six months. I duly did and had to pay $250 entrance fee when I was only earning $475.' (Katherine Mattock, 1990, p. 65.)

CHAPTER NINE

1. In a letter dated 2 August 1971 to Betsy Treadgold, Noel referred to a friend called Johnson, of the Chartered Bank. 'I think he was in the Bank when Leiper was there. I had my office on the first floor of the Bank as long ago as

1930, but left when it was being rebuilt.' G.A. Leiper wrote *A Yen for my Thoughts* about Hong Kong in World War II. See Chapter Ten of this book.

2. 'The Gripps is slang for the Hongkong Hotel. No one knows why, though there are many theories; fanciful, coarse or libellous, according to the size of the speaker's hotel bill.' (C.S. Archer, p. 73.)

3. Ball description from Paul Gillingham, pp. 57–8. Noel was an active member of the society in post-war years but records cannot confirm when exactly he joined.

4. Letter dated 31 May ?1968 to Joan Scrivener.

5. *The Cambridge Biographical Encyclopaedia,* p. 522. See also Paul Gillingham, p. 56.

6. Elizabeth Sinn, 1994, p. 12. See also Caroline Courtald and May Holdsworth, p. 43. Lady May Ride believes Noel was not present at the wedding. She was a good friend of Noel's and attended the wedding herself.

7. Gillian Chambers, pp. 52–3.

8. Gillian Chambers, pp. 52–3.

9. The Hong Kong Jockey Club has found no record of Mr Croucher's membership before World War II, but anecdote, photographs and logic suggest Noel was already a horse-owner before the war.

10. Telephone interview with Kai-bong Chau on 26 November 1997.

11. Austin Coates, 1994, p. 242. See also the Cartoon of Potts, Austin Coates, 1994, p. 163, and Austin Coates' use of Jack's picture of Mimi Hayim, p. 159: 'Mimi Hayim leading in Comedy King, Shanghai derby, 1920. This was the first year lady owners were admitted to the Shanghai Race Club. Mimi Hayim certainly lent weight to the proceedings. The Hayim family took over from their relatives, the Benjamins, in the brokerage firm of Benjamin and Potts.'

12. See Chapter Thirteen of this book.

13. Paul Gillingham, p. 153.

14. 'His [Alec Potts'] photographs of the Fanling Hunt survived the Japanese occupation of Hong Kong hidden in a tin box placed in the rafters of a Kowloon godown. Unlike most other private photograph collections, they were not used as fuel.' (Paul Gillingham, p. 156.)

15. Interview with Rosie Potts in Hong Kong on 19 November 1997.

16. Interview with Lord Lawrence Kadoorie in Hong Kong on 20 June 1985.

17. Interview with Ian MacCallum in London on 2 July 1996.

18. Thanks to journalist and writer Damien McElroy for his researches into the Wallem family.

19. Paul Gillingham, p. 87.

20. Interview with Peter Vine on 26 February 1997.

21. Noel Croucher attended the following company meetings in 1930: Hong Kong, Canton & Macao Steamboat; Hong Kong Tramways; Green Island Cement (the last meeting of which was held in the Shewan, Tomes offices, where a younger Noel had been a junior clerk); Hong Kong & Shanghai Hotels; Hong Kong Engineering & Construction; Union Insurance and its associated concerns, China Fire Insurance Company Ltd.; and British Traders' Insurance Company Ltd.

22. Noel Croucher attended the following company meetings:

Canton Insurance Office; China Underwriters; Star Ferry; Hong Kong & Shanghai Bank; Hong Kong Realty & Trust; Hong Kong, Canton & Macao Steamboat; Hong Kong Rope Manufacturing (1931/32);

Star Ferry; Peak Tramways; Hong Kong Tramways; Hong Kong Bank; Hong Kong Realty & Trust; Hong Kong & Shanghai Hotels (1933);

Hongkong Land; Hong Kong Bank; Hong Kong Rope Manufacturing; China Provident; Union Insurance (1934).

23. *South China Morning Post*, 12 March 1932.

24. See previous chapter, re HK Tug & Lighter Company.

25. *South China Morning Post*, 30 June 1932.

26. *South China Morning Post*, 30 June 1932.

27. *South China Morning Post*, 30 April 1933.

28. *South China Morning Post*, 19 May 1934.

29. *South China Morning Post*, 5 June 1935.

30. *South China Morning Post*, 20 May 1937.

31. *South China Morning Post*, 25 February 1933.

32. At the 1934 Dairy Farm meeting, Noel actually proposed *higher* directors' fees, but then, there had been no increase for the directors since 1918. (*South China Morning Post*, 21 February 1934.) Noel attended his first shareholders' meeting of A.S. Watson & Company Ltd. in 1934. (*South China Morning Post*, 18 April 1934.)

33. For years without headquarters of its own, the Hong Kong Stock Exchange moved into 10 Ice House Street, an imposing nine-storey building formally opened on 11 May 1934 by Mr G.H. Potts, chairman of the stock exchange. (*South China Morning Post*, 29 May 1934.) This building was the first in the colony with gearless signal control lifts, among other innovations. (Paul Gillingham, p. 95.)

34. *The Directory & Chronicle for China, Japan, Corea, Indo-China, Straits Settlements, Malay States, Siam, Netherlands, India, Borneo, the Philippines, etc.,* Annual, 1934, pp. F165, A613.

35. Despite this, Noel stood on the left of the then chairman of the stock exchange, George Potts, at the opening of the exchange's new building in 1934.

36. Interview with Guy Sayer in London on 10 March 1997.

37. Norman Miners, pp. 119–20.

38. Fax dated 13 November 1996 from Norma Rasmussen, now in Italy.

39. Interview with Robert Minnitt in England in June 1996. Richard Croucher says his father once pointed out a junk in Aberdeen fishing village as their future home, but they never moved there. Noel merely wanted to show his son that riches are temporal. (*South China Morning Post,* 16 March 1980.)

40. Norman Miners, pp. 121–2.

41. Letter dated 23 October 1997 from Miss Leonia Tai, for Director of Administration, Government Secretariat, Lower Albert Road, Hong Kong.

42. Ai Wu, quoted by Barbara-Sue White, pp. 190–1.

43. James Pope-Hennessy, p. 48.

44. *The Directory & Chronicle for China, Japan, Corea, Indo-China, Straits Settlements, Malay States, Siam, Netherlands, India, Borneo, the Philippines, etc.,* Annual, 1941, pp. A611–2.

45. Interview with Peter Vine on 26 February 1997.

46. *South China Morning Post,* 13 March 1935.

47. *South China Morning Post,* 18 April 1935.

48. Report of Lane Crawford's Annual General Meeting, *South China Morning Post,* 1 July 1935.

49. *South China Morning Post,* 30 December 1936.

50. *South China Morning Post,* 29 March 1940.

51. Interview with Guy Sayer in London on 10 March 1997.

52. Annual Report by the Hong Kong General Chamber of Commerce, 1937.

53. *South China Morning Post,* 15 December 1938.

54. *South China Morning Post,* 9 March 1939.

55. *South China Morning Post,* 9 March 1939.

56. *South China Morning Post,* 18 May 1940. See also Chapter Thirteen of this book.

57. *South China Morning Post,* 30 March 1940 and 4 April 1940.

58. According to his son Richard, the search for the right school involved a tour on which Noel would inform the headmaster of his immense wealth and his big name in Hong Kong expecting this to open the gates to his son. Another source says Noel asked a friend to try to get young Richard into Winchester — 'but there was no way we could do it'. In the end, Richard was signed up for a public school whose name says it all: Bigshotte.

59. *South China Morning Post,* 7 January 1937.

60. Gillian Chambers, p. 60.

61. Speech by Noel Croucher, *South China Morning Post,* 28 October 1940.

62. *South China Morning Post,* 28 October 1940.

63. Interview with Robert Minnitt in England in June 1996. He became assistant to Frank Gimson, the incoming Colonial Secretary of Hong Kong, who arrived only in time to wield his uncertain authority in Stanley Internment Camp.

64. Interview with Robert Minnitt in England in June 1996.

65. Interview with Robert Minnitt in England in June 1996.

66. Gillian Chambers, pp. 66–7.

67. Interview with Robert Minnitt in England in June 1996.

68. Walter H. Young, pp. 156–8. See also G.H. Gompertz, p. 112.

69. Interview with Pat Loseby in Easebourne on 5 July 1996.

70. The funding for the home came from Lady Clara Ho Tung. (Paul Gillingham, p. 120.) Interview with Pat Loseby in Easebourne on 5 July 1996.

71. Emily Hahn, 1944, p. 228.

72. Interview with Pat Loseby in Easebourne on 5 July 1996.

73. 'My mother had a dogs' home for the SPCA and she ran it from the 12th of December 1933 to the 12th of December 1941, because 1941 is when the Japs came in, in December. They came in and took over on my mother's birthday, and she was the last woman, the last person I think to leave Kowloon on the last ferry that went over, because she was looking after her dogs and trying to put them to sleep, as many as she could, before she was taken away by the police and told to come over with them.' (Interview with Pat Loseby in Easebourne on 5 July 1996.)

74. See Dennis J. Duncanson, p. 84.

75. Gillian Chambers, p. 67.

76. Gillian Chambers, p. 68.

CHAPTER TEN

1. Annual Report, Hong Kong General Chamber of Commerce, 1937, pp. 9–10.

2. *South China Morning Post*, 27 March 1939.

3. *South China Morning Post*, 27 February 1939.

4. *South China Morning Post*, 27 February 1939.

5. See Nigel Cameron, 1986, p. 128.

6. *South China Morning Post*, 29 April 1939.

7. *South China Morning Post*, 29 March 1939.

8. Company chairman, D.F. Landale. (*South China Morning Post*, 19 May 1939.)

9. Far from indulging in profiteering, the company said dividends were possible only because of its reserves. (*South China Morning Post*, 12 April 1940.)

10. Paul Gillingham, p. 171.

11. See G.B. Endacott, 1964, pp. 299–300.

12. Paul Gillingham, p. 175.

13. Jean Gittins, 1969, p. 113.

14. Mimi Lau was the girlfriend of Wing Commander Steele-Perkins, and also happened to work for a company which secured a contract for making pre-cast concrete breeze blocks. Strangely, forty-six out of a hundred of her product failed engineering tests and hence became known as 'Mimi Laus'. Even the air raid shelters became seen as a waste as the city was shelled much less than expected. The commission of inquiry's report into the ARP scandals made its way into Stanley Internment Camp and was never seen again. (See Paul Gillingham, p. 176.)

15. Emily Hahn, 1944, pp. 230–2.

16. Paul Gillingham, p. 176.

17. 'Diary', B.C. Redwood, quoted by Michael and Mun Him Wise, pp. 232–3.

18. John Luff, 1967, pp. 49–50.

19. G.B. Endacott, 1964, p. 302.

20. George Wright-Nooth, pp. 92, 113.

21. G.A. Leiper, pp. 89–94, 97–9. See Noel's letter dated 2 August 1971 to Betsy Treadgold, quoted in previous chapter.

22. John Luff, 1967, p. 166.

23. G.B. Endacott, 1964, p. 303.

24. 'When Noel went to camp, he took one book with him: Palgrave's *Golden Treasury.*' (Interview with Leslie Wright on 5 August 1997.)

25. George Wright-Nooth, p. 89.

26. *Captive Colony* by John Stericker, formerly administrative secretary at Stanley Internment Camp, Hong Kong. Typescript.

27. Carl T. Smith Collection.

28. Noel said in his letters to close friends that he had done so.

29. Noel later remembered the Comptons when the widow and daughter were in difficult straits and approached Noel for help. (Letter dated 4 June 1978 to Joan Scrivener.) He seemed puzzled as to why they needed help, noting that the Sassoons were a 'very very rich family'. (Letter dated 20 August 1978 to Joan Scrivener.) On 2 September 1978, he wrote: 'Harry Compton was Manager of Sassoons in 1918 and married Mimi about 1924. She had 2 children, Ronnie and Suzette. Harry was interned by the Japs with me in 1941 and released in 1945 and re-formed [rejoined ?] Sassoons. Then after a few months he retired to England and died.'

30. Noel Croucher's writings, as reproduced by John Luff, 1967, pp. 184–6.

31. Nigel Cameron, 1986, pp. 138–9. The story was not exclusive to Noel, of course — the Japanese-run, English-language *The Hong Kong News* also reported it.

32. Indeed, they do fill several books, notably Jean Gittins' *Stanley: Behind Barbed Wire.*

33. George Wright-Nooth, p. 121.

34. Barbara-Sue White, 1996, p. 216.

35. G.A. Leiper, p. 157.

36. G.B. Endacott and A. Birch, pp. 204–5.

37. Telephone interview with George Wright-Nooth on 5 December 1997.

38. Interview with Robert Minnitt on 5 July 1996.

39. George Wright-Nooth, pp. 139–41.

40. Nigel Cameron, 1986, pp. 139–42.

41. Interview with Lord Todd in Cambridge, 9–10 July 1997. 'We all heard the story of the bomb under his bed,' says Pat Loseby. (Interview in England on 5 July 1996.)

42. Noel Croucher's writings, reproduced by John Luff, 1967, pp. 221–2.

43. Noel Croucher's writings, as reproduced by John Luff, 1967, pp. 221–2.

44. George Wright-Nooth, pp. 242–3.

45. From John Stericker (no page numbers).

46. From John Stericker (no page numbers).

47. Jean Gittins, 1982, pp. 147–8.

48. George Wright-Nooth, p. 253.

49. Phone call with Michael Rawlinson on 19 August 1996 and interview on 29 October 1996.

50. Letter dated 1 March 1962 to Joan Scrivener.

51. It is believed (by May Ride, among others) that Noel was one of the donors, after the war, for a new chapel at St. Stephen's College. Though likely, this cannot be confirmed as no list of individual donors was kept.

52. John Luff, 1967, p. 215.

53. Letter dated 23 November 1962 to Joan Scrivener.

54. George Wright-Nooth, p. 248.

55. John Luff, 1967, pp. 204–13.

56. Nigel Cameron, 1986, p. 147.

57. Thanks to Richard Croucher for this and other correspondence.

58. Many stories exist of the miraculous survival of brandy (or whiskey) bottles. See Dick Wilson, p. 129. Duncan Graham also recalls Noel telling the story of his own brandy bottle.

59. Interview with Elizabeth and Allen Mills in London on 16 July 1996.

60. Interview with the late Leslie Wright in Hong Kong on 5 August 1997. Sister Barbara O'Sullivan recalls Noel telling her that the Japanese had covered the safe with newspapers and used it as a stand for their kettle. (Interview on 20 March 1998.)

61. Interview with G.O.W. Stewart in the Cotswolds on 20 March 1997.

62. G.A. Leiper details the shifts to which he and his colleagues at the Standard Chartered Bank resorted to in this endeavour. See G.A. Leiper, pp. 37, 77.

63. George Wright-Nooth, p. 153.

64. Interview with Marjorie Bray in Hong Kong on 23 April 1997.

65. 'I was in Singapore after the war, and Borneo and Kuala Lumpur. Noel's name was known. He was generally known as the richest white man east of Suez. I believe he also had business interests in Singapore.' (Interview with Revd John Chynchen in Hong Kong in August 1996.) Also: 'In 1946, he was

already venerable.' (Interview with Sir Jack Cater in Hong Kong on 11 February 1997.)

CHAPTER ELEVEN

1. Interview with Lord Lawrence Kadoorie in Hong Kong on 20 June 1985.

2. Acknowledgements, Chapter 13: 'The Road to Recovery' (pp. 75–88), John Luff, 1968.

3. Henry J. Lethbridge, 1969, p. 78.

4. 'First Annual Report of the Hong Kong War Memorial Fund Committee, 1947, Section 9, Ordinance 10/47', Health and Welfare Branch, Government Secretariat.

5. John Luff, 1968, p. 88.

6. Robin Hutcheon, 1983, p. 100. Back in 1940, Noel had lent his name to a controversy with this leading English-language daily. An unofficial member of the Legislative Council and fellow businessman, S.H. Dodwell wrote to the editor alleging the newspaper had German sympathies. Noel Croucher and A.L. Shields, the principal of Shewan Tomes & Company, supported Dodwell's views. The paper was outraged and published the correspondence, ignoring the complaint thereafter. See Robin Hutcheon, pp. 84–5.

7. Interview with Guy Sayer in London on 10 March 1997.

8. Interview with Wong Yue-nam on 24 September 1996.

9. Gillian Chambers, p. 75.

10. Gillian Chambers, p. 70.

11. Croucher papers; also Gillian Chambers, pp. 78, 82.

12. Interview with Richard Hownam-Meek in Hong Kong on 21 April 1997.

13. Interview with Gerald Carey in England on 13 July 1996.

14. Interview with Richard Croucher on 7 November 1996. Richard was at Oxford University after the war — Noel must have been pleased — but it did not last.

15. Anthony Lawrence, p. 158.

16. *Far Eastern Economic Review*, 16 October 1946.

17. *Far Eastern Economic Review*, 23 October 1946.

18. *Far Eastern Economic Review*, 12 March 1947.

19. See Chapter Nine of this book.

20. Robin Barrie and Gretchen Tricker, p. 51.

21. J.P. Braga, p. 259.

22. J.P. Braga, p. 259.

23. Francis Zimmern, as quoted in Stock Exchange of Hong Kong, pp. 14–5.

24. Interview with Lord Michael Sandberg at St. James' Square on 3 July 1996.

25. Interview with F.A. Silva on 28 October 1996.

26. Interview with Allen Mills on 16 July 1996.

27. Interview with Francis Zimmern on 25 September 1996.

28. Interview with G.O.W. Stewart on 20 March 1997.

29. Telephone call with Florence Lo on 2 October 1996.

30. Interview with Florence Lo on 6 June 1996.

31. Company Registration Records, Number 2700, 1948, and 1989.

32. Interview with Joyce Symons at Royal Overseas Club in London on 17 June 1996.

33. See Wong Siu-lin.

34. Robin Barrie and Gretchen Tricker, p. 55.

35. Noel later referred his son to a Wheelock Marden firm, Dominion Insurance, where Richard Croucher worked for a while. Noel later chided Richard for failing to build on this opportunity to be with one of the biggest firms in the East.

36. Interview with Guy Sayer in London on 10 March 1997.

37. Interview with Edward Lawrence on 5 November 1996.

38. John Marden, quoted in Robin Hutcheon, 1987, p. 78.

39. *Far Eastern Economic Review*, 2 December 1954.

40. Report of Annual General Meeting for Wheelock Marden & Company, *Far Eastern Economic Review*, 15 November 1956.

41. Telephone interview with George Cam, London, on 7 March 1997.

42. Interview with Peter Vine on 16 February 1997.

43. Robin Barrie and Gretchen Tricker, p. 56.

44. *South China Morning Post*, 16 March 1980.

45. Robin Hutcheon, 1987, p. 78.

46. Interview with Michael Rawlinson on 29 October 1996. Howard Rough, the Royal Society's founder, was a keen Freemason as are many society members — but not Noel.

47. Interview with John Marden on 15 November 1996.

48. Interview with Anne Marden on 15 November 1996.

49. If one lacked breeding, it helped to be a Freemason. There was marked overlap through the years between office-bearing Freemasons, office-holding members of the Royal Society of St. George, committee members at St. John's Cathedral, and rankings at the top of team sports. Top Freemasons were often top policemen. Even in the 1980s and '90s, some St. George Society members admit its leadership was then dominated by police and freemasonry. But Noel was not a Mason.

50. Phone call with Michael Rawlinson on 19 August 1996.

51. See Chapter Three of this book.

52. 'St George goes to the rescue', *Eastern Express*, 12 December 1995. In 1995, the society repatriated a young English bricklayer after he lost his job at the new airport, and a seriously ill former journalist was sent home.

53. Interview with Pat Loseby on 5 July 1996.

54. Minutes, the Royal Society of St. George, Hong Kong Branch, 30 June 1974. With thanks to the Society for permission to read the minutes.

55. Phone call with Michael Rawlinson on 19 August 1996.

56. Interview with Guy Sayer on 10 March 1997. Guy Sayer's father, G.R. Sayer, was a government cadet in Hong Kong from 1908, and Guy himself had a lifelong career in the Hong Kong & Shanghai Banking Corporation.

CHAPTER TWELVE

1. Richard Hownam-Meek confirms, 'Yes, Coote was a good friend of Noel's.' A Cable & Wireless publication (received thanks to Alan Hooper) recorded Frederick Stanley Coote's death in 1967. A New Zealander, he reached Singapore with the Eastern Extension Australasia and China Telegraph Company by 1930, serving also in Batavia (now Jakarta). He arrived in Hong Kong in 1935, Shanghai in 1937 and was back in Hong Kong after the war where he was appointed divisional manager for the Far East of what was then Cable & Wireless in 1951. He stayed in Hong Kong after retirement in 1956, managing Redifusion (HK) Ltd. His war work with the ambulance service resulted in his knighthood.

2. From Croucher's own papers, translated by Carl T. Smith and Dolly Dabuco.

3. Interview with Richard Hownam-Meek in Hong Kong on 21 April 1997.

4. Gillian Chambers, 1993, p. 87.

5. Gillian Chambers, 1993, p. 88.

6. Interview with Bill Hancock on 20 July 1996.

7. Gillian Chambers, 1993, pp. 91–3.

8. Gillian Chambers, 1993, p. 93.

9. This, and the previous paragraph, from Gillian Chambers, 1993, p. 104.

10. In 1996–97, the club was split on whether royal patronage of the club should continue following China's resumption of sovereignty over Hong Kong.

11. Interview with Pat Loseby on 5 July 1996.

12. Interview with Richard Hownam-Meek on 21 April 1997.

13. Interview with Brian McElney in Bath on 5 March 1997 and phone call with Dr Freddie Watson on 24 March 1997.

14. Phone call on 23 March 1997 with Bridget Corrie-Hall, daughter of the former Mrs Dalziel and Jack Armstrong.

15. Interview with Richard Hownam-Meek in Hong Kong on 21 April 1997.

16. Interview with Gerald Carey on 13 July 1996.

17. Letters to Joan Scrivener dated 19 May 1957 and 21 October 1957.

18. Many thanks to Sir Gordon MacWhinnie, 4 February 1997.

19. Spencer Robinson, pp. 100–1.

20. Interview with Leslie Wright on 5 August 1997.

21. Interview with Peter Vine on 26 February 1997.

22. Letter dated 6 September 1997 from Ansie Lee Sperry.

23. See Chapter Nine of this book.

24. Letter dated 22 February 1997 from Brian Johnson.

25. Letter dated 6 September 1997 from Ansie Lee Sperry.

26. Interview with Bunny Browne, 18/19 July 1997.

27. Interview with Bill and Betty Hancock in Combe Flory, England, on 20 July 1996.

28. Phone call with Brian Tisdall on 21 November 1996.

29. Letter dated 22 February 1997 from Brian Johnson.

30. Interview with Joyce Symons at Royal Overseas Club in London on 17 June 1996.

31. 'Mr Croucher could count to ten and say hello in Cantonese.' (Interview with Wong Yue-nam and Florence Lo on 24 September 1997.)

32. Noel Croucher later wrote a reference for Wong Yue-nam on 20 July 1979, citing his long and devoted service. Noel described Wong as 'an honest,

hardworking and reliable man to whom I can entrust any duty and his work is always very satisfactory. I can guarantee he will be an excellent office boy to any employer...'

33. Interview with Cheung Kam-chuen on 30 October 1996.

34. Interview with Richard Stoneman on 27 August 1996.

35. See letter dated 1 May 1961 from Noel Croucher to Joan Scrivener.

36. Fax dated 13 November 1996 from Norma Rasmussen from Italy. Noel knew Norma's father-in-law, M.C. Rasmussen, who from 1906 worked at Green Island Cement Co., then managed by Shewan Tomes. Her husband was B.R. Rasmussen.

37. Interview with Ian MacCallum on 2 July 1996.

38. Interview with Wynne Ward on 25 February 1997.

39. Interview with Anne Sorby in Markbeech Kent on 13 July 1996. Terence Sorby was born in Hong Kong. His father, Vincent, was with Hong Kong Electric (see Austin Coates, 1977) but was killed in 1941. Terence had been fighting in Europe but came back after the war to find his mother. She, being Irish, had spent it in Macao.

40. Interview with Leslie Wright on 5 August 1997.

41. Letter dated 15 May 1977 to Joan Scrivener.

42. Letters to Joan Scrivener dated 19 May 1977 and 13 June 1977.

43. See Johannes Nieuhof.

44. '17th Century China survey is Fascinating Reading Today', by Jill Doggett, *South China Morning Post,* 8 June 1972.

45. Kevin Sinclair, *South China Morning Post,* 16 March 1980.

46. Interview with Teresa Price on 11 June 1996.

47. Phone call with George Wright-Nooth on 5 December 1997.

48. Letters dated 28 September 1976 to Richard Croucher.

CHAPTER THIRTEEN

1. A typical comment of many who knew Noel then was that from Robert Minnitt: 'I don't think he was terribly active in the public sphere but he was always there.' (Interview in England on 5 July 1996.)

2. F.D. Ommanney, 1962a, p. 207.

3. Interview with Marjorie Bray in Hong Kong on 23 April 1997.

4. Thanks to Lilianna Lau, Juvenile Care Centre, for her fax dated 18

November 1997. Ms Lau also confirms that Noel donated $150,000 to the JCC premises at 1a Lower Albert Road, circa 1951.

5. Thanks to Sir Y.K. Kan, vice-patron of Stanley Sea School. Phone call, 12 January 1998.

6. Phone call with Captain David Wright on 15 March 1998.

7. Former Executive and Legislative Councillor, Jimmy MacGregor, also recalls occasions on which Noel promised to match others' contributions, 'dollar for dollar', but that when the time came, 'Noel's memory came unstuck. He gave me a rough time over Sandy Bay and should have been working with me.' (Interview with Jimmy MacGregor on 23 January 1997.)

8. Interview with Sister Barbara on 20 March 1998.

9. Interview with Jenny Hodgson in Hong Kong on 16 January 1997.

10. Thanks to Barbara Rogers for her fax dated 1 February 1997.

11. Clipping is undated, but probably from 1965 or 1966. Sir David Trench was Governor, 1964–71.

12. Phone call with Brian Tisdall on 21 November 1996.

13. Interview with Lord Michael Sandberg in London on 3 July 1996.

14. Interview with Peter Vine on 26 February 1997.

15. Interview with Sister Barbara on 20 March 1998.

16. Interview with Richard Stoneman on 27 August 1996. See E.H. Paterson for more about the hospital.

17. Letter dated 22 February 1997 from Brian Johnson.

18. Phone call with Bernard Mellor on 19 March 1997.

19. See Geoffrey C. Gunn, p. 87: 'The Banco Ultramarino dealt with the Persian opium export monopoly ... and, in turn, their resident broker in Macao, a certain Nemazee.' See also Emily Hahn, 1944, p. 323: 'Nemazee's house was a clearing ground for prison-camp news.'

20. *South China Morning Post*, 9 November 1954.

21. Letter dated 20 August 1996 from Ms Ada Kwan, director, Hong Kong Society for the Protection of Children.

22. Interview with Betty Forsgate at the Peak, Hong Kong, on 20 February 1997.

23. Phone call with Sir John Cowperthwaite on 7 March 1997.

24. Sir John Cowperthwaite, quoted in *Asian Wall Street Journal*, 30 June 1997.

25. Letter dated 9 January 1962 from Noel Croucher to Joan Scrivener.

26. From Rola Luzzato. P.C. Lee's *Hongkong Album* (p. 62) features Noel Croucher, adding his home address (555 The Peak), telephone no. (96013) and birthday.

27. *Far Eastern Economic Review,* 2 April 1959.

28. Robin Barrie and Gretchen Tricker, p. 58.

29. Phone call with Jose Olbes on 10 June 1997.

30. 'Hong Kong Hongs with Long Histories & British Connections' by Dan Waters, *Journal of the Hong Kong Branch of the Royal Asiatic Society* 30 (1990), p. 253.

31. *Far Eastern Economic Review* 21 (1956).

32. Phone call with Brian Tisdall on 21 November 1996.

33. Interview with Leslie Wright on 5 August 1997.

34. Interview with Duncan Graham in Hong Kong on 4 September 1996.

35. Interview with Richard Hownam-Meek on 21 April 1997.

36. Interview with Brian Johnson on 5 March 1997.

37. Interview with Allen Mills on 16 July 1996.

38. Interview with Guy Sayer in London on 10 March 1997.

39. Interview with Peter Vine on 26 February 1997.

40. Interview with Leslie Wright on 5 August 1997.

41. Interview with Sir Sidney Gordon on 27 September 1996.

42. Interview with Nigel Rigg in Forest Row, England, on 6 March 1997.

43. Interview with Sir, now Lord, Michael Sandberg at St. James Square in London on 3 July 1996.

44. Interview with G.O.W. Stewart in the Cotswolds on 20 March 1997.

45. Alan Chalkley, p. 37. Guardian Assurance merged with Royal Exchange Assurance and became Guardian Royal in 1968.

46. See Appendix: Letters to Joan Scrivener.

47. Letters to Joan Scrivener dated 11 March 1957 and 10 August 1960.

CHAPTER FOURTEEN

1. Poem *Finis* by Walter Savage Landor (1775–1864), quoted by Noel Croucher in a letter dated 1 March 1962 to Joan Scrivener.

2. Interview with Wynne Ward on 25 February 1997. Wynne Ward used to play gin rummy every week or so with Noel at his house and remembers several curry lunches there on a Saturday, in the company of Jack and Greta Hobbs.

3. *Far Eastern Economic Review* 33, fourth issue (1961).

4. Interview with Rosie Potts on 19 November 1997.

5. Interview with Guy Sayer in London on 10 March 1997.

6. Interview with Guy Sayer in London on 10 March 1997.

7. Interview with Leslie Wright on 5 August 1997.

8. Interview with Francis Zimmern on 25 September 1996.

9. Was Noel Croucher a taipan? H.M. Gerald Forsgate replied, 'No, no, certainly not! That's for managers of companies. I was general manager of Kowloon Wharf from 1959 and captain of the rugby!' (Interview on 20 February 1997.)

10. Telephone interview with Jose Olbes on 10 June 1997.

11. Interview with Ronnie Ross in Hong Kong on 22 April 1997.

12. Interview with Eddie Lawrence on 5 November 1996.

13. Telephone interview with George Cam, London, on 7 March 1997.

14. Interview with Pat Loseby on 5 July 1996.

15. Telephone interview with Joy Dickinson on 16 October 1996.

16. The Croucher Index Book. Details from the British Post Office's *Directory*, and *Kelly's Directory*, 1967.

17. Interview with Bill and Betty Hancock in Combe Flory on 20 July 1996.

18. Letters to Joan Scrivener dated 26 May 1967 and 14 July 1967.

19. Letters to Joan Scrivener dated 2 August 1967 and 24 August 1967.

20. Robin Hutcheon, 1983, pp. 126, 134.

21. 'I have not been able to ascertain what sum Mr Croucher donated in 1961, nor the precise use to which it was put, the usual Library resources having failed me...' (Letter dated 4 February 1997 from Dr E.S. Leedham-Green, deputy keeper, Cambridge University Archives.)

22. Noel had little connection with Oxford University. On 11 February 1966, he was approached by the Oxford Colonial Records Project (established in 1963), which offered a home to papers in private hands which could be useful for future research into the colonial period. Noel's name had been forwarded by Colonel Owen Hughes. But Noel replied in August 1966 to say he had nothing to offer the project. (Thanks to Amanda Hill, Rhodes House Library Archivist, for her letter dated 17 March 1997.)

23. *The Times* published a Letter to the Editor, 12 November 1966. *The Times Literary Supplement*, 24 November 1966, also carried coverage of the crisis. See *Magdalene College Magazine and Record* New Series, No. 11: 1966–67.

24. Letter on Boxing Day, 1975, from Noel Croucher to his son Richard. When Noel wrote, 'the manuscript remained at Cambridge', he was probably referring to the fact that after the first appeal was made to keep the Ovid manuscript in England, the decision was taken to preserve it by producing a facsimile edition of the entire fifteen books of Caxton's Ovid. *The Times*, 18 September 1968, reported that 'at the British Museum yesterday with grateful oratory a group of eminent British scholars presented two massive, leather-bound gold-tooled tomes to an American businessman, and so ended one of the most extraordinary stories in the history of publishing.'

25. Letter dated 4 February 1997 from Dr E.S. Leedham-Green, deputy keeper, Cambridge University Archives.

26. A.B. Emden, p. 170.

27. Doreen King, p. 38. See also *St. John's Review* (September 1949), p. 290: 'Mr N.V. Croucher has signified that he is willing to give a part or the whole of the cost either of restoring the former East Window or purchasing a new one. Several of the best English firms have been consulted...'

28. *St. John's Review* XXIII, no. 11 (November 1956). See also *St. John's Review* (March 1956).

29. Letter dated 26 February 1997 from The Revd John W. Foster.

30. Letter dated 26 February 1997 from The Revd John W. Foster.

31. Letter dated 5 July 1980 from The Very Revd S.F. Sidebotham, Dean, St. John's Cathedral. Emphasis added. Mrs Marjorie Bray, a long-standing member of the Cathedral Council says, 'When Dowbiggin was there, he was the Big Old Man of the Cathedral. In a way, Noel stepped into his shoes.' (Interview in Hong Kong on 23 April 1997.)

32. Letter dated 8 June 1962 to Joan Scrivener. Joan Fontaine confirms the acquaintance: 'I believe I met Mr Croucher and he assisted me in obtaining a lovely Guache painting by a Chinese artist and sending it to me in New York. I still have the painting, signed in Chinese characters. ... It has been in my bedrooms — Brentwood, New York City or Carmel — ever since it arrived from Hong Kong. Lovely to see upon awakening.' (Letters from Joan Fontaine postmarked 21 August and 2 September 1998.) Also, see Chapter Eight of this book.

33. Letter dated 8 March 1963 to Joan Scrivener.

34. Letter dated 31 May 1961 to Joan Scrivener.

35. Letter dated 16 October 1962 to Joan Scrivener.

36. 'Dear Joan... If you were here I'd give you a kiss. Now I come to think of

it, I never have kissed you have I? ...' (Letter dated 5 January 1966 to Joan Scrivener.) Note: this contradicts his recording of a kiss circa 1957/58.

37. Letter dated 31 May 1961 to Joan Scrivener. Emphasis is Noel's own.

38. Letter dated 16 November 1961 to Joan Scrivener.

39. Letter dated 7 May 1964 to Joan Scrivener.

40. Letter dated 8/9 August 1968 to Joan Scrivener.

41. Letters dated 30 April 1966 and 12 May 1966 to Joan Scrivener.

42. Letter dated 13 July 1968 to Joan Scrivener.

CHAPTER FIFTEEN

1. Letter dated 3 April 1970 to Joan Scrivener.

2. His fascinating life is the subject of a forthcoming biography by Frank Bren. A more lurid account is *Donald of China* by Earl Albert Selle. It was Donald who persuaded General and Madame Chiang to go on a national tour in 1934 to increase their popular support. In particular he was credited with resolving the Sian (Xi'an) incident in December 1936. The Young Marshal's troops had kidnapped Chiang Kai-shek, in disagreements over whether republicans should be fighting the communist Chinese or the invading Japanese, and it was Donald who mediated an accord on uniting China.

3. Letter dated 12 November 1970 from Noel Croucher to Mrs Mary Donald, care of Mrs Nunley of California.

4. 'He [Donald] was as reticent about the details of his own personal life as he was about the lives of others. He said that he was married to an Australian girl in Hong Kong in 1905. Their daughter was born a few years later. Around 1912, his wife said to him, "Don, you are married more to China than to me." With the daughter, she had left him forever.' (Earl Albert Selle, p. 8.) A Sydney newspaper piece in about 1945, titled ' "Chinese" Donald—Mystery Man', states: 'Not generally known is the fact that Donald is married, with a daughter, Muriel, now nearing 30. He was married, in China, to Mary Wall, of Sydney'.

5. Letter dated 6 November 1970 from K.C. Yu to Noel Croucher.

6. Earl Albert Selle, p. 155.

7. Earl Albert Selle, pp. 214–6.

8. Letter dated 12 November 1970 from Noel Croucher to Mrs Mary Donald, care of Mrs Nunley of California.

9. Letter dated 14 January 1971 from Muriel Donald to Noel Croucher.

10. Letter dated 2 January ?1976 to Richard.

11. Interview with Dr Diana Siu on 10 September 1996. Curiously, Dr Siu's husband was to become a recipient of Noel's posthumous generosity, securing a grant from The Croucher Foundation.

12. Noel's letters to Joan Scrivener, in this case on 5 February 1976.

13. 'This I still feel is one of the main purposes of The Croucher Foundation. I always think that our mission, if we can call it such, must be to bring up the young people, and bring up the outstanding among the young people.' (Interview with Rayson Huang in Cambridge on 9 July 1996.)

14. Letter dated 3 October 1996 from Tracy Poon, administrative officer, Ebenezer School and Home for the Blind, Hong Kong.

15. Letter dated 4 September 1978 from Lore Spilker, acting principal, Ebenezer School and Home for the Blind, to Mrs Roberts, a Hong Kong Bank Trust Officer, acknowledging receipt of the money; and letter dated 8 September 1978 from Mrs Roberts to Noel Croucher.

16. Interview with Keith Marshall in Merseyside on 4 March 1997.

17. Letter dated 12 June 1975 from M. Pratt, assistant secretary of the society, to Miss M.B. Spooner of the university, Hong Kong University Registry Files.

18. Letter dated 10 July 1976 to Richard Croucher.

19. Robin Hutcheon, 1983, pp. 126, 147.

20. Robin Barrie and Gretchen Tricker, p. 65.

21. Interview with Malcolm Surry, formerly at the Securities Commission, and Business Editor at the *South China Morning Post*, Hong Kong, on 21 June 1996.

22. Robin Barrie and Gretchen Tricker, p. 65.

23. Interview with Duncan Graham in Hong Kong on 4 September 1996.

24. Letter dated 2 June 1973 to Joan Scrivener.

25. Robin Barrie and Gretchen Tricker, p. 81.

26. See Nigel Cameron, 1986, Chapter 10.

27. Interview with Malcolm Surry in Hong Kong on 21 June 1996.

28. Minutes of the board meeting held on 10 July 1975 at 9.30 a.m., in the boardroom of the Lee Hysan Estate Company Limited, 25th Floor, Prince's Building, Hong Kong. Many thanks to Malcolm Mathews, managing director, HK and China Gas Company for his letter dated 24 October 1996.

29. Minutes of the board meeting of HK and China Gas Company held on 19 August 1975.

30. Interview with Francis Zimmern on 25 September 1996.

31. Letter dated 4 July 1977 from Noel to Richard Croucher.

32. Letter dated 5 October ?1976 from Noel to Richard Croucher.

33. Letter dated 2 November 1976 to Joan Scrivener.

34. See *Private Eye*, August to November 1976, March 1977 and July 1977. A series titled 'Changi Jim Rides Again' ran on 14 October, 28 October, 11 November, 25 November, and 23 December 1977. A critique of the financing for the Mass Transit Railway Corporation in Hong Kong — a subject we know from Noel's column in *The Star* that he also felt strongly about — was printed in *Private Eye*, 26 November and 10 December 1976. Also, the 'Gulf Arabian debacle in Hong Kong' mentions broker Alan Knapp and Jardine Fleming on 2 September 1977.

35. N.M. Rothschild & Sons were at pains to reimburse clients, but the episode altered Noel's plans. (Letter dated 17 August 1998 from Victor Gray, The Rothschild Archive.) See also 'Clash of the Corporate Titans — Some leading names in Hongkong and international finance are still squabbling over a seven-year-old dispute' by James Bartholomew, *Far Eastern Economic Review*, 12 June 1980. See also Guy de Rothschild, pp. 158–9.

36. *Far Eastern Economic Review*, 3 March 1979.

37. Interview with Duncan Graham in Hong Kong on 4 September 1996.

38. Interview with Sir Jack Cater in Hong Kong on 11 February 1997.

39. 'Of the civilians in Hong Kong, all that we shall say is that some are nicer than others. The number ones, twos and even threes of the great commercial firms are sometimes social successes. There are distinctions, however, that are not easy to understand. Why should pig-iron turn up its nose at twopenny nails? To this distant land people come with double names that sound formidable until it is discovered that the double-barrelled ones discharge very small shot at home. The Service people call the civilians dollar-snatchers, and the latter think of the former as dollar-lackers.' (The Revd E.J. Hardy, chaplain to the British Forces in Hong Kong, in Barbara-Sue White, 1996, pp. 142–3.)

40. Interview with Joyce Symons at Royal Overseas Club in London on 17 June 1996.

41. Interview with Peter Vine on 26 February 1997.

42. Letter to the Editor, *South China Morning Post*, Hong Kong, 12 April 1980.

43. Interview with Elizabeth and Allen Mills (the latter being Assistant Commissioner for Securities in Hong Kong 1977–84) in London on 16 July 1996. Yuen Lai, Noel's amah for fourteen years, outlived her boss and was mentioned in his will.

44. Thanks to Elizabeth Mills' diary, we know the Mills dined with Noel on 16 August 1978; had lunch on 5 April 1979, when Elizabeth had to pick Noel up as there were no buses running on the Ching Ming Festival; lunched again on 6 April 1979; and dined at the Hong Kong Club on 24 August 1979.

45. Interview with Peter Vine on 26 February 1997.

46. Fax dated 13 February 1997 from Judy Green.

47. Telephone interview with Joy Dickinson, Spain, on 16 October 1996. Also: 'On my 25th wedding anniversary my husband and I put a little notice in the paper. Then there was a little parcel for me in the office. It was a five shilling piece, dated from the year we were married. So thoughtful! It was from Noel. And I remember I got on a bus once to go somewhere, and there was Croucher! He said his car was out of order. But for him to be on the bus!'

48. *South China Morning Post*, 16 March 1980.

49. Interview with Gerald Carey on 13 July 1996.

50. Interview with Sir Jack Cater in Hong Kong on 11 February 1997.

51. Letter dated 29 September 1976 to Richard Croucher.

52. Letter dated 23 June 1976 to Richard Croucher.

53. Letter dated 4 July 1971 to Joan Scrivener.

CHAPTER SIXTEEN

1. Letter dated 22 February 1997 from Brian Johnson.

2. *Wanted*, written by Josiah Gilbert Holland, 1819–81, American editor, writer and poet. This was a favourite poem of Noel Croucher's — he kept a copy of it all his life and had it printed on Christmas cards he sent to friends.

3. Phone call with Brian Tisdall on 21 November 1996.

4. Noel might have recalled that John Crowcher was at Gonville in the 1400s.

5. Letter dated 27 May 1977 to Joan Scrivener.

6. Interview with Lady May Ride in Bournemouth on 18 July 1996.

7. See Alexander Robertus Todd, 1983.

8. Letter dated 19 June 1978 to Joan Scrivener.

9. Interviews in Cambridge on 9 and 10 July 1996. Lord Todd died on 10 January 1997. Lord Todd's first letter dated 23 June 1978 began: 'Dear Mr Croucher, I have just had a letter from Lady Ride who is a very old friend of ours in which she tells me that you wish to do something to help finance students from Hong Kong...'

10. Dr Joseph Needham, 1900– , historian of science, had a consuming interest in the Chinese tradition of medicine, science and technology, and published *Science and Civilisation in China* in seven volumes from 1954.

11. The liquidation of Croucher's Commonwealth Investments (Panama) Inc. was required to realise the money for the foundation. This, being more complex than originally hoped, was not completed until March 1984. (See Alexander Robertus Todd, 1984.)

12. Letter dated 29 November 1978 to Lord Todd.

13. Interview with Lord Sandberg in London on 3 July 1996. Noel put it differently in his letter dated 8 January 1979 to Lord Todd: 'When I told Mr Sandberg, Chief Manager of the H.K. & Shanghai Bank that you and Lady Todd were among my guests he was very, very pleased and in the circumstances I asked him to be our host and he was delighted...'

14. Interviews with Lord Todd on 9 and 10 July 1996.

15. *The Cambridge Biographical Encyclopaedia*, p. 705.

16. Thanks to Richard Marshall, finance director, The Nuffield Foundation, 28 Bedford Square, London, for his letter dated 27 February 1997. See also The Nuffield Foundation.

17. Letter dated 7 June 1979 from Lord Todd to Noel Croucher.

18. Letter dated 3 December 1979 from Lord Todd to Noel Croucher.

19. Fax dated 14 March 1998 from Ian MacCallum.

20. Letter dated 12 February 1980 from Lord Todd to Noel Croucher.

21. Interview with Rayson Huang in Cambridge on 9 July 1996.

22. Letter dated 27 November 1996 from Sir Robert Black.

23. This story could not be confirmed, but is certainly possible.

24. Letter dated 14 July 1996 from Lord MacLehose of Beoch, Ayrshire. Noel had kept a letter from Governor MacLehose which thanked him for his gift of an 'album of cuttings from newspapers about the visit [to Hong Kong] of the previous Duke of Edinburgh'. This note, dated 9 May 1975, followed the visit of the Queen and Prince Philip to Hong Kong in 1975.

25. Interview with Lord Lawrence Kadoorie in Hong Kong on 20 June 1985.

26. The source is a close friend of Noel's who would prefer to remain nameless. Interview in Hong Kong on 24 August 1996.

27. See Chapter 2, ' "Kindness and Reasons": William Lovett and Education', by Brian Harrison, in Gordon Marsden, pp. 13–29.

28. Letter dated 20 January 1980 to Richard Croucher.

29. Letter dated 20 January 1980 to Richard Croucher.

30. Letter dated 20 January 1980 to Richard Croucher.

31. Letter dated 24 January 1980 from Noel to Richard Croucher.

32. Interview with Ian MacCallum on 2 July 1996.

33. An Internet search shows she may have died in 1991.

34. Interview with Lady May Ride on 18 July 1996.

35. Interview with Brian McElney in Bath on 5 March 1997.

36. Interview with Hans Michael Jebsen in Hong Kong on 10 September 1997.

37. Gweilo, literally male devil; originally a derogatory term for white men, but now a general colloquial term for expatriates used by expats themselves.

38. Interview with Wong Yue-nam on 24 September 1996.

39. Interview with Lady May Ride on 18 July 1996.

40. Interview with Florence Lo on 6 June 1996.

41. Interview with Ian MacCallum in London on 2 July 1996. Anderson & Partners could not confirm or deny the story of Noel's death but the evidence of Wong Yue-nam among others is convincing.

42. *South China Morning Post,* 16 March 1980.

43. Jack and Johanna Jones, 1987, p. 40.

44. The office of Li Ka-shing was unable to confirm the appointment: 'We regret to inform you that Mr Li has no recollection of an acquaintance with the late Mr Croucher...' (Letter dated 18 June 1997 from Amy Au, manager, chairman's office, Cheung Kong (Holdings) Limited.)

45. 'Businessman's Final Farewell', *South China Morning Post,* 13 March 1980.

46. Interview with May Ride in Bournemouth on 18 July 1996.

47. Phone call with Richard Croucher on 20 November 1996.

48. When Jack Hobbs said he wanted to be stockbroker, Noel said: 'Right you have to do two things — you have to join the HK club, which he arranged, and, you must open an account with the HK Bank, which I did...' Jack then decided to stay in government. (Interview on 11 June 1996.)

BIBLIOGRAPHY

DOCUMENTS AND PERIODICALS

The Archivo Historico de Macao
Asian Wall Street Journal
British Post Office's *Directory*
China Mail
Daily Press
Far Eastern Economic Review
Financial Times
Hong Kong Company Registration Records
Hong Kong General Chamber of Commerce (annual reports)
Hong Kong Standard
Hong Kong Tatler
Hong Kong Telegraph
Hong Kong University Registry Files
Journal of the Hong Kong Branch of the Royal Asiatic Society
Kelly's Directory
Legislative Council (proceedings, 1890–91)
Private Eye
The Royal Society of St. George, Hong Kong Branch (minutes)
South China Morning Post
Special 1992–97. From the Macau Government Media Bureau, Avenida da
    Amizade, 876, Edificio Marina Gardens, 15/E, Macau.
St. John's [Cathedral] *Review*
The Stock Exchange of Hong Kong (annual reports)
The Times (London)

REFERENCE WORKS

The Cambridge Biographical Encyclopedia. David Crystal. Cambridge University Press,
    1994.

The Concise Oxford Dictionary

The Directory and Chronicle for China, Japan, Corea, Indo-China, Straits Settlements, Malay States, Siam, Netherlands, India, Borneo, the Philippines, etc., 1903–41, annual. Hong Kong Daily Press Office.

Golden Guide To Hong Kong and Macau. Hong Kong: Far Eastern Economic Review Ltd., 1969.

Webster's Biographical Dictionary. USA. 1953.

Who's Who 1993. A & C Black, 145th annual edition.

Who's Who in the Far East 1906–7. Hong Kong: China Mail.

Who's Who in Hong Kong. 1980, 1988. Kevin Sinclair.

BOOKS

Airlie, Shiona. *Thistle and Bamboo, The Life and Times of Sir James Stewart Lockhart.* Hong Kong: Oxford University Press, 1989.

Archer, C.S. *China Servant.* London: Collins, 1946.

Bard, Solomon. *Traders of Hong Kong: Some Foreign Merchant Houses, 1841–1899.* Hong Kong: Urban Council, 1993.

Barrie, Robin and Gretchen Tricker. *Shares in Hong Kong.* Hong Kong: The Stock Exchange of Hong Kong, 1991.

Bartholomew, James. 'Clash of the Corporate Titans — Some leading names in Hongkong and international finance are still squabbling over a seven-year-old dispute.' *Far Eastern Economic Review* (12 June 1980).

Bird Angus, Marjorie. *Bamboo Connection, Recollections of the China Coast.* Hong Kong: Heinemann Asia, 1985.

Bird, Isabella. *The Golden Chersonese.* London: Century Publishing, 1983. (First published by John Murray in 1883.)

Blyth, Sally and Ian Wotherspoon. *Hong Kong Remembers.* Hong Kong: Oxford University Press, 1996.

Bowie, Dr Gavin G.S. *Eastleigh, Bishopstoke and Chandlers Ford.* European Library — Zaltbommel/Netherlands MCMLXXXVI.

Braga, J.M., ed. *Hong Kong Business Symposium.* Hong Kong: South China Morning Post Publications, 1957.

Cameron, Nigel. *The Hongkong Land Company Ltd. — A brief history.* Hong Kong: Hongkong Land, 1979.

—— *The Milky Way, The History of Dairy Farm.* Hong Kong: The Dairy Farm Company Ltd., 1986.

Chalkley, Alan. *Adventures and Perils, The First 150 Years of Union Insurance Society of Canton, Ltd.* Hong Kong: Union Insurance, 1985.

Chambers, Gillian. *Eastern Waters, Eastern Winds — A History of the Royal Hong Kong Yacht Club.* Hong Kong: Royal Hong Kong Yacht Club, November 1993.

Chan, Anthony B. *Li Ka-Shing, Hong Kong's Elusive Billionaire.* Hong Kong: Oxford University Press, 1996.

Chan, W.K. *The Making of Hong Kong Society, Three Studies of Class Formation in Early Hong Kong.* Oxford: Clarendon Press, 1991.

Cheng, Irene (Ho Tung). *Clara Ho Tung, a Hong Kong Lady, her Family and her Times.* Hong Kong: Chinese University of Hong Kong, 1976.

Chesney, Neville, ed. *The Clubs of Hong Kong.* Hong Kong: Illustrated Magazine Publishing Co. Ltd., 1981.

Clarke, Kathleen. *Civic Pride Engendered and Remembered.* Southampton: K.M. Clarke, 1995.

Coates, Austin. *Prelude to Hong Kong (Macao and the British 1637–1842).* London: Routledge & Kegan Paul, 1966.

—— *A Mountain of Light. The Story of the Hong Kong Electric Company.* Hong Kong: Heinemann, 1977.

—— *Whampoa — Ships on the Shore.* Hong Kong: Hong Kong & Whampoa Dock Company Limited, 1980.

—— *China Races.* Hong Kong: Oxford University Press, 1983, 1994.

—— *Quick Tidings of Hong Kong.* Hong Kong: Oxford University Press, 1990.

Coe, Jonathan. *What A Carve-Up.* London: Penguin, 1994.

Cohen, Paul A. *History in Three Keys — The Boxers as Event, Experience, and Myth.* New York: Columbia University Press, 1997.

Cooper, John. *Colony in Conflict, HK Disturbances May 67–Jan 68.* Hong Kong: Swindons, 1970.

Corner in Ropes, The History of the 'Corner' together with a Report of the Sensational Trial, Potts v. Rustomjee, reprinted from *Hong Kong Telegraph,* 16 July 1889.

Courtauld, Caroline and May Holdsworth. *The Hong Kong Story.* Hong Kong: Oxford University Press, 1997.

Cox, Gordon Daubney. *Eastleigh, The Archive Photographs Series.* UK: Chalford Publishing Company, 1996.

Cremer, R.D., ed. *Macau City of Commerce and Culture.* Hong Kong: University of East Asia Press Ltd., 1987.

Craik, Mrs (aka Dinah Maria Mulock). *John Halifax, Gentleman.* England: Collins, 1954. (First published in 1856.)

Crisswell, Colin. *The Taipans, Hong Kong's Merchant Princes.* Hong Kong: Oxford University Press, 1981.

Crisswell, Colin and Mike Watson. *The Royal Hong Kong Police 1841–1945.* Hong Kong: Macmillan, 1982.

Crocombe, Leonard. *Slow Ship to Hong Kong.* London: Edward Stanford Limited, 1951.

Cumine, Eric. *Hong Kong Ways & Byways.* Hong Kong: Belongers' Publications, 1981.

Duncanson, Dennis J. 'Ho Chi Minh in Hong Kong 1931-32'. *China Quarterly,* 1974.

Edel, Leon. *Writing Lives, Principia Biographica.* New York: W.W Norton & Company, 1959, 1984.

Emden, A.B. *A Biographical Register of the University of Cambridge to 1500.* Cambridge University Press, 1963.

Endacott, G.B. *A History of Hong Kong.* Hong Kong: Oxford University Press, 1964.

—— *Government & People in Hong Kong.* Hong Kong: Oxford University Press, 1964.

Endacott, G.B. and A. Birch. *Hong Kong Eclipse.* Hong Kong: Oxford University Press, 1978.

Feldwick, Walter, editor-in-chief. *Present Day Impressions of the Far East and Prominent and Progressive Chinese at Home and Abroad: the history, people, commerce, industries and resources of China, Hong Kong, Indo-China, Malaya and Netherlands India.* London: Globe Encyclopaedia, 1917.

Field, Ellen. *Twilight in Hong Kong.* London: Frederick Muller Ltd., 1960.

Forster, L. *Echoes of Hong Kong and Beyond.* Hong Kong: Ye Olde Printerie, 1933.

Freemasonry in Northern China 1913–1937, History of. 1938. Privately printed in Shanghai.

Gilbert, Martin. *First World War.* London: Harper Collins, 1994.

Gillingham, Paul. *At the Peak — Hong Kong Between the Wars.* Hong Kong: Macmillan, 1983.

Gittins, Jean. *Eastern Windows — Western Skies.* Hong Kong: South China Morning Post Publications, 1969.

—— *Stanley: Behind Barbed Wire.* Hong Kong: Hong Kong University Press, 1982.

Gompertz, G.H. *China in Turmoil, Eyewitness 1924–1948.* London: J.M. Dent & Sons Ltd., 1967.

Grafton, F.M. *Freemasonry in Shanghai and Northern China.* 1894. Updated by Robert S. Ivy in Tientsin in 1913.

Graham, John. *The Lowe Bingham Story 1902–1977.* Hong Kong, 1977.

Grantham, Alexander. *Via Ports, From Hong Kong to Hong Kong.* Hong Kong: Hong Kong University Press, 1965.

Grout, Donald Jay. *A History of Western Music.* London: J.M. Dent & Sons Ltd., 1960.

Gull, B. Manico. 'The Story of the Chinese Labor Corps'. *Far Eastern Review* XIV, no. 4 (April 1918), Shanghai.

Gunn, Geoffrey C. *Encountering Macau, A Portuguese City-State on the Periphery of China 1557–1999.* USA: Westview Press, 1996.

Hacker, Arthur. *Arthur Hacker's Wanchai.* Hong Kong: Odyssey Publications, 1997a.

—— *The Hong Kong Visitor's Book, A Historical Who's Who.* Hong Kong: Odyssey Publications, 1997b.

Hahn, Emily. *China To Me, A Partial Autobiography.* USA: Blakiston Company, 1944. (Reprinted by Virago Press, London, in 1987.)

—— *Hong Kong Holiday.* USA: Doubleday & Company, 1946.

Hall, Peter. *In the Web.* Published by Peter Hall, Beech House, 27 Quarry Road East, Heswall, Wirral L61 6XD, 1992.

Hayim, George. *Thou Shalt Not Uncover Thy Mother's Nakedness.* London: Quartet Books, 1988.

Hibbert, Christopher. *The Illustrated London News Social History of Victorian Britain.* London: Book Club Associates, 1976.

Higham, Charles. *Wallis, Secret Lives of the Duchess of Windsor.* London: Pan Books, 1988.

Hoe, Susanna. *The Private Life of Old Hong Kong — Western Women in the British Colony 1841–1941.* Hong Kong: Oxford University Press, 1991.

Hughes, Richard. *Hong Kong, Borrowed Place, Borrowed Time.* London: Andre Deutsch, 1968.

Hunter, William C. *Fan Kwae at Canton.* (Reprinted as *An American in Canton 1825–44* by Derwent Publications, Hong Kong, 1994.)

Hutcheon, Robin. *SCMP, The First Eighty Years.* Hong Kong: South China Morning Post Publications, 1983.

—— *Wharf, The First Hundred Years.* Hong Kong: The Wharf (Holdings) Limited, 1986.

—— *The Blue Flame, 125 Years of Towngas in Hong Kong.* Hong Kong: The Hong Kong and China Gas Company Limited, 1987.

—— *First Sea Lord, The Life & Work of Sir Y.K. Pao.* Hong Kong: The Chinese University Press, 1990.

Ingrams, Harold. *Hong Kong.* London: Her Majesty's Stationery Office, 1952.

Jarratt, P.E. *Whitwell An Island Village, Glimpses of the Past.* (ISBN: 0 9519142 0 0)

Jarvie, I.C. and Joseph Agassi, eds. *Hong Kong: A Society in Transition.* London: Routledge & Kegan Paul, 1969.

Jones, Jack and Johanna. *The Isle of Wight, An Illustrated History.* Dorset: The Dovecote Press, 1987, 1995.

Kelly, Fred. *The Diary of Inspector Fred Kelly of the Royal Hong Kong Police Force:* compiled during his internment in Stanley Detention Camp (21 January 1942–31 August 1945). Hong Kong: Public Records Office, 1974.

Kent, Simon. *Ferry to Hong Kong.* London: Arrow Books, 1959.

King, Doreen. *A Short History & Guide, St John's Cathedral, Hong Kong.* Hong Kong, 1987.

King, Frank H.H. *History of the Hongkong and Shanghai Banking Corporation.* Four volumes. UK: Cambridge University Press, 1988.

Kipling, Rudyard. *From Sea to Sea.* A poem. 1888.

Klein, Daryl. *With the Chinks: 2nd Lieutenant in the Chinese Labour Corps, with Illust.* London: John Lane, 1933.

Ko Tim Keung and Jason Wordie. *Ruins of War, A Guide to Hong Kong's Battlefields and Wartime Sites.* Hong Kong: Joint Publishing (HK) Ltd., 1996.

Laidlaw, E.F. *The Story of the Royal National Hospital, Ventnor.* Isle of Wight: E.F. Laidlaw, 1990.

Laufer, Berthold. *Sino-Iranica: Chinese Contributions to the History of Civilisation in Ancient Iran; with Special Reference to the History of Cultivated Plants and Products...* Chicago: Field Museum of Natural History, 1919.

Lawrence, Anthony. *Foreign Correspondent.* London: George Allen & Unwin Ltd., 1972.

Lee, P.C. *Hongkong Album.* Hong Kong: Sin Poh Amalgamated (HK) Ltd., 1960.

Leiper, G.A. *A Yen for My Thoughts.* Hong Kong: South China Morning Post Publications, 1982.

Lethbridge, Henry J. 'Yellow Fever'. *Far Eastern Economic Review* (2 May 1968).

—— 'Hong Kong under Japanese Occupation'. In *Hong Kong: A Society in Transition,* I.C. Jarvie, ed. London: Routledge & Kegan Paul, 1969.

—— 'Condition of the European Working Class in Nineteenth Century Hong Kong'. *Journal of the Hong Kong Branch of the Royal Asiatic Society* (1975).

—— *Hong Kong: Stability and Change.* Hong Kong: Oxford University Press, 1978.

—— Introduction in *The Hong Kong Guide 1893.* Hong Kong: Oxford University Press, 1982.

Lilius, Aleko. *I Sailed with Chinese Pirates.* Hong Kong: Oxford University Press, 1991.

Ljungstedt, Anders. *An Historical Sketch of the Portuguese Settlements in China and of the Roman Catholic Church and Mission in China & Description of the City of Canton.* Hong Kong. First published in 1932, reprinted by Viking Hong Kong Publications in 1992.

Luff, John. *The Hidden Years.* Hong Kong: South China Morning Post Publications, 1967.

—— *Hong Kong Cavalcade.* Hong Kong: South China Morning Post Publications, 1968.

Luzatto, Rola, ed. *Hong Kong Who's Who, 1958–1960.* Hong Kong: Ye Olde Printerie, 1960.

Macnair, Harley Farnsworth. *The Chinese Abroad, Their Position and Protection, A Study in International Law & Relations.* Shanghai: The Commercial Press Limited, 1924.

Marsden, Gordon, ed. *Victorian Values, Personalities and Perspectives in Nineteenth Century Society.* USA: Longman, 1990.

Mattock, Katherine. *Hong Kong Practice, Drs Anderson & Partners — the first hundred years*. Hong Kong: Drs Anderson & Partners, 1984.

—— *Partners in Law, The History of Johnson Stokes & Master*. Published for Johnson Stokes & Master. Hong Kong, 1990.

Maugham, Somerset. *The Painted Veil*. UK: Mandarin/Viking Penguin, first published in 1925.

Maurois, Andre. *Call No Man Happy*. London: Jonathan Cape, 1950.

Miners, N.J. *The Government & Politics of Hong Kong*. Hong Kong: Oxford University Press, 1975.

—— *Hong Kong Under Imperial Rule 1912–1941*. Hong Kong: Oxford University Press, 1987.

Morris, Jan. *Hong Kong: Epilogue to an Empire*. London: Penguin/Vintage, 1989.

Murphey, Rhoads. *The Outsiders — The Western Experience in India & China*. USA: University of Michigan Press, 1977.

Nash, Nancy. *Rewarding Success, The First Hundred Years of Jebsen & Company 1895–1995*. Hong Kong: Jebsen & Co. Ltd., 1995.

Nieuhof, Johannes. *Gezantschap der Neerlandtsche Oost-Indische Compagnie aan den grooten Tartarischen Cham, den tegenwoordigen keizer van China* (An embassy from the East-India Company of the United Provinces, to the Grand Tartar Cham Emperor of China, deliver'd by Their Excellencies Peter de Goyer and Jacob de Keyzer). With an appendix of several remarks taken out of Father Athanasius Kircher. English'd, and set forth... 1665.

Norton-Kyshe, James William. *The History of the Laws and Courts of Hong Kong, from the Earliest Period to 1898*. Two volumes. Reissue of 1898 edition by Vetch & Lee Ltd., Hong Kong, 1971.

Nuffield Foundation, The. *The Nuffield Foundation, Review of the First Ten Years 1943–1954*. Oxford: Oxford University Press, 1953.

Ommanney, F.D. *Eastern Windows*. London: Longmans Readers Union, 1962a.

—— *Fragrant Harbour, A Private View of Hong Kong*. London: Hutchinson & Co., 1962b.

Palgrave, Francis T. *The Golden Treasury, Selected From the Best Songs and Lyrical Poems in the English Language and Arranged with Notes*. Macmillan & Co., Limited, 1946 (first edition: 1861).

Parkin, George R. *Round the Empire*. London: Cassell's Educational Works, 1892.

Parr, Donald A. *Newport in Old Photographs*. UK: Alan Sutton Publishing Limited, 1994.

—— *Ventnor & District*. UK: Sutton Publishing Limited, 1996.

Paterson, E.H. *A Hospital for Hong Kong — the Centenary History of the Alice Ho Miu Ling Nethersole Hospital*.

Peplow, S.H. and M. Barker. *Hong Kong Around and About*. Hong Kong: Ye Olde Printerie, 1931.

Pittis, Donald and Susan J. Henders. *Macao: Mysterious Decay and Romance.* Hong Kong: Oxford University Press, 1997.

Pope-Hennessy, James. *Half-Crown Colony, A Hong Kong Notebook.* London: Jonathan Cape, 1968.

Poy, Vivienne. *A River Named Lee.* Canada: Calyan Publishing Ltd., 1995.

Price, Eunice. *A History of the Hong Kong Post Office 1841–1991.* Hong Kong: Hong Kong Post Office, 1991.

Rich, P.J. *Chains of Empire: English public schools, Masonic cabalism, Historical causality and Imperial clubdom.* 1991.

Ride, Lindsay and May. *An East India Company Cemetery, Protestant Burials in Macao.* (Edited by Bernard Mellor.) Hong Kong: Hong Kong University Press, 1996.

Robinson, Spencer. *Festina Lente, A History of the Royal Hong Kong Golf Club 1889–1989.* Hong Kong: The Royal Hong Kong Golf Club, 1989.

de Rothschild, Guy. *The Whims of Fortune.* England: Granada, 1985.

Sayer, Geoffrey Robley. *Hong Kong 1862–1919: Years of Discretion.* Hong Kong: Hong Kong University Press, 1975.

—— *Hong Kong 1841–1862: Birth, Adolescence and Coming of Age.* Hong Kong: Hong Kong University Press, 1980. (First published by Oxford University Press, Hong Kong, in 1937.)

Senelick, Laurence, et al. *British Music Hall 1840–1923.* USA: Archon Books, 1981.

Selle, Earl Albert. *Donald of China.* Sydney: Invincible Press, 1948.

Seth, Mesrovb Jacob. *Armenians in India.* Calcutta: Armenian Holy Church of Nazareth. First published in 1937, reprinted in 1983.

Sewell, William. *Strange Harmony.* UK: Edinburgh House Press, 1946.

Silva, Frederic A. *Todo O Nosso Passado, All Our Yesterdays — The Sons of Macao, Their History and Heritage.* Macao: Livros Do Oriente, 1996.

Sinn, Elizabeth. *Power and Charity, Early History of the Tung Wah Hospital.* Hong Kong: Oxford University Press, 1989.

—— *Growing with Hong Kong, The Bank of East Asia 1919–94.* Hong Kong: Hong Kong University Press, 1994.

Smith, Carl T. *Chinese Christians: elites, middlemen, & the Church in HK.* Hong Kong: Oxford University Press, 1985.

—— *A Sense of History — Studies in the Social and Urban History of Hong Kong.* Hong Kong: Hong Kong Educational Publishing Company, 1995.

Somers, Geoffrey Vincent. *The Royal Hong Kong Jockey Club: the story of racing in Hong Kong.* Hong Kong: Royal Hong Kong Jockey Club, 1975.

Stein, Sir Aurel. *On Alexander's track to the Indus: personal narrative of explorations...* London: Macmillan, 1929.

Stericker, John. *Captive Colony, The Story of Stanley Camp Hong Kong 1941–45.* Xerox.

Stevens Smith, Joyce. *Matilda, Her Life and Legacy.* Hong Kong: Matilda and War Memorial Hospital, 1988.

Stock Exchange of Hong Kong. *A Glimpse of the Past.* First publication of the Hong Kong Stock Market History Project. Hong Kong: Centre of Asian Studies, the University of Hong Kong, 1998.

Strachey, Lytton. *Eminent Victorians.* London: Penguin, 1918, 1948.

—— *Queen Victoria.* London: Peguin, 1921, 1971.

Summerskill, Michael. *China on the Western Front.* London: Michael Summerskill, 1982.

Symons, A.J.A. *The Quest for Corvo, An Experiment in Biography.* London: Penguin, 1979.

Symons, Catherine Joyce. *Looking at the Stars.* Pegasus Books, 1996.

Todd, Alexander Robertus. *A time to remember: the autobiography of a chemist.* Cambridge University Press, 1983.

—— 'Origins of The Croucher Foundation'. In *First Report 1980–84.* The Croucher Foundation, 1984.

Vare, Daniele. *The last of the Empresses; Passing from the Old China to the New; The Maker of Heavenly Trousers; The Temple of Costly Experience;* etc.

Veronica (pseudonym). *The Islanders of Hong Kong: Being a Series of Open Letters Dealing with the Immortal Types to be found in Hong Kong.* Xerox. Hong Kong University Library, Special Collection, 1907.

Ward, Lock & Co. *A Pictorial & Descriptive Guide to the Isle of Wight.* London, 1906.

Welsh, Frank. *A History of Hong Kong.* London: Harper Collins, 1994.

Wharton-Tigar, Edward. *Burning Bright.* UK: Metal Bulletin Books Limited, 1987.

White, Barbara-Sue. *Turbans & Traders, HK's Indian Communities.* Hong Kong: Oxford University Press, 1994.

—— (ed.). *Hong Kong, Somewhere Between Heaven and Earth.* An anthology. Hong Kong: Oxford University Press, 1996.

Whitworth, Phoebe. *Memoir.* Xerox, The Helena May Library, Hong Kong.

Wilson, Dick. *Hong Kong! Hong Kong!* London: Unwin Hyman, 1990.

Wise, Michael and Mun Him, eds. *Travellers' Tales of Old Hong Kong and the South China Coast.* Brighton: In Print Publishing, 1996.

Wong Siu-lun. *Emigrant Entrepreneurs, Shanghai Industrialists in Hong Kong.* Hong Kong: Oxford University Press, 1988.

Wright, Arnold, ed. *Twentieth Century Impressions of Hong Kong, Shanghai, and other treaty ports of China: their history, people, commerce, industries, and resources.* London: Lloyd's Greater Britain Publishing, 1908. Repirnted in part by Graham Brash, Singapore, in 1990.

Wright-Nooth, George and Mark Adkin. *Prisoner of the Turnip Heads: horror, hunger and humour in Hong Kong, 1941–1945.* London: Leo Cooper, 1994.

Young, Walter H. *A Merry Banker in the Far East (& South America).* John Lane, 1916.

INDEX

Trustees of The Croucher Foundation

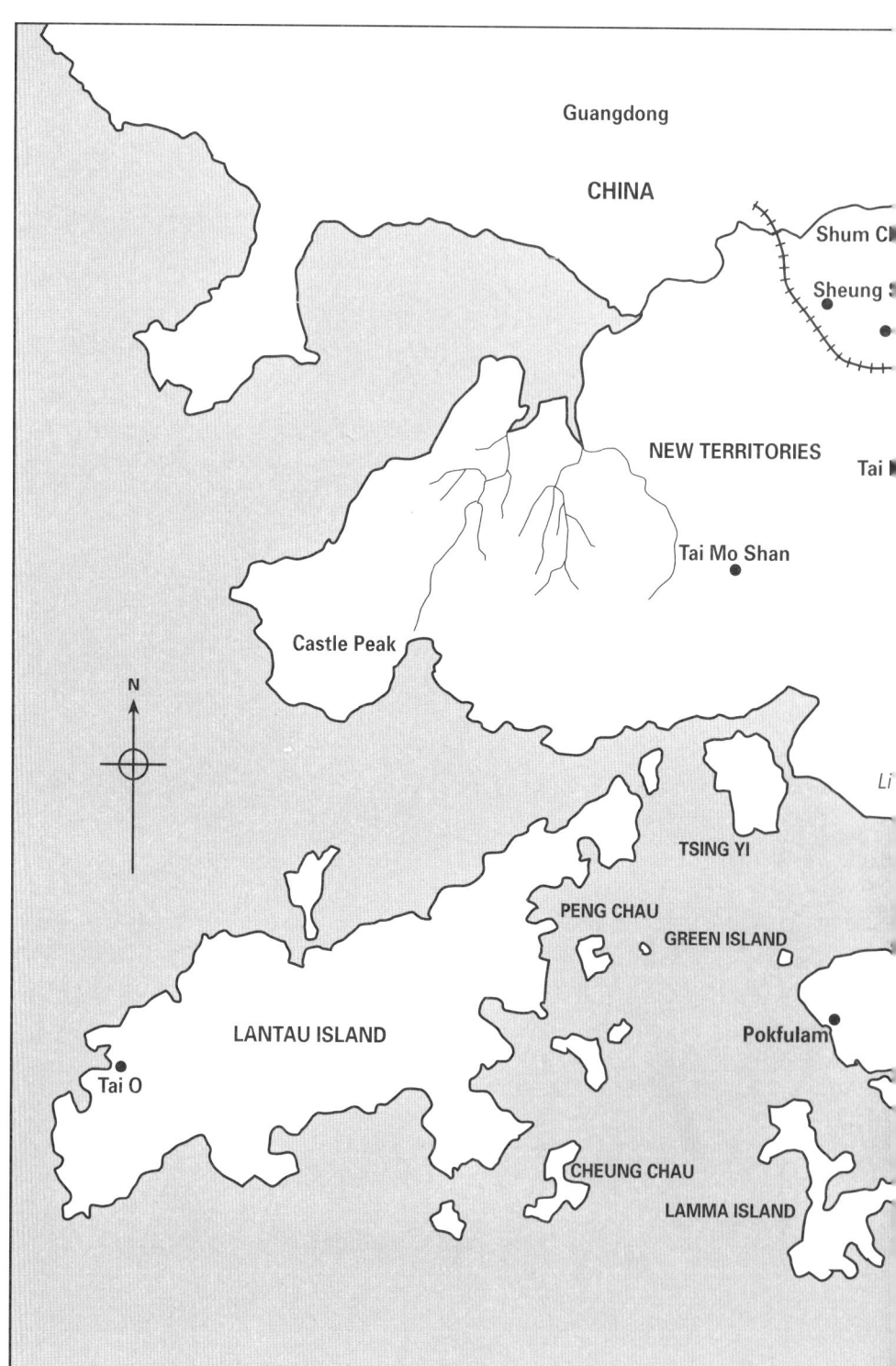

Guangdong

CHINA

Shum C[

Sheung S

NEW TERRITORIES

Tai

Tai Mo Shan

Castle Peak

N

Li

TSING YI

PENG CHAU

GREEN ISLAND

LANTAU ISLAND

Pokfulam

Tai O

CHEUNG CHAU

LAMMA ISLAND